Spenser's Allegory

. . . . . because the ear repeats,
Without a voice, inventions of farewell.

Spenser's Allegory

The Anatomy of Imagination

ISABEL G. MACCAFFREY

PRINCETON UNIVERSITY PRESS

PRINCETON, NEW JERSEY

Copyright © 1976 by Princeton University Press
Published by Princeton University Press,
Princeton, New Jersey
In the United Kingdom: Princeton University Press,
Guildford, Surrey
All Rights Reserved
Library of Congress Cataloging in Publication Data will
be found on the last printed page of this book
This book has been composed in Linotype Baskerville
The lines on page ii are from Wallace Stevens, *The Owl
in the Sarcophagus*
Printed in the United States of America
by Princeton University Press, Princeton, New Jersey

Preface

This book is not a comprehensive reading of *The Faerie Queene*. Such readings are already available, performed with finesse by critics who have participated in the renaissance of Spenserian studies over the past two or three scholarly generations. I think of surveys by writers such as A. C. Hamilton, William Nelson, Maurice Evans, and Kathleen Williams, as well as readings of individual books of the poem in works by Harry Berger, Donald Cheney, Angus Fletcher, Thomas Roche, Humphrey Tonkin, and others. No one who, at this late date, puts forward yet another book on Spenser can do so without the awareness of a debt that must go far beyond footnote documentation. No theoretical work could possibly proceed without the strong base provided by critics and scholars who, with attentive care and learning, have opened the text of *The Faerie Queene* to our understanding. We can now say, I think, that some consensus has been achieved, on fundamentals of the poem if not on details. We know much of what *The Faerie Queene* is "about," its richness, complexity, and strangeness; we know much concerning the formal modes that directed the poet's proceedings. "We" includes, of course, myself. From almost all the books on Spenser produced over the past few decades, as well as more general works in relevant areas of Renaissance studies, I have derived pleasure and profit in varying degrees; by many items in the voluminous journal materials, I have been enlightened. In the following pages, particular indebtedness has been, as far as possible, specified. But no honest critic can avoid the disclaimer that must now be *de rigueur* for all students of the major English poets: the myriad filiations of one's intellectual life over the years of composition can no longer be completely unraveled, and as people of good will in the community of

v

scholars, we must often be content with general acknowledgment rather than specific documentation.

One of my principal debts cannot, however, go unmentioned. I have found myself continually returning, for refreshment, inspiration, and understanding, to the late Rosemond Tuve's great book, *Allegorical Imagery*. Indeed, my positive intention in the present book could be understood as an exploration of her remark (p. 106) that "allegory does not equate a concretion with an abstraction, but shadows or mirrors essences." Her book is avowedly a prolegomenon to Spenser, the chief member of the "posterity" to whom her "medieval books" point. That she did not live to write on *The Faerie Queene* itself cannot be sufficiently lamented. This book, though it is not the one she would have written, would have been received by her with the generosity she accorded to so many younger scholars, and I would like to regard it as another contribution to the prolific scholarly "posterity" of her spirit.

Readers will find that *The Faerie Queene* looks, in the following pages, something like one of those maps of the United States attributed to New Yorkers or Californians— some parts afflicted with an unnatural gigantism, others perplexingly foreshortened or shrunken. I have chosen illustrative passages with my main theoretical argument in view, and though in Chapters II, III, and IV I have maintained a roughly chronological progress through the poem, many salient episodes, themes, and cantos remain unnoticed. Throughout, I have been principally concerned to show a relationship between the protean formal resources of Spenserian allegory and what is, to my mind, the poet's underlying thematic purpose: to explore the ways of knowing available to human beings "in the middest," and thereby to define more precisely the possibilities of moral action. Among these ways, I have argued, the energizing core is the power that we have learned from Wordsworth to call "Reason in her most exalted mood": the Imagination.

This book has been long in the making, and detailed

vi

acknowledgment of private indebtedness would amount to an intellectual autobiography, a tedious genre at best. I have learned from my students and colleagues at Bryn Mawr College, Tufts University, and Harvard University more than I can ever fully acknowledge, even to myself. Friends at other institutions, both in conversation and in print, have provided stimulus, contradiction, and inspiration. Ann Berthoff gave the first chapter her searching attention, and its present obscurity is much less deep than it would have been without that enlightening scrutiny. Robert Burlin also read the first chapter, and called my attention to the Blake drawing of Spenser, but those details are neither the beginning nor the end of his contribution to this book. Its deepest roots lie in the years of our acquaintance, and without them it could never have thrived, or even existed.

The book was written largely in a year's leave supported by a grant from the John Simon Guggenheim Memorial Foundation—a gift of time that no scholar can ever sufficiently repay. Other kinds of support were provided by my husband, Wallace MacCaffrey, in that year and every other year.

Acton, Massachusetts
July, 1975

Contents

Abbreviations

CQ	*Cambridge Quarterly*
EC	*Essays in Criticism*
EETS	Early English Text Society
ELH	*ELH, A Journal of English Literary History*
ELR	*English Literary Renaissance*
HLQ	*Huntington Library Quarterly*
JEGP	*Journal of English and Germanic Philology*
JWCI	*Journal of the Warburg and Courtauld Institutes*
LCL	Loeb Classical Library
MLQ	*Modern Language Quarterly*
MP	*Modern Philology*
PMLA	*Publications of the Modern Language Association*
RES	*Review of English Studies*
SEL	*Studies in English Literature*
SP	*Studies in Philology*
SR	*Studies in the Renaissance*
TSLL	*Tennessee Studies in Language and Literature*
Var.	*The Works of Edmund Spenser: A Variorum Edition,* ed. Edwin Greenlaw *et al.*, 11 vols. (Baltimore, 1932-1957)

The following texts are used for writers frequently cited.

The Works of Geoffrey Chaucer, ed. F. N. Robinson, 2nd ed. (Boston, 1957)

Dante Alighieri, *Inferno, Purgatorio, Paradiso,* tr. J. A. Carlyle, Thomas Okey, and P. H. Wicksteed, The Temple Classics, 3 vols. (London, 1941, 1946)

The Poems and Letters of Andrew Marvell, ed. H. M. Margoliouth, 2 vols. (Oxford, 1952)

The Student's Milton, ed. F. A. Patterson, rev. ed. (New York, 1933)

The Riverside Shakespeare, ed. G. B. Evans *et al.* (Boston, 1974)

Spenser's Faerie Queene, ed. J. C. Smith, 2 vols. (Oxford, 1964)

Spenser's Minor Poems, ed. E. de Selincourt (Oxford, 1910)

The Poetical Works of William Wordsworth, ed. E. de Selincourt and Helen Darbishire, 5 vols. (Oxford, 1940-1949)
William Wordsworth, *The Prelude,* ed. E. de Selincourt and Helen Darbishire, 2nd ed. (Oxford, 1959)

The archaic u, v, i, and j have been conventionally modernized.

Spenser's Allegory

Imaginatio vero est vis qua percipit homo figuram rei absentis.
Hec habet principium a sensu quia quod imaginamur, imaginamur vel ut vidimus vel ad similitudinem alterius rei iam vise
ut ille virgilianus Titirus ad similitudinem sue civitatis Romam
imaginabatur.

Guillaume de Conches, 12th Century

All things acted on Earth are seen in the bright Sculptures of
Los's Halls & every other Age renews its powers from these Works
With every pathetic story possible to happen from Hate or
Wayward Love & every sorrow & distress is carved here
Every Affinity of Parents Marriages & Friendships are here
In all their various combinations wrought with wondrous Art
All that can happen to Man in his pilgrimage of seventy years.

Blake, Jerusalem, 1804-1810 (?)

Surely . . . we must cry out that imagination is always seeking to
remake the world according to the impulses and the patterns in
that Great Mind, and that Great Memory? . . . What we call
romance, poetry, intellectual beauty, is the only signal that the
supreme Enchanter, or some one in His councils, is speaking of
what has been, and shall be again in the consummation of time?

Yeats, Ideas of Good and Evil, 1901

Introduction

The architect Louis Kahn has described his vocation as the attempt to create "a society of spaces the client never dreamed of."[1] Art not only embodies our dreams, it directs our dreaming; Kahn's realized spaces demonstrate for his clients what they should have dreamed of. If, as Yeats said, art is a vision of reality, it is also a vision of possibility at the point where it intersects actuality. For us, the unrealized is also the unreal, but for the traditional cosmologies and ontologies of western thought, the invisible world that attracts our dreams and our yearning for realization could be more "real" than the visible.

> But what sort of things shall we say subsist? Are they the intelligible or the visible? Certainly they are the intelligible, and this is the judgment of Plato, who puts things visible in the genus of non-being, and puts the intelligible only in the genus of being.[2]

[1] *The New York Times*, October 23, 1972, p. 40.

[2] Tasso, *Discourses on the Heroic Poem*, II.11; *Literary Criticism: Plato to Dryden*, ed. Allan H. Gilbert (Detroit, 1962), p. 477. I shall assume throughout this study the widespread acceptance, by Spenser and most of his lettered contemporaries, of some such "Platonic" metaphysic as Tasso here expresses. At its most general, this means simply a belief in the reality of an invisible realm of being; ontological descriptions of that realm varied widely. I agree with the thesis of Robert Ellrodt in *Neoplatonism in the Poetry of Spenser* (Geneva, 1960), who credits the "persistent strain of Platonic inspiration" running through the poet's works rather to "an older tradition inherited from the Middle Ages" than to the recovered works of Plato himself and his redactors in the *Quattrocento* (p. 11).

A succinct account of the fortunes of the Platonic Idea and its repercussions for the theory of art in the centuries preceding Spenser is given by Erwin Panofsky in the early chapters of *Idea: A Concept in Art Theory*, tr. J.J.S. Peake (Columbia, S.C., 1968).

To give body to this invisible realm is the task of poetic imagination, in particular of allegory. Shakespeare's
Theseus, at the end of a dream play, speaks of how "imagination bodies forth / The forms of things unknown" (*MND*
V.i.14-15). Dreams give us access to a normally hidden
realm, and the waking dream of art produced by miracu-
lously blinded bards makes visible the secret powers that
rule our lives. These powers were re-named by Freud:
Eros, Ananke, and their cohorts. Spenser's contemporaries
called them Fate or Providence, or identified them with
constellations in the sky. They included angelic intelli-
gences that moved the planets and mediated between heav-
en and earth; a realm of ideal essences or "ideas"; and the
fathomless regions of the human soul inhabited by a variety
of psychic energies. The mind of man contemplates, contains, and names these forces:

> And thus, from divers accidents and acts
> Which do within her observation fall,
> She goddesses and powers divine abstracts:
> As Nature, Fortune, and the Virtues all.[3]

To these "powers divine" must be added the invisibles of
the temporal dimension: the vanished past and the unpene-
trated future. Past and future are aspects of God's design
and are visible to him, but for human beings they can be
"seen" only with the inward sight of memory or prophecy.
Behind all these unseen realities is the ultimate reality,
dwelling "in that realm of eternal truth from which all
things temporal were made, [which] we behold with our
mind's eye."[4]

The process of imagining alluded to in the preceding
paragraph involves, in fact, several distinct, even mutually
exclusive, operations of the mind; these mental operations

[3] Sir John Davies, *Nosce Teipsum; The Complete Poems*, ed. A. B.
Grosart, Early English Poets Ser. (2 vols., London, 1876), I, 43-44.
[4] St. Augustine, *De Trinitate*, vii; *The Later Works*, tr. John Burnaby
(Philadelphia, 1955), p. 65.

4

have been differently described and evaluated at different stages in the history of ideas. Consideration of them has always been affected by prevailing metaphysical and onto-logical theories, though the relationships between ontology and imagining were not always clearly discerned or spelled out. Before proceeding to the particulars of Spenser's poem, it will be necessary to unravel some complications of the imagination's life with respect to certain philosophical prin-ciples. The speculations which undergird all theories of imagination are introduced above in the reference to dreams, which can be regarded ambivalently—and were so regarded throughout the Middle Ages—depending upon whether they are the products of self-generated illusion, or divinely implanted vision. And the ambiguity of dreams, in turn, is a vividly focused instance of a larger problem, the central issue of epistemology. Does the mind (or the imag-ination) make or merely apprehend what it perceives? Is there, as Tasso insists (following Plato), a realm of "intel-ligible" being more ultimate than that which we project upon the world in our imaginative structures? And, if there is, what is the relation between these structures and that actuality?

When Coleridge, in 1802, proclaimed that "in our life alone does Nature live," he was giving radical expression to the "projectionist" view of the epistemological puzzle.[5] He did not succeed in convincing himself, and a significant part of his intellectual life was devoted to the long wrestle with the subject/object distinction. For Spenser and his contemporaries, the notion that "Nature lives" insofar as we perceive and evaluate it could not have been formulated in

[5] The classic account of this subject for the Romantic period is M. H. Abrams, *The Mirror and the Lamp* (New York, 1953), especially Ch. 3. The history of the mind's commerce with the world has been traced by Owen Barfield in *Saving the Appearances: A Study in Idolatry*. I shall be discussing the phenomenon he calls "original participation": "the sense that there stands behind the phenomena, *and on the other side of them from man*, a represented, which is of the same nature as man" (Harbinger ed. [New York, 1965], p. 111).

the same way. If the eye (including the mind's eye) "makes" the object it perceives, it does so, they would hold, by making sense of it, understanding and locating it. This process can occur because an intelligible "outer" world and a sense-making "inner" world are aspects of a single divinely-designed universe. In the sixteenth century the subject/object, creative/visionary issue, though extremely complex, was not yet insoluble. It had been solved in the great intellectual systems of the high Middle Ages. Allegory considers the life of man as it unfolds within the assumptions provided by these systems; this means that allegorical fictions develop within a "mental space" which is analogically related to the spaces realizing God's "great idea," the macrocosmic spaces of the universe.

"Mental space" is Coleridge's identifying phrase for the locale of *The Faerie Queene*: it is liberated from "all material obstacles"; "it is truly a land of Fairy, that is, of mental space."[6] Speculation about the character of this interior human world, and about its most elusive indwelling power, imagination, has a long history, some high points of which will be indicated in the first chapter, as a prolegomenon to the argument that an allegory—at any rate, Spenser's allegory—is a model of the mind's life in the world. It is a model in Susanne Langer's sense: "A model . . . always illustrates a principle of construction or operation; it is a symbolic projection of its object which . . . must permit one to match the factors of the model with respective factors of the object, according to some convention."[7] In allegory, mind makes a model of itself; more accurately, imagination offers a model of the imagining process. *The Faerie Queene*

[6] *Coleridge's Miscellaneous Criticism*, ed. T. M. Raysor (Cambridge, Mass., 1936), p. 36.

[7] *Mind: An Essay on Human Feeling*, Vol. I (Baltimore, 1966), p. 59. *Model* in this context is distinguished from *image*, "a rendering of the appearance of its object in one perspective out of many possible ones. It sets forth what the object looks or seems like." *The Faerie Queene* is a model that contains images and discloses the principles of their operation.

mirrors the mind's very structure, as well as its principalities and powers; it is at once a treatise upon, and a dazzling instance of, the central role that imagination plays in human life.

This thesis does not entail, as I hope to demonstrate, neglect of the concerns traditionally attributed to "grave moral Spenser." His allegory records significant points of contact between what we now call "subjective" and "objective" realms, and therefore involves epistemological principles which rapidly become moral principles. What we see is what we think, and what we see and think interact to bring about what we do. The "vertuous and gentle discipline" that Spenser set out to exemplify in his poem is a moral discipline, but it cannot be that without also being an epistemological and imaginative discipline. His schoolmaster, Richard Mulcaster, connected the human "prerogative of understanding beyond sense," which I have identified with imagining, with the proper conduct of "this our mortall life."

> Last of all our soull hath in it an imperiall prerogative
> of understanding beyond sense, of judging by reason,
> of directing by both, for deutie towards God for societie
> towards men, for conquest in affection, for purchace in
> knowledge, and such other things, whereby it furnisheth
> out all maner of uses in this our mortall life, and be-
> wraieth in it self a more excellent being, then to con-
> tinew still in this roming pilgrimage.[8]

"This roming pilgrimage" can yield to an existence in which dreams become truth, and one function of imagination is to give us practice in dreaming such dreams, so that we may be ready for unveiled reality. But if we are to understand high dreams, we must first understand and rehearse the humbler, originating stages in the life of the

[8] *Mulcaster's Elementarie*, ed. E. T. Campagnac (Oxford, 1925), pp. 36-37.

mind. Another of allegory's tasks is to reproduce what Whitehead, describing the genesis of mental life from the flux of "illimitable" ordinary experience, calls "complete occasions": comprehended experiences, rescued from submergence in the confusion of the quotidian. "Memory, anticipation, imagination, and thought" separate the occasion from its spatio-temporal continuum and envelop it in an illuminating manifold.

> A complete occasion includes that which in cognitive experience takes the form of memory, anticipation, imagination, and thought. These elements in an experient occasion are also modes of inclusion of complex eternal objects in the synthetic prehension, as elements in the emergent value.[9]

To relate such occasions to "complex eternal objects": this is what we mean by knowledge, and upon this mysterious but familiar process, the allegorizing imagination turns its powerful self-regarding gaze. Like the *Commedia, Pearl,* and at least one thread of *Piers Plowman, The Faerie Queene* is about processes of coming to know. It dramatizes the adventures of the wit of man, through all its many powers, drawing upon a traditional scenario repeatedly rehearsed—for example, in some prolix couplets by Lydgate:

> Wher as man, in sentence,
> By reson hath intelligence,
> To make his wytt to enclyne,
> To knowe thinges that be dyvyne,
> Lastyng and perpetuel,
> Hevenly and espirituel,
> Of heven and of the firmament,
> And of every element,
> Whose wyt ys so clere y-founde,
> So perfyt pleynly and profounde,

[9] A. N. Whitehead, *Science and the Modern World* (New York, 1925), p. 246; Whitehead is discussing the process of abstraction.

> That he percethe erthe and hevene
> And fer above the sterris sevene,
> So that he hath of every thing
> Verray perfyt knowlechyng
> In his secret ynwarde syghte.[10]

In *The Faerie Queene,* Spenser shows us the "secret ynwarde syghte" doing what it does.

It is my conviction that Spenser has a more conscious and systematic notion of imagination's proper function than any we find in most of his contemporaries. He repeatedly insists upon its implications for the theory of knowledge, and loses no opportunity to describe the upward mobility of the imaginative power. Among the dreary iterations of *The Teares of the Muses,* Urania celebrates "the mindes of men borne heavenlie," made capable of understanding what they cannot literally observe by virtue of the human ability to "see" with the inward eye.

> From hence wee mount aloft unto the skie,
> And looke into the Christall firmament,
> There we behold the heavens great *Hierarchie,*
> The Starres pure light, the Spheres swift movement,
> The Spirites and Intelligences fayre,
> And Angels waighting on th'Almighties chayre.
>
> $\qquad\qquad\qquad\qquad$ (505-10)

This book will consider some of the ways in which Spenser's sophisticated conscious and self-conscious allegory deals with epistemological problems, including the capacities and limitations of fictions as vehicles of truth—for example, the fiction of *The Faerie Queene.* The poem looks at itself and offers an eloquent argument for its own existence, commenting in the process upon how metaphors work, what is implied by various metaphorical and iconographical strategies, and how far we may trust the basic medium, language.

[10] John Lydgate, *Reson and Sensuallyte,* ed. Ernst Seiper, EETS (Ex. Ser.) LXXXIV (London, 1901), pp. 20-21.

It is often said that self-referring fictions are peculiar products of the introspective "modern mind." But modernity and self-consciousness are themselves recurrent historical phenomena. Readers of Dante, of Chaucer, of Spenser, know that imagination's most appropriate personification has always been Narcissus.

PART I

Allegory and Imagination

1. The Universe of Allegory

The power of imagination is described by Michael Drayton at the climax of *Endimion and Phoebe*, that curious amalgam of Ovid and Plato.

> And now to shew her powerfull deitie,
> Her sweet *Endimion* more to beautifie,
> Into his soule the Goddesse doth infuse,
> The fiery nature of a heavenly Muse,
> Which in the spyrit labouring by the mind
> Pertaketh of celestiall things by kind:
> For why the soule being divine alone,
> Exempt from vile and grosse corruption,
> Of heavenly secrets comprehensible,
> Of which the dull flesh is not sensible,
> And by one onely powerfull faculty,
> Yet governeth a multiplicity,
> Being essentiall, uniforme in all;
> Not to be sever'd nor dividuall,
> But in her function holdeth her estate,
> By powers divine in her ingenerate,
> And so by inspiration conceaveth
> What heaven to her by divination breatheth.[1]

Drayton's last couplet neatly acknowledges the subjective origin of conceptualizing, while allowing, in the etymological progress from *inspiration* to *breatheth*, for the dependence of imagining upon divine origins. The historical process that led up to this and similar eulogies of the heavenly Muse in the Renaissance is a lengthy and tangled skein. I propose to unravel only its main thread, as a preface to the argument that the allegorical method and the theory of

[1] *The Works of Michael Drayton*, ed. J. W. Hebel *et al.* (5 vols., Oxford, 1961), I, 142; lines 505-22.

imagination are inseparably related during the centuries which sustained belief in both the objective reality of an invisible realm, and a required relation between that realm and the realities perceived by sense.

"The history of imagination is the account of the process by which rightful recognition was given to that function of the mind in virtue of which we have pictures."[2] The slowness of the process and the tardiness of recognition can be traced to the lowly origin of *phantasia* in the material body of man; it belonged to the sensible soul, the soul which man shares with the brutes. In a dualistic metaphysic like Plato's —a dualism never completely solved by Aristotle, and endemic in western philosophy—imagination inevitably bore an hereditary stigma. A philosopher dedicated to escape from the bonds of materiality must cast a cold eye on *phantasia*, irrevocably shackled to the objects of sense from which its second-class images are derived. In the faculty-psychology of classical philosophy which survived in various versions through the lifetime of Spenser, imagination was a humble mediating power. The younger Pico could declare, as a "proposition which in the eyes of philosophers and theologians is a clear and admitted fact," that

There exists a power of the soul which conceives and fashions likenesses of things, and serves, and ministers to, both the discursive reason and the contemplative intellect; and to this power has been given the name *phantasy* or *imagination*.[3]

Spenser depicts this power as the melancholic man Phantastes, "that mad or foolish seemd," in the third chamber of

[2] Murray W. Bundy, *The Theory of Imagination in Classical and Medieval Thought* (Urbana, 1927), p. 96.

[3] Gianfrancesco Pico della Mirandola, *On the Imagination*, tr. Harry Caplan (New Haven, 1930), p. 37. A useful summary of the theory of imagination in relation to the psychology of the late Middle Ages can be found in Morton Bloomfield's discussion of Langland's Imaginatif, *Piers Plowman as a Fourteenth-Century Apocalypse* (New Brunswick, 1961), Appendix III.

Alma's turret (II.ix.52). Toiling at its menial, though necessary, tasks, *phantasia* looks uninteresting and harmless
enough. But it has some interesting features, as Aristotle
noted. "For imagining lies within our own power whenever
we wish (e.g. we can call up a picture, as in the practice of
mnemonics by the use of mental images)."[4] Though dependent, ultimately, on sense experience, imagination can function in the absence of sensation; Aristotle cites the example
of dreams. In this partial independence of the image-mak-
ing power lie the seeds of many future developments.

But this is not the whole story about imagination for classical philosophy. Both Plato and Aristotle recognized that
the imagining power plays an essential role in even the loftiest ranges of human thought, the realm of "the contemplative intellect"; and both, in different ways, made room for
it in their epistemologies. In certain of Plato's late dialogues, there is discussion of images as reflections, divinely
implanted in the soul, of the ideal realm.[5] And Aristotle
acknowledged that even the rational soul cannot function,
in man, without imagination. "To the thinking soul images
serve as if they were contents of perception. . . . That is why
the soul never thinks without an image."[6] The notion that
imagination, though in origin a "lower" faculty, is an ingredient in man's knowledge even of divine truth, appears
in many medieval descriptions of the rational soul; the account by Hugh of St. Victor is especially pertinent.

> The third power of the soul appropriates the prior
> nutritional and sense-perceiving powers, using them, so
> to speak, as its domestics and servants. It is rooted en-
> tirely in the reason, and it exercises itself either in the
> most unfaltering grasp of things present, or in the under-
> standing of things absent, or in the investigation of

[4] *De Anima*, III.3 (427b); *The Basic Works of Aristotle*, ed. Richard
McKeon (New York, 1941), p. 587.
[5] See Bundy's discussion of the *Sophist* and *Timaeus*, *Theory of Imagination*, pp. 48-53.
[6] *De Anima*, III.6 (431a); *BW*, p. 594.

15

things unknown. This power belongs to human-kind alone. . . . This divine nature is not content with the knowledge of those things alone which it perceives spread before its senses, but, in addition, it is able to provide even for things removed from it names which imagination has conceived from the sensible world, and it makes known, by arrangements of words, what it has grasped by reason of its understanding.[7]

Hugh's classification of invisible realities accessible to the soul follows a tripartite scheme which corresponds to man's life in time and space. In the moment, we grasp "things present"; to the past or regions remote in space belong "things absent"; to the future, "things unknown." Spenser provides an expansive version of the last notion in his stanza on the voyages in the Proem to Book II of *The Faerie Queene*.

> But let that man with better sence advize,
>   That of the world least part to us is red:
>   And dayly how through hardy enterprize,
>   Many great Regions are discovered,
>   Which to late age were never mentioned.
> (II.Pro.2)

The great regions include the new-found lands of the Americas, but the poet goes on to speculate audaciously of the "other worlds" in the stars or beyond, which may also be discovered by imagination.

The relationship, in imagining, between sense experience and the knowledge of invisible reality is paradoxical and crucial. It appears to be based upon an analogy between the soul's humblest function—recording and reproducing sensory images—and its most exalted—intuiting ultimate essences in those realms of deep truth that are imageless though not inapprehensible. The analogy derives from an

---

[7] *The Didascalicon of Hugh of St. Victor: A Medieval Guide to the Arts*, tr. Jerome Taylor (New York, 1961), pp. 49-50.

introspectively derived truth: that knowledge of transcendent reality is "like" knowledge of images in being immediate and non-discursive. Accommodation of epistemology to this fact can be found in Plato's extrapolation of fantasy as "the very faculty which, rightly informed by light from above, results in vision higher than reason can attain,"[8] and in the medieval notion of an *intellectus* superior to *ratio* or discursive reason. To the threefold hierarchy of faculties is added a fourth which transcends them all.

> Sense, imagination, reason and understanding
> [*intelligentia*] do diversely behold a man. For sense
> looketh upon his form as it is placed in matter or
> subject, the imagination discerneth it alone without
> matter, reason passeth beyond this also and considereth
> universally the species or kind which is in particulars.
> The eye of the understanding is higher yet. For surpassing the compass of the whole world it beholdeth
> with the clear eye of the mind that simple form in itself.[9]

Boethius' *intelligentiae oculus* "sees" simple forms; it therefore seems somehow akin to the sub-rational power, imagination, which also "discerns" forms *sine materia*. Poetry, Milton said, is simple, sensuous, and passionate. In that simplicity lies its claim to kinship with the high visionary powers of the transcendent intellect. References to an eye in the mind underline this relationship. "The mind has, as it were, eyes of its own, analogous to the souls' senses. . . . I, Reason, am in minds as the power of looking is in the eyes."[10] From here it seems but a short step, logically if not chronologically, to the notion of "Wit the pupil of the Soul's clear eye,"[11] the erected wit of the *Apologie for Poetry*.

In fact, of course, the concept of imagination as the art-

---

[8] Bundy, *Theory of Imagination*, p. 53.

[9] Boethius, *The Consolation of Philosophy*, Bk. V, Prosa 4, tr. "I.T.," rev. H. F. Stewart; *Boethius*, LCL (London, 1953), p. 389.

[10] Augustine, *Soliloquies*, I.vi.12; *The Earlier Writings*, tr. J.H.S. Burleigh (Philadelphia, 1953), p. 30.

[11] Davies, *Complete Poems*, I, 75.

ist's special gift was very slow to emerge. The nature of poetic fictions was a subject of debate in the twelfth century, but it was treated in the course of more general discussions concerning the nature of the symbolic method and the interpretation of Scripture. Wit (*ingenium*) or imagination was a way of knowing before it was a power of making.

> *Ingenium* . . . is a vital link in human consciousness,
> uniting the highest and the basest capacities of will
> and curiosity. It is closely related to imagination,
> the power of mind by which things absent are
> perceived, and thus to "fantasies" of all sorts, from
> the wildest dream to the highest state of vision.[12]

Nevertheless, although members of the so-called School of Chartres both analyzed and produced poetic fictions which embodied visionary truth, imagination as an aesthetic principle was regarded even by them as of minor importance, and as potentially dangerous. Hugh of St. Victor included among the functions of the soul not only the power to understand, but the power to record the fruits of understanding by providing *names* "which imagination has conceived," but this activity is quite narrowly defined. Later in the *Didascalicon* there is a disparaging chapter on "the songs of the poets" as "mere appendages of the arts," unworthy of being counted among the true *artes*.[13]

A strong renewal of interest in imagination, as both a noetic and a creative faculty, accompanied the recovery of neo-Platonic and "occult" symbolisms in the Renaissance. These reinforced

> a profound conviction that man, the image of the
> greater world, can grasp, hold, and understand the

[12] Winthrop Wetherbee, *Platonism and Poetry in the Twelfth Century* (Princeton, 1972), pp. 94-95.

[13] *Didascalicon*, pp. 87-88. The Chartrians, however, attributed a higher seriousness to secular literature than that allowed by Hugh; see Wetherbee, *Platonism and Poetry*, pp. 49ff.

18

greater world through the power of his imagination. We come back here to that basic difference between Middle Ages and Renaissance, the change in the attitude to the imagination. From a lower power which may be used in memory as a concession to weak man who may use corporeal similitudes because only so he can retain his spiritual intentions towards the intelligible world, it has become man's highest power, by means of which he can grasp the intelligible world beyond appearances through laying hold of significant images.[14]

The use of imagination to "grasp the intelligible world" is one side of the picture. The other is confidently asserted by Tasso, who cites "the Areopagite" to support the highest possible claim for the poet as a maker of images.

That part of occult theology that is contained in the signs, and has the power of making one perfect, is fitting to the indivisible part of our soul, which is the intellect at its purest. The other, eager for wisdom, which brings proofs, he attributes to the divisible part of the soul, much less noble than the indivisible. Thence it leads to the contemplation of divine things; and to move readers in this way with images, as do the mystic theologian and the poet, is a much more noble work than to teach by means of demonstrations, which is the function of the scholastic theologians.[15]

This is a lofty flight indeed; and interest in the creative faculty was not confined to "mystical theology." Imagination improves our prospects in this life as well as the next.

Sure He that made us with such large discourse,
Looking before and after, gave us not

[14] Frances Yates, *The Art of Memory*, Peregrine ed. (London, 1969), pp. 226-27.
[15] *Discourses*, I.10; Gilbert, p. 476.

That capability and godlike reason
To fust in us unus'd.

(Hamlet, IV.iv.36-39)

These words of Hamlet draw what to us seems a necessary conclusion from the presence in man of discursive reason, his peculiar intellectual faculty: we know in order to use our knowledge. An aspect of "discourse," the ability to look "before and after," alludes to those mnemonic and prophetic powers that also dwell with imagination. The godlike capability of man manifests itself in the making and carrying-out of plans, like Hamlet's plot to kill the king, or the state as a work of art; and also in monuments of unaging intellect which outlast many individual life-spans and enable us to triumph over mortality. Among these monuments are the alternative worlds of art, societies of spaces that remain unrealized until the maker's fiat causes them to become tangible in paint or stone or words.

Sidney's *Apologie for Poetry* is both the culmination of the movements of thought I have been tracing, and a portent of things to come. Sidney speaks of alternative worlds and the power of the poet to create *ex nihilo* in terms that may strike us as very modern. And, in fact, the audacity of such a position was acknowledged and deplored by writers in the following century, who saw that the poetic imagination was to be feared not simply because it dealt with licentious subjects and sensuous images, but because it presumptuously, even blasphemously, preferred its own creations to the divine handiwork.[16] Sidney's saucy comparison could lead to fearfully dangerous consequences. The poet,

lifted up with the vigour of his own invention, doth
grow in effect into another nature, in making things

[16] These attitudes are discussed by Perry Miller in *The New England Mind: The Seventeenth Century,* Beacon Press ed. (Boston, 1961), pp. 257-59. Richard Sibbes, for instance, denounced imagination for disparaging "the work of God in the creatures, and everything else, for it shapes things as itself pleaseth" (p. 258).

either better than Nature bringeth forth, or, quite anew, forms such as never were in Nature. . . . Her world is brazen, the poets only deliver a golden.[17]

"Freely ranging only within the zodiac of his own wit," he can escape the limits that constrain ordinary mortals and enjoy the powers of a god in the little world he has made. Nevertheless, if we read on, we must agree that Sidney does not press the implications of this paragraph. The passage that begins by setting the poet beside God ends with a reminder of the Fall.

> Neither let it be deemed too saucy a comparison
> to balance the highest point of man's wit with the
> efficacy of Nature; but rather give right honour to
> the heavenly Maker of that maker, who having made
> man to His own likeness, set him beyond and over all
> the works of that second nature: which in nothing he
> showeth so much as in Poetry, when with the force of a
> divine breath he bringeth things forth far surpassing
> her doings, with no small argument to the incredulous
> of that first accursed fall of Adam: since our erected wit
> maketh us know what perfection is, and yet our infected
> will keepeth us from reaching unto it.[18]

Although Sidney celebrates the poet's power to invent, he makes a crucial connection between invention and the intuition of uninvented reality: "our erected wit maketh us know what perfection *is*." A perfected but invisible reality exists; the poet adumbrates it in the "new" forms of his golden worlds. But these new forms are really reminders of old forms, since we once lived in an actual golden world.[19] As

[17] Sir Philip Sidney, *An Apology for Poetry*, ed. Geoffrey Shepherd (London, 1965), p. 100.

[18] Ibid., p. 101.

[19] The implications of Sidney's theory of poetic imagination have recently been analyzed by Michael Murrin in Ch. 7 of *The Veil of Allegory* (Chicago, 1969). He distinguishes the "oratorical" tradition of the *Apologie* from the theories of "the allegorists," including Spenser,

Sidney's editors have noted, sixteenth-century poets, like their medieval counterparts, were reluctant to detach the poet's golden worlds from the actuality of the divine Creation or to claim absoluteness for poetic creativity. The notion of making, making-up, or feigning opens a Pandora's box of fraudulent visions—fictions that mislead deliberately or inadvertently, prove deceptive or self-deceiving.[20] To ground poetic fiction in an ideal realm—ordinarily obscured by the waywardness of the infected will and the opaqueness and hostility of the fallen environment—is to insure its validity. In a sense, therefore, all valid art is imitative or visionary, though, as Sidney suggests, the objects of imitation are inaccessible to any but an erected wit. Verisimilitude gives way to the stratagems of a higher mimesis, and to Touchstone's paradox that the truest poetry is the most feigning.

The complexities of relationship between invention and imitation can be endlessly debated. Many readers in the sixteenth century were no doubt satisfied by the cheerful compromise of Puttenham, who concluded that the poet "is both a maker and a counterfaiter: and Poesie an art not only of making, but also of imitation."[21] More interesting questions arise when we consider the kind of commerce that can exist between visible and transcendent reality, and between the material resources available to the artist and the impalpable truth apprehended by imagination. The answers lie in the theory of metaphor. For if it is the case, as I have been arguing, that imagination's task has traditionally been to render visible the realms of being apprehended by the "secret ynwarde syghte," then it is no wonder that allegory,

---

but agrees that the two points of view approach each other in the notion that "the poet practised anamnesis; he recalled to man what in fact he had once experienced" (p. 187).

[20] A succinct account of sixteenth-century views concerning the nature of fictive illusion can be found in William Nelson, *Fact or Fiction: The Dilemma of the Renaissance Storyteller* (Cambridge, Mass., 1973).

[21] *The Arte of English Poesie*, I.i; ed. G. D. Willcock and A. Walker (Cambridge, 1936 [1970]), p. 3.

the most important of the metaphorical modes, dominated fiction-making for many centuries.

Poets themselves, of course, have always been interested in these problems and in the kind of claims that can be made for their fictions. The loftiest role in which they have cast themselves has been that of the seer or visionary; for Christian authors, the model is the author of the Apocalypse.

> The Revelation of Jesus Christ, which God gave unto him, to shew unto his servants things which must shortly come to pass; and he sent and signified it by his angel unto his servant John:
> Who bare record of the word of God, and of the testimony of Jesus Christ, and of all things that he saw.
> (Rev. 1:1-2)

An angel, or a Muse, dictates: "What thou seest, write in a book" (Rev. 1:11). It is this visionary power for which Milton prays in Book III of *Paradise Lost*: that his inward eye may be cleared, that he "may see and tell / Of things invisible to mortal sight" (III.54-5). The genre of the dream vision enabled medieval poets, when they dared, to imply a similar kind of literalness for their fictions: I saw this. The *Divine Comedy* is the greatest example in European poetry;[22] in English one must look to Blake for a comparable absoluteness in claiming the mantle of the prophetic bard, able to pierce heaven and survey ultimate reality with unmediated vision.

When Richard Blackmur calls allegory "the highest form of the putative imagination," he is connecting it with the power to objectify the realm of possibility. But possibility must be grounded in potential realization; therefore, "suc-

---

[22] On the "literalness" of Dante's fiction, see the Appendix to Charles Singleton, *Commedia: Elements of Structure* (Cambridge, Mass., 1965). The discussion is extended in Richard H. Green, "Dante's 'Allegory of the Poets' and the Mediaeval Theory of Poetic Fiction," *CL* IX (1957), 118-28; and Singleton, "The Irreducible Dove," Ibid., 129-35.

cessful allegory—*La Vita Nuova* and *Pilgrim's Progress*—
requires the preliminary possession of a complete and sta-
ble body of belief appropriate to the theme in hand."[23] The
same may be said of all symbolic modes; if symbols do not
directly mirror "reality," they must at least refer to it
obliquely. The "body of belief" which lay behind Spenser's
poem and its ancestors assumed an integral relationship
among the various modes of being, though that relationship
would be differently described, according to the writer's
purposes. One version led to visionary and "literal" fictions:
the *Commedia* or *Paradise Lost*; another, to allegory itself,
further removed in the "putative" realm, and darkly
shadowed.

"Symbolism" is a mode of experience; allegory is a mode
of thought.[24] Both assume an "objectively" valid relationship between material and transcendent being; for the sym-
bolist, this is grounded in a metaphysic—associated with
various versions of neo-Platonism, such as the writings of
the pseudo-Dionysius—that looks upon the universe as a
"sacred emanation" from the "inaccessible One." Fr. Chenu
explains that, for these thinkers, "upwards reference" was
built into things, part of their very natures, and to read

[23] *The Lion and the Honeycomb* (New York, 1955), p. 131.

[24] I am deliberately alluding to the formula of C. S. Lewis in *The Allegory of Love* (Oxford, 1936): "Symbolism is a mode of thought, but allegory is a mode of expression" (p. 48). Lewis's distinctions in this famous passage are curiously asymmetrical, and it is odd that, osten-sibly sharing the theology and ontology of the great allegorical poets, he should perpetuate an essentially incompatible post-romantic view of the inferiority of allegory. I am assuming that allegory and symbol-ism are two ways of dealing with the "fact" of a genuine congruence between visible and invisible reality, and that they are not mutually exclusive. A "symbolic" situation can be allegorized, and an allegory can eventuate in symbolic vision; both these processes can be seen in *The Faerie Queene*. I concur with Angus Fletcher, however, in thinking the allegory/symbol issue an "unhappy controversy" (*Allegory: The Theory of a Symbolic Mode* [Ithaca, 1964], p. 13). Fletcher's dissection of it in his Introduction is helpful; his subtitle suggests a single source for these "two" modes.

symbols was to unfold a meaning that God had written into the world.

> This *anagoge*, this upwards reference of things, was constituted precisely by their natural dynamism as symbols. The image of the transcendent was not some pleasant addition to their natures; rather, rooted in the "dissimilar similitudes" of the hierarchical ladder, it was their very reality and reason for being. The symbol was the means by which one could approach mystery; it was homogeneous with mystery and not a simple epistemological sign more or less conventional in character.[25]

Coleridge's famous definition of symbolism gives a modern version of this principle: a symbol "is always itself a part of that, of the whole of which it is representative." The relation is metonymic, not metaphorical; indeed, Coleridge's example is one of the schoolbook instances of metonymy: " 'Here comes a sail',— (that is a ship) is a symbolic expression."[26] Such symbols can and do exist in "real life," and everyone has experienced intensifications of significance which seem to be focused in some natural object or phenomenon. Metaphors, on the other hand, are never found in nature; they are logical contrivances of the imagination, forced to provide substitutes for rare direct experience of

[25] M.-D. Chenu, *Nature, Man, and Society in the Twelfth Century*, tr. Jerome Taylor and Lester K. Little (Chicago, 1968), p. 123.

[26] *Miscellaneous Criticism*, p. 29. The metaphor/metonymy distinction has been studied by Roman Jakobson in his work on aphasia, most accessibly in "The Cardinal Dichotomy in Language," *Language: An Enquiry into Its Meaning and Function*, ed. R. N. Anshen (New York, 1957). Metaphor is based on similarity, metonymy on contiguity. Jakobson remarks that "The primacy of the metaphorical way in the literary schools of romanticism and symbolism has been generally acknowledged, but it is still insufficiently realized that it is the predominance of metonymy which underlies and actually predetermines the so-called 'realistic' trend" (p. 171). This principle would account for the fact that the dominance of "realistic" modes produces an enthusiasm for symbolism and an undervaluation of allegory.

unsensed reality. And metaphorical fictions, including the major kind, allegory, are based upon a view of reality offered by Milton's Raphael; earth and heaven are "each to other like," but not identifiable. Milton does not allow the archangel to claim for his retrospective narrative the truth of ultimate vision appropriated by the blind bard; he adopts the more modest method of analogy:

> what surmounts the reach
> Of human sense, I shall delineate so,
> By lik'ning spiritual to corporal forms,
> As may express them best, though what if Earth
> Be but the shadow of heav'n, and things therein
> Each to other like, more than on earth is thought?
> (V.571-76)

Raphael's rhetorical question both defines and solves the problem of fiction as a mode of truth-telling. If we can assume that the phrase, "earth the shadow of heaven," points to genuine ontological fact, then the maker's corporal forms assume a reliability superior to any that inventiveness alone can claim. "Likeness" legitimates fictions; but we are to remember that a metaphorical gap always exists. So Aquinas:

> From material things we can rise to some sort of
> knowledge of immaterial things, but not to a perfect
> knowledge; for there is no proper and adequate
> proportion between material and immaterial things,
> and the likenesses drawn from material things for
> the understanding of immaterial things are very
> unlike them.[27]

These distinctions have been helpfully unraveled by Winthrop Wetherbee in his study of twelfth-century allegory; his discussion of "rationalist" and "symbolic" modes is relevant to later literary developments as well.

[27] *Summa Theologica*, Bk. I, Q. 88, Art. ii; *Basic Writings of St. Thomas Aquinas*, ed. A. C. Pegis (2 vols., New York, 1945), I, 848.

Metaphor was a fundamental tool of those rationalist philosophers who sought knowledge of God from the study of the structure of the universe and the complex laws, causes, and analogies by which it is linked with the human mind. Symbolism, on the other hand, lent itself to an "anagogical," an open-ended, and ultimately mystical view, closely related to the traditions of biblical exegesis, but tending increasingly to embrace the natural world as well, under the influence of a renewed interest in the cosmic sacramentalism of the pseudo-Dionysius and John Scotus Eriugena. In this view *naturalia* were of value to the extent that they could be seen as directly reflective of God.[28]

Both metaphor and symbol are grounded in a relationship of intelligibility between seen and unseen worlds. Metaphor expresses the relation in the form of an analogy, which, though God and the angels may perceive it intuitively, can only be *expressed* for man through a conscious rational process.

As the quotation from Aquinas indicates, analogical relationships must take account of distinction as well as likeness, or at any rate must not conceal them. There must always be two or more terms in an analogy, and from this fact many misunderstandings about allegory have arisen. When Empson writes that "part of the function of allegory is to make you feel that two levels of being correspond to each other in detail, and indeed that there is some underlying reality, something in the nature of things, which makes this happen,"[29] he is describing accurately the analogical relation. But, although phrases like "two levels of being" are almost inevitable in discussions of allegory, the problem of how to describe the relation between them continues to plague literary theory. It is probably best solved *ad hoc* in the process of concrete analysis, but a few negative remarks need to be made here. There is something wrong

---

[28] *Platonism and Poetry*, p. 17.
[29] *The Structure of Complex Words* (London, 1951), p. 346.

with sentences like this one by Graham Hough: "Allegory
. . . abstracts certain qualities from experience, and then
looks for sensible images . . . to bring them vividly to the
mind of the reader." Hough sees one of the objections himself: "What principle have we for deciding whether the
image or the concept came first?"[30] Precisely. Terms like
"came first" are both presumptuous and meaningless. They
imply temporal priority, and any formula that assumes such
priority presumes an access to the creator's imagination for
which there is no warrant. But the nature of the relationship between "image" and "idea" is also misconceived. The
notion that the writer moves from "experience" to "abstraction" and then back to the "sensible" realm is untrue not
only to the imaginative process, but also to the universe
which allegory reflects. There is an inauthentic arbitrariness about this picture of the poet casting about for some
sort of "sensible image" in which to clothe his abstractions,
for "ideas" and visible objects all belong to the same universe and are elements in the providential scheme of Creation. A cosmic poem like *The Faerie Queen* or *Piers Plowman*—and lesser allegories to a lesser degree—depicts this
intelligible world as it looks to the eye of the mind. The
crooked is made straight, the rough places plain; or rather,
the crookedness, roughness, and obscurity of the ordinary
fallen world are reproduced in a context where nothing is
without meaning, and there is access to that meaning.
Everything is "visible," and when everything becomes accessible to sense, we can see that the relationships between
aspects of reality are not arbitrary. This is not to say that
the poets employ a conventional vocabulary of symbols
with fixed and invariable significances; it is to say that sig-

---

30 *A Preface to "The Faerie Queene"* (London, 1962), pp. 102-103.
Some of these matters are discussed by Morton Bloomfield in "A Grammatical Approach to Personification Allegory," *Essays and Explorations*
(Cambridge, Mass., 1970). He observes that priority in the poet's mind
"is extremely difficult to determine exactly, and his mental procedures
could be the same in both personification allegory and symbolism"
(p. 256).

nificances and their embodiments are rationalized and justified within an ontological system where different grades of reality are continuous and congruent at different points on the scale; to the imaginative eye of the allegorist, all become part of an apprehensible "nature." "The writer of an *allegoria* breaks down his figure for me into that which my senses can apprehend."[31]

Description of the metaphorical situation in allegory can be amended by shifting the notion of priority from temporal to logical. Neither the poet nor the reader "starts from" one realm of being and moves on to another. Rather, we are made aware of a relation of dependence between what we see directly and what we "see" only indirectly through the metaphor. Logical priority in a loose sense can be understood to involve a primary claim on our attention. In a stricter sense, logical priority is causative, as Aristotle explains.

> In those things, the being of each of which implies
> that of the other, that which is in any way the cause
> may reasonably be said to be by nature "prior" to
> the effect. . . . The fact of the being of a man carries
> with it the truth of the proposition that he is, and the
> implication is reciprocal. . . . The true proposition,
> however, is in no way the cause of the being of the man,
> but the fact of the man's being does seem somehow to be
> the cause of the truth of the proposition, for the truth
> or falsity of the proposition depends on the fact of the
> man's being or not being.[32]

"Cause" in this context implies entailment or dependency, and this is precisely what is implied by the "meaning" of an allegory with respect to its *visibilia*. The existence of the material or visible (sometimes called literal) aspect of an allegorical fiction is entailed by the existence of its non-visi-

---

[31] Rosemond Tuve, *Elizabethan and Metaphysical Imagery* (Chicago, 1947), p. 107.
[32] *Categoriae*, xii (14b); *BW*, p. 35.

ble meaning. To put the matter in this way is, in some degree, to insure against forcing a resolutely non-allegorical fiction into a mode alien to the assumptions its form presupposes. It also absolves us from trespass upon the writer's creative process. And, finally, it does least violence to the intimacy of the relation among the different so-called levels of the meaning, which are in fact stages on an ontological continuum.

The usefulness of conceiving of allegorical relationships as logical rather than chronological can be confirmed by recalling Coleridge's formulation of "the law of the dependence of the particular on the universal, the first being the organ of the second, as the lungs in relation to the atmosphere, the eye to light."[33] To conceive of particulars as "organs" whereby universals are apprehended, dependent but accessible avenues of approach to the ultimate immanifest, permits us to speak of allegory's fictive particularities more accurately than a vocabulary of "levels" will allow. The existence of a particular—within an appropriate metaphysical system—assumes the existence of a universal. This is the model for logical subordination. So, for instance, the existence of a word assumes some sort of referent for it. The relation between language and the "language" of allegorical metaphor has been pointed out by Owen Barfield.

> When we use language metaphorically, we bring it
> about of our own free will that an appearance means
> something other than itself, and, usually, that a manifest
> "means" an unmanifest. . . . We use the phenomenon as
> a "name" for what is not phenomenal.[34]

It is interesting to recall Hugh of St. Victor's comment that imagination "is able to provide even for things removed from it *names* which imagination has conceived from the

[33] *The Statesman's Manual*, Appendix B; *The Complete Works of Samuel Taylor Coleridge*, ed. W.G.T. Shedd (7 vols., New York, 1884), I, 462 n.
[34] *Saving the Appearances*, p. 126.

sensible world." To conceive of metaphor as an allegorical "language" is helpful because it includes *both* the idea of separateness between word and referent *and* the notion of the referent's inaccessibility without the word. Words, and allegorical images that are like words, are the body of thought and as such they are, of course, indispensable, since disembodied reality is not for us. "The soul never thinks without an image."

Imagination is the generator of images, and allegory gives us insight into the life-processes of those images. But, as this capsule history has, I hope, suggested, imagination must not therefore be considered an insignificant "aesthetic" faculty on the fringes of consciousness. It lies at the center of human understanding and, as Mulcaster said, "furnisheth out all manner of uses in this our mortall life." These uses may be moral; they may be literary; they may be practical or scientific. Jacques Monod has recently reiterated the importance of imaginative experience for the scientist.

> Tous les hommes de science ont dû, je pense, prendre conscience de ce que leur réflexion, au niveau profond, n'est pas verbale: c'est une *expérience imaginaire*, simulée à l'aide de formes, de forces, d'interactions qui ne composent qu'à peine une "image" au sens visuel du terme. . . . Je ne crois pas en effet qu'il faille considérer les images non visuelle sur lesquelles opère la simulation comme des symboles, mais plutôt, si j'ose ainsi dire, comme la réalité subjective et abstraite, directement offerte à l'expérience imaginaire.[35]

[35] "I am sure every scientist must have noticed how his mental reflection, at the deeper level, is not verbal: to be absorbed in thought is to be embarked upon an *imagined experience*, an experience simulated with the aid of forms, of forces, of interactions which together only barely compose an 'image' in the visual sense of the term. . . . Indeed, the nonvisual images with which simulation works would be more rightly regarded not as symbols but, if I may so phrase it, as the subjective and abstract 'reality' offered directly to imaginative experience." (Translation by Austryn Wainhouse, from Knopf edition of Monod, *Chance and Necessity*). *Le hasard et la necessité* (Paris, 1970), p. 170. Monod's chapter can be regarded as an updating of Henri Bergson's

31

These remarks are valuable in reminding us that imagination, even in poetry, is not exclusively an affair of visible "images," though it may employ them in expressing its insights. It concerns, in fact, "la réalité subjective" in all its ramifications. And subjective reality is characterized, above all, by its lust for unexperienced perfections, a lust satisfied by the creation of artificial paradises, societies of perfect spaces, models and theorems of total visibility and intelligibility. *The Faerie Queene,* too, is a world of possibility, where the eternal invisible powers take on flesh, and the gardens and groves they inhabit draw closer. At the same time, it is the world of each of us, in which we hope to have our happiness. The mind turns inward in order that it may return with a more powerful sense of identity and purpose to its own experience in a bewildering universe, which may yet be remade in the image of the heart's desire. Like Wordsworth, Spenser was interested in imagination as the maker of poetic worlds; also like Wordsworth, he deals at a deep level with the universal human power of imagining. His poem accomplishes for his age the goal Wordworth set before himself: to

> describe the Mind and Man
> Contemplating; and who, and what he was—
> The transitory Being that beheld
> The Vision.
>
> (*PW* V.6)

---

classic account of the *fonction fabulatrice* in *Les deux sources de la morale et de la religion* (Paris, 1933), an effort to rationalize the persistence of imagination in terms of evolutionary theory.

2. The Fallen World: Analytical Allegory

> Unutterable providence . . . has set two ends before
> man to be contemplated by him; the blessedness, to wit,
> of this life, which consists in the exercise of his proper
> power and is figured by the terrestrial paradise, and the
> blessedness of eternal life, which consists in the fruition
> of the divine aspect, to which his proper power may not
> ascend unless assisted by the divine light.[1]

The first of these two ends is the one that Spenser sets
before himself in his great poem. *The Faerie Queene* unfolds "in the middest"; to follow it to its end requires patience of both poet and reader. For a human being vacillat-
ing between erected wit and infected will, awareness of the
gap between *might be* and *is* may lead to an effort to escape
altogether from his lamentable condition but, as Spenser
was to show repeatedly, premature simplifications lead to
dead ends. We must find the blessedness of this life—
understanding—before we ascend higher. The Red Cross
Knight is assured by the old man Contemplation that his
"painefull pilgrimage" will end, that there "is for thee
ordaind a blessed end" (I.x.61). Nevertheless, though cosmic and apocalyptic intimations are always relevant to the
action of *The Faerie Queene*, its main locale is the "thurgh-
fare ful of woe" that is life itself. A consciousness of where
and how we live as fallen human beings governs the nature
of Spenser's rhetorical mode, allegory, and directs his conduct of it in the poem.

We come to diverse ends, Dante said, by diverse means.
The way to the terrestrial paradise is "by the teachings of
philosophy, following them by acting in accordance with

[1] Dante, *De Monarchia*, III.xvi; *The Latin Works*, tr. P. H. Wicksteed, The Temple Classics (London, 1904), p. 277.

the moral and intellectual virtues," and by the exercise of man's "proper power." Allegory belongs to the fallen world, the world of Plato's cave-dwellers; it is an invention of mind on its own, trying to make sense of experience in a benighted universe.

> But the universe to the eye of the human understanding is framed like a labyrinth, presenting as it does on every side so many ambiguities of way, such deceitful resemblances of objects and signs, natures so irregular in their lines, and so knotted and entangled. And then the way is still to be made by the uncertain light of the sense, sometimes shining out, sometimes clouded over, through the woods of experience and particulars. . . . In circumstances so difficult neither the natural force of man's judgment nor even any accidental felicity offers any chance of success.[2]

Human understanding has suffered a decline in perspicuity and ease, an increase in opacity and laboriousness, since the Fall. Sir John Davies, urging his readers to know themselves, prefaced *Nosce Teipsum* with an account of epistemological disaster.

> But then grew Reason dark, that she no more
> Could the fair forms of Good and Truth discern:
> Bats they became that eagles were before.[3]

For an explanation of this predicament, one could turn to Plato, whose ontological hierarchy has "darkness" built into it; the demi-urge became increasingly deformed as it descended further into base matter. The Christian version adds a temporal dimension to the fundamentally static Platonic scheme. God describes himself as outside time, but

[2] Francis Bacon, Preface to *The Great Instauration; Selected Writings*, ed. H. G. Dick, Modern Library (New York, 1955), pp. 433-34.
[3] *Complete Poems*, I, 16-17.

also as time's informing principle, the cause of grammatical tense. "Ego sum et principium et finis, dicit Dominus Deus, qui est, et qui erat, et qui venturus est, omnipotens" (Rev. 1:8). The Fall of Man was both a fall into time and a fall from lucid to imperfect vision, from univocal to equivocal language, from a world of light to a cloudy grove. The toil of growing up involves a recognition that knowledge, for us, is bound to the wheel of time: it is emergent, progressive, and very slow.

The power of understanding that we have lost, and must now painfully reconstruct, was symbolized, for many Renaissance writers, by Adam's naming of the beasts: "the pure knowledge of nature and universality, a knowledge by the light whereof man did give names unto other creatures in Paradise, as they were brought before him, according unto their proprieties."[4] Time, that has carried man farther away from the light of Paradise, may eventually return him to it, however. Even in this cloudy place, he has inklings of better things, a once and future state of beatitude, wisdom, and felicity.

> Certes also ye men, that ben erthliche beestes, dremen alwey your begynnynge, although it be with a thynne ymaginacioun; and by a maner thought, al be it nat clerly ne perfitly, ye loken from afer to thilke verray fyn of blisfulnesse. And therfore naturel entencioun ledeth yow to thilke verray good, but many maner errours mystorneth you therfro.[5]

This "natural intention," a kind of instinct for Paradise, offered grounds for qualified optimism when it came to devising educational programs designed to re-convert bats into eagles. Bacon, assuring man that "whensoever he shall be able to call the creatures by their true names, he shall again

---

[4] Bacon, *Advancement of Learning; Selected Writings*, p. 161.
[5] Chaucer's translation of Boethius, Bk. III, Pr. 3; *The Works of Geoffrey Chaucer*, ed. F. N. Robinson (2nd ed., Boston, 1957), p. 343.

command them,"[6] designed a method to ascertain whether the human understanding "might by any means be restored to its perfect and original condition."[7] Milton, a few decades later, sketched out a regime that would "repair the ruins of our first parents" (*SM*, p. 726). The notion that, through education in the *artes*, man can regain something of his original rectitude and wisdom was not invented in the Renaissance. The *opus restaurationis* of the Middle Ages was to bring about "la réintégration de tout le genre humain dans l'unité primordiale."[8]

> This, then, is what the arts are concerned with, this is what they intend, namely, to restore within us the divine likeness, a likeness which to us is a form but to God is his nature.[9]

Four hundred years later, Fulke Greville composed a *Treatie of Humane Learning* which, despite its gloomy Calvinist bias, suggested that man can refashion himself through study, particularly of the arts of eloquence and their powerful controlled dreams. They can "play noble parts," helping us to overcome the defects of our fallen nature. So poetry,

> Teacheth us order under Pleasure's name,
>   Which, in a glasse, shows Nature how to fashion
>   Her selfe againe, by ballancing of passion.[10]

[6] *Of the Interpretation of Nature; The Works of Francis Bacon*, ed. J. Spedding, R. L. Ellis, and D. D. Heath (7 vols., London, 1870), III, 222.

[7] Proemium to *The Great Instauration; Selected Writings*, p. 423.

[8] Wetherbee, *Platonism and Poetry*, p. 208; quotation from Chenu, *La théologie au douzième siècle*. For further discussion of the *opus restaurationis*, see R. W. Southern, *Medieval Humanism and Other Studies* (Oxford, 1970), Essay 4; and E. B. Greenwood, "Poetry and Paradise: A Study in Thematics," *EC* XVII (1967), 13.

[9] Hugh of St. Victor, *Didascalicon*, p. 61.

[10] *Poems and Dramas of Fulke Greville*, ed. Geoffrey Bullough (2 vols., New York, 1945), I, 182.

Pressed into the service of the *opus restaurationis*, literature was forced to take account of the special disabilities of its audience, confronting the ambiguities of experience with powers of knowing that were weakened, slowed, and easily distracted by will and sense, but nonetheless capable of envisaging "what perfection is." Allegory is a mode well adapted to deal with man's epistemological dilemma. In Spenser's allegory, especially, we can see the poet accepting his double responsibility: to re-fashion Paradise in imagination, embodying the dreams of "erthliche beestes"; and to provide a clue to the labyrinth of this world, where we are perplexed by hints, guesses, lights that go out, a language that continually betrays us.

In the first place, allegory is an *analytic* mode. The poet demonstrates how we explicate the objects confronting our fallen understanding. Some of his images imitate these objects, by being inherently ambiguous or deceitful, but at the same time, as Bacon advocated, he provides "helps to the senses"; the fiction includes an analysis of how it is to be read. Northrop Frye says that in allegory "a poet explicitly indicates the relationship of his images to examples and precepts." The key word is *explicitly*, which need not be taken literally. It is a shorthand term, distinguishing what the allegorist does from what any maker of fictions does. Every successful literary work teaches us the rules by which it is to be understood. The allegorist does this in a particularly self-conscious and thoroughgoing way; *explicitly* has the force of *designedly, self-consciously*. In an allegory the process of explication and self-contemplation becomes part of the metaphorical fiction. Frye says that the self-interpretation of allegory inhibits us, as readers, from adopting the techniques we are used to bringing to bear upon literary texts. He is right, I think, in locating the distaste for allegory in the fact that "continuous allegory prescribes the direction of . . . commentary, and so restricts its freedom."[11] If this distaste has diminished recently, it may

---

[11] *Anatomy of Criticism* (Princeton, 1957), p. 90.

be because we have learned that richness of interpretive potentiality is as interesting as the freedom permitted by "symbolic" forms. And, in any case, the restrictions placed on "freedom" by Spenser are qualified by other aspects of his allegory.

Allegory is analytic in another sense as well. One of its procedures involves the definition or "unfolding" of complex concepts (as distinct from the visible seemings of experience) by identifying their attributes with various elements in the visible fiction. The explication of Despair in Book I is accomplished through description of the setting and the personification; through action—the encounters and conversations between the two knights and Despair; and through narrative sequence—the fact that the Red Cross Knight comes upon Despair at this point in his career rather than another. In the explication of Pride, Spenser follows a similar method, but complicates it by doubling the personification, so that different aspects of pride are exposed in the contrasting *visibilia* of Lucifera and Orgoglio. This process is the opposite of poetic ambiguity, whereby meaning is concentrated in "lightning flashes" of dense linguistic implication—a point made by Empson, in his classic paragraphs on the Spenserian stanza. Ambiguity exploits implication; the counter-process of analytical allegory unpacks the multiple meanings of appearances and sorts out alternatives. The result Empson describes as "an alternative to, or peculiar branch of ambiguity";[12] what C. S. Lewis has called "iconographical ambiguity"[13] is solved within the poem itself by the poet.

Allegory's explication of its own metaphors formally imitates the process of discursive reasoning, which characterizes human understanding as distinct from angelic intellectuality. For fallen man, in particular, the syllogistic process of discursiveness is laborious, a halting quest entangled

[12] *Seven Types of Ambiguity* (2nd ed., London, 1947), p. 34.
[13] *Studies in Medieval and Renaissance Literature* (Cambridge, 1966), p. 160.

38

with temporality. "The light which we have gained was given us, not to be ever staring on, but by it to discover onward things more remote from our knowledge" (*SM*, p. 748). Milton's sentence might be a description of the career of the Red Cross Knight in Book I of *The Faerie Queene*. In his first dragon-battle, his armor provides only "A little glooming light, much like a shade" (i.14); after the last battle, he looks upon the bright countenance of Truth unveiled. In between, there is the gradual discovery of "onward things more remote," figured in the basic ground-plan of allegory, the pilgrimage or quest. More than mere fashion dictated the popularity of this narrative pattern during the centuries of allegorical writing. The quest is a figure for the progressive, ongoing nature of our understanding, "as the state of man now is." It makes us aware of the temporal categories under which we must contemplate reality, and thus reinforces the analytic approach to images and concepts. Whether or not allegory actually uses a journey as narrative base, it always implies a discursive "plot"—if it is not always a *Bildungsroman*, it invokes *Bildung* as the critical procedure of the narrative.[14]

The epistemological precision of allegory can be identified in part, then, with its imitation of the process whereby we analyze, categorize, and give names to the opaque realities, both "external" and "internal," of experience. But this is not the whole story, for opaqueness itself plays an important prescriptive role in the allegorical method, as well as a descriptive one. We need only recall Spenser's characterization of his poem as a "dark conceit," and consider the implications of Puttenham's defense of darkness as an essen-

---

[14] I do not mean to imply that *Bildung* in *The Faerie Queene* entails "character development" in the novelist's sense; on the other hand, to argue as William Nelson does that "stability of character" is absolute in Spenser's heroes seems to me to deny the experience of almost every reader, particularly of Book I. (See *The Poetry of Edmund Spenser* [New York, 1963], pp. 122-23.) Spenser does not examine motives in a novelistic way, but the consequences of experience are often manifested as an advance in the hero's strength, competence, or understanding.

tial aspect of what he calls "full Allegorie." He begins with an example of "mixt" allegory, a quotation from Gascoigne.

> The cloudes of care have covred all my coste,
> The stormes of strife, do threaten to appeare. . . .

Puttenham comments:

> I call him not a full Allegorie, but mixt, bicause he discovers withall what the *cloud, storme, wave,* and the rest are, which in a full allegorie shoulde not be discovered, but left at large to the readers judgement and conjecture.[15]

Rosemond Tuve extends this rhetorical analysis to allegory's structure, insisting that *"good allegory never tells* in so many words" what the images mean.[16] Her statement appears to contradict the explicitness of interpretation which I have identified as a primary characteristic of allegory, following Frye's observation that the allegorical poet "explicitly indicates the relationship of his images to examples and precepts." The two statements are not really irreconcilable, but they point to a genuine complication. Spenser's allegory is designed to demonstrate the darkness of our situation as fallen human beings, with special reference to the accessibility of truth; the demonstration proceeds by introducing us to a fictive world whose enigmatic surface darkly reflects the everyday darkness in which we grope. It also provides us with clues, simple, complex, obvious, subtle, and above all, diverse, for penetrating that surface. The result is a

---

[15] *Arte of English Poesie,* III.xviii; p. 188. The distinction between "pure" and "mixed" allegory goes back to Quintilian's *Institutes,* VIII.vi, and is not infrequently noted in Elizabethan rhetoric books. Henry Peacham in *The Garden of Eloquence* (1593), observes that "Sometime an Allegorie is mixt with some words retaining their proper and usual signification" (Facsimile ed., introd. W. G. Crane [Gainesville, Fla., 1954], p. 26).

[16] *Allegorical Imagery* (Princeton, 1966), p. 290.

model for us in learning to fathom our own lives. There always *are* clues in allegory—what Miss Tuve calls "parallel statements in another form of discourse, that give us hints of what path to take to a meaning." But they are not "declarations" of meaning; the reader is always required to do some of the work.

One kind of "darkness" in allegory, therefore, is the mimetic phase of the fiction; it imitates everyday, ill-informed experience. Here Puttenham's rule for "full Allegorie" is helpful, in insisting that the continued metaphor of an allegory is peculiar insofar as the author does not "discover" the tenor of his images—"what the *cloud, storme, wave,* and the rest are." The nature of the images is discovered slowly and by intricate means, in a process which initially imitates ordinary discursive understanding but eventually departs from it in the intensity and completeness of illumination that is achieved. At the outset, clues are postponed. So we read, at the beginning of the first hero's first adventure:

> Thus as they past,
> The day with cloudes was suddein overcast.
> (I.i.6)

Spenser does not speak of a storm of anger, or divine displeasure, or natural malevolence, and indeed this storm is none of these. Its meaning is complex and gradually revealed, beginning with the next line, which speaks of "angry *Jove*" and the relationship of loving hate between nature and supernature. The unraveling continues for many stanzas; but before we unravel, we *see,* and what we see or experience is first of all opaque and enigmatic to our vision.

I have said "first of all," and the relation of presentation to explication is usually though not invariably a temporal one in Spenser's narrative. It should be understood that temporality in this case is working *within* the fiction; I am not now speaking of a process whereby the poet finds his images—having argued, above, that this procedure should *not* be described in terms of *first . . . then*. But the experience of the human characters in *The Faerie Queene* moves in time as Milton recommended, from a little light to the discovery of "more remote" meanings, from one opaque image to another, slightly more transparent one, and finally into the light of truth. In this respect, as I suggested earlier, Book I is paradigmatic. "Darkness" for the Red Cross Knight is deep at the beginning. The point of greatest transparency in the images comes at the House of Holiness in Canto x, and the narrative subsequently moves into a new dimension and another kind of "darkness," this time a visionary opacity, "dark with excessive bright."

The sequential character of knowledge in Spenser's allegory can be illustrated on a small scale from the fourth canto of Book II, in which Guyon approaches a disorderly scene.

> It fortuned forth faring on his way,
> > He saw from farre, or seemed for to see
> > Some troublous uprore or contentious fray,
> > Whereto he drew in haste it to agree.
> > A mad man, or that feigned mad to bee,
> > Drew by the haire along upon the ground,
> > A handsome stripling with great crueltee,
> > Whom sore he bett, and gor'd with many a wound,
> > That cheekes with teares, and sides with bloud did
> > > all abound.
> > > (II.iv.3)

The stanza records the hero's gradual approach, from a point so distant that he is not sure what he is seeing ("seemed for to see" refers to Guyon's uncertain effort to interpret his own perception), to a close-up in which the tears on the stripling's cheeks are visible. The alternative phrases in the third line are not quite synonymous; the second more exactly approximates the true situation, marking the hero's, and the reader's, improvement of understanding as a closer look reveals not a mere unspecified "uprore," but a "contentious fray," a contest between two persons, who will be described in the second quatrain. This procedure is typical of Spenser's method in many episodes of *The Faerie Queene*, where we are kept closely bound to the perceiving character's point of view and the verse consists almost entirely of noncommittal descriptive phrases with a minimum of commentary, explicit or implied, by the poet. The phrase, "or that feigned mad to bee," is prophetic, since one of the things Spenser wants us to note about Furor is that it resembles madness in its dangerous irrationality, but cannot be excused as true madness might be, since it expresses the willful short-circuiting of reason by the "affections" in a furious man ("reason blent through passion," iv.7). But when we first encounter the phrase it contributes naturally enough to the peering, conjectural effort of Guyon to work out just what is going on.

The focus, therefore, gradually sharpens in the course of these nine lines, but what we see is still not a figurative meaning; it is a violent visible happening, and it is followed by another stanza of description, this time of "a wicked Hag . . . In ragged robes, and filthy disarray." This stanza's second half allows the metaphor to begin to shape itself behind the noncommittal surface, not through explicit comment, but by appealing to the reader's familiarity with the emblem for Occasion:

> Her lockes, that loathly were and hoarie gray,
> Grew all afore, and loosely hong unrold,
> But all behind was bald, and worne away,
> That none thereof could ever taken hold.
> (II.iv.4)

It is not until several more stanzas describing Guyon's struggle with the "madman" have absorbed our attention, however, that the nature of the characters is fully unfolded. The Palmer names them:

43

That same is *Furor,* cursed cruell wight,
That unto knighthood workes much shame and woe;
And that same Hag, his aged mother, hight
Occasion, the root of all wrath and despight.

(II.iv.10)

He continues for another stanza, advising Guyon how to cope with these odd enemies; his remarks confirm what we have already noticed in attending to the details of the battle, and make explicit the *kind* of commentary that is relevant to the action, by exposing the tenor of the metaphorical vehicle. The exposure is not altogether explicit, of course; some of the Palmer's details require further explication by *us*—for example, the mother-son relationship between Occasion and Furor, one of Spenser's favorite ways of indicating logical connection.[17]

The Palmer's role in this episode descends from that of the helpful hermits who turn up conveniently to unravel the confusions of Sir Lancelot and others in the Arthurian romances. The knight undergoes experiences; the hermit, standing in for the author, who stands in for God, tells him what they mean. In explaining how to read the allegories in which they appear, such characters are also elucidating the part played by the analytic, categorizing intelligence in the psychic world of each of us. We turn our own lives into allegories when we contemplate their meaning. The Palm-

[17] This episode is discussed at some length by Paul Alpers, *The Poetry of "The Faerie Queene"* (Princeton, 1967), pp. 209-14. He argues convincingly for the iconographical unorthodoxy of Spenser's Occasion, a point which, if acceptable, supports my suggestion that the poet deliberately darkens his surfaces at the outset of this and other adventures. "The reader's initial inability to identify Occasion means that he does not see this episode from the vantage point of the Palmer, but to some extent comes to his knowledge by participating in Guyon's experience" (p. 212). My disagreement with Alpers hinges on his insistence that as readers we are always as close to the action as we are here; legitimate intervention by the poet between reader and image is much commoner than he allows. I also depart from his position, of course, in arguing that local effects in *The Faerie Queene* are part of a comprehensive design for the poem that has philosophical import.

er's speech in Canto iv is the pivot of Spenser's episode, the point at which the continued metaphor emerges from darkness into the light of analysis and explicitness. The relation between implicit and explicit meanings is not often so clearly definable as it is here; but always there *is* such a relation, and here lies the special power of allegory as a mirror of our fallen condition. It reflects its maker's knowledge of his own perplexity as a fallen being, and also his confidence in the power of *ingenium*, the erected wit, eventually to make sense of the situation.

The didacticism of the allegorical mode is a function of the special kind of response that allegory exacts from its readers. Insofar as the careful analysis of truth-seeking made manifest in allegory has general force, it becomes exemplary. The referential power of the fiction is turned directly upon us, the readers, urging introspection into our own ways of knowing. The traditional way of encouraging self-reference was to shape the allegory around a dreamer who could serve as surrogate for the reader. The pilgrim "Dante" is the best example; another is the dreamer of *Pearl*, making his slow, painful, self-deceiving, humble way toward comprehension of an otherworldly mystery. Puttenham's stress on "the readers judgement and conjecture" in his defense of allegorical darkness is a reminder that allegory's didactic purpose is best served when the reader is forced, by the poet's rhetorical manipulation, to enter and participate in the fiction. The most satisfactory and interesting allegories are those in which the writer has been most ingenious in contriving clues that will lead us toward meaning without resort to repetitive explicitness, and thus allows the reader's resourcefulness its full scope.

It is one of the purposes of this book to distinguish among and reflect upon the various ways in which a reader's response is elicited and directed in Spenserian allegory. There is, however, another aspect of this process that requires elucidation before we proceed. A reader is required to notice, not only local rhetorical effects in each stanza, but a sequence of images and their relation to each other: he must attend to a narrative pattern. This aspect of allegory is always stressed, with good reason, in official definitions in the Renaissance. Allegory is a *continued* metaphor, and its continuousness offers us, as readers, our chief means of access to the unstated meanings it makes visible. Darkness is a consequence of the shrouded metaphorical tenor, Una behind her veil. But we are gradually enabled to make out the meaning because events and personages stand in relationship to each other. As Roger Hinks has pointed out, isolated "allegorical" figures in classical art no longer yield up their significance; "the individual personifications . . . cannot be accurately assessed at this distance in time." It is only when we "concentrate upon the relations between them invented by the artist" that they become accessible; "this is the only practicable way of discovering how he and his contemporaries envisaged them."[18] The literary context of Spenserian allegory is not so distant from us that we cannot reconstruct it and learn to read icons like Occasion. But though we may identify her through iconographical details, we discover her *meaning* only when we see what she does in the context of her relationship to Guyon her conqueror, to Phedon her victim, and to Furor her son. Genuine allegories must be continued metaphors in which "the whole narrative structure implies, and is conditioned by, the metaphorical intention."[19] They belong to Aristotle's fourth type of metaphor, the most complex and interesting. "Metaphor by proportion occurs when the second term is related to the first as the fourth to the third; then the poet may use the second in lieu of the fourth, or vice versa."[20] In a complex metaphor where the tenor is wholly or partly unexplicated,

[18] *Myth and Allegory in Ancient Art* (London, 1939), p. 18.

[19] Ibid., p. 13. These and related matters are discussed by Thomas Roche in the opening section of *The Kindly Flame* (Princeton, 1964). He notes that we are not asked to attend to point-for-point correspondences between events and meaning in "continued metaphors"; "the continuity is not vertical but horizontal" (p. 10).

[20] *Poetics* xxi (57b), tr. Gerald F. Else (Ann Arbor, 1967), p. 57.

46

only the third and fourth terms of the analogy will be visible, but their relationship can indicate, implicitly, the direction commentary should take.

The *action* of an allegory is, therefore, a main avenue of accessibility to its possible meanings. But Spenser's method as a story-teller has certain striking peculiarities which are analogous, on the narrative plane, to the alternations of "darkness" and "brightness" on the plane of rhetoric, noted above. The reader's attentiveness, patience, and ingenuity are solicited to unravel sequential relationships between episodes in the narrative, as between the surfaces and meanings of particular images. Spenserian narrative, like Spenserian rhetoric, mimes the epistemological experience of fallen man, and in forcing the reader to participate in this mimesis, observing its darkness and its distracted incompleteness, the allegory makes its self-regarding didactic point.

Spenser's principal narrative strategy in *The Faerie Queene* is causal inexplicitness. "Causes," including those inner causes that we call motives, are among the invisible aspects of human experience which allegory exists to elucidate. They fall within the purview of imagination, as "daily life" testifies; those who are least practiced in the exercise of imagination are always those who are most surprised by turns of events or revelations of motive to which "inward sight" could have provided an anticipatory clue. So allegorical narrative, as we should expect, dissects and dramatizes causality. But it ordinarily does this in an oblique fashion. As Paul Alpers and others have insisted, there are no plots, as Conrad or Henry James would understand that term, in *The Faerie Queene*. Plotlessness is a characteristic not merely of Spenser's poem, but of allegory as a mode; allegorical episodes tend to be paratactically related, while the characteristic of plots is causal linkage. Erich Auerbach's analysis of paratactic *styles*—preeminently, that of the Bible—has shown that such styles create an enigmatic surface, demanding the participation of the reader to interpret the unexpressed relations—causal or otherwise—between the juxtaposed syntactic elements.[21] A paratactic *narrative* functions in a similar way, joining its elements in a noncommittal, purely temporal sequence, for which E. M. Forster has provided the elementary paradigm in *Aspects of the Novel*: "The king died and then the queen died."[22] *And then* is at once the most unrevealing and the most suggestive of narrative links. In allegory, it has the effect of compelling us to recognize the significance of cause by seeing it unfolded in an unfamiliar way.

The special tacit communicativeness embodied in paratactic narrative can be illustrated by a charmingly primitive allegorical scrap dating from the reign of Henry VIII.

> The knight knocked at the castle gate;
> The lady marvelled who was thereat.
>
> To call the porter he would not blin;
> The lady said he should not come in.
>
> The portress was a lady bright;
> Strangeness that lady hight.
>
> She asked him what was his name;
> He said, "Desire, your man, madame."
>
> She said, "Desire, what do ye here?"
> He said, "Madame, as your prisoner."
>
> He was counselled to brief a bill,
> And show my lady his own will.

[21] See Erich Auerbach, *Mimesis: The Representation of Reality in Western Literature*, tr. Willard Trask (Princeton, 1953), Ch. 1. Maurice Evans observes in *Spenser's Anatomy of Heroism* (Cambridge, 1970), that "narrative sequence always implies cause and effect" in *The Faerie Queene* (p. 62).

[22] (New York, 1927), p. 130. "Plot," of course, in Forster's formula, requires causal explicitness: "The king died, and then the queen died of grief." The fascination of plotting, for writer and reader, lies in how and when causality rises to the surface.

"Kindness," said she, "would it bear,"
"And Pity," said she, "would be there."

Thus how they did we can not say;
We left them there and went our way.[23]

In this miniature *cul-de-sac* of the great labyrinth of the *Roman de la Rose,* several characteristics of Spenserian allegory are visible in rudimentary form. The narrative begins abruptly, "in the middest," with a lack of prefatory material like the blankness of "A gentle Knight was pricking on the plaine." It proceeds in linear fashion, leaving the reader to fill in the white spaces between the distichs, to ask (and answer) such questions as, Why and how did he become her prisoner? What does "prisoner" mean? There are clues, notably in the speakers' names and in the general familiarity of the situation—an over-familiarity, in fact, which may be responsible for the poet's loss of interest in the whole affair; and indeed, the story hardly needs to be pursued. The paradigm is made so entirely visible in the few highly charged details of setting and action, that we know at once "how they did"; the poet need not "say." These particular gaps in the paratactic narrative are bridged by our knowledge of a literary background, a grid of unspecified allusion. In the more complexly charged interstices of the Spenserian lattice, interpretation ordinarily has more to

[23] *Early English Lyrics,* ed. E. K. Chambers and F. Sidgwick (London, 1907), p. 56. The editors attribute these verses to William Cornish, an interesting if shadowy figure whose name is associated, as Master of the Children, with various entertainments at the early Tudor courts. In the Twelfth Night revels of 1494, for instance, Cornish played St. George; at his entry he was followed by "a ffayer vyrgyn attyrid lyke unto a kyngys dowgthyr, and ledyng by a sylkyn lace a Terryble & huge Rede dragun, The which In Sundry placys of the halle as he passyd spytt ffyre at hys mowth." Sydney Anglo, "William Cornish in a Play, Pageants, Prison, and Politics," *RES* (N.S.) X (1959), 349. This article and the book by the same author, *Spectacle, Pageantry, and Early Tudor Policy* (Oxford, 1969), help us to reconstruct the facility with which iconographical language was used and understood in the sixteenth century.

draw on (a multiplication of clues often making for deliberate ambiguity), but the principle is the same. Narrative sequence is a vehicle of tacit meaning, calling upon the reader to supply the intervening material that the narrator fails to provide, and thereby to understand the need for such imaginative exercise in the interpretation of his own experience. It is an aspect of the virtuous and gentle discipline which allegory inculcates.

It is worth noting that the effect produced by paratactic narrative is responsible for the recurrent comparisons of *The Faerie Queene* to a dream: "a copy of the mind's conceptions in sleep." But—Lamb continues—"what a copy!" An ordinary dream seems to us, on waking, "reasonless" and "unliked"; in Spenser's poem, on the other hand, "the transitions . . . are every whit as violent as in the most extravagant dream, and yet the waking judgment ratifies them."[24] The waking judgment—the alert reader's participatory imagining—reaches out to touch the poet's designing silence.

Significatio in Spenserian allegory is variously incarnated in the poem's elements: in rhetorically defined images, narrative sequence, allusion, and also the so-called commentary of the poet. All of these belong to the *vehicle* of the continued metaphor, not to its tenor, which emerges only from the totality of parallel (or congruent) "statements" in the allegory. Spenser is comparatively reticent about pressing overt comment upon us. Unlike Dante, he "shows no sign of letting the commentary engulf the action"; unlike Ariosto, he avoids an "attitude of absolute domination of

[24] *Var.* II, 249. A sensible discussion of *The Faerie Queene* as a dream poem is Graham Hough's in *Preface*, pp. 97-99 and 134-35. His analogy is based partly upon the presence of paratactic elements in both dream and poem. "Causal relations are expressed in dreams by mere succession; alternatives by taking both members of the alternative into the same context. In fact the ample array of logical relations is reduced to a simple parataxis" (p. 135). For interesting comments on Spenser's variation upon medieval dream-vision, see Michael Murrin's review article, "The Varieties of Criticism," *MP* LXX (1972-73), 349.

the poem in favor of a more modest approach."[25] But, though he may resort to direct address more sparingly than these poets do, he is resourceful in contriving other means of address, including a system of allusions—names, places, *topoi*—whose familiarity allows them to branch into traditional contexts and add the rich relevance of such contexts to the poem's penumbra of meaning. All such layers of significance stand in complementary rather than iterative relation to the visible events, or images, of the narrative. They are mutually cooperative elements in a total *significatio*, and should not be confused with the "level of ideas," even when they take the form of discursively framed propositions.

It is necessary to insist that no element of the verbal surface in *The Faerie Queene* bears more than a tangential, oblique, or parabolic relation to what is called the "allegorical sense." Alpers says that "physical and moral formulas have equivalent status in the verbal reality" of the poem;[26] a more satisfactory word than *formulas* might be found (utterances? expressions?), but the point is well taken. All Spenser's locutions, whether they concern "objects," moral formulas, gestures, fictive speech, or behavior (and often they refer to more than one) cooperate to make us aware of an unarticulated hidden sense, a sense that never reveals itself explicitly as a whole, though explicit statements about aspects of it form part of the verbal fabric. Spenser's allegory triumphantly conforms to the elegant description by Edgar Wind: "Persuasive allegory does not duplicate. . . . It releases a counterplay of imagination and thought by which each becomes an irritant to the other, and both may grow through the irksome contact."[27] The presence of "thought" in Spenser's poem—discursively explicit commentary, proverbial saws, generalization, moralized interpretation—is less an intervention by the poet than a reminder of

---

[25] Fletcher, *Allegory*, p. 319; Robert M. Durling, *The Figure of the Poet in Renaissance Epic* (Cambridge, Mass., 1965), p. 224.

[26] *Poetry of "The Faerie Queene,"* p. 203.

[27] *Pagan Mysteries in the Renaissance* (Rev. ed., Harmondsworth, Mx., 1967), p. 279.

the part that such formulations play in intellectual life. Explicit abstract verbalizing has a role in our understanding of the world, but not a solo part; it is neither sufficient in itself nor ultimate. As Wind says, it should exist in "counterplay" with imagination. In incorporating such utterances into his fiction, Spenser indicates their proper relation to the total epistemological process; this is another aspect of his allegory's analysis of the confused manner in which we proceed toward unconfusion. Discursive verbalization punctuates the process, summing up a conscious position at a particular stage, but it must be, and always is, superseded by a renewed complexity of imaginative apprehension and a further, more adequate clarification. The moralized stanzas that Spenser sets at the beginning of many cantos are either confirmed or disconfirmed by the action that surrounds them; always there is a counterpoint, a mutual irritation, between their simplicity and the complexity of intellectual experience mirrored in the narrative and images. Take, for instance, the stanza at the opening of III.iii, where Spenser distinguishes between the "sacred fire" of true love and the inflammation of "filthy lust," a distinction earlier dramatized in the encounter of Britomart and Malecasta. He concludes with a reference to

> that sweet fit, that doth true beautie love,
> And choseth vertue for his dearest Dame,
> Whence spring all noble deeds and never dying fame:
> (III.iii.1)

It is a doctrine reiterated by a dozen Renaissance philosophers and familiar to a large literate public who enjoyed the dialogues of the *Cortegiano* and similar popularized versions of neo-Platonism. But the complexities of "choosing virtue" and choosing a wife are yet to be worked out in the Artegal/Britomart plot of *The Faerie Queene*, and when they are, the smooth elision of the quotation's second line will have been unpacked, and we shall have seen how intricate a system of resemblances can lie behind an innocent-looking quasi-personification like "choseth vertue for his dearest Dame." We shall also have had explored for us some relationships between love and "noble deeds," and the sense in which falling in love can be called a "sweet fit."

There is yet another respect in which passages of overt commentary fit into the poem's analytic pattern. These few lines, like other instances of "statement" in *The Faerie Queene*, are examples of "ordinary language." They move on the level of discursive abstraction and generalization; at the same time they are, inevitably, full of half-conscious or moribund metaphors, which the fiction is to dramatize. Their presence is, therefore, an aspect of the poem's linguistic self-consciousness, another significant element in allegory. Because it is "continued" and analytic, allegory can dissect the metaphors that lie unnoticed and imperfectly understood in our daily speech. In literalizing the metaphorical implications of language, it exposes and disinfects its natural fallen duplicity. We are seldom attentive enough to the implications of what we say, in particular to the metaphorical edge hidden in commonplace locutions. To be made to attend to them is to repair the ruins of our first parents by regaining some intimation of an originally perfect linguistic lucidity.[28] Examples of this "unmetaphoring"[29] can be found in every book of the poem: for instance, in Book IV, where Spenser elaborately unravels the mean-

[28] The most acute treatment of this aspect of *The Faerie Queene* is the essay by Martha Craig on "etymological puns": "The Secret Wit of Spenser's Language," *Elizabethan Poetry: Modern Essays in Criticism*, ed. Paul Alpers (New York, 1967), pp. 447-52. See also K. K. Ruthven, "The Poet as Etymologist," *CQ* XI (1969), 9-37. Spenser's etymologizing of his names is discussed in Alice Blitch, *Etymon and Image in "The Faerie Queene"* (Dissertation, Michigan State, 1965). Many hares are started in A. C. Hamilton's interesting article, "Our new poet: Spenser, 'well of English undefyld,'" *A Theatre for Spenserians*, ed. J. M. Kennedy and J. A. Reither (Toronto, 1973), pp. 101-23.

[29] This is Rosalie Colie's term for Shakespeare's unpacking of linguistic implication in dramatic action. See *Shakespeare's Living Art* (Princeton, 1974), e.g., pp. 145-46 on "unmetaphoring" in *Romeo and Juliet*.

ings of the "bonds" of love and their opposite, "loose love."
In the girdle of Florimell, these terms become symbolically
incarnate.

> That girdle gave the vertue of chaste love
> And wivehood true, to all that did it beare.
>
> (IV.v.3)

If an unchaste wife tries it on, however, "it would loose, or
else a sunder teare"; Venus, to whom it belongs, lays it aside
"when so she usd her looser sport." Its function is "to bind
lascivious desire, / And loose affections streightly to re-
straine" (4). False Florimell, naturally, cannot wear the
belt:

> For ever as they fastned it, it loos'd
> And fell away, as feeling secret blame.
>
> (IV.v.16)

"Ungirt unblest," remarks the Squire of Dames sardonically
(18). False Florimell is a "discordfull Dame" (IV.iv.3) who
stirs up strife between comrades and breaks the bonds of
friendship. When Spenser turns an adjective into a verb,
wise saws about loose love are dramatized as the binding
and loosing of friends and lovers; allegorical action brings
to life the latent metaphor.

All the important characteristics of allegory reflect and
encourage an awareness that we live in a radically deformed universe. In this fallen world, the universe of discourse is as severely warped as any other aspect of reality.
Satan was the first dissembler, the first liar, and the first
user of equivocal language, "scoffing in ambiguous words"
(*PL* VI.568). A false tongue is the instrument of a false appearance, and in a world of false appearances falsity or ambiguity of language must be assumed. Adam's tongue expressed a univocal relation between word and thing, but a

confusion of tongues has fallen upon us. The story of Babel is a myth of the Fall of Language; more accurately, of the failure or disinclination of human beings to make themselves mutually intelligible. We must use a tainted medium to express our apprehensions of a deceptive world, and our own deceitfulness. There is a darkness in things that makes them opaque to the moral vision; there is a darkness in the soul that makes it incapable of seeing accurately. Servants of this double darkness, words, not surprisingly, "slip, slide, perish."

The verbal medium itself, therefore, may be said to have degenerated from its primal innocence, along with the human wills that employ it and the objects (whether visible or intellectual) to which it refers. For the poet this myth has far-reaching implications. One of them is that, since words have been warped away from accuracy of meaning, he must employ imperfection to defeat itself, bending the medium still further until, "by a commodious vicus of recirculation," it ends where it ought to have begun. A forked tongue is the poet's stock in trade, and all the figures of rhetoric abuse language in order to use it more effectively. Puttenham, beginning his discussion, "Of the figures which we call Sensible," explains that "first, single words have their sence and understanding altered and figured many wayes, to wit, by transport, abuse, cross-naming, new naming, change of name. This will seeme very darke to you, unlesse it be otherwise explaned."[30] Violence is the keynote of his discussion; like Aristotle, Puttenham regards figurative language as the "wresting" of significances. It is all "dark"; it emerges from the darkness of our condition, and signifies the necessity whereby we attain the light by enduring and mastering the darkness.

The dark conceit of allegory wrests significances so violently, so visibly, that it achieves a paradoxical, ironic plainness. Puttenham calls it "the Figure of false semblant":

[30] *Arte of English Poesie*, III.xvii, p. 178.

"when we speake one thing and thinke another, and that our wordes and our meanings meete not." Referring to the figure's "duplicitie," he warns:

> And ye shall know that we may dissemble, I meane speake otherwise then we thinke, in earnest aswell as in sport, under covert and darke termes, and in learned and apparant speaches, in short sentences, and by long ambage and circumstance of wordes, and finally aswell when we lye as when we tell truth.[31]

Allegory is a double-edged weapon, serving both lies and truth. Tyndale, who called allegory a "subtle and pestilent thing . . . to persuade a false matter," admits that,

> contrariwise, there is not a better, vehementer, or mightier thing to make a man quick witted and print wisdom in him, and make it to abide, where bare words go but in at the one ear and out the other.[32]

"Bare words," worn by use and abuse, can be both adorned and elucidated by the darkening and twisting of metaphorical translation. Tyndale also stresses the power of allegory to stimulate a man's wit and take him through the dark forest of earthly meanings—a point made by Boccaccio in defending allegory, and before him by Augustine. The composer of allegorical fictions makes complicated lies, inviting us to enter his world only to cause it to turn on us and declare, in devious ways, its own duplicity.

The allegorist is the most honest of fabulators, since, though his basic figure is the one in which "our wordes and our meanings meete not," by providing clues to unlock the

---

[31] Ibid., III.xviii, p. 186.

[32] *Doctrinal Treatises and Introductions to Different Portions of the Holy Scriptures*, ed. Henry Walter, Parker Society (Cambridge, 1848), p. 428.

allegory's secret truth, he confesses his awareness of the fiction's lying fictiveness. Allegory offers a complication of means for self-examination by the poet, as well as grounds for analogy between what the poet does and what we all do in trying to make sense of the world. Classical theorists linked allegory with *ironia*; in an allegorical poem the maker can be ironic at his own expense and also at the expense of blundering mankind. Irony, and allegory, are thus methods of self-correction, scourges of folly both ethical and linguistic. The ironist uses words deviously to uncover deviousness in the object of his attention; *his* deviousness, as Quintilian remarked, is both illusory and clear.

> That class of allegory in which the meaning is
> contrary to that suggested by the words, involves an
> element of irony, or, as our rhetoricians call it,
> *illusio*. This is made evident to the understanding
> either by the delivery, the character of the speaker or the
> nature of the subject. For if any one of these three is out
> of keeping with the words, it at once becomes clear that
> the intention of the speaker is other than what he
> actually says.[33]

The allegorist speaks through an illusion but takes care to make himself clear. His own procedure thus becomes an object lesson for those in his audience who may see less clearly, or employ illusion irresponsibly.

To these ends, clear vision and responsible illusion, Spenser directs the fiction of *The Faerie Queene*. Each reader of the poem is encouraged to become a "noble person in vertuous and gentle discipline," to recognize in the details of the fiction an unfolding of the ordinary processes of his life in a manner that will persuade him to understand their underlying nature and, having understood, to amend them. The degree and kind of self-discovery demanded by allegory may be said to violate the prevailing aesthetic canons

[33] *Institutes of Oratory*, VIII.vi.54; *Quintilian*, tr. H. E. Butler, LCL (4 vols., London, 1953), III, 333.

of modern literary criticism, for which fictions are autotelic: closed systems or self-sufficient "worlds" of discourse. To adopt such an aesthetic theory, however, still leaves the theorist in a position of debating the relationship between fictive and "actual" worlds. This relation may itself be a subject for fictive treatment, since we cannot exclude any subject-matter from the raw material of art. To incorporate the argument within the fiction is to create a paradoxical situation for which the breaking of the fiction's boundaries is the formal expression. The peculiar didacticism of allegory is one version of the open-ended fiction that makes a statement about the relation between literature and life, that is, about its own status as fiction. If allegory "is a by-product of the philosophic mind,"[34] it may be so in this respect: that the allegorist's concern with his own method, and with the validity of his poem's existence, characterizes also the introspectiveness of philosophical system-makers.

The relation assumed in allegory between reader and fiction entails a degree of identification between fictive and "real" events that seems to blur the lines we normally draw between these two realms. If we wish to save appearances in order to maintain a Kantian aesthetic, we can say that the fiction invites us to enter into its world and become for the time being a fictional character. This notion is alluded to in *Through the Looking-Glass*, as well as in earlier dream-visions. The incorporation of the dreamer into the poem solicits the willingness of the reader to submit to the same process; the immediacy of relationship between reader and fiction is itself drawn into the fiction, and the breaking of boundaries becomes a "fictional" event, like the melting of the mirror's surface in the first chapter of the *Looking-Glass*. Dante and Langland, by making themselves heroes of their own stories, acknowledge this propensity of allegorical fictions to devour their contemplators. Coleridge's remarks on *The Faerie Queene* suggest that we should read it, too, as a dream vision; that, in effect, we fall asleep when

34 Hinks, *Myth and Allegory*, p. 16.

we read it, and thus enter its world. "The poet has placed you in a dream, a charmed sleep, and you neither wish, nor have the power, to inquire where you are, or how you got there."[35]

The position I have outlined is an ingenious but sophistical solution to some theoretical problems, and I do not insist upon it, or even entertain it, except intermittently. What is important is that philosophical fictions are open-ended, and that open-endedness is built into allegory both formally and thematically because, by calling attention to the process whereby we understand the fiction itself, it sheds light upon the process whereby all understanding takes place, and because it invites its readers to correlate what it "unfolds" with certain realities concealed in the unrevealing confusion of their own lives and identifiable only through introspection. Such correlation *occurs*, in fact, when we read any fiction, "realistic" or "unrealistic"; what is peculiar to allegory is the frankness with which the invitation is extended, and a congruence of patterning whereby the correspondence between invented and experienced reality is demonstrated.

[35] *Miscellaneous Criticism*, p. 36.

3. The Transcendent World: Synthetic Allegory

I have been speaking about the darkness of allegory as part of its conceitedness, and as a reflection of dark, labyrinthine fallen experience. But there is another kind of darkness in poetry, one which is often detached altogether from allegory and discussed as a separate mode. It is related to our apprehension of a realm not merely invisible, but transcendental. The main events of allegory take place "in middest of the race"; they do not, like the archetypal occurrences of myth, refer to the trans-historical realm where we locate beginnings and ends. Of *The Faerie Queene* we can say, as Dante said of the *Commedia*,

> the *branch of philosophy* which regulates the work
> in its whole and in its parts, is morals and ethics,
> because the whole was undertaken not for speculation
> but for practical results.[1]

Yet this statement qualifies a preceding sentence describing "the *end* of the whole": "to remove those living in this life from the state of misery and lead them to the state of felicity." "This life" is not the *exclusive* concern of any important allegory we can think of, if only because, as Milton and everyone else has said, human beings are immortal as well as mortal creatures, and the soul longs always for its true home. "Nothing can be recounted justly among the causes of our happiness, unless in some way it takes into consideration both that eternal life and this temporal life" (*SM*, p. 1121). Milton's sentence echoes Dante's distinction between eternal and terrestrial blessedness, the state of felicity and "this life." The greatest allegories—the *Divine*

---

[1] *Latin Works*, p. 351; from *Epistola X*, the "Letter to Can Grande."

60

Comedy, Piers Plowman, The Faerie Queene—are encyclo-pedic fictions, models of a total human reality; it is inevita-ble that such poems should include transcendental refer-ence. But even allegories less ambitious in scope—*Pearl* or *Pilgrim's Progress*—must make reference to "that eternal" as well as "this temporal," the poles of truth for amphibious mankind. And therefore allegory refers "upward" to the final truths of God, as well as outward to the multiple truths of human life in the middest, and forward to figurally an-ticipated futures.[2] Insofar as they deal with the causes of our happiness and unhappiness, allegorical fictions legiti-mately include, among their metaphorical patterns, images —sometimes called "mythic"—which are sources, rather than instances, of metaphorical discourse.

The relation between a human fiction and transcendent reality necessarily differs from the relation between fiction and "interior" reality—the psychic processes of fallen man. Therefore, the description of the "mental space" of Spen-ser's poem suggested in the preceding section must be am-plified, to accommodate the presence of envisioned ultimate truth and the unanalyzed images that adumbrate it. There is a synthetic as well as an analytic aspect to Spenser's alle-gory, which corresponds to the human soul's awareness of its permanent alternatives: Heaven and Hell, felicity and damnation. The poles of the Christian universe constitute a realm of changeless, uninvented being which in "ordinary life" we never encounter in unmediated form. The mediator is imagination; the result is a visionary poetry in which the

[2] The presence of a "vertical" pole is visible in the earliest Christian allegories. See Bloomfield's description of the orientation of the early medieval "allegorical or symbolic tradition": "Characters and actions are explicable in terms of an overarching realm of meaning, which is Christian and which directs everything to above. The meaning of events and episodes is found in an overhanging layer of significance which tends to isolate them in terms of the sequence of history and nature" (*Essays and Explorations*, p. 120). Spenser was, of course, deeply interested in "history and nature," and one of his special con-cerns in *The Faerie Queene* is to explore the interaction of *two* "realms of meaning."

61

images imitate a complex simultaneity of experience associated with mystical rapture and poetic inspiration. *Paradise Lost* is composed almost completely in this visionary mode, and in certain important respects it is a simpler poem than *The Faerie Queene,* where "that eternal life" and "this temporal life" exist in a counterpoint which Spenser's readers apprehend as an alternation between different fictional techniques, or different versions of metaphor. Both poems eventuate in dark conceits, but in Spenser the darkness usually gives way to unanalyzed transparency; in Milton, darkness marks the triumphant limit of human intellectual and imaginative power.

Almost every defender of allegory in the Renaissance insists that its darkness is a way of concealing the deep and high truths of ultimate reality from the profane vulgar. Their further insistence that special learning and initiation were required to comprehend this darkness suggests that they understood the images themselves to be essential, not accidental, mediators of meaning.[3] This aspect of allegory links it with magic, with "pagan mysteries" and their analogues in Christian thought. Some essential spadework on this subject has been done by Edgar Wind, and, as many critics have discovered, his account is of great value in helping us to understand literary allegory. Wind points out that in its most sophisticated forms allegory attempts to educate its readers in the realities of *both* the temporal and the transcendental worlds. Because "God has placed his dwelling in darkness," darkness becomes a means of apprehending

[3] The hiddenness of allegory's sense was often defended at the same time on opposing grounds. Boccaccio writes: "Such then is the power of fiction that it pleases the unlearned by its external appearance, and exercises the minds of the learned with its hidden truth; and thus both are edified and delighted with one and the same perusal" (*Boccaccio on Poetry,* ed. C. G. Osgood [Indianapolis, 1956], p. 51). The unlearned are fended off, the learned exercised, by the same images. The most serious justification of allegory, which Boccaccio derives from Augustine, stresses the "strong intellectual effort and various interpretation" required for understanding; as a result, truth is made "more precious" (p. 60).

light. The complex "knots" of imagery in certain Renaissance emblems represent the re-absorption of previously articulated meanings into their sources.

The "unfolded" figures, which appeared familiar
because they were closer to exoteric terms, are
united—"infolded"—in a mysterious cypher which
comprises the contraries as one; and when "complication" reaches its height, and the opposites
become indistinguishable, all multiplicity vanishes
in the One beyond Being—the absolutely unfamiliar,
for which there is no fitting image or name.[4]

Spenser never attempted so high a flight, but Wind's paragraph exposes some of the tacit assumptions that explain the existence of "mythic" passages in *The Faerie Queene*. In these, the images conform to what Wind describes as an "intermediate state" of being; they invite "further 'complication' above and further 'explication' below." "Explication" or "unfolding" is the analytic process I have already discussed and linked with the imitation of discursive reasoning. "Complication," which Wind also calls "infolding," depends, rather, upon intuitive comprehension and points toward a trans-temporal reality. Creating opaque complex images, the poet imitates and anticipates the finalities of heavenly truth, where the attributes that we "see" on earth as separate are absorbed into a single vision.

The visionary or vertical dimension of *The Faerie Queene* is most vividly manifest, as Frye has said, in mountain-top epiphanies like those of Books I and VI;[5] extra-temporal reference is present, too, in the taciturn enigmatic cantos where the narrative slows and we are presented with complex uninterpreted images characterized by *both* "resistance to rationalization" and "signifying power."[6] These epi-

---

[4] *Pagan Mysteries*, p. 206.

[5] For "images of ascent," see *Fables of Identity: Studies in Poetic Mythology* (New York, 1963), pp. 58-62.

[6] The phrases of Angus Fletcher, describing the "shift from allegory to myth" (*Allegory*, p. 321).

sodes have attracted special attention and, with it, disagreement, from critics: Belphoebe's first appearance in Book II; the Cave of Mammon; the Garden of Adonis; the Masque of Cupid; the Temple of Isis and Britomart's dream. There are many lesser examples where the poem's atmosphere thickens and illumination dims; some of these are demonic, such as the underworld visitations of Cantos i and v of Book I, and most of them are anagogic, pointing to some version of conclusiveness, whether "heavenly bliss" or doom, or a secular apocalypse within history.

These episodes and images are fully incorporated into the body of Spenser's allegory and should not be extracted from it by the use of a radically distinct terminology. Wind's account is valuable because it recognizes that "unfolding" and "infolding" are distinguishable but functionally inseparable stages in a process of understanding a world that presents itself to us darkly.

> Contrary to the divine intelligence which the
> reading of hieroglyphs is supposed to foreshadow,
> the intuitive grasp of them depends on discursive
> knowledge. Unless one knows what a hieroglyph
> means, one cannot *see* what it says. But once one has
> acquired the relevant knowledge, "unfolded" by more
> or less exoteric instruction, one can take pleasure in
> finding it "infolded" in an esoteric image or sign.[7]

Most of the major "infolded" images in *The Faerie Queene* occur fairly late in their respective books, after "one has acquired the relevant knowledge" through exposure to a sequence of images analytically "unfolded" in the temporal plane. The structures of individual books thus imitate another aspect of the plain man's pathway to knowledge: the dependence of intuitive visionary moments on the unvisionary experience of ordinary coming-to-know. The compatibility of vision with allegory is everywhere apparent in

[7] *Pagan Mysteries*, p. 208.

the great allegorical fictions, not merely in the *Divine Comedy* which, as Singleton has said, claims a thoroughgoing literalness within the fiction. The authority of visionary experience informs also those parts of other works where the poet's inventiveness melts into the ecstatic passivity of the seer. *Piers Plowman* offers many examples; in *The Pilgrim's Progress*, which for most of its length is a continued metaphor, fictiveness opens into vision at the climax of both Parts. In fact, the conclusions of Bunyan's stories represent that moment when the figurative intimations of our lives are absorbed into the actualities that stand behind them. Part I ends with the dreamer's vision:

> Now just as the gates were opened to let in the men, I looked in after them, and behold, the city shone like the sun; the streets also were paved with gold, and in them walked many men, with crowns on their heads, palms in their hands, and golden harps to sing praises withal.
>
> There were also of them that had wings, and they answered one another without intermission, saying, "Holy, holy, holy, is the Lord." And after that, they shut up the gates; which when I had seen, I wished myself among them.[8]

These images are understood to exist in a dimension of reality distinct from that of the earlier images of the Interpreter's House or Doubting Castle; they are not metaphors. Yet they can inhabit the same story because Bunyan and his reader know that the invented truths of allegory and the achieved truths of vision are complementary. The "behold!" of Bunyan's dreamer follows upon a careful metaphorical progress. Spenser's Red Cross Knight is allowed a vision of the Heavenly City, but only after he has visited Cleopolis, the fairest city "that might be seen" by a mere mortal eye. Cleopolis' major feature, the "towre of glas," Panthea, is a

[8] *The Pilgrim's Progress*, ed. James B. Wharey, rev. Roger Sharrock (2nd ed., Oxford, 1960), p. 162.

house of earthly fame and a mirror for all earthly cities (I.x.58). It is also a reminder that a well-ruled mortal commonweal resembles our ultimate felicity, so that a "literal" city can become, in a fiction like *The Faerie Queene*, part of a vision of man's life as an effort to reconstruct and anticipate his true heavenly home.

The validity of non-metaphorical visions within allegory is likely to depend upon assumptions about the historicity of the Bible, and most such visions are, like Bunyan's, directly modeled upon biblical texts. The irruption of visionary moments into the fiction can also be made plausible by setting the entire allegory within the matrix of a dream. Spenser, for reasons we cannot now know, chose not to compose *The Faerie Queene* as a dream-vision, but he shows great inventiveness in finding substitutes for the sense of historicity, of fictive literalness, which that genre promotes. The self-consciousness of his poem derives, in part, from his special sense of himself as a participant in an historical process and of his poem as itself an historical fact, the latest contribution to a literary sequence that included the fictions of Virgil, Dante, and Chaucer: "Poets, even as Prophets, each with each / Connected in a mighty scheme of truth." I am not speaking now of "Spenser's historical allegory," though that certainly must be considered in any complete account of the poem's historicity, and its sovereign pertinence to a valid reading of *The Faerie Queene* is better understood than it used to be, chiefly as a result of two fine essays by Frank Kermode.[9] From both the historical and the visionary planes, the fictive boundaries open to let us see the true boundaries which give our lives meaning: an ever-present realm of unseen reality, and the vanished but accessible past, especially the history of imagination's efforts to make sense of human life.

A syncretistic turn of mind enabled Spenser, like many other artists in the Renaissance, to subdue into a continuum

[9] "Spenser and the Allegorists" and "*The Faerie Queene* I and V," now collected in his *Shakespeare, Spenser, Donne* (New York, 1971).

any or all of the images in which men have labored to realize their sense of truth. This generated a technique of allusion which locates the poem in the history of human imagining and thereby offers us another means of approach through the allegory to uninvented reality.

The "mental space" of the poem has, therefore, an historical as well as a metaphysical or visionary dimension; and the two are related to each other. Their interaction can perhaps best be described by considering the idea of "Fairy Land" itself, a fictive "place" that still contains a good deal of *terra incognita*. A critical muddle has confused the universe of discourse in which the poem unfolds, and a fictive place actually referred to from time to time by the poet as "Fairy Land." These two are not identical, and failure to recognize their non-identity has resulted in misconceptions about the nature of Spenser's undertaking, and complaints about inconsistencies. Spenser speaks at greatest length about Fairy Land in Book II (itself a significant hint as to the nature of that book's theme): in the Proem and in his account of the volume *Antiquitie of Faery lond*, which Guyon reads at the House of Alma. But these two references point in different directions, to the *two* senses in which we are to take this crucial concept.

Most writers on the subject have taken their cue from Guyon's book, and from the "Faerie" characters in the poem. Fairy Land, says Miss Rathborne, is "a land of fame, which reveals the meaning of world history." For Roche, it is "the ideal world of the highest, most virtuous *human* achievements"; for Frye, "the world of realized human nature."[10] These descriptions share an emphasis on ideality,

[10] Isabel E. Rathborne, *The Meaning of Spenser's Fairyland* (New York, 1937), p. 206; Roche, *Kindly Flame*, p. 45; Frye, *Fables of Identity*, p. 73. See also Frye's essay, "The Rising of the Moon: a Study of 'A Vision,'" where Fairy Land is called "a world of moral realisation, like Dante's purgatory, where the good is separated from the bad" (*An Honoured Guest: New Essays on W. B. Yeats*, ed. Denis Donoghue and J. R. Mulryne [London, 1965], p. 11). This is really a description of Spenserian allegory, and hence is close to what I shall call the "larger" Fairy Land, the entire poetic "world."

the realization of the possibilities inherent in human nature and history. And the emphasis is justified by *Antiquitie of Faery lond*, which is set over against *Briton moniments*, the melancholy chronicle of British history from its beginnings in a "salvage wildernesse" to the coming of Arthur. The contrast between them forces upon us the disastrousness of "real" history by juxtaposing it with the orderly utopian progress of the Elfin emperors. The founder of the line, Elfe, was created by Prometheus, and the story of his descendants does not include that historical declination recorded by human mythographers, classical as well as Christian. The Elfin race did not fall, nor endure the vicissitudes of Hesiodic subsidence from gold to iron. The keynote of its history is mastery and control, symbolized by the "bridge of bras," "built by art upon the glassy See" by the emperor Elfinor. The next stanza is typical, in tone and content, of the Elfin chronicle.

> He left three sonnes, the which in order raynd,
> And all their Ofspring, in their dew descents;
> Even seven hundred Princes, which maintaynd
> With mightie deedes their sondry governments.
> (II.x.74)

Order and *dew descent*, legitimate rule *maintaynd*: such principles are the realized norm in Fairy Land. *Briton moniments* records, on the other hand, monotonously reiterated chaos, bloody usurpations, and the ruination of kingdoms. It is not much like Fairy Land; but then, neither is the wild landscape of the poem itself, where grotesque monsters, untamed beasts, licentious giants, wicked enchantresses, and vile enchanters roam almost at will. To equate the events that transpire in this "world" with the lucid decorums of Guyon's book is to call in question the veracity of Faerie historians.

When the poet speaks in his own voice about Fairy Land,

he leaves a somewhat different impression. He begins the Proem to Book II by invoking history; his poem is "this famous antique history," the account of events long past, like *Antiquitie of Faery lond*. But by the time the five stanzas of the Proem are over, we are situated in a fore-ground, a "present time," both fictive and actual.

> And thou, O fairest Princesse under sky,
> In this faire mirrhour maist behold thy face,
> And thine owne realmes in lond of Faery,
> And in this antique Image thy great auncestry.
> (II.Pro.4)

Fairy Land is the mirror of Elizabethan England as the "antique Images" of history are mirrors of every unfolding present moment. They show us our own faces, ugly or beau-tiful, made intelligible by the receding perspective of his-tory, "back in a time made simple by the loss / Of detail." But the mirror of history never reflects merely the ideal. It is rather a mirror of possibility, and its didactic force is wit-nessed in that Elizabethan best-seller, the *Mirror for Magis-trates*.[11] Spenser suggests a different sort of possibility in the bewildering shiftiness of his Proem's middle stanzas. Recent discoveries vouch for the conjectural existence of other worlds that "no body can know" at first hand, it may be, for many aeons.

> Yet all these were, when no man did them know;
> Yet have from wisest ages hidden beene:
> And later times things more unknowne shall show.
> Why then should witlesse man so much misweene
> That nothing is, but that which he hath seene?

[11] In his interesting book, *Idea and Act in Elizabethan Fiction* (Princeton, 1969), Walter R. Davis characterizes the fictive worlds of sixteenth-century literature in terms of "possibility": "such fiction will remain as close to Ideas, ideals, or ideas as to actions; and it will thus, instead of rendering for us the probabilities of life as we know it, at-tempt to enlarge our sense of the possibilities of life" (p. 44).

What if within the Moones faire shining spheare?
What if in every other starre unseene
Of other worldes he happily should heare?
He wonder would much more: yet such to some appeare.

(II.Pro.3)

The stanza describes the slow movement of providential history, truth emergent from the womb of time to be consummated in some unimaginable future when the possible and the actual shall be one. The final phrase is perhaps merely clumsy; but Spenser seems to be saying that unseen, merely heard-of worlds can *appear*, in visible, imagined form, "to some." The stanza's argument conflates three invisibles, three versions of the heterocosm: past, future, and envisaged or imaginary reality. And these are indeed the dimensions of Fairy Land in its larger sense, the locale of the poem itself.

A distinction between two meanings of Fairy Land was recognized among earlier readers of the poem, for example its eighteenth-century editor John Hughes.

> It is plain that by the literal Sense of *Fairy-Land*, he only design'd an *Utopia*, an imaginary place; and by his *Fairies*, Persons of whom he might invent any Action proper to human Kind, without being restrain'd, as he must have been, if he had chosen a real Scene and historical Characters. As for the mystical Sense, it appears . . . that his *Fairy-Land* is *England*, and his *Fairy-Queen*, Queen Elizabeth.[12]

12 *Var.* I, 316-17. Greenlaw makes the distinction in another way: "The realm of Gloriana is two-fold: England in the historical allegory; the Celtic Otherworld in the fairy aspect" (*Var.* I, 352). However we name the "two" realms, Spenser's blurring of geographical outlines repeatedly works against simple identification of the *poem's* setting with Fairy Land in the narrow sense. Arthur and Guyon travel together "Long . . . through wastefull wayes"; "Full many Countries they did overronne, / From the uprising to the setting Sunne." In the next stanza, with no specification of what "countrey" they have reached, "At last, as through an open plaine they yode," they meet Britomart (III.i.3-4). In III.ii, Spenser shifts the scene to Britain for the episodes

To distinguish the two Fairy Lands in terms of two allegorical "senses" is not to describe exactly what is going on in the poem; but Hughes' recognition of an ideal and a "real" signification is useful. And Spenser's desire to "invent any Action proper to human Kind" is pertinent to the larger meaning of Fairy Land that I want now to discuss. This Fairy Land is wider, deeper, more confused and confusing than the limited realm of Guyon's book. "It is our land, hard, multiform, unsatisfactory, greatly and poignantly beautiful. It is where we are right now."[13] Certainly it is where Spenser was in 1590. And where he was, was in the mind of Europe, or at any rate the mind of England. There have been many discussions of the sense in which the action of *The Faerie Queene* occurs "in the mind"; they all go back to Coleridge's observations, glanced at earlier.

> You will take especial note of the marvellous independence and true imaginative absence of all particular space and time in *The Faerie Queene*. It is in the domains neither of history or geography; it is ignorant of all artificial boundary, all material obstacles; it is truly in land of Fairy, that is, of mental space.[14]

Spenser loosens the spatio-temporal net in order to admit *un*particular and *im*material space-time: the space of what Stevens calls "the heavens, the hells, the longed-for lands," and the time that survives for our perusal in the heaped-up mythologies of civilization.

For a description of the "mental space" of Spenser's poem, we might turn to Hazlitt's celebrated account of Coleridge's own intellectual landscape.

---

at King Ryence's castle and Merlin's cave; but the quality of the events there rehearsed do not differ noticeably from those in "Fairy Land"; the borders of the two realms obviously march together. So do the frontiers of (the specific) Fairy Land and those of "Eden lands" where the dragon-battle takes place (II.i.1).

[13] Hayden Carruth, "Spenser and His Modern Critics," *Hudson Review* XXII (1969), 140.

[14] *Miscellaneous Criticism*, p. 36.

Mr. Coleridge has "a mind reflecting ages past"; his
voice is like the echo of the congregated roar of the
"dark rearward and abyss" of thought. He who has seen
a mouldering tower by the side of a crystal lake, hid by
the mist, but glittering in the wave below, may conceive
the dim, gleaming, uncertain intelligence of his eye: he
who has marked the evening clouds uprolled (a world
of vapours) has seen the picture of his mind, unearthly,
unsubstantial, with gorgeous tints and ever-varying
forms. . . .
Our author's mind is . . . *tangential*. There is no subject in which he has not touched, none on which he has
rested. . . . He is a general lover of art and science, and
wedded to no one in particular. He lends himself to all
impressions alike; he gives up his mind and liberty of
thought to none. . . . Hardly a speculation has been
left on record from the earliest time, but it is loosely
folded up in Mr. Coleridge's memory, like a rich, but
somewhat tattered piece of tapestry: we might add . . .
that scarce a thought can pass through the mind of man,
but its sound has at some time or other passed over his
head with rustling pinions.[15]

Let us retranslate this romantic description of a mental
landscape into the fictive landscape of Spenser's poem. Hazlitt's passage dovetails with Coleridge's own description of
Spenser's "land of Fairy, that is, mental space." Mental
space is the space which imagination inhabits and sustains.
It is "ignorant of all artificial boundary," preeminently the
spatio-temporal boundaries that circumscribe first-hand
experience. In consequence, mental space can accommodate
not merely remote places, but what Hazlitt, misquoting *The
Tempest*, calls "the 'dark rearward and abyss' of thought,"
and Spenser, "this famous antique history." The past lies in
the mind, "folded up" in memory, to be unfolded when an
appropriate stimulus occurs. And memory functions, for
someone like Coleridge (or the collective mind of Renais-

[15] *The Spirit of the Age; The Complete Works of William Hazlitt,*
ed. P. P. Howe (21 vols., London, 1932), XI, 29.

sance Europe figured in *The Faerie Queene*), with ontological impartiality. It entertains history and speculation on
equal terms, what man has actually made and what he has
only thought of making, the truths of being and the truths
of imagining. When St. Augustine described spiritual vision, "by which we think of corporeal things that are absent," he recognized that the corporeal things need not ever
have possessed literal bodies.

> We think of heaven and earth and the visible things
> in them even when we are in the dark. In this case
> we see nothing with the eyes of the body but in the
> soul behold corporeal images: whether true images,
> representing the bodies that we have seen and still
> hold in memory, or fictitious images, fashioned by
> the power of thought.[16]

Spenser's personification of memory, Eumnestes, remem-
bers the "infancies" of *both* Nestor and Methuselah
(II.ix.57); his library contains volumes of both "true" history, *Briton moniments*, and fictive "history," *Antiquitie of
Faery lond*. And just so, Puttenham remarks, the poet, inventing "Counterfait places," may describe "any true place,
citie, castell, hill, valley or sea, & such like"; *or* he may
"fayne places untrue, as heaven, hell, paradise, the house
of fame, the pallace of the sunne, the denne of sleepe, and
such like which ye shall see in Poetes."[17]

"Scarce a thought can pass through the mind of man," but
it finds a home in *The Faerie Queene*, that mirror which,

---

[16] "Nec illud alterum, quo absentia corpora corporalia cogitantur, in-
sinuare difficile est; ipsum quippe caelum et terram et ea, quae in eis
videre possumus, etiam in tenebris constituti cogitamus, ubi nihil
videntes oculis corporis, animo tamen corporales imagines intuemur,
seu vera, sicut ipsa corpora vidimus et memoria retinemus, seu fictas,
sicut cogitatio formare potuerit." *De Genesi ad litteram libri duodecim*,
XII.vi.15; ed. and tr. P. Agaësse and A. Solignac (2 vols. [Bruges], 1972),
I, 348. The translation in the text is by J. H. Taylor, in *The Essential
Augustine*, ed. V. J. Bourke, Mentor ed. (New York, 1964), p. 94.

[17] *Arte of English Poesie*, III.xix; p. 239.

like the eye of the poet in Hazlitt's description, reflects "a mouldering tower by the side of a crystal lake, hid by the mist," in which dwell all those speculations "left on record from the earliest time," all the possibilities that man has ever envisaged for himself, whether realized or unrealized. Here are the past visions of Eumnestes' chamber, and the "Infinite shapes" in that of Phantastes, "Some such as in the world were never yit" (II.ix.50), like "The *Amazons* huge river now found trew," in the manner of Adam's dream (II.Pro.2) Fairy Land "is" the human imagination itself, hospitable to solicitations from the world without and the world within, those visitings recorded by Wordsworth which emerge in the imagination's depths into a seamless expressive truth.[18] The reader who enters the world of *The Faerie Queene* assents to a journey within, which yet leaves nothing behind or "outside" that he would wish to retain: "what I would not part with I have kept." Like the young Wordsworth, we rejoice

> To sit within some solitary wood,
> Far in some lonely wood, and hear no sound
> Which the heart does not make, or else so fits
> To its own temper that in external things
> No longer seem internal difference
> All melts away, and things that are without
> Live in our minds as in their native home.
>
> (*PW* V.343)

I have quoted Wordsworth not to romanticize Spenser's poem, but to suggest that it is legitimate to speak of Fairy Land as "the human imagination" if we use the term in a comprehensive Wordsworthian sense. "Imagination" for Wordsworth includes nearly everything that the mind does except immediate perception in the present moment, and even that readily gives way to the inward-turning gaze.

---

18 "Faeryland is a model, a geography, of the world of poetic fiction" (Humphrey Tonkin, *Spenser's Courteous Pastoral* [Oxford, 1972], p. 100).

For Spenser, the human imagination was deeply implicated in an awareness of the past—the past of human imagining as well as the past of human history. And for him the
past implied the future as well, for what was formerly only
imagined may become actual; Merlin, in Book III, prophe-
sies the "future" of Britain, but it is a confirmed prophecy,
a future that for the reader of *The Faerie Queene* has become history. And behind Spenser's poem is a further implication: that in the timeless realm beyond history, in which
all things shall one day be upfolded, the imagined and the
real will become one, the crooked images be absorbed into
their archetypes. This is the ultimate justification for the
leveling of mythologies that goes on in the poem. All significances point beyond themselves, and all of them, even
the most serious and sacred, in the end will dissolve and be
made new—"the solemn temple, the great globe itself"—
and history will give way to the truths toward which it has
been leading us. Spenser's name for Truth is Una, and his
poem is a great labyrinth with a single center. The labyrinth is made up of efforts to transcribe humanity's sense of
its own meaning: in actions, in words, in images, in institutions, in edifices, in prayers (the poem ends, like *The
Tempest*, with a prayer). But all the turnings lead ultimately to the same place, the source where we shall be made
whole again beyond confusion. The system of historical allusions and the envisioned truths they shadow are twin coordinates of "mental space" in *The Faerie Queene*. The
poem holds within its depths the history of the human
race's strivings and its dreams—the products of infected
will and erected wit, both books of *Utopia*. Its concordant
inclusiveness makes it what, Cowley said, "a true piece of
Wit" should be, a "strange *Mirror* of the *Deitie*." The Deity
made man's mind, or imagination, capable of reflecting the
divine glory, and reflecting upon it. So *The Faerie Queene*
is necessarily a mirror of the human mind as it contemplates
the Deity in its progress through history.

Spenser tells us something about the nature of his poem

75

—of poetry itself in relation to ultimate truth—at one of the high points of *The Faerie Queene*. When the Red Cross Knight has done his penance in the House of Holiness and been led by Mercy to the hermitage of the old man Contemplation, he is granted a vision "that never yet was seene of Faeries sonne," though similar visions have been witnessed by the sons of human fathers. Indeed, the Knight's vision is a token of the fact that he is "sprong out from English race," not Fairy Land, as he is about to discover (I.x.60). The object of the vision, the heavenly Jerusalem, as I have already suggested, takes us out of fiction and into the realm that fictions reflect. And at this crucial visionary moment, Spenser pauses to speak to us about the place, the Mount of Contemplation itself. His description follows the three-fold pattern of allusion that so often testifies, in Renaissance literature, to the reconciliation of mythologies. There is first an Old Testament analogue: this Mount is "Such one as that same mighty man of God . . . Dwelt fortie dayes upon." Typologically, Moses' forty days prefigure the sojourn of Christ in the wilderness, and Spenser may intend us to recall that. But he speaks explicitly rather of the prophecy of Moses' death; this is the mount

where writ in stone
With bloudy letters by the hand of God,
The bitter doome of death and balefull mone
He did receive, whiles flashing fire about him shone.

(I.x.53)

The New Testament analogue in the following stanza is the Mount of Olives, scene of Christ's agony, when he too received "the bitter doome of death." Spenser begins predictably in solemn vein, but the stanza's conclusion, though keeping decorum with a larger purpose, has often startled readers.

Or like that sacred hill, whose head full hie,
    Adornd with fruitfull Olives all arownd,

76

Is, as it were for endlesse memory
Of that deare Lord, who oft thereon was fownd,
For ever with a flowring girlond crownd:
Or like that pleasaunt Mount, that is for ay
Through famous Poets verse each where renownd,
On which the thrise three learned Ladies play
Their heavenly notes, and make full many a lovely lay.

(I.x.54)

There was ample precedent for invoking what Dante calls "the scripture of the pagans" to underline and amplify Scriptural references; Dante's editor remarks on his "characteristic habit of taking parallel illustrations from sacred and profane stories."[19] Spenser's allusion to the Muses on Parnassus is an instance of that assimilation of pagan myth I have been discussing; like many similar allusions in *The Faerie Queene*, it indicates that all human imaginings deserve serious attention as genuine attempts to figure forth ultimate truth. This purpose is accomplished in the first instance by the *ordering* of the reference, its juxtaposition, in triptych form, with the two Scriptural episodes. Spenser could have "said" the same if he had chosen a more predictable classical analogue—say, the doom of Hercules on Mt. Œta. It is the source in *pagan* myth that is significant.

But in choosing Parnassus, Spenser "says" more; he does not merely affirm the seriousness of pagan imaginings, but speaks directly of poets and poetry. We are to ponder the content, not merely the form, of this allusion; to consider the relation between the "thrise three learned Ladies" and their lays, and the awful events on Sinai and the Mount of Olives. To encourage this, Spenser makes a gradual tonal modulation away from the terrible dooms and flashings of Stanza 53, toward the delicate harmonies of the Parnassus lines. The bridge by which the modulation is effected is the

---

[19] *Latin Works*, p. 362. Spenser's practice of this traditional technique is discussed by James E. Phillips, "Spenser's Syncretistic Religious Imagery," *ELH* XXXVI (1969), 110-30. See also Douglas Bush, *Mythology and the Renaissance Tradition* (Minneapolis, 1932), pp. 94-96.

passage on the Mount of Olives, where Spenser refers to the *consequences* of Christ's presence rather than his "bitter doome." The appropriateness of this emphasis is evident, though Spenser as usual does not spell it out. This hill, despite or because of the scene of agony it witnessed, blossoms and is "Adornd with fruitfull Olives"; Christ by his death turned death into the portal to life. In this genial air, the stanza's conclusion in the pleasance of Parnassus is not tonally shocking; and a moment's reflection will show that it is not doctrinally so, either. Poets' verses commemorate *this* hill, as the garland that crowns "that sacred hill" commemorates the Lord. That garland itself, through a reflexively metaphorical twist, is like a poet's garland, though since it is part of the divine allegory, its meaning lies in *res*, not *verba* only. Poets' songs look to their source in divine inspiration; but all sacred sources spring ultimately from the same fountain, as the interwoven allusions insist, including the reference to God's hand engraving its letters upon stone in Stanza 53. The Ladies' notes, which inspired the poets, are "heavenly"; and there is only one Heaven. "Divine Wisdom spoke not only on the Mount of Olives, but also on Parnassus," and on Sinai.[20]

Spenser's pause in his narrative for the space of two stanzas draws us briefly away from the Red Cross Knight's story, but when we return, our sense of the story's gravity has been deepened. The fictive mount from which this fictive character (shortly, however, to be identified with an historical personage) is to receive a vision of his "blessed end" (x.61), is an *example* of "famous Poets verse," whose source in the Muses' heavenly notes has just been revealed; and the model for *those* notes is suggested by the flowering garland that speaks of Christ's sacrifice, the event which made it possible for our words and fictions to adumbrate the truth. A few stanzas later, Spenser uses a traditional allusion to underline the idea of communication between man and God. The Red Cross Knight sees Jerusalem,

[20] C. S. Lewis, *Spenser's Images of Life* (Cambridge, 1967), p. 14.

As he thereon stood gazing, he might see
The blessed Angels to and fro descend
From highest heaven, in gladsome companee,
And with great joy into that Citie wend,
As commonly as friend does with his frend.

(x.56)

It is the ladder of Jacob's dream, an image that was consistently read, from the early Middle Ages through the Reformation commentaries, as a figure for the mediating power of the Incarnation, the preeminent example of God's willingness to "converse" with man in human terms, "as friend does with his frend."[21]

Spenser has thus surrounded the moment of *anagnoresis* in Book I with a system of concentric and parallel allusions whose effect is to ground his poem in history by linking poetry with God's perpetually recurrent visitations of humanity. At the same time, he is establishing the allusive mode of *The Faerie Queene*, a mode in which the "matter of just memory" contained by his poem will be revealed as the entire panorama of human experience, experience that includes words spoken to him and words spoken by him, the designs of Providence and Fortune, and the self-created designs of his own snares, labyrinths, and strange mirrors. The substance of the fiction is not visionary or "literal"; the Red Cross Knight cannot be ever staring on the City where his destiny lies. He must descend again to the plain of ordinary human life, to "Abet that virgins cause disconsolate." "A Gentle Knight was pricking on the plaine"; here the poem unfolds. It is a plain, or plane, where truth must speak obliquely. But the fiction, being conscious of itself as a fiction, can relax its boundaries to allow the *direct* light to shine through from time to time. Allegory admits vision; it also admits quotidian actuality in the form of the reader's

---

[21] References to the commentaries, and discussion of Milton's allusion to Jacob's Ladder, can be found in my article, "The Theme of *Paradise Lost*, Book III," *New Essays on "Paradise Lost,"* ed. Thomas Kranidas (Berkeley and Los Angeles, 1969), pp. 58-85.

meditations on the images and their conformity to his own experience. The allegorist incorporates within his fiction the two limits of art: an upward limit where fiction merges with transcendent reality in vision; and a downward or inward limit where fiction touches clumsy life at her stupid work. Both of these limits point to the fiction's sources, for boundaries are drawn in order to stem the flow of "real" light and darkness so that the artist can achieve his fictive authenticity. In allegory, the "philosophical" poet contrives to remind us continually of the boundaries, and therefore of the sources, of his poem. Some instances of this formal reflexiveness in *The Faerie Queene* are now to be examined.

4. Reader and Character

The intersecting axes of "mental space" in *The Faerie Queene* are glimpsed from time to time throughout the poem. The characters, including the heroes, move primarily in the horizontal plane, but Spenser's readers have their attention repeatedly drawn to the upper and lower limits of reality which are also the sources of the poem's truth. This vertical dimension is ordinarily beyond the horizon of the characters, but visible to us; as always when a distance develops between fiction and reader, the effect is to make us aware of fictiveness itself and to ponder the nature and relevance of fictions. Episodes also occur *within* the fiction in which an invisible reality impinges upon the hero's consciousness, and is recognized for what it is, so that he (or she) becomes a witness to the drama being played out within and around his own psyche. Both kinds of actions will be noticed in this section in examples drawn from the first two books, where Spenser seems to be making a distinction between the amount of transcendental light which he allows to filter through to the respective heroes.

I begin, however, with a simple instance of allegorical self-consciousness which is also visibly a moment of self-consciousness for the hero of Book II. In the parlor of the House of Alma, Guyon and Arthur encounter "A lovely bevy of faire Ladies." They are seen in characteristic attitudes: singing, laughing, frowning, blushing. "Some plaid with strawes; some ydly satt at ease" (II.ix.35). Each knight finally confronts a particular lady. Guyon's damsel blushes and casts down her eyes when he speaks, and he, disturbed to see her "So straungely passioned" (though it is her nature, since she *is* a passion), asks what he may do "to ease you of that ill."

> She answerd nought, but more abasht for shame,
> Held downe her head, the whiles her lovely face
> The flashing bloud with blushing did inflame,
> And the strong passion mard her modest grace,
> That *Guyon* mervayld at her uncouth cace:
> Till *Alma* him bespake, Why wonder yee
> Faire Sir at that, which ye so much embrace?
> She is the fountaine of your modestee;
> You shamefast are, but *Shamefastnesse* it selfe is shee.
>
> (II.ix.43)

Guyon is introduced to an aspect of himself, or rather to the source of self in him, the essence to which his life gives existential being. In the stanza's last line, an adjective is introduced to its abstract noun. The noun/adjective relation is a basic grammatical and ontological foundation-stone of allegory; in making it explicit here as part of the fiction, Spenser is exposing one of the crucial processes underlying his composition of the poem. He is also making visible, as all allegories must, the Platonic or anti-nominalist ontology which the fiction assumes. The process is not uniquely Spenserian. There is a charming example in Bunyan's allegory, where Great-Heart speaks with an old gentleman awakened from a nap under an oak tree. Asked his name, he gives no answer; Great-Heart responds:

> I deem I have half a guess of you; your name is old Honesty, is it not? So the old gentleman blushed, and said, Not Honesty in the abstract, but Honest is my name; and I wish that my nature shall agree to what I am called.[1]

Bunyan's episode makes clear another point: the honest man, who embodies the quality attributively, is related to the quality or noun as to an impossible ideal. His nature may "agree to" the abstraction Honesty, but cannot be

---

[1] *Pilgrim's Progress*, p. 247.

totally transparent because there is always a residue of other non-honest attributes in the mixed reality of a human being. Spenser's heroes are temperate and praise-desiring men, but Guyon *is* not Temperance or Shamefastness and never will be. Even the Red Cross Knight, who as a saint may one day rejoin his archetype, remains, in the poem's world, a "man of earth," holy but not Holiness. He is, as the poem is careful to tell us, "The *Patrone* of true Holiness" (I.i.Arg.).

The encounters in Alma's chamber are self-revealing in a simple but profound way. And the entire episode, if we read it carefully, can tell us a good deal about the nature of Spenser's fiction. The noun/adjective contrast, focused in Alma's reply to Guyon, is also exemplified in the different methods of portraying two kinds of characters in Canto ix. The two main female figures are presented in much detail, both visual and conceptual. Prays-desire wears "a long purple pall" and holds a poplar branch, emblematically related to Hercules; she further characterizes herself in a stanza-long speech about the "desire of glory and of fame." Shame-fastness wears a blue "garment" and carries a mysterious bird (nightingale? owl?). She does not speak, and her passionate silence suggests further characterization. Figures like these are recognizably related to analogues in the visual arts, and in masques, and masque-like representations in literature, there are similarly embodied concepts whose attributes point toward conceptual analysis.[2] Because they do not express propositions, they do not perform significant actions in the "plot," but merely repeat their characterizing gestures, which must be sufficiently informative to make up for the lack of dramatized meaning. Spenser offers a further

[2] The two maidens of II.ix are rather low-pressure instances of the densely metaphorical personages, the "massive allegorical figures with wide symbolic import," that Spenser regularly employs to embody essences. An ultimate instance is Nature in the *Mutabilitie Cantos*. The most careful analysis of such figures is by Rosemond Tuve; see *Images and Themes in Five Poems by Milton* (Cambridge, Mass., 1957), p. 57, and the chapter on Milton's *Nativity, passim.*

comment on Alma's parlor in his description of its hangings, a "royall arras richly dight," but strangely blank.

> In which was nothing pourtrahed nor wrought;
> Not wrought nor pourtrahed, but easie to be thought.
> (II.ix.33)

This enigmatic tapestry expresses the purely intellectual nature of concepts, which are "easie to be thought" but not to visualize, unless we are thinking metaphorically.[3] And that, of course, is what the allegorical poet does; he causes visible shapes to form on the blank screen of the mind's eye. To these he gives names like Shamefastness and Prays-desire, and attributes which anatomize their essences.

Personifications of qualities in Spenser's allegory are usually accompanied by descriptions of these attributes; that is, their function is to help us "unfold" a complex conception, more completely explicated in the heroic plot. Prays-desire and Shamefastness are ordinary in this respect. What is not ordinary is their relationship to the other characters. In setting Guyon face to face with Shamefastness, Spenser is analyzing allegorical process itself, allowing the fiction actually to portray what ordinarily it *does*. By introducing "adjectival" characters, the Temperate Man or the Just Man, into a sequence of adventures, Spenser causes them gradually to become transparent to the reader's vision, so that behind each of them we come to see the outlines of a noun: Temperance, Justice. This noun becomes a character itself in Shamefastness, and the encounter therefore points toward the nature of the fiction as well as the nature of the hero. But in addition to the relation between the reader and the event, there is the hero-event relation to be considered. Guyon confronting Shamefastness, observing her attributes and finally hearing her name, is in the usual position of the

[3] The argument that Spenser is here describing "the initial stages of perception" is advanced by Jerry Leath Mills, "Symbolic Tapestry in *The Faerie Queene*, II.ix.33," *PQ* XLIX (1970), 568-69. Things "easy to be thought" are "sensory forms awaiting conceptualization."

reader of an allegory learning to "see" the nature of its fictional characters. This is even clearer in Arthur's encounter with his lady.

> The Prince by chaunce did on a Lady light,
>   That was right faire and fresh as morning rose. . . .

After a passage describing her appearance—what Arthur *sees*—there is a conversation between them, in which the lady describes her "great desire of glory and of fame," and insists that Arthur himself shares the same "mood," or "fault."

> The Prince was inly moved at her speach,
>   Well weeting trew, what she had rashly told;
>   Yet with fair semblaunt sought to hide the breach,
>   Which chaunge of colour did perforce unfold,
>   Now seeming flaming whot, now stony cold.
>   Tho turning soft aside, he did inquire,
>   What wight she was, that Poplar braunch did hold:
>   It answered was, her name was *Prays-desire*,
> That by well doing sought to honour to aspire.
>   (II.ix.39)

The hero's reactions have significance within the fiction; his hot and cold shivers relate him to Pyrochles and Cymochles, the passionate brothers who divide the "forward" and "froward" impulses, but whose fraternity intimates a relationship between apparent opposites.[4] In Arthur the potentially destructive irascible and concupiscent passions moderate each other and are in turn controlled by his higher faculties; this control has been demonstrated by the Prince's defeat of Cymochles and Pyrochles in Canto viii. Thus ideally composed in him, they become Prays-desire, the thirst for fame, honor, and Gloriana that fuels the Prince's magnificence, or magnanimity.

---

[4] These terms are developed as controlling concepts in William Nelson's discussion of the design of Book II, *Poetry of Spenser*, pp. 178-203.

We, the audience, "see" something more in the episode than the hero himself does. But also displayed in him is a process of coming to understand that imitates *our* relation to the poem's personified or embodied concepts. We observe a sequence of visual attributes, which are then confirmed by the character's speech or gestures; finally, a name serves to summarize what we have learned, synthesizing an analytic process. And, if the allegory is effective, like Arthur we are "inly moved" by the truthful relevance of the image to ourselves. The force of this part of Canto ix can be indicated by noticing that it violates one of the "rules" of allegory, as stated by C. S. Lewis.

> To the characters participating in an allegory,
> nothing is allegorical. . . . Our own experience when
> reading an allegory is double. It is divided between
> sharing the experiences of the characters in the story
> and looking at their life from somewhere outside it.[5]

In fact, this paradigm is violated or invaded or deformed more than once by Spenser in *The Faerie Queene*. And such violations are an aspect of the poem's self-consciousness. In most fictions, the author in one way or another manipulates the distance that separates character from reader; in the analytic mode of Spenser's allegory, he draws attention to the distance itself—the "doubleness" that Lewis speaks of— in order to point to one of his embracing themes, the ways imagination has contrived for understanding experience, and for expressing that understanding. Fictions invent lives, or versions of life, that enable us to observe psychic reality in a way that we cannot normally do with respect to ourselves. We know more about a fictive character than he knows about himself, and this knowledge can work reflexively to make us aware of a penumbra of unapprehended reality that invisibly surrounds and controls our own lives. Arthur's meeting with Prays-desire is (among other things)

[5] *Images of Life*, p. 29.

an example of the self-contemplation that is the ultimate purpose of allegory. We are spectators *ab extra* during a great part of most allegories, seeing a meaning that the characters do not see; for them, most of the time, as Lewis says, "nothing is allegorical"; their experiences are opaque to their own understanding.[6]

Spenser often disposes his personifications—the static, frankly emblematic figures who have their being toward the abstract end of the ontological scale—in order to indicate when the reader of his allegory must become a spectator. The procession of the Deadly Sins in Book I is an obvious example. In presenting the Sins, and other figures like them, Spenser addresses himself directly to a reader (or sometimes, as we shall see, to a character who temporarily assumes the role of spectator rather than actor). This is plain in the colloquy between knights and ladies at the House of Alma; it is also plain, though a little more complicated, in the stanzas on Lucifera's Counselors in Book I. They go forth to take the air while the book's hero, the Red Cross Knight, is mingling with the company, "mongst the middest crowd" (I.iv.15). We are not told where he is while the procession passes by—only, after twenty stanzas of description, that he deserted his companions.

> But that good knight would not so nigh repaire,
> Him selfe estraunging from their joyaunce vaine,
> Whose fellowship seemd far unfitt for warlike swaine.
>
> (iv.37)

His response can hardly be called an epiphany; it is rather a fit of the sulks, as Spenser suggests in having the Knight encounter, immediately afterward, Sansjoy. He wants to be noticed for the redoubtable knight he is; if he cannot fight,

[6] Discussing "the darkness in which the hero moves," Harry Berger remarks that "the hero is our scapegoat: he errs, sins, suffers, is alienated from the world of common day *so that* we may interpret" ("Spenser's *Faerie Queene*, Book I: Prelude to Interpretation," *Southern Review* [Adelaide], II [1966], 26).

he becomes merely one of the mob, so he pridefully absents himself. It is doubtful whether the repellent figures on their "unequall beasts" have made any impression on him except to make him feel neglected and therefore joyless. The Knight's "estrangement" from the uncongenial company thus makes good sense psychologically. But in emphasizing his removal from the scene, and his lack of interest in the procession, Spenser *also* stresses the fact that the procession itself has unfolded for the benefit of the reader, not of any character, and his descriptions of the Sins underline this point. The details that reveal the nature of each figure are in the first instance visual: this is what we would see if we were on the spot. Like Chaucer's pilgrims, each figure rides a suitable mount and is characteristically clothed. But, like Chaucer, Spenser immediately moves away from the visual surface to give us details that no spectator could observe. Sloth's breviary is "worne, but . . . little redd"; Envy is a backbiter, hostile especially to "the verse of famous Poets witt"; Lechery's wiles for gaining ladies' love are given almost a stanza. In particular, Spenser looks inward to show us the invisible filthiness of these characters; each is the victim of an appropriate disease—"shaking fever," "a dry dropsie," and so on. In addition, the stanzas draw on a long tradition of representations of the Sins, pictorial and homiletic.[7]

All these traditional details—allusions, pathological analyses, remarks on habitual behavior—are beyond the range of a spectator like the Red Cross Knight, even if he were watching. They speak over his head to an audience outside the poem. The whole episode takes up at least half

[7] See Adolf Katzenellenbogen, *Allegories of the Virtues and Vices in Medieval Art*, tr. A.J.P. Crick (London, 1939); Samuel C. Chew, "Spenser's Pageant of the Seven Deadly Sins," *Studies in Art and Literature for Belle da Costa Greene* (Princeton, 1954), pp. 37-54; *Essays by Rosamond Tuve: Spenser, Herbert, Milton*, ed. T. P. Roche (Princeton, 1970), pp. 73-74, and Ch. 2 of Tuve, *Allegorical Imagery*; Morton W. Bloomfield, *The Seven Deadly Sins* (Michigan State, 1952).

of Canto iv, though it is not functional in what is often called the education of the hero. It is part of a larger allegorical design, which can be known in its entirety only by its maker, and those who are endowed temporarily with the maker's vision. There is an analogy here with God's surveying of his own works "at one view," and with the privileged visionary poet, but for the moment I shall not press it. Spenser's procession of the Deadly Sins is supposed to remind us of what we already know about sin, from Scripture, from sermons, from looking at pictures and reading poems and watching interludes and pageants, as well as from introspection. The descriptions call upon all these "sources," or analogues. Their function is to remind us of the *total* context within which the Red Cross Knight is blindly making his way toward disaster or triumph, damnation or salvation. He has lost truth, but we have not, because we are still companioned by the poet and, through him, by all the earlier admonitory fictions that he is here summing up and making plain to the mind's eye. We have access to a wider range of "experience" than does any character *in* the poem, because we move in the realm of imagination: Fairy Land in its broad rather than its narrow sense. The Red Cross Knight, even if he sees Idleness, "the nurse of sin," riding before Lucifera's chariot, does not grasp the relationship between Sloth and Pride, nor the relevance to himself of such a personage.

> From worldly cares himself he did esloin
> And greatly shunned manly exercise.
>
> (iv.20)

Idleness in these lines is the prophetic mirror of the Knight as he will shortly afterward appear to us,

> Pourd out in loosnesse on the grassy grownd,
> Both carelesse of his health, and of his fame.
>
> (vii.7)

The hero is made to enact this relationship by virtue of being a character in an allegorical fiction. We, as its readers, observing both Idleness and the idle Knight from "outside," understand the fiction's meaning. With the poet's help, we recognized Idleness as itself, and will go on to watch the noun becoming an adjective in a knight who has abandoned his quest. The hero himself, totally "inside" the fiction in these episodes, is not allowed to participate in either insight.

The estrangement of the Red Cross Knight from Lucifera's procession is the equivalent, in the narrative pattern, of a character's distance from the reader of a fiction. A similar point is made, with reference to a different source of "distance" in the hero—that is, a different kind of imperviousness to the experience being portrayed—when, in the third canto of Book II, the poet makes a narrative detour on which Guyon does not accompany him. The principal figure in this episode appears to the reader and to a couple of comic characters hiding under a bush. The hero this time is not just absentminded or willful; he is literally absent, so he does not see Belphoebe. Still less does he hear the ten stanzas of luxuriant verse lavished upon her, blazoning her beauty and surrounding her with analogues. The effects of this "conspicuous irrelevance" in the fabric of *The Faerie Queene* have been exhaustively analyzed by Harry Berger and need not be rehearsed again.[8] What is important is the frequency in the poem of such "irrelevances," long and short. They occur whenever Spenser strays away from the foreground of his fiction, where the focus is on the characters' experience, to address his audience directly and ges-

---

8 *The Allegorical Temper* (New Haven, 1957), pp. 121-60. Berger holds that "The technique of conspicuous irrelevance is the basic strategy of Spenser's allegorical method" (p. 123). For him, it is a means of reconciling "fable and allegory," or "ornament and argument" (p. 122). For me, it would be more exact to say that "conspicuous irrelevance" is a self-referring technique that calls attention to Spenser's basic allegorical strategy. Its significant feature is its conspicuousness— the force with which it asks us to notice peculiarities of modes of being within the poem.

ture toward the picture's background—where, beyond the hero's range of vision, stand in receding planes Dante's dark wood, Penthisilea, Diana, the golden chain that knits Heaven and Earth, the Cave of Night, or the Garden of Adonis where *no character*, during the foreground time of the poem, actually is seen.

In pointing to the non-relationship between Guyon and Belphoebe in Book II, Spenser is telling us something about his hero, and even more about the cosmic setting, not merely fictive, in which he moves. Belphoebe, Spenser informs us in the Letter to Ralegh, is related to Gloriana insofar as they are both unfoldings of "the most excellent and glorious person of our sovereign the Queen." Guyon bears on his shield an *image* of Gloriana, which thus stands at two removes from that Glory or Honour embodied in her and in Belphoebe, as well as in the historical personage Elizabeth. Prince Arthur, also dedicated to the service of Gloriana, has had a vision of her in a dream; but Guyon does not "see" Belphoebe. Arthur's access to a realm of being that is closed to Guyon is confirmed in Book II by his rescue of the unconscious knight (Canto viii) and by his conquest of Maleger (Canto xi).

The focus of the difference between the two characters comes in the two books they read at the House of Alma. For Guyon, a native of Fairy Land in its narrow sense, "history" is mere chronology, a sequence of glorious reigns, as recorded in *Antiquitie of Faerie lond,* or expressed by reiterated demonstrations of virtue on the personal level. Although he does become more completely perfected in, or transparent to, virtue (in particular, but not exclusively, the virtue of Temperance) in the course of Book II,[9] this fact

[9] I concur with Frank Kermode in thinking that the crucial episode in the perfecting of Guyon as an instance of Heroic Virtue is his experience in Mammon's Cave; see "The Cave of Mammon," in *Shakespeare, Spenser, Donne,* pp. 60-83. I do not believe that the hero undergoes any sort of "fall" in Canto vii, as argued by, e.g., Berger, who speaks of Guyon's "idle curiosity" (*Allegorical Temper,* pp. 27-28); and Maurice Evans, "The Fall of Guyon," *ELH* XXVIII (1961), 215-224.

is visible to the audience rather than to him. Guyon does not exist in a teleological realm of becoming: that kingdom of ends that is providential history. The Red Cross Knight's story ends with a prophecy of apocalypse, and Arthur, if the poem had been completed, would have been united with the Queen whom he had previously experienced in his vision. It is a definition of apocalypse that in it vision and reality become one. But for Guyon there really is no end; Book II opens into further adventures, in a conclusion without a conclusion, as the characters prepare to leave the erstwhile Bower of Bliss.

> Let *Grill* be *Grill*, and have his hoggish mind,
> But let us hence depart, whilest wether serves and wind.[10]
> (II.xii.87)

There are few finalities in Guyon's world. In the whole course of his adventures, he does not kill any adversary, though he triumphs over many. He is the prisoner of a linear temporarity, non-teleological and essentially monotonous: the realm of More's *Utopia*. The Utopians' glad reception of Christian revelation must eventually have shaken their commonwealth to its foundation, for Christianity endows history with significance as a process, moving toward an end: an infolding of images, a reunion of ectypes with archetypes, and the death of *chronos* in *kairos*. The temporality of *The Faerie Queene*, Book I, embraces all three aspects of time recognized by the theologians; what Aquinas calls the "measurement" of being is accomplished in all three modes in the Red Cross Knight.

---

[10] It is true that the Red Cross Knight cannot regard his victory over the dragon as a final stopping-place; in accordance with the advice of Contemplation, "He nought forgot, how he whilome had sworne, . . . / Unto his Farie Queene backe to returne" (I.xii.41). He does so "shortly," but the pause has been long enough to make its prophetic point; and the stanza that rounds off Canto xii (42) leaves the narrator in "a quiet rode," in strong contrast to the hasty launching of Guyon and the Palmer.

> Spiritual creatures, as regards successive affections
> and acts of understanding, are measured by time.
> Hence Augustine says that to be moved through
> time is to be moved by the affections. But as regards
> the being of their nature, they are measured by
> aeviternity; whereas as regards the vision of glory,
> they share in eternity.[11]

Guyon, making his affectionless way through the cyclical processes of pagan temporality, is denied the visions of Gloriana and Una that give meaning to the quests of the Christian knights. And he is denied, as well, the sight of Belphoebe, though she pertains to "the being of his nature." She comes from the realm of *aevum* that prefigures the last things and gives exemplary resonance to present things. *Aevum* in Book II is made apparent to the reader and to certain other characters, and it touches Guyon at many points without his knowledge. He moves within a providential scheme that is invisible to him; but there is "care in heaven" for him nonetheless. The tableau of the unconscious knight, brought to the limit of his Herculean power by his ordeal in Mammon's Cave, watched over by the angelically "faire young man," is an exact and moving image of his situation. And this Angel belongs to the same realm as does Belphoebe, also unseen by Guyon. Similar heroic similes, and similar cadences, are prompted by the two.

> Such as *Diana* by the sandie shore
> > Of swift *Eurotas*, or on *Cynthus* greene,
> > Where all the Nymphes have her unwares forlore,
> > Wandreth alone with bow and arrowes keene,
> > To seeke her game: Or as that famous Queene . . .
> > > > > (iii.31)
> Like as *Cupido* on *Idaean* hill,
> > Who having laid his cruell bow away,
> > And mortall arrowes, wherewith he doth fill

[11] *Summa Theologica*, Bk. I, Q. 10, Art. 5, Reply Obj. 1; *Basic Writings*, I, 81.

> The world with murdrous spoiles and bloudie pray,
> With his faire mother he him dights to play,
> And with his goodly sisters, *Graces* three . . .
>
> (viii.6)[12]

I do not suggest that Spenser intended his reader to make a connection between these two characters on the basis of similar rhetorical patterns; I do suggest that his rhetoric in both cases points to a similar status for his two figures. The allusions to classical deities endow both with numinous power, also symbolized by their possession of irresistible weapons now temporarily "laid away." The Angel and Belphoebe are charged with an ontological energy, and come from an order of reality distinct from that expressed in the personifications at the House of Alma. Prays-desire and Shamefastness reveal concepts, "easie to be thought"; they are notations, visual and discursively verbal, for quite complex but abstract ideas that we do not encounter directly except in fictions. Belphoebe is the Spenserian equivalent of a mythical being, a pagan deity in its pristine mysteriousness before its power has been drained away by naive allegorizing. She is not the visual representation of an invisible principle; she will not be dissolved into an essence when she returns to her native habitat, any more than the Angel will dissolve. That habitat has no precise name, though it has been many times described by poets. It is the home of Milton's Attendant Spirit, "Before the starry threshold of *Joves* Court"—

> those happily climes that ly
> Where day never shuts his eye,
> Up in the broad fields of the sky.
> (*Comus*, 976-78)

---

12 R. M. Cummings has argued for the presence in Spenser's angel of iconographical attributes attached to Mercury in Renaissance art; this suggestion reinforces the allusion of the episode to the epic motif of the "heavenly messenger." "An Iconographical Puzzle: Spenser's Cupid at *Faerie Queene*, VII [*sic*], viii," *JWCI* XXXIII (1970), 317-21.

94

It is not quite Heaven, and Milton tactfully avoids identifying it with ultimate reality. It is what Eliot calls "the world of . . . the *high dream*"; Dante's Earthly Paradise is the definitive literary model, and the fourth section of *Ash Wednesday* gives us another glimpse of a reality poised "in the time between sleep and waking."[13]

In his essay on Dante, Eliot also observes that "the resurrection of the body has perhaps a deeper meaning than we can understand," and this meaning is reflected in the poetic modes which realize "the high dream." Spenser's rhetoric for Belphoebe and the Angel is concrete, densely allusive, and above all *uninterpreted*, compared with the stanzas on the Deadly Sins, or Alma's ladies. There is much meaning in the allusions and the traditional details of Spenser's descriptions, as critics have shown; but the meanings remain inexplicit, the images taciturn.

> His snowy front curled with golden heares,
> Like *Phoebus* face adornd with sunny rayes,
> Divinely shone, and two sharpe winged sheares,
> Decked with diverse, plumes, like painted Jayes,
> Were fixed at his backe, to cut his ayerie wayes.
>
> (II.viii.5)

Some of the details allude to Tasso, others to visual representations of angels and of Cupid. Phoebus is a weighty figure in *The Faerie Queene*, but his implications here are not spelled out. The conjunction of *snowy front* and *sunny rayes* hints at the concordance of opposites characteristic of such mythical beings.[14] The suggestiveness of the passage, as of the next stanza and the elaborate description of Belphoebe in Canto iii, remains incarnate in the image,

---

[13] Phrases from Eliot's "Dante" in *Selected Essays 1917-1932* (New York, 1932), pp. 223, 212; *Ash Wednesday, Collected Poems 1909-1962* (New York, 1963), p. 90.

[14] These images are positive versions of the fire/water references that pervade Book II and are negatively embodied in the siblings Pyrochles and Cymochles.

however; and this method is a signal to the reader. He is to read the image in a certain way; and the manner of apprehension in turn signifies the nature of the being that is apprehended. These are figures in which meaning has been "upfolded"; in revealing them, the poet moves back up the scale of being, toward more complete versions of reality. They do not point beyond themselves, though they *come* from regions that are accessible only to the "inward sight" of the visionary. These revelatory symbols have been penetratingly described by Gombrich.

> The symbol that presents to us a revelation cannot be said to have one identifiable meaning assigned to its distinctive features. All its aspects are felt to be charged with a plenitude of meanings that can never be exhaustively learned, but must be found in the very process of contemplation it is designed to engender. . . . The very experience of meaning after meaning which is suggested to our mind as we contemplate the enigmatic image, becomes an analogue of the mode of apprehension in which the higher intelligences may not only see one particular proposition as in a flash, but all the truth their mind can encompass—in the case of the Divine Mind the totality of all propositions.[15]

Enigmatic images like Belphoebe adumbrate intuitive, not discursive, understanding; and it is precisely this visionary experience that is closed to Guyon, who must make do with his reason, a crucial, grave, and even heroic faculty, but one that does not involve dreaming or imagining. When unconscious, he lies "In senceles dreame" (viii.4), unlike the Red Cross Knight, who dreams of demons, or Arthur, who dreams of Gloriana. The removal of Guyon from the scene, through unconsciousness or narrative detour, is informative within the "plot" of the hero's adventures, but it is more largely informative in terms of Spenser's thematic design,

[15] E. H. Gombrich, *Symbolic Images: Studies in the Art of the Renaissance* (London, 1972), p. 159.

which imitates the conceptual frameworks the human imagination has devised in order to understand the world and
its own situation as a dweller in that world. Guyon's vision
is confined to the waking realm of rational heroism. He
lacks imagination, in the large sense in which I have been
using that term; being gifted only with mortal sight, he cannot see the things invisible to it. But we, as readers, do see
them, and are thus encouraged to define the differences between seeing and not-seeing and to identify ourselves as
seers, with the aid of the allegory. Implied comparisons between Guyon and the Red Cross Knight, deliberately urged
upon us by the poet, raise complex questions about time
and history, Nature and Grace. The discussions initiated by
Woodhouse's brilliant article have given these problems
sufficient critical currency. I am concerned here less with
"ideas" than with Spenser's explication of them in terms of
the allegorical resources available to him, and new resources contrived by him.

Participation by reader or audience in an unspoken commentary upon the fiction is not a technique invented by
Spenser. But the fact that he is writing allegory enables him
to make visible as part of the fiction this particular aspect
of fictional meaning. Such meaning *exists*, for example, in
Chaucer's *Knight's Tale*, but it is not visibly imagined.
Chaucer awards Emelye to Palamon through the agency of
a famous speech by Theseus on the inevitability of events
and the need to join ourselves to the will of the universe,
to accept "that to us alle is due" (A.3044). His speech is,
among other things, a sermon on mutability:

> The brode ryver somtyme wexeth dreye;
> The grete tounes se we wane and wende.
> Thanne may ye se that al this thyng hath ende.
> (A.3024-26)

The world-view offered by Theseus is in many ways identical with that of Chaucer's audience, and stoic submissive-

97

ness is not very distant from the Christian virtue of patience. But it is bound into an ultimate hopelessness; the
historic cycles that cause civilizations to "wane and wende"
never cease, and the end of every being is no end, but a
point on an eternally revolving wheel; this is Guyon's view
of history as well. The story of *The Knight's Tale*, circled
by this dark river, must take on a special coloring for an
audience of Canterbury pilgrims, who are going from *here*
to *there*, toward a blessed end that is truly a consummation.
We sense something of the poignancy of human nobility
within the strait limits of pagan philosophy, and something
of the joy in the renewal of aspiration and potentiality that
comes with the Christian promise. Chaucer's wordless
meanings are so delicate that such commentary must seem
heavy-handed; but few careful readers will deny their presence. Pagan or pre-Christian fables could readily be made
to acquire such resonances for a Christian audience, for
imagination is always nourished by its own earlier tri
umphs. Milton exploits the relationship again in *Samson
Agonistes*. And so Spenser gives us Guyon, his nobility necessarily less than that of the Red Cross Knight but closer to
ours in its naked humanness, and also a moving instance of
the limits imposed by disbarment from the eschatological
dimension of imagining.

The alternatives to Theseus' philosophy remain invisible
behind the surface of *The Knight's Tale*, but Spenser, in the
explicit mode of allegory where total visibility is the rule,
can *show* us Belphoebe and the Angel in bowers and on
Idean hills where Guyon cannot go. This is part of allegory's un-subtlety; but subtlety can be a rationalization of
human inarticulateness, and we can also regard allegory as
the triumph of an articulate audacity over the ordinary limits of human speech. And Spenserian visibility is not always
unsubtle; the crucial seventh canto of Book II inevitably
comes to mind. As Guyon approaches Mammon's Cave, he
is alone:

> of none accompanide;
> And evermore himselfe with comfort feedes,
> Of his owne vertues, and prayse-worthy deedes.
> (II.vii.2)

In the context of Guyon's range of virtues, this self-esteem is not reprehensible pride; it is what Milton called a right honoring of oneself. The solitary hero has nothing to rely on except his own powers; to recall past deeds is to arm himself for those to come. And, in fact, he succeeds heroically in this most difficult encounter. Spenser indicates the limits of his power in his faint and rescue by the unseen Angel; the limits of his knowledge are suggested by two meetings in the Garden of Proserpina. Among the wailing souls eternally imprisoned in the infernal river, one attracts special attention.

> Deepe was he drenched to the upmost chin,
> Yet gaped still as coveting to drinke
> Of the cold liquor, which he waded in.
> (II.vii.58)

Questioned by the Knight, he reveals his name: "Lo *Tantalus*, I here tormented lye." Guyon's response puts Tantalus in his place as an object-lesson in possibility, to be contemplated and rejected by the temperate man.

> Nay, nay, thou greedy *Tantalus* (quoth he)
> Abide the fortune of thy present fate,
> And unto all that live in high degree,
> Ensample be of mind intemperate,
> To teach them how to use their present state.
> (II,vii.60)

Guyon is "reading" Tantalus allegorically, as an icon that has reached its final place in the scheme of things ("the fortune of thy present fate") and henceforth serves as an "en-

99

sample" to those still in the middest, in the "present state." Present state observes ever-present fate and, if it is wise, profits by its examples. The relation of instance to concept, adjective to noun, is accessible to reason; two cantos later Guyon will be brought to see himself as a counter-instance to Tantalus, an example of Shamefastness, having rejected the over-reaching which was Tantalus' special form of intemperance.

But Guyon does not "read" the second figure he confronts.

> I *Pilate* am the falsest Judge, alas,
> And most unjust, that by unrighteous
> And wicked doome, to Jewes despiteous
> Delivered up the Lord of life to die,
> And did acquite a murdrer felonous;
> The whiles my hands I washt in puritie,
> The whiles my soule was soyld with foule iniquitie.
>
> (II.vii.62)

At the end of Pilate's speech, Guyon says nothing; the narrative moves back and away from him, leaving the Christian reader to meditate upon the meaning of this revelation, and to consider the relationship between the man who washed his "handes . . . in puritie" and the baby of Canto i whose bloody hands could not be cleansed by the Knight or his Palmer. Pilate, implicated in the most crucial event in history, is an uninvented archetype; he is the source *in history* to which types point, and Guyon as a denizen of Fairy Land is unprepared for this kind of meaning. Those "who Calumniate & Murder under Pretence of Holiness & Justice"[16] are descended from Pilate, who himself participates in the bloody-handedness that derives from Cain (and is re-embodied in Ruddymane). The allusion prepares *us* for Spenser's reference a few stanzas later to man as the "wicked foe" of God (viii.1). The phrase has given offense

---

[16] Blake, *A Vision of the Last Judgment; The Poetry and Prose of William Blake*, ed. David V. Erdman (Garden City, N.Y., 1968), p. 547. Blake adds that "Pilate has bloody hands that never can be cleansed."

to those who assume that it refers to Guyon. But though it includes him, it does not refer to him simply or exclusively. "To many sad purposes, and in many heavy applications Man is an enemy to God."[17] This principle is axiomatic within the Christian scheme, to which Spenser alludes in the figure of Pilate. Guyon falls silent before him, but that silence for the Christian reader is full of resonance, which becomes articulate at the beginning of the next canto in the reference to human sinfulness and God's merciful response to it. "Care in Heaven," manifested in the Angel's descent, is also manifested in Christ's redemptive entrance into history, one episode of which Guyon's temptation by Mammon imitates.[18]

To understand the meaning of Pilate, Guyon must become a man of faith, and possess the vision that is the token or reward of faith. I do not believe that this happens during his career in the poem, though others have argued that it does.[19] An admission of Spenser's willingness to address his readers tacitly over the heads of his characters can relieve us, however, of having to identify everything that happens in the poem with experiences transpiring exclusively within the fiction. The fact that a character's experience occurs in a particular setting and a particular pattern that

[17] *The Sermons of John Donne*, ed. Evelyn M. Simpson and George R. Potter (10 vols., Berkeley & Los Angeles, 1953-1962), X, 135. Donne's whole argument in this paragraph is relevant; he goes on to remind his audience that "for Man to adhere to Man, to ascribe any thing to the power of his *naturall faculties*, to think of any beame of clearnesse in his own understanding, or any line of rectitude in his owne will, this is to accumulate and multiply enmities against God."

[18] Patrick Cullen is accurate on this subject: Guyon "faints not because he has sinned, but because Adam sinned and because he has reached the limitations of his own virtue. . . . Guyon's faint, therefore, is not so much an indictment of him as it is a statement of the necessity of grace" ("Guyon *Microchristus*: The Cave of Mammon Revisited," *ELH* XXVII [1970], 168). The later part of Cullen's argument, which suggests a parallel between the Harrowing of Hell and Guyon's rescue of Verdant in the Bower of Bliss, seems to me, however, unsupported by the text.

[19] For example, Evans, *Anatomy of Heroism*, p. 132, and Ch. 6, *passim*.

is allusive *need not* (and ordinarily *does* not) signify its dramatic "meaning" in the character's consciousness. Rosemond Tuve says of the Mammon episode:

> It does not turn Guyon into a "Christ-figure" when
> in canto vii.9 Spenser directs us to see the parallels
> with Christ's three temptations. Rather, this indicates
> the amplitude of the issue and states a doctrine
> about the relation between all human temptations
> and Christ's. Spenser uses classical images similarly,
> to extend through their history the significance of
> his fiction.[20]

Guyon is not trying to imitate Christ, and Spenser does not, I think, give us grounds for inferring that he realizes that he has done so. *We* realize it, as we realize that in Canto xii the same hero is sailing on a sea that Ulysses traversed before him. Guyon's rejection of Mammon's temptations is to be "explained" not by assuming that he is modeling his behavior on a biblical prototype, but by recognizing that within Spenser's system of assumptions all instances of a virtue necessarily resemble each other, and all partake of the archetype definitively embodied in the Word that assumed flesh in order to give redemptive significance to particular mortal instances of virtuous behavior.

The "distance" between Guyon and the reader is, therefore, used by Spenser to indicate different ways of reading experience. Insofar as Guyon exists within an atemporal, counter-historical world, he does not comprehend the divine providential scheme which employs historical events to reveal ultimate truth. Insofar as he is cut off from visionary or imaginative "reality," he cannot see figures like Belphoebe, who embody the human yearning for an ideal realm which can be experienced only in imagination. In the case of Pilate, Spenser depends on prior knowledge in his reader to bridge the gap between what Guyon sees and

20 *Allegorical Imagery*, pp. 32-33.

what the experience signifies; in the case of Belphoebe and the Angel, he uses narrative digression and allusion to divide us from his hero.

Allusions are the rhetorical equivalent of Spenser's narrative detours. Together or separately, these techniques take us out of the geographical and temporal limits that straiten the characters. Allusions open up a temporal perspective; they "extend through their history the significance" of the fiction. Spenser's handling of allusion in *The Faerie Queene* resembles Milton's in *Paradise Lost* in that it enables us to perceive in the myriad shapes of myth and human imagining a pattern of constantly reiterated archetypes. But, since the foregrounds of the two poems are established, respectively, within and outside history, the allusive method works for them in opposite directions. When Milton links Eve to Proserpina, he allows us to look down into history to witness the dispersion of the archetypes. When Spenser says that the Angel is like Cupid and Phoebus and Mercury, he is causing us to look back toward the prototype in the mythic *aevum* and observe the reabsorption of the instance in its Idea. The physical separation of character from character, or of reader from character, in the narrative pattern, opens up a "spatial" perspective that, like allusion in the temporal dimension, refers to the various realms of being accessible or inaccessible to mortal sight. The Red Cross Knight divided from Una, Scudamour divided from Amoret, narrator and audience divided from the absent or unconscious Guyon: in all these separations a distinction is made between psychological, imaginative, and spiritual experience.

5. Mirrors of Fiction: The Ecphrastic Image

Spenser's manipulation of the distance between the fiction and its audience often allows him to comment upon the kind of reality that fictions possess, and upon the varying attitudes we should adopt toward them. But he has other resources for introducing reflexive commentary. The ecphrastic image has a long history in both the literature and the painting of Europe.[1] A work of art becomes the subject of a work of art; Keats writes a poem about a Grecian urn, or Courbet paints himself painting a picture.[2] The intricate passageways of self-commentary opened by this technique are almost infinite. Shakespeare explores some of them in the play within a play, and Spenser, too, experiments with setting a fiction inside a fiction. One such instance—which also shows the poet establishing the audience-character relationship with great care—is the climactic episode of Book III, when Britomart visits the House of Busirane and observes, first, the series of tapestries depicting "all Cupids warres," and then the Masque of Cupid. Both tapestries and masque are the products of an enchanter's artfulness which intends to deceive, though both, in the context of the larger fiction, can be seen to figure a kind of truth. The presence of the heroine and her wariness as she confronts a series of ambiguous contrived images combine with the enveloping presences of poet and reader to create

---

[1] See Jean H. Hagstrum, *The Sister Arts* (Chicago, 1958); John B. Bender, *Spenser and Literary Pictorialism* (Princeton, 1972).

[2] In *L'Atelier du Peintre*; Courbet called the work an "Allégorie réelle." See Kenneth Clark, *Looking at Pictures* (New York, 1960), pp. 167-77. For comment on the picture as "a complete allegory," cf. the conclusion of Roland Barthes' essay, "The World as Object," *Critical Essays*, tr. Richard Howard (Evanston, 1972), p. 12.

a hall of mirrors in which complicated epistemological and ethical issues can be observed. These cantos offer a particularly clear instance, therefore, of the way in which our understanding of the *nature* of particular images essentially affects our grasp of Spenser's themes. The narcissism of allegory is part of its ethical and metaphysical seriousness.

The reader and the protagonist view these pageants together. Britomart, unlike the Red Cross Knight at Lucifera's court, does not absent herself, but "busily" attends to what she sees, and Spenser's handling of the tapestry-figures identifies the character's experience with the reader's in a simultaneous foreground. The percentage of non-visual detail and commentary is very much less than that in the Deadly Sins passage. Instead, Spenser keeps us constantly aware that we are *looking at pictures*, literally "visible" in the fiction; in other words, we are in the same situation as Britomart. This stanza on the loves of Apollo is typical:

> So lovedst thou the lusty *Hyacinct*,
>> So lovedst thou the faire *Coronis* deare:
>> Yet both are of thy haplesse hand extinct,
>> Yet both in flowers do live, and love thee beare,
>> The one a Paunce, the other a sweet breare:
>> For griefe whereof, ye mote have lively seene
>> The God himselfe rending his golden heare,
>> And breaking quite his gyrlond ever greene,
> With other signes of sorrow and impatient teene.
>
> (III.xi.37)

The first five lines leave us uncertain whether Spenser is merely telling us the stories, or describing the tapestry, though the use of present tense at ll. 3-5 leaves the second possibility open. At any rate, there is a firm return to the visual in the stanza's second half, where the god's conventional, emblematic gestures are graphically rendered. Sometimes when he seems to be digressing into an emotion, Spenser insists that, after all, he is telling us what we are *seeing*, as in the lines on Europa.

105

Ah, how the fearefull Ladies tender hart
Did lively seeme to tremble, when she saw
The huge seas under her t' obay her servaunts law.

(xi.30)

"Did lively seem to tremble": it is the description of a melo-dramatic, mimetic art-form, of the kind that pleased Spenser and his contemporaries, as it pleases the princes in Kalender's house in the *Arcadia*, or causes Leontes' courtiers to praise "that rare Italian master, Julio Romano, who, had he himself eternity and could put breath into his work, would beguile Nature of her custom, so perfectly he is her ape." (V.ii.97-100)[3] And so Spenser continues to keep our eyes on the object. "Then shewd it how . . . ," "Twise was he seene . . . ," "And thou, faire Phoebus, in thy coulours bright / Wast there enwoven," "All which in that faire arras was most lively writ," "There was he painted. . . ." Such reminders keep us constantly aware of the visible visual surface; in the middle (st. 40-41) there is a particularly striking description of Neptune and his chariot, so circumstantial that it appears to allude to an actual tapestry that Spenser and his audience might have seen—or if not, to incorporate a dozen or so conventional tapestry motifs.[4]

[3] The taste for verisimilitude in the visual arts is easy to document. John Dee praises the "divine power" of the painter who can "bring with him, home (to any mans Judgement) as Paternes lively, of the thinges rehearsed," "Cities, Townes, Fortes, Woodes, Armyes, yea whole Kingdomes" (quoted from Dee's Preface to Euclid, in Peter J. French, *John Dee: The World of an Elizabethan Magus* [London, 1972], p. 152). For another Shakespearean example, see the elaborate description of the painting of the Siege of Troy, beginning at 1.1366 of *The Rape of Lucrece*: "A thousand lamentable objects there, / In scorn of nature, art gave liveless life" (1373-74).

[4] This is the conjecture of Frederick Hard, "Spenser's 'Clothes of Arras and of Toure,'" *SP* XXVII (1930), 176. But the fondness for the lifelike, referred to above, is sufficient to explain Spenser's stanzas, which also directly echo their source in the *Metamorphoses*, VI. 104: "Maeonis elusam designat imagine tauri / Europam: verum taurum, freta vera putares" (Ovid, *Metamorphoses*, tr. Frank J. Miller, LCL [2 vols., London, 1928], I, 294). Ovid's lines, of course, also describe a

In this episode, we are being shown what the heroine sees, or what she can see if she is attentive enough. "Her busie eye" peruses "each secret of that goodly sted," including the powerfully expressive, enigmatic idol of the blindfolded Cupid on a profane altar. Britomart is being introduced to the religion of love, presided over by a ruthless god. But it is an introduction, not an initiation. She is already in love with Artegal, has suffered for her love, and will suffer more. At the House of Busirane she is called upon to consider from "outside" the nature and consequences of her emotions, or rather one aspect of them. Her position in relation to the tapestries and the masque is analogous to the position of the reader of an allegory, observing, meditating, understanding. Earlier in Book III, Spenser tells us that she has restlessly followed "the guidance of her blinded guest" (iv.6)—the same blind Cupid whose idol she now sees, but does not worship. A movement from unconscious submission to feeling, then to conscious power over feeling, has occurred. The tapestries present Britomart with the equivalent of a cosmic vision, a universe enthralled to love, "To shew Dan *Cupids* powre and great effort" (xi.46), a power which can overthrow rational order as Britomart's own spear unhorsed Guyon. The four gods whose loves are most extensively portrayed —Jupiter, Apollo, Neptune, and Saturn—belong to the four elements, so that we sense behind the particular myths a universal power pervading the entire cosmos, coming to rest finally in human lovers, "Kings, Queenes, Lords Ladies, Knights and Damzels gent . . . heap'd together with the vulgar sort."

At the same time, however, that Britomart and the reader are being instructed by the icons in Busirane's tapestries, they are receiving a lesson in the deceitful potency of art. The illusion of life which the tapestries produce is matter

work of art, Arachne's web. For a description stressing the rhetorical contribution to the effect, see Claud A. Thompson, "Spenser's 'Many Faire Pourtraicts, and Many a Faire Feate,'" *SEL* XII (1972), 21-32.

for admiration but also, potentially, for deception. The *amores* of the pagan gods exemplify the genuine power of "cruell *Cupid*," but their maker is an enchanter and the tapestries do not only "entreat," deal with, the subject of love: they also "entreat" the observer's participation in and assent to its pleasures.

> And in those Tapets weren fashioned
>> Many faire pourtraicts, and many a faire feate,
>> And all of love, and all of lusty-hed,
>> As seemed by their semblaunt did entreat.
>>> (III.xi.29)

"Entreat" has some of the force Spenser gives it at II.vii.53, where Proserpina whiles away the hours of Hell in her arbor, "Her selfe to shroud, and pleasures to entreat." An *Oxford English Dictionary* example of 1526 makes "entreat" synonymous with "perswade," a meaning relevant to Busirane's purposes. Spenser's line is syntactically awkward and redundant if "entreat" simply means "treat of"; it does not seem far-fetched to suppose that these "semblaunts" are also soliciting approval of love and "lusty-hed." It is interesting, too, that Spenser stresses that they *are* "semblaunts," for in the preceding stanza the enchanter's efforts to delude have been explicitly indicated.

> For round about, the wals yclothed were
>> With goodly arras of great majesty,
>> Woven with gold and silke so close and nere,
>> That the rich metall lurked privily,
>> As faining to be hid from envious eye;
>> Yet here, and there, and every where unwares
>> It shewd it selfe, and shone unwillingly;
>> Like a discolourd Snake, whose hidden snares
> Through the greene gras his long bright burnisht
>>>> backe declares.
>>>> (III.xi.28)

This much-admired stanza, an admonition by the poet before he reveals the subjects of the tapestries, alerts us to the sinister power of art to misinterpret, deliberately or unconsciously, the phenomena of experience. In a wider sense, the tapestries suggest the self-confounding, illusion-making power of imagination when it is enthralled to love, a power which has threatened the heroine from the beginning of Book III, and which she will conquer when, in the final canto, she captures the enchanter and causes "all that fraud" (xii.43) to vanish (though Spenser characteristically makes her regret its loss: "Sight of such a chaunge her much dismayd," III.xii.42). Cupid's cruel power is made to appear grand ("great majesty"), seductive, and irresistible. Since these are genuine aspects of love, the tapestries tell a true story. But the implications of the truth can be assessed only by those who remain outside it, like Britomart: those who know that they are seeing an image of life which demands interpretation and must not be taken at face value. Dangerous works of art reveal their illusory nature "unwares" and "unwillingly" to the discerning ("envious"?) eye of the poet; their genuine substance "lurks" beneath a potentially misleading surface.

Both art and love are elucidated in the next canto, where Britomart's role, at first, is again that of a spectator. The Masque of Cupid refers more immediately than do the tapestries to her own condition, culminating as it does in the figure of the tortured Amoret who, as the incarnation of "goodly womanhead," is a generalized version of an aspect of the knight herself. In developing Britomart's response, Spenser exploits some special features of the masque, which was the most self-conscious of dramatic forms. It was to be used in the generations after Spenser by Ben Jonson to comment on the relation between the fiction and its audience, and by Milton to intimate the identity between the spectators' lives and his heroine's woodland wanderings. The mingling of audience and masquers in the

dance at the conclusion of a masque, and the participation
of courtly persons as actors who in their roles as Virtues
speak about themselves, became in Jonson's hands devices
to efface the mirror's surface and allow fiction and "reality"
to interpenetrate.[5] In Spenser's Masque of Cupid a rudimentary form of this technique is visible; the presence of
Amoret, an undisguised actual woman, among the personified abstractions at the masque's center, owes its shocking
force not only to the grisly detail of the exposed heart, but
to the collapse of the conventional barrier dividing Britomart as spectator from the spectacle itself. The intimacy
of the relation between her and Amoret parodies the concord between actors and audience in a masque; on the
other hand, upon Britomart's resistance to the traditional
participation in the masquers' revels depends the success
of her mission. Spenser exploits the genre's characteristics
in several ways, all involving distortion, resistance, or
parody; so art probes its own pathology.

Spenser's description of Amoret also emphasizes the sinister power of Busirane's fiction to metamorphose those
whom it constrains.

> She dolefull Lady, like a dreary Spright,
> Cald by strong charmes out of eternall night,
> Had deathes owne image figurd in her face,
> Full of sad signes, fearefull to living sight.
>
> (xii.19)

"Deathes owne image" effaces Amoret's human countenance
to make her an animated "signe." We have once before seen
a "Spright" summoned from Hell by an enchanter: when
Archimago "cald out of deepe darknes dread" the spirits
who would become actors in the false dream of the Red
Cross Knight (I.i.38). Spenser's stanza in Book III touches
on the same point: that imagining, which permits the

---

[5] This principle is carefully worked out in Stephen Orgel's fine book,
The Jonsonian Masque (Cambridge, Mass., 1965), e.g., pp. 102, 118-19.

erected wit to perceive and manipulate invisible reality, can transform its material into the imagery of Hell as well as Heaven, can conjure up diabolic as well as angelic beings as models for vulnerable human actors.

This fiction has its source in "eternall night," and there is no ambiguity about that phrase, nor any doubt as to the genuine existence of sprites, though Amoret is not literally possessed, but only seems so. The fiction points to its source, and this effect is enhanced when Spenser says that Amoret is followed in the procession by "the winged God himself"— the actual Cupid whose idol Britomart saw worshipped in the preceding canto and whose power she has *experienced*. At the masque's end, the "rude confused rout" trails off into a comment by the poet.

> There were full many moe like maladies,
>   Whose names and natures I note readen well;
> So many moe, as there be phantasies
> In wavering wemens wit, that none can tell,
> Or paines in love, or punishments in hell.
>   (xii.26)

The narrator first identifies himself as a member of the audience at the masque, "reading" the natures of the fictive personages. He then recites a sequence of analogues for these personages: fantasies, the pains of love, the punishments of hell—a related sequence that deepens in seriousness and in degree of "reality." The blurring of ontological distinctions results in the superimposing of planes, so that psychological, emotional, and spiritual phenomena are seen to have a common center. And so with imaginative and actual truth: fantasies—of Amoret, of Busirane, of the poet —are engendered by and rooted in a source that eventuates in the torments or joys of ultimate reality, Hell or Heaven.

The Masque of Cupid, as several critics have indicated, literalizes the metaphors of a religion of love.[6] The potent

6 Notably Roche, *Kindly Flame*, pp. 74-77.

icon of Amoret and her pierced heart projects a meaning spelled out by Spenser in the *Hymne in Honour of Love*; Cupid's darts

> Rest not, till they have pierst the trembling harts,
> And kindled flame in all their inner parts,
> Which suckes the blood, and drinketh up the lyfe
> Of carefull wretches with consuming griefe.
>
> (123-26)

Instead of literary references to arrows that "have pierst the trembling harts," a palpitating pierced heart is presented to our very eyes, as we share with Britomart the lurid imaginings of Busirane. We are probably meant to recall Malecasta, stricken with love for a strange knight, whose "wound still inward freshly bled" (III.i.56), and Britomart's reference to her own "bleeding bowels" as she complains "That all mine entrailes flow with poysnous gore" (III.ii.39). The power of art to make these invisible or psychic sufferings "real" by embodying them in dramatic images, is manifest in Busirane's magic. For Britomart, the dramatization is an exorcism. The autonomy and health of imagination, its unsparing urge, once it is released, to uncover and fix upon the truth of things, however distasteful, is evident in the apparition of Amoret as the poet-narrator controls and presents it. The dream will appear as the nightmare it is when it is endowed with the loving literalness of fiction.

But the fiction looks and feels different to those who read it and understand its meanings, and those who are condemned to enact it and be uncomprehendingly victimized by it. Both Scudamour and Amoret are prisoners of a description of "love" that has become prescriptive; they are compelled to enact roles written for them by the human imagination, enshrined in a code of "courtly love." From Chaucer onward, poets had enjoyed the comedy of lovers who took seriously the rule-books of loving; Spenser is here concerned with the very un-comic results of such serious-

ness when it is pushed to the point of delusion. The metaphors of the courtly tradition are no longer true descriptions of these lovers' emotions; Amoret does not wish to be
a cruel mistress enjoying an adulterous love affair; she
wants only to be the faithful wife of Scudamour.

> And the sharpe steele doth rive her hart in tway,
> All for she *Scudamour* will not denay.
>
> (III.xi.11)

Both lovers are tortured "By strong enchauntments and
blacke Magicke leare" (III.xi.16), exaggerated dramatiza-
tions of love as a cause of suffering and "consuming griefe."
Love *is* a source of grief, but it is not only, and not ultimately, that. The imagination is diseased which sees in Cupid an
hypostatized external, uncontrollable power, rather than
the figure for an emotion that must be confronted in oneself; it will make a religion of love and prostrate itself before an idol. Britomart, though marveling at Busirane's mis-
created pleasures, has outgrown this view of love, so she is
"Neither of idle shewes, nor of false charmes aghast"
(xii.29); she is able to penetrate the sanctum and find the
sorcerer alone with his shoddy trappings and his obsessed
victim.

If Britomart's demolition of Busirane's castle reminds us
of Guyon's laying waste the Bower at the climax of Book II,
we are seeing something Spenser wants us to see. Busirane,
like Acrasia, is an enchanter, a framer of frauds (xii.43);
both characters embody and dramatize the power of the
infected will to distort love into monstrousness. We are not
asked to transplant these mighty figures into any particular
human will—that is, to read the allegory in exclusively psychological terms. Enchanter and enchantress are larger
than life-size; they come from Hell itself, where in pure
archetypal form live those essences in which human beings
participate adjectivally. Busirane's victims, Scudamour and
Amoret, are not unvirtuous; they are deluded victims who

113

assent to what certain fiction-makers have told them about
love—that it is an exclusively physical submissiveness, a
way to cheat death and seize the passing day; or that it is
a "Monster fell," a torturer who enthralls us to guilt and
"continuall feare" (III.xi.16).

The plight of Scudamour and Amoret is set before us,
and before the heroine of Book III, as Mortdant and Verdant are set before Spenser's readers, and Guyon, in Book
II. In these climactic episodes, the total significance of intemperance and unchastity is "upfolded." Both vices involve
delusion, the will's imprisonment in self-created imaginings
about love. In the House of Busirane are enacted the consequences of a view of love which possesses Britomart herself
at the beginning of her story, and which Glauce identifies
with the monster-creating imagination. Britomart's description of her own suffering after she fell in love with "th' only
shade and semblant of a knight" and was "subjected to loves
cruell law," looks ahead, as I have already suggested, to the
Masque of Cupid and its grisly climax.

> Sithens it hath infixed faster hold
>   Within my bleeding bowels, and so sore
>   Now ranckleth in this same fraile fleshly mould,
>   That all mine entrailes flow with poysnous gore,
>   And th'ulcer groweth daily more and more;
>   Nor can my running sore find remedie,
>   Other then my hard fortune to deplore,
>   And languish as the leafe falne from the tree,
> Till death make one end of my dayes and miserie.
>   (III.ii.39)

The languishing Scudamour, hopelessly deploring his hard
fortune, enacts in Canto xi a part of this description; the
irremediable sore finds dramatic embodiment in Amoret in
Canto xii. But Britomart, by the time she witnesses the
pageant, has been inoculated against its delusions. Glauce
answers her melodramatic self-portrait with the suggestion

that imagination has run riot and presented her with monsters, not truth.

> Daughter (said she) what need ye be dismayd,
> Or why make ye such Monster of your mind?
> Of much more uncouth thing I was affrayd;
> Of filthy lust, contrarie unto kind:
> But this affection nothing straunge I find.
>
> (ii.40)

"This affection" is, in fact, perfectly natural. "No guilt in you, but in the tyranny of love." Love's power *is* tyrannical in the sense of irresistible; it is like Britomart's own irresistible spear with which she overthrows all opponents. But it is not "contrarie unto kind"; the remedy of chaste and faithful marriage exists within nature, and its fruits will be revealed by a benevolent enchanter, Merlin, in the next canto. Love properly understood does not lead to death, and the imagination which sees it thus is self-destructive.[7]

In dissolving Busirane's charms, Britomart destroys one of imagination's destructively persistent fictions, and Spenser insists once more that every artist must unlock the dream and release the audience if his art is not to become a rival to the "real" world and, therefore, a prison. Prospero does this willingly, Busirane under constraint. The insubstantial pageants vanish, and their makers as well, as the audience acknowledges the limits of art. The presence of diabolical fictions in Spenser's invented universe helps to chasten and make innocent the great fiction that is *The Faerie Queene*. When he turns, himself, to pageant-making, the poet devises not a Masque of Cupid, art aspiring to magic, but the River-Marriage that concludes Book IV with

---

[7] As Kathleen Williams writes, Glauce's comment sets up "a norm of health and sanity against which the monsters of Britomart's mind . . . can be seen for what they are—fictions made by our own unbalance, which misunderstands the nature of love" (*Spenser's World of Glass* [Berkeley & Los Angeles, 1966], p. 93).

a vision of great creating nature. Busirane's enchantments are balanced by a healthier, self-knowing art. An attentive look at the central figure confirms this judgment, especially if the tormented Amoret hovers in the background.

> Then came the Bride, the lovely *Medua* came,
> Clad in a vesture of unknowen geare,
> And uncouth fashion, yet her well became;
> That seem'd like silver, sprinckled here and theare
> With glittering spangs, that did like starres appeare,
> And wav'd upon, like water Chamelot,
> To hide the metall, which yet every where
> Bewrayd it selfe, to let men plainely wot,
> It was no mortall worke, that seem'd and yet was not.

> Her goodly lockes adowne her backe did flow
> Unto her waste, with flowres bescattered,
> The which ambrosiall odours forth did throw
> To all about, and all her shoulders spred
> As a new spring; and likewise on her hed
> A Chapelet of sundry flowers she wore,
> From under which the deawy humour shed,
> Did tricle downe her haire, like to the hore
> Congealed litle drops which doe the morne adore.

> (IV.xi.45-46)

The first of these stanzas declares a mystery, an enigmatic image of the kind that make up the programs of so many Renaissance paintings. "Unknowen" and "uncouth" introduce the vision: the garment the Medway wears expresses, by its very nature, the hiddenness of its sense.[8] The stanza's last three lines are especially significant, though paradoxically so, since they express the fact that this *significatio*,

---

[8] Spenser, if indeed he had read the *De planctu*, could be thinking of the robe of state of Alain's Natura, whose "appearance perpetually changed with many a different color and manifold hue," to suggest the interplay of the four elements. Alain de Lille, *The Complaint of Nature*, tr. Douglas M. Moffat (New Haven, 1908), p. 11.

though visible to men, is inaccessible, or difficult of access, to their understanding. They echo Spenser's description of a genuinely "mortall worke," in the preceding book, and the contrast with Busirane's tapestry where "the rich metall lurked privily, / As faining to be hid" is instructive. The mysterious garment of Medway insists upon its own fictiveness. The "metall" of which it is made is hidden by being "wav'd upon" (overtraced with a wavelike pattern, as in watered silk; compare Duessa's "tinsell trappings, woven like a wave," I.ii.13), but it lets its nature be known, as the gold mingled with the silk in the tapestry does not; anyone scrutinizing it will "plainely wot" that he is seeing an object that stands in for what it represents. The alexandrine is not entirely unambiguous, but its gist refers to any "mortall worke" whose nature is to seem what it is not. The river's "unknowen geare," on the other hand, is figurative by design; its seeming is not an illusion, but a fiction, a veil that can intimate the truth it conceals, like *The Faerie Queene* itself.

In these lines, therefore, Spenser comments upon the formal nature of fictions which give an oblique intimation of a more distant reality, and suggests that they are harmless —indeed, valuable—as long as they "let men plainely wot" what they are. If we turn from the form to the substance of the Medway image, we observe the poet composing in a mode familiar to us in the visual arts of the Renaissance. Some of the information necessary for a full interpretation is withheld; enough is revealed to make clear the direction in which interpretation must move, and to locate the image in a context sufficiently conventional to supply, without stating, the probable implications of the details. Wind's analyses of Botticelli's programs in his two most famous paintings show how far a learned commentator can go in understanding the painter's meaning, but we cannot be absolutely certain that all the details are correct, and Wind's interpretation has, of course, been challenged. Spenser's stanzas should be placed within the same general context as that of the *Primavera* and the *Birth of Venus*. Medway has affinities with the right-hand figures in both pictures— the group of Flora, Chloris, and Zephyr in *Primavera*, the Hours of Spring in *Venus*. In both, flowers are scattered or blown about to indicate the burgeoning of life under the impulse of the generative power. Wind writes of the latter picture:

> While the general atmosphere is that of a
> cosmogonic myth, and shows how the divine spirit,
> in the words of Plutarch, is "changed and distributed
> into winds and water", the moment chosen for
> representation is that following the cosmic birth: the
> new-born Venus, already risen from the sea, is blown to
> the shore by the winds of spring. And as if to suggest,
> through a poetic after-image, that the sea has been
> fertilized by the sky, a mystical rain of roses issues from
> the breath of the wind-god—"the spirit moving over the
> waters."[9]

It is not necessary to see Medway as another avatar of Venus (though that may well be the case) to accept the relevance of such analysis to Spenser's river-maiden,

> with flowres bescattered,
> The which ambrosiall odours forth did throw
> To all about, and all her shoulders spred
> As a new spring.

The Marriage of Canto xi expresses the triumph of the concordant powers that have struggled through Books III and IV of *The Faerie Queene* to establish their hegemony over the disruptive forces led by Ate. Spenser's great images, and notably this one of the Medway, make us see that triumph as something profoundly natural, as natural as the

---

[9] *Pagan Mysteries*, p. 137; the two paintings are discussed in Chs. 7 and 8, respectively. For another interpretation, and a consideration of the problems involved in reading these programs, see Gombrich's essay, "Botticelli's Mythologies," now in *Symbolic Images*, pp. 31-81.

coming of spring, and at the same time infinitely mysterious, as mysterious as the original *fiat* of the Spirit. It eventuates in a union of the elements, figured in Medway's garment decorated with "spangs," "like starres . . . like water."
When Spenser comes to sum up "the seas abundant
progeny," too numerous to be named, he refers to "three
thousand more . . . Of th' Oceans seede, but *Joves* and *Phoebus* kinde" (xi.52). These are the fresh waters whose nature
participates in that of both sea-god and sky-gods, a mingling of attributes often at war with each other.

Spenser's drift in the Medway stanzas is, then, clear
enough, but any attempt to restate the sense adumbrated
in them is likely to seem incomplete, and such a consequence is compatible with Spenser's design. The phenomena
which the image reflects are themselves delicate, unstable,
and evanescent. As Roche points out, Spenser is rendering a visual experience that corresponds to familiar
psychic experiences—"that curious state where sunlight and
waves become nothing and everything all at once, where
things are just about to become ideas."[10] He goes on to call
this "the realm of mythic vision," an exact phrase for the
kind of "reading" such images demand. In the Medway,
Spenser has copied into his poem a phenomenon which
would be recognized by those who saw in Nature a divine
hieroglyph, upon which the hieroglyph of the poem is
modeled. The inarticulateness of the images therefore goes
beyond the instability of the subject-matter; it is a function
of that opaqueness in things which is one of the results of
the fall. The mirror of Nature is obscured when we breathe
our sinfulness upon it. Yet in this darkened mirror we can
still catch glimpses of the truth, as Michael promises Adam
at the end of *Paradise Lost.*

> Yet doubt not but in valley and in plain
> God is as here, and will be found alike
> Present, and of his presence many a sign

[10] *Kindly Flame*, p. 183.

> Still following thee, still compassing thee round
> With goodness and paternal love, his face
> Express, and of his steps the track divine.
>
> (XI.349-54)

But we do not now look on God's face; his footsteps are signs of a presence no longer directly visible. Nature is "no mortall worke"; it is what it seems to be, itself and yet the herald of a further reality, which makes "men plainely wot" that behind and within its *visibilia* there is a range of meanings that cannot otherwise come to us at all.

An image related to that of the Medway, but differently presented and approached, is one of the symbolic cruxes of *The Faerie Queene*: the statue of Isis, and Britomart's dream about it, in Book V. Canto vii begins with a commentary by the poet on the nature of what we are about to see. This takes the form of a little dissertation on the origin of myths as explanations of invisible but significant reality. The idea of Justice on earth derives from an awareness of the orderly heavens, "rul'd by righteous lore / Of highest Jove." (V.vii.1) Such speculation leads to a hypostatizing of Justice as a divine principle incarnate in a human hero; hence develops a myth.

> Well therefore did the antique world invent,
>   That Justice was a God of soveraine grace,
>   And alters unto him, and temples lent,
>   And heavenly honours in the highest place;
>   Calling him great *Osyris*, of the race
>   Of th' old Ægyptian Kings, that whylome were;
>   With fayned colours shading a true case:
>   For that *Osyris*, whilest he lived here,
> The justest man alive, and truest did appeare.
>
> (V.vii.2)

The rhyme-word of the first line, *invent*, carries the full weight of Elizabethan usage. Invention is explicated by Sidney as the "finding of the matter" in which to embody a "conceit" or idea. Such finding is also a making:

> Whereas other arts retain themselves within their subject, and receive, as it were, their being from it, the poet only bringeth his own stuff, and doth not learn a conceit out of a matter, but maketh matter for a conceit.[11]

Imagination receives its "conceits" from the invisible world; it is a visionary power, dwelling on earth, which incarnates its insights in whatever "stuff" it can find. Spenser is not so fastidious as Sidney about the nature of the "matter" used by the poet; the imagination can seize on an actual living man and, seeing through his justness to the perfect Justice available to inward sight, make him a god. The "god" then takes the name of the man: "Calling him great *Osyris*." Nevertheless, though it uses uninvented "matter," Spenser's imagination is here seeking and finding the means to express a sense of the reality that dwells beyond *visibilia*. This is the import of the seventh line: "With fayned colours shading a true case." The colors are at once the colors of rhetoric and the "visible" signs—those made by a painter or a painterly poet from his colors—created in language. The result of the process is exemplified in the idol of Isis Church.

The critical problem here is to distinguish between the way in which this numinous image is offered to the reader, and the presentation of the Medway in the previous book. "Then came the bride, the lovely *Medua*," says Spenser in IV.xi, cheerfully enough but without elaborate preamble. He is the presenter of the masque, not its interpreter. But Britomart is led through the precincts of a temple (like Scudamour at the shrine of Venus in IV.x) to gaze upon a

---

[11] *Apology for Poetry* (Shepherd), p. 120.

work of art wrought by the "cunning hand" of a mortal artist, an ecphrastic image. And the poet's voice explicates the meaning of the details as they become visible to an observer;

> Uppon her head she wore a Crowne of gold,
> To shew that she had powre in things divine.
>
> (vii.6)

The iconography is extended in the next stanza; the statue beats down wickedness under its feet, like Christ trampling the serpent.

> One foote was set uppon the Crocodile,
>   And on the ground the other fast did stand,
>   So meaning to suppresse both forged guile,
>   And open force.
>
> (vii.7)

"Such was the Goddesse," the concluding phrase, sets the description in a narrative frame, formally offered to both the heroine and the reader as an opaque, revealing, carefully designed icon. Thus did Botticelli compose his "mythologies," but the poet can be more explicit than the painter.

Britomart's dream later in the canto is "a wondrous vision, which did close implie / The course of all her fortune and posteritie" (V.vii.12). The vision is an enigma, enigmatically described, but Spenser does not leave us to puzzle over it. "The gravest wight" among Isis' priests expounds the dream, after the manner of the helpful hermits of the romances.[12] The interpreter is "fild with heavenly fury" (20), a rapture not unlike the "divine instinct and unnatural rage" that, according to E.K., possesses the poet. Spenser's insistence that these interpreters speak with the voice

12 I am not suggesting that the vision's import is exhausted by the official explanation. The various layers of the dream are effectively unwrapped by Lewis, *Images of Life*, pp. 99-104.

of divine authority makes Britomart's dream a holy fiction, to be carefully distinguished from those other instances throughout *The Faerie Queene* where he has dissected the vanity of fancy, its pandering to self-deception, its willingness to enlist in the cause of pride. There is another such instance of imagination used for sinister purpose in Book V; Geryoneo, overcome by Arthur, has perpetuated his wickedness in an idol demonically related to the statue in the Temple of Isis—

> an Idole of great note and name,
> The which this Gyant reared first on hie,
> And of his own vaine fancies thought did frame.
>
> (V.xi.19)

Under this idol's altar there lives a monster resembling the crocodile of Britomart's vision; but this creature is "real." Summoned by the strokes of Arthur's sword, it issues forth in its awful literalness, to be subdued only by the utmost efforts of the hero. At last it lies dead in "a puddle of contagion." Thus did the tyrant make his dream truth; his fantasy is one that feeds on human flesh. The Crocodile at Isis' Temple is subdued both by the goddess's "long white sclender wand" (7) and by the hand of the maker, which created a genuine fiction, a statue that remains a statue, a vision that remains in the visionary realm.[13] But vision allowed to rampage in the world, uttering its "fowle blasphemous speaches" (V.xi.28), is as dangerous as bad Genius's snares in the Bower of Bliss, or the Masque of Cupid, and must be similarly dealt with her. So Arthur treats "that Idoll deem'd so costly dere":

> he did all to peeces breake and foyle
> In filthy durt, and left so in the loathely soyle.
>
> (V.xi.33)

---

[13] The statue's apparent movement, "as it were inclining" and moving its wand "with amiable looke" (vii.8), takes place as Britomart

Spenser's control of the vision in Canto vii provides further evidence for his understanding of the limits of fiction; it is at the same time a demonstration that he himself observes those limits, and that they are honored by his virtuous fictive characters. The Temple in which the vision is unfolded is the emblem of an ideal mimetic relationship between art and the visible universe, which in turn offers many portals into ultimate meanings. The things of Nature point beyond themselves; properly understood, they open into infinite perspectives, like the cosmic "Scenes" that Jonson and Inigo Jones were to devise for court masques. The Temple in Spenser's Isis canto is an equivalent of these symbolic centers in the masque. Britomart is conducted into it by the priests:

> Whose goodly building when she did behould,
> Borne uppon stately pillours, all dispred
> With shining gold, and arched over hed,
> She wondred at the workemans passing skill,
> Whose like before she never saw nor red;
> And thereuppon long while stood gazing still,
> But thought, that she thereon could never gaze her fill.
>
> (V.vii.5)

The priests who serve this Temple honor Isis, but Spenser is careful to remind us also of Osiris. God and goddess, Sun and Moon, rule the heavens, the visible reminder of the "heavenly Commonweale" ruled by Jove and Jove's Maker. Britomart after her vision lies wakeful until dawn,

> Untill she spide the lampe of lightsome day
> Up-lifted in the porch of heaven hie.
>
> (vii.17)

---

prays, preparatory to falling asleep; Spenser does not bother to resolve our uncertainty about its literalness, but the movement, if anything, heightens the statue's artificiality rather than suggesting that it is alive.

"The porch of heaven" is a relatively conventional phrase; Milton gives a variation of it in the first line of *Comus*: "Before the starry threshold of Jove's court." The Masque at Ludlow is contained by references to Jove's court and the blissful Gardens of Adonis, heavenly mansions fictively named by the poet but alluding to "real" cosmic. powers. The context of *Comus* is the universe itself; and so with the vision of Britomart in *The Faerie Queene*. "The porch of heaven," "th' hevens themselves," are figured in the Temple with its golden pillars arched like the night sky. In his earliest verses, Spenser had described the heavens as the roof of the Creator's temple:

> He bade me upwarde unto heaven looke.
> He cride to me, and loe (quod he) beholde,
> What under this great Temple is containde,
> Loe all is nought but flying vanitie.[14]

The Temple of Book V, a shrine to the moon-goddess, is a cosmic fiction, a reminder that the mortal artisan's ultimate responsibility is to model his miniature world on the great World.[15]

In this house of the gods, things are seen as they are; as the chief priest explains, divine vision can penetrate every secret place, much as the poet "sees" every corner of his fictive universe.

> Can from th'immortal Gods ought hidden bee?
> They doe thy linage, and thy Lordly brood;

---

[14] I give the version in *A Theatre for Voluptuous Wordlings*, Sonnet I, later somewhat altered for *The Visions of Bellay*, ll. 7-14, in the *Complaints* volume.

[15] Female deities in *The Faerie Queene* are often endowed with cosmic reference. This is most obvious and explicit in the case of Venus, for whom Spenser's chief model was Lucretius (perhaps in Boethius' version). In one of the tapestries, she is given a "mantle, colour'd like the starry skyes" (III.i.36). Isis, of course, is the Venus of the Egyptian pantheon.

They doe thy sire, lamenting sore for thee;
They doe thy love, forlorne in womens thraldome see.

(V.vii.21)

The next stanza expounds the dream, which thus becomes
an allegory within an allegory, an instance of the way in
which dark conceits emerge into light under the gaze of divinely gifted seers. The gods "discover" hidden truth to the
dreamer as Spenser himself makes his readers see invisible
reality. The dream does not yield all its secrets, however,
and the fact that it *is* a dream indicates an intimate relation
between these images and Britomart, who dreams her own
hopes and fears and wakes to find them truth. Two cantos
later, some of the concepts embodied in the idol and the
crocodile are made publicly manifest in Mercilla,[16] who unlike the goddess in her sanctum, sits "on high, that she
might all men see, / And might of all men royally be seene"
(V.ix.27). Arthur and Artegal, who do not—or cannot—
dream Britomart's dream, participate in the public occasion, which is devised not by the gods, but by their surrogates on earth. But in the dream canto, Spenser reminds us
of the conditions that undergird his great allegory: the
weakness of our vision, and the power of the erected wit
which can take us through obscurity to a place of unshad-
owed truth.

Other instances of *aenigma*[17] are scattered through *The*

---

[16] This argument does not depend upon precise identification of the
allegorical import in the two episodes. Several scholars have recently
distinguished Equity, the principle explicated in the Idol, and Mercy
or *Clementia*, embodied in Mercilla. See, e.g., James E. Phillips, "Renaissance Concepts of Justice and the Structure of *The Faerie Queene*,
Book V," *HLQ* XXXIII (1970), 103-20. The fact that both principles
are made visible as feminine beings indicates that Spenser conceived of
them as close and compatible, though not identical.

[17] Puttenham considers *aenigma* the darkest of the figures: "We dis-
semble againe under covert and darke speaches, when we speake by
way of riddle (*Enigma*) of which the sense can hardly be picked out,
but by the parties owne assoile" (*Arte of English Poesie*, III.xviii;
p. 188).

Faerie Queene; a rough index of their presence is the wealth of critical explication they have attracted. Critics' constant return to these episodes points to an inexhaustibility in the images that is a function of the poet's deliberate inexplicitness and his skill in devising—"inventing"—images that imply a number of different kinds of meaning. Britomart's dream, in its obviously sexual dimension, can admit Freudian interpretation, and legitimately so as long as we recognize that we are translating the images into a discursive vocabulary unfamiliar to the poet. The process can be legitimate because no single explication exhausts these images' richness; they do not tolerate any interpretation we choose, but they are hospitable to, and can render compatible, several different descriptions. The priests' interpretation of the dream is authoritative in the sense that it offers an explication that no reader can ignore, but it is the beginning, not the end, of our understanding, and its function is partly to insist that the images belong to a kind that *demands* intelligent "reading."

The peculiarity of these enigmatic images is dictated by their role in Spenser's anatomy of imagination. The Medway and the Temple of Isis are approached from different directions by the poet, as I have tried to show. But they are alike in shadowing a meaning that is not immediately yielded at the poem's surface, a meaning which we penetrate only by repeated and leisurely contemplation of that surface. We keep coming back to these images, actually re-reading them or reviving them in our memory of the poem. They provide evidence for Yeats's remark that man can embody truth but cannot know it. The imagination makes or finds—invents—what it cannot completely explain; a residue or penumbra remains, or, better, revives, welling up through any conceptual grid we lay over the image, with each rereading. It is possible to offer explanations of this curious overreaching tendency of imagination—theological, psychological, and otherwise—but that is not the task of this book. I want merely to point to the fact that in *The Faerie Queene* this tendency is acknowledged, as it must be if Spenser is to deal adequately with his great subject.

The critical role of the narrator is to indicate the sort of reading appropriate to various parts of the poem. Spenser's aspiration to write an epic, his claim to heroic dignity, rests only in part upon the chivalric setting and the "magnificence" of his personages. It is also based on the poem's comprehensive variety, a criterion gradually developed in the literary criticism of the sixteenth century. Macrobius awarded Virgil godlike status among the poets, "a disposition divine rather than mortal," because his epic united variety with unity.

> With the universal mother, Nature, for his only
> guide he wove the pattern of his work—just as in
> music different sounds are combined to form a single
> harmony. . . . You will find a striking resemblance be-
> tween the handiwork of the divine craftsman and that
> of our poet.[18]

Discordia concors became a familiar term of praise in the Renaissance. Harmonious comprehensiveness was a criterion that seemed good to Milton, and he embraced it successfully in *Paradise Lost*, encompassing in a colossal mythic fiction, as Marvell wrote, "Heav'n, Hell, Earth, Chaos, All." The fine confidence of that "All" cannot be matched by Spenser, but *The Faerie Queene* is comprehensive in some ways that *Paradise Lost* is not, and notably in its anatomy of imagination, of the many ways in which the human understanding makes sense of the world. I stress *many*, because there has been some tendency in recent criticism to insist that there is *a* way of reading *The Faerie Queene*. There is, but it involves a willingness to surrender

---

[18] *Saturnalia* V.i.18-19; tr. Percival Vaughan Davies (New York & London, 1969), p. 285. The *locus classicus* in the Renaissance for the poem as a "world" is in Tasso's *Discourses*, III.31; *Literary Criticism* (Gilbert), pp. 498-501.

to the poet's guidance; once we have done that, we shall find that he demands of us a continuous intellectual and imaginative agility, a willingness to tack and veer, to inflect, unfold and upfold, that challenges the most sophisticated literary training. It is true that there is a simplicity in *The Faerie Queene*, long ago accurately noted by C. S. Lewis and reiterated by many sympathetic critics rightly suspicious of oversophistication. But that simplicity is a function of the depth at which Spenser engages his subject; he is concerned, as Lewis says, with "the fundamental tendencies of human imagination as such."[19] The mere idea of a poem on such a subject is vertiginous; to imagine Spenser confronting it is like imagining Milton contemplating the abyss from which would rise his unborn poem, the obscure source of worlds. Milton's formula for poetry, "simple, sensuous, and passionate," best suggests what we mean by calling *The Faerie Queene* simple. It is a simplicity that for human beings unable to participate in angelic vision must express itself in staggering complexity and subtlety of invention. Any critical position that would reduce such inventiveness to a single mode is to be eschewed. The pages that follow will attempt to indicate how a reading that is alertly attentive to the poem's sweet variety ought to proceed.

[19] *Allegory of Love*, p. 313.

PART II

Re-Mythologizing: Book I as Context

1. The Vertical Axis

Book I provides the context for all the other books of *The Faerie Queene*. It has the longest reach, the deepest resonance, the most highly generalized structure. As Harold Bloom has said, it includes the basic points of reference for the poem.

> If we isolated Book I . . . we would still have all the
> essential states of being; the redeemed City of the
> Faerie Queene, the paradisal garden of Una's
> parents, . . . the post-lapsarian generative universe
> in which the knight undergoes trials, deceptions,
> and unsanctified sexual experience, and the self-
> absorbed Ulro, or hell-within-nature, of Archimago's
> hermitage, Duessa's bowers, and Fradubio's vegetative
> prison.[1]

The history of the Red Cross Knight in the poem traces a pattern more inclusive than that enacted by any other of the heroes; it exemplifies the *imitatio Christi*, that "retrospective typology" made available by the New Covenant, expressed in the lives of the Apostles, and preserved in the Book of Acts.

> The typological presentation signals a life which
> grows out of a spiritual conformity to Christ and
> which participates in the new existence which God
> opens up. It signals a life that is in this way the fruit
> of redemption, an ethical existence, "righteousness",

[1] *The Visionary Company* (New York, 1961), p. 19. Similar points are made by many critics, e.g., A. C. Hamilton, *The Structure of Allegory in "The Faerie Queene"* (Oxford, 1961), p. 128; Williams, *World of Glass*, p. 8.

which is given from heaven . . . through faith, and
whose only form is the form Christ gave it.[2]

Righteousness, or Holiness, is grown into by the Red Cross
Knight, as his life gradually assumes its destined form within "the post-lapsarian generative universe." The world of
The Faerie Queene is, like our own, a vale of soul-making,
in Keats's beautifully accurate phrase. Spenser's concern
with soul-making was part of his underlying concern with
the ways in which human beings come to terms with their
lives, learning to locate, describe, and understand the context ("reality") within which they are constrained to exist,
including the problematic realm of self-generated or invented "reality." Coming to know is a major aspect of the
theme in Book I.

At the poem's outset, both the Knight and the reader
must enjoin themselves, with Yeats:

> Now shall I make my soul,
> Compelling it to study
> In a learned school.[3]

The Red Cross Knight, of course, does not understand, as
he rides across the horizon in the first line, that study in a
learned school is necessary. His most immediate context, his
armor, might provide some lessons, but it is the poet who
informs us of its provenance, and the Knight himself courts
disaster by laying it aside at a later crisis. Dante wrote that
"the adolescent who enters into the wandering wood of this
life would not know how to keep the right path if it were
not shown to him by his elders."[4] He would not even recog-

2 A. C. Charity, *Events and Their After-Life* (Cambridge, 1966), pp.
152-53. The term "retrospective typology" is that of John MacQueen,
who gives a good brief account in his little book, *Allegory* (London,
1970), pp. 41-43.
3 "The Tower," *The Collected Poems of W. B. Yeats* (New York,
1952), p. 197.
4 *The Convivio of Dante Alighieri*, IV.xxiv; tr. P. H. Wicksteed, The
Temple Classics (London, 1903), pp. 350-51.

134

nize it *as* a wandering wood. But the Red Cross Knight has
no elders; his truth is a woman, a passive and nearly helpless truth in bondage to the fallen nature of her protector
and mounted on a "palfrey slow"; even when she does speak,
he does not heed, or not soon enough. But we, the poem's
readers, by the very act of reading are listening all the time
to our elders, and above all to the poet who speaks for "the
mighty scheme of truth" devised through time by men of
imagination. We have an advantage over the Knight, for
we, like the poem's maker, have studied in a learned school;
have opened a book and read:

> Nel mezzo del cammin di nostra vita
> mi ritrovai per una selva oscura,
> che la diritta via era smarrita.

Or, if not this, have read:

> Lancelot . . . took up his pursuit through the thick
> of the forest, keeping to neither track nor path, but
> following where fortune led. The darkness of the
> night served him ill, for he could make out nothing,
> either near or far, by which to steer his course.[5]

Or we have read in a fairy tale of the witch who dwells in
the wood. The Red Cross Knight must find the thread of
the labyrinth without the aid of literary analogues. Nor can
he make use of the poet's rhetorical clues, mediating between event and meaning. Like Lancelot, he is benighted,
but in more than one sense of the term; and it is Spenser
who gives us the senses.

> Thus as they past,
> The day with cloudes was suddein overcast,
> And angry *Jove* an hideous storme of raine
> Did poure into his Lemans Lap so fast,

[5] *The Quest of the Holy Grail*, tr. P. M. Matarasso (Baltimore, 1969),
pp. 81-82.

> That every wight to shrowd it did constrain,
> And this faire couple eke to shroud themselves
> were fain.
>
> (I.i.6)

The last two lines assimilate the "faire couple" to "every wight"; they are not exempt from the common fate, such as bad weather, but like everyone else are constrained by it. "Angry Jove" exemplifies the indifferent or hostile Nature that is the home of fallen man; its elemental sexuality is dangerously significant, too. If we like, we can identify Jove with the followers of the Prince of the Power of the Air, given dominion over the lower world at the Fall. The infinitive *to shroud* is essentially innocent, but its repetition gives it an uneasy charge that projects a sense of the ominous, if nothing more. The sense deepens as we read on and hear Spenser describing the wood itself.

> Whose loftie trees yclad with sommers pride,
> Did spred so broad, that heavens light did hide,
> Not perceable with power of any starre:
> And all within were pathes and alleies wide,
> With footing worne, and leading inward farre:
>
> (I.i.7)

There are direct warnings here to the reader, such as the second and third lines; we do not know exactly what will lurk in this wood, but any attentive reader will expect such an unenlightened place to be the dwelling of monsters.

The total effect of these stanzas is to make us aware of a complicated set of meanings that define for us, but not for him, the hero's situation.

> To a half-blind man, even when the sun is shining
> its brightest the sky looks cloudy. Some things are
> naturally so profound that not without difficulty
> can the most exceptional keenness in intellect sound

136

their depths; like the sun's globe, by which, before
they can clearly discern it, strong eyes are sometimes
repelled.[6]

Boccaccio's paragraph condenses two justifications for allegory; its "veil" both imitates the infirmity of our eyesight
and shields it from a truth it cannot master. There is a natural obscurity in the things of this world, and we are all
half-blind men, obliged to regard truth through a veil.
Veiled truth is thus a figure for the limits of human understanding in two senses; it is also a description of the allegorical fiction which mirrors the process of understanding.

> O pardon me thus to enfold
> In covert vele, and wrap in shadowes light,
> That feeble eyes your glory may behold,
> Which else could not endure those beames bright.
> (II.Pro.5)

This is a conventional apology for dark conceits, in the context of *The Faerie Queene* linking Gloriana with Una and
poetic truth with revealed truth, of which Spenser permits
us several glimpses in Book I. It blazes out at the betrothal-
feast when the hero is at last ready to look upon the "celestiall sight" of Una unveiled (I.xii.23); and Arthur's veiled
shield, the work of Merlin, symbolizes both heavenly light
and the magic arts (including this poem) which make that
light visible on earth. Its "blazing brightnesse" daunts the
eye (I.vii.19); it is the cause of epiphanies.

> But all that was not such, as seemd in sight,
> Before that shield did fade, and suddein fall.
> (I.vii.35)

We might say the same of *The Faerie Queene*. But unveil-
ings can occur only rarely; through most of the fiction the

---

[6] *Boccaccio on Poetry*, p. 59.

137

poet's method must mediate between the glory and our feeble sight; it must, that is, be allegorical. Allegory teaches us how to read and how to imagine beneath the cloudy skies of everyday life; this is the virtuous and gentle discipline to which we are first asked to submit.

The epistemological orientation of Book I is evident in Spenser's construction of contexts for his own metaphors. Turns of phrase which are repeatedly used to describe his characters' psychological situation are grounded in images —most often of "places"—which have literal force within the fiction: they are located along the axes of "reality" in the poem's visionary geography. The result is to call attention to the power of metaphor to put us in touch with truth; figures become more than mere rhetorical strategies when we are led to see their origin in mythic under- or over-worlds. An especially clear instance is the treatment of Sleep in Book I, which begins in the first canto with the descent to Morpheus' dwelling. Many readers have noticed the dangers that attend falling asleep in *The Faerie Queene*. The soul, its defenses down, is exposed to dangers from within and without; heroes and anti-heroes alike are assaulted by threatening powers as they lie "all drownd in deadly sleepe" (I.i.36). The metaphor of drowning is Spenser's favorite version of the commonplace which links sleep with death, and it is animated when Archimago sends a bad spirit to Morpheus' house, the source of dreams and other unconscious impulses. In quest of the god of Sleep, the spirit descends into "the world of waters wide and deepe."

> Amid the bowels of the earth full steepe,
> And low, where dawning day doth never peepe,
> His dwelling is; there *Tethys* his wet bed
> Doth ever wash, and *Cynthia* still doth steepe
> In silver deaw his ever-drouping hed,
> Whiles sad Night over him her mantle black doth spred.
>
> (i.39)

To fall asleep is to commit oneself to the sad kingdom of
Night (visited again in Canto v), a world of unacted desires, including sexual desires. The dreamer's brain "Is tost
with troubled sights and fancies weake" (i.42) ; *phantasia*
is released to its irresponsible revels. Archimago's charms
unlock this underworld. They "trouble sleepy mindes,"
Spenser says, and he then proceeds to show us the archetypal sleepy mind, the god Morpheus in his soundless
cavern. He is "devoide of carefull carke" (44), having removed himself "farre from enemyes" (41); the famous
stanza on "his slumber soft" seductively touches all our
deep impulses to retreat into protected infancy, to abandon
heroic quests and the pain of growing up. The spirit
descends,

> And unto *Morpheus* comes, whom drowned deepe
> In drowsie fit he finds: of nothing he takes keepe.
>
> (40)

Sleepy minds are those which surrender the attentiveness
appropriate to successful progress through the wood of the
world. They appear in allegories but do not read them.

Later instances of sleepy minds among the human characters of *The Faerie Queene* draw some of their resonance
from this mythic context in the poem's first canto. To have
seen the waters under the earth is to have been provided
with a key for unlocking many later allegorical metaphors.
"You in careless sleepe are drowned quight," says the false
Una to the Red Cross Knight (i.53). Other instances follow:
Fradubio "drownd in sleepie night" (ii.42) as the first stage
of his arboreal paralysis; those benighted in Corceca's hovel
who "all in deadly sleepe did drowned lye" (iii.16); Idleness at the head of Lucifera's train, "Still drownd in sleepe,
and most of his daies dead" (iv.19). Examples in Book II
imply a similar knot of meanings. It is not surprising to find
that Cymochles, "in joyes . . . dround," is also "in ladies lap

entombed" (II.v.36). And Guyon's condition upon emerging from the Cave of Mammon, though not blameworthy, is symptomatic; it reiterates the point, made at large in Canto vii, that he has visited the realm of death and that the path to this realm is traversed wherever we descend into psychic darkness in sleep. Unconscious, he is still "there," though to observers in the upper world of daylight he looks like the brother of sleep:

> cloudes of deadly night
> A while his heavy eylids cover'd have,
> And all his sences drowned in deep senceless wave.
> (II.viii.24)

Guyon's submission to the senseless night of sleep is a sign of his human frailty, his vulnerability to the assaults of the passionate twins Cymochles and Pyrochles. But Spenser interestingly inflects his myth of sleep in Canto vii when the hero first descends into Mammon's underworld. It is adjacent to Morpheus' cave, and Spenser insists on a similar topographical literalness as Mammon leads Guyon to his door, "that to the gate of Hell, which gaped wide / Was next adjoyning" (24).

> Before the dore sat selfe-consuming Care,
> Day and night keeping wary watch and ward,
> For feare least Force or Fraud should unaware
> Breake in, and spoile the treasure there in gard:
> Ne would he suffer Sleepe once thither-ward
> Approch, albe his drowsie den were next;
> For next to death is Sleepe to be compard:
> Therefore his house is unto his annext;
> Here Sleep, there Richesse, and Hel-gate them both betwext.
> (II.vii.25)

Lines 7-8 make explicit the relationship between a comparison—the metaphorical yoking of sleep and death—and its literalized equivalent in the geography of Fairy Land:

140

"*Therefore* his house is unto his annext." And *because* these houses are "annext," the poet can frame his comparisons with some confidence. There is a suggestion that the figure is not figurative at all, but a condensed, allusive description of what truly exists. Such passages are informative in a rather Blakean way, hinting that the imagination's work of making metaphors is a valid epistemological activity.

The anchor in the poem's fictive literalness which Spenser provides in II.vii completes a curve begun in the poem's opening canto. Sleep's kingdom has been located on the map of Fairy Land with respect to false dreams, fantasies, death, "Richesse, and Hel-gate." But the stanza on Guyon's descent includes an interesting variation: Care, Mammon's porter, *wards off* sleep lest the treasure be despoiled. "Day and night keeping wary watch and ward": the line might be describing the hero of Book II himself, dedicated to the wary maintenance of rational waking consciousness. "Watch and ward" are among the principal duties of the Knight of Temperance; he must guard himself against the assaults of sleep and his own tendency to become a "sleepy mind" in the embraces of Phaedria or Acrasia. His posture thus resembles the watchfulness of "selfe-consuming Care," and it is reasonable, I think, to suggest that Spenser is here presenting Guyon with a perverted equivalent of his own wary virtue, on guard against "carelesse ease" (II.vi.13).[7] Care is guarding the wrong sort of treasures, never to be laid up in heaven; the sleepless denizens of Mammon's kingdom warn us that even an alert will can be fatally misdirected. The energy that powers Guyon's temperance is

[7] "Carelesse ease" is one of the names of Phaedria; Guyon's voyage to her island in the Idle Lake establishes one pole of the extremes, Ease and excessive Care (occupying adjacent cantos), between which the temperate hero moves. Spenser makes us see what fertile ground idleness and ease offer to the self-indulgent imagination; Phaedria has a "fantasticke wit" (II.vi.7), especially adept at fiction-making. This wanton damsel "greatly joyed merry tales to faine, / Of which a storehouse did with her remaine." Her fundamental frivolity turns this "pleasant purpose," like all the others, "to a scoffing game" (6).

manifested in demonic form as a corruption of his goodly nurture, in the "ugly shapes" laboring at these underground forges:

> Deformed creatures, horrible in sight,
> And every feend his busie paines applide,
> To melt the golden metall, ready to be tride.
>
> (II.vii.35)

After such nightmare visions, Guyon's swoon is almost welcome, a return to his mere humanity as a man in the middest.

The whole action of *The Faerie Queene* is played out in the context of a reality normally inaccessible to us, but made visible by the poet's translation of what his imagination sees.[8] By allowing us glimpses of ultimate "realities"—places and personages—Spenser illuminates the continued metaphor in the main action. We come to see that metaphor is a necessary way of speaking about events and experience in our world, where much of reality is invisible. We cannot "see" the experience from which the metaphor, "drowned in deadly sleep," derives, but the imagination of the poet can. In exposing the sources of the linguistic medium through which our experience is refracted, he offers us a clue to the labyrinth in which we all wander. The animation of dead metaphors, through the process of fictive literalizing which I have been examining, works similarly to instruct the reader in the allegorical mode and to indicate the

---

[8] The spinning-out of Book I's contexts continues throughout the poem, and there are many later inflections of the sleep/drowning metaphor. The hidden music for the Masque of Cupid produces a "delitious harmony" that confounds Britomart's senses, "And the fraile soule in deepe delight nigh dround" (III.xii.6). The line helps us to see the masque as a fantasy, a waking dream, manifesting imagination's most sinister powers. The episode is countered when Britomart experiences "a wondrous vision" as she sleeps "Under the wings of *Isis*." Here, entrancement of the senses is a prelude to a true dream; "whilest her earthly parts with soft delight / Of sencelesse sleepe did deeply drowned lie," her "heavenly spright" is released to its vision (V.vii.12).

relevance of imagining to the moral life.[9] By letting us "see" psychic and spiritual experience within the conceptual framework that supports our ordinary ontological decisions, the imagination persuades us to attend to them with a seriousness we may ordinarily be unwilling to bestow upon invisible truth.

The axis of this pseudo-visionary reality in *The Faerie Queene* is the vertical coordinate of Spenser's imagined world in Book I. Its poles are the Cave of Night and Avernus in Canto v (to which Morpheus' house is annexed), and the Mount of Contemplation in Canto x. At each of these poles there reigns a different kind of darkness, marking the limits of ordinary human power, whether active or contemplative. The two cantos establish points of reference for the intervening and ensuing action. They also clarify—if that is the word—certain puzzling aspects of the actions that lead up to them, for our illumination, like the hero's, is progressive. The darkness of the underworld is a willful recoil from light. Old Night, "with visage deadly sad, / That *Phoebus* chearefull face durst never vew," retreats, ironically, from Duessa's false light:

> She greatly grew amazed at the sight,
> And th' unacquainted light began to feare:
> For never did such brightnesse there appeare;
> And would have backe retyred to her cave.
> (I.v.21)

This is an echo of (and a source for) the similar response of Error in Canto i:

> She lookt about, and seeing one in mayle
> Armed to point, sought backe to turne againe;

---

[9] The process is akin to Spenser's resurrection of moribund etymologies, noted above p. 53. Hamilton describes the poem as "translating itself" and writes several paragraphs on the animation of metaphor: "what might become clichés in another writer, stock phrases dulled by repetition, become alive with significance" (*Structure of Allegory*, pp. 212-15).

> For light she hated as the deadly bale,
> Ay wont in desert darknesse to remaine,
> Where plain none might her see, nor she see any plaine.
> (I.i.16)

The last line is pertinent to Night as well, who is not only hard to see, but cannot herself "see" Duessa for what she is. The Red Cross Knight's entanglement with Error enacts his own blindness, which in Canto i takes the form of adolescent overconfidence: "Vertue gives her selfe light through darknesse for to wade" (i.12). In a sense, all that follows is an ironic comment on this naive maxim, which is not so much untrue as empty at this point in the poem. *Light* and *darkness* must be more fully unfolded, in all their complexity, before the Knight's remark can be properly assessed.

The many meanings of darkness begin to exfoliate from this point on, and they are focused in Canto v, where Spenser reveals the "roote of *Duessaes* race" (v.27). Duessa is "the daughter of Deceipt and Shame" (26); her grandmother is Night, mother of falsehood. The recitation of genealogies is one of Spenser's habitual methods of indicating relationships along the ontological scale; the temporal hierarchy of generations becomes a metaphor for the "spatial" hierarchy of the abstraction ladder. So, in this underworld, the Sans brothers are identified as "old *Aveugles* sonnes" and thus the cousins of Duessa (23). Night is, in fact, "most auncient Grandmother of all" (22), and Spenser develops this Hesiodic idea in his allegory as a means of indicating the participation of every fallen being in primitive darkness. Old Night is the ancestress of all the earthly nights, "grisly" and "loathsome," that overtake the characters of the poem; she is grandmother of the "suddein overcast" of rain-clouds in Canto i that prefigures the Red Cross Knight's pilgrimage into his own spiritual and intellectual darkness. Old Aveugle is the ancestor of the negative principles that assault the Knight and represent fallings-off from those positive movements of the will that can lead us toward truth: allegiance to order or law, faith, joy. He also stands behind the toads that Error vomits, "which eyes did lacke" (i.20); behind Corceca, Blind Devotion, who "Sate in eternall night" (iii.12); and behind the porter Ignaro, encountered by Arthur in Orgoglio's castle, whose "eye sight him fayled long ygo" (viii.30).

The action of Canto v is perfectly intelligible, *unless* we assume that the allegory must refer solely to the hero. But Spenser is not concerned only with the education of the Knight; he is educating his audience as well, and that involves explication of the principles underlying the action in the foreground. The generative energy of *The Faerie Queene*, as of all great cosmic fictions, is the urge to make sense of the world's shapeless welter; for Spenser this involves rationalization, the unraveling and tracing to their sources of the varied threads of being. The poem lays a great network of meaning over a world that appears meaningless to the veiled sight, the only faculty we command in ordinary life. Canto v of Book I is one of the points at which this unraveling, unveiling, and reknitting can be clearly observed; and it is performed for the benefit of the reader, not the Knight, who is lying in bed recovering from the wounds inflicted by Sansjoy.

One of the purposes of the descent in Canto v is to unfold the meaning of the biblical allusion at the opening of Canto iv, where Lucifera's palace is said to be built on sand, like that of the parable in *Matthew* 7:26. At the end of Canto v, this shaky foundation is shown to be a miniature version of Hell, the kingdom of darkness and nothingness. Spenser gives two accounts of an "underworld" in Canto v, and, far from being a meaningless duplication, the doubling makes a necessary, though hardly subtle, point about the relation of human action to ultimate reality. Within the great circle of Hell itself are traced the lesser but concentric circles of the smaller hells that terminate each prideful action. Hell is full of famous challengers of the gods, and the mighty are present in Lucifera's dungeon too—"that great proud king of *Babylon*," Croesus, Nimrod, and Alexander. The catalogue of notorious sinners ends with a quietly menacing stanza, depicting

> the endlesse routes of wretched thralles,
> Which thither were assembled day by day,
> From all the world after their wofull falles,
> Through wicked pride, and wasted wealthes decay.
> But most of all, which in that Dongeon lay
> Fell from high Princes courts, or Ladies bowres,
> Where they in idle pompe, or wanton play,
> Consumed had their goods, and thriftlesse howres,
> And lastly throwne themselves into these heavy stowres.
>
> (v.51)

The dwellers in "high Princes courtes, or Ladies bowres" make up the audience of the poem: *tu quoque*. With the next stanza, we move to the narrative foreground, where "day by day" the Knight pursues his quest. The underworld we have just witnessed has defined one of his possible destinations; he himself realizes that he is "in perill of like painefull plight" (52). Not even the Dwarf, who is "ever last" (i.6), can miss the import of Lucifera's ruinous hinderparts. The place is finally revealed as "that sad house of *Pryde*" (53); and we, who have seen not just *a* hell, but Hell, know that Sansjoy has been healed and lives everlastingly, to make the House of Pryde forever "sad."

The foreground of Spenser's poem is populated with instances; the receding planes and the under- and overworlds, with principles. Avernus in I.v is the prototype for the later (or earlier) hells of the poem, and it "contains" as well, by virtue of allusion, the hells previously imagined by older poets, chiefly classical but also Christian. One *exemplum* in particular attracts Spenser's attention. The story of Hippolytus is a notable instance of "conspicuous irrelevance," though it leads into the moving dialogue be-

146

tween Aesculapius and Night.[10] The small inset-story, four stanzas long, retains, however, its own integrity and is not "interpreted" by the poet. It records the waste of human talent, the meaningless, self-destructive passion of lives led in ignorance of the right relation between human and divine principles. "The gods," for Phaedra and Theseus, are mere extensions of their own power; even Hippolytus, who scorns love, is thereby abusing divinity, and the wrath of Venus produces the catastrophe. Aesculapius, who usurped the power of Jove, is a preeminent example of what a man may become who uses his god-given talents as if they were his own. Prospero restores his magic to its source and is saved; and so too the Red Cross Knight, confirmed in sainthood, confronts Guyon and the Palmer with words that demonstrate that he has not chosen the way of Aesculapius.

> His be the praise, that this atchiev'ment wrought,
> Who made my hand the organ of his might;
> More then goodwill to me attribute nought:
> For all I did, I did but as I ought.
>
> (II.i.33)

As so often in *The Faerie Queene*, the "allegorical point" of the Hippolytus/Aesculapius digression is not very subtle or recondite when reduced to a moral maxim; but Spenser "always means something subtler and broader than one says he does."[11] In the living world of the poem these figures display the special power of an inexplicit fable. The episode is a good illustration of what Boccaccio meant when he said that truths become "more precious" when we find our own way to them through the darkness by way of "strong intellectual effort."

This fable speaks to Spenser's audience by invoking their

---

[10] The interesting and sympathetic discussion of the episode by Alpers (*Poetry of "The Faerie Queen,"* pp. 345-47) is one of the few to have made sense of it.

[11] Thomas M. Greene, *The Descent from Heaven: A Study in Epic Continuity* (New Haven, 1963), p. 310.

prior knowledge of a myth, for the story omits some of the
details, and two of the principals' names are not specified
(Theseus has been mentioned, two stanzas earlier [35], as
"condemned to endlesse slouth by law"). The myth is in
turn knitted into the poem's fabric, not only in the sense
that it helps us to understand the choices confronting the
hero, but also by an allusion that ties it to this book's major
chain of references. Night adjures Aesculapius:

> Goe to then, O thou farre renowmed sonne
> Of great *Apollo*, shew thy famous might.
> (I.v.43)

The reverberations elicited by the revelation that this suf-
ferer is a son of Apollo are very potent in Book I.[12] There
is an immediate irony, if we place the allusion next to
Night's sour comment a few stanzas earlier: "The sonnes of
Day he favoureth, I see" (25). The sons of Day can end
their days in the kingdom of eternal Night. Bunyan's
dreamer sees "that there was a way to hell, even from the
gates of heaven"; Aesculapius and Phaethon, children of
great Apollo, go down to darkness. And so light becomes
the fire of Hell. Phaethon

> inflames the skyen
> With fire not made to burne, but fairely for to shyne.
> (I.iv.9)

Aesculapius' labors in Hell are described in a deliberate
ambiguity which speaks of how a life-giving power can become deadly:

> he did alwaies strive
> Himselfe with salves to health for to restore,
> And slake the heavenly fire, that raged evermore.
> (I.v.40)

---

12 They are discussed by Alastair Fowler in his chapter on Book I
as the "Book of the Sun," *Spenser and the Numbers of Time* (London,
1964), especially pp. 72-73.

"The heavenly fire" is the fire of Jove's vengeance, the dark side of the holy light. Gaston Bachelard has written pertinently about the protean symbolism of fire:

> Among all phenomena, it is really the only one to which there can be so definitely attributed the opposing values of good and evil. It shines in Paradise. It burns in Hell. It is gentleness and torture. It is cookery and it is apocalypse. . . . It is a tutelary and a terrible divinity, both good and bad. It can contradict itself; thus it is one of the principles of universal explanation.[13]

The dark fires of Hell and the dazzling light of Heaven are counterparts of the poles of darkness; they are all self-contradicting "principles of universal explanation," and all are made manifest in *The Faerie Queene*. They are also present *in potentia* in the microcosm of man, and mingle bafflingly on Middle Earth, where we lead our lives.

The duplicity of the phenomenal world is incarnate in Duessa. She takes it with her to the Cave of Night and there, where unambiguous principles rule, she is not recognized. " 'I, that do seeme not I, *Duessa* ame,' " she announces (26), and the stanza that follows epitomizes with a fine complication the bewilderment of seemings that confronts us daily. Night bends to kiss "the wicked witch,"

>   saying; In that faire face
> The false resemblance of Deceipt, I wist
> Did closely lurke; yet so true-seeming grace
> It carried, that I scarse in darkesome place
> Could it discerne, though I the mother bee
> Of falshood, and root of *Duessaes* race.
> O welcome child, whom I have longd to see,
> And now have seene unwares. Lo now I go with thee.
>
>   (I.v.27)

[13] *The Psychoanalysis of Fire*, tr. A.C.M. Ross (Boston, 1964), p. 7.

These shifty phrases imitate the sleight-of-hand inherent in the subject. To "resemble" Falsehood or Deceit is a contradiction in terms, conveyed in the transposed modifier ("false resemblance of Deceipt"). Yet this false resemblance carries "true-seeming grace" (the rhyme-word bearing ironic weight), the appearance of truth—and thus Deceit is true to itself, since its "truth" is false-seeming. But this "truth" is so true that it can hardly be discerned by Night "in darkesome place"—or is it the *resemblance* that can hardly be discerned? Night suggests that she should have been able to see "it" (whatever *it* is), since she is "the mother . . . Of falshood"; but just because she is who she is —the essence of darkness and every sort of concealment— she cannot "see." In particular, she cannot see because she is dazed by the appearance that Duessa bears—"th' unacquainted light" (21) from which she shrank when the false sun first appeared. The stanza closes on another paradox: Night has "seene unwares" Duessa's "false resemblaunce," the true false-seeming beneath Duessa's true-seeming appearance. To see unwares is to see not at all, as the Red Cross Knight learns to his cost; but such seeing is the rule in this kingdom of negations. It is beset by the paradoxes that Donne struggled to express in his *Nocturnall upon S. Lucies day*, a place that is the home "Of absence, darknesse, death; things which are not."

Yet these things which are not—absence, darkness, the prospect of death—impinge upon our lives, and we can observe their fearful negative power in the career of Book I's hero. At this very moment, having absented himself from truth, he is lying in the darkness of "that sad house of *Pryde*," from whose false light obscurity and death emanate; when the Sins ride forth,

> still before their way
> A foggy mist had covered all the land;
> And underneath their feet, all scattered lay

> Dead sculs and bones of men, whose life had
> gone astray.
>
> (I.iv.36)

The power of the poet's vision can pierce these foggy mists and let us see the unspeakable things they conceal. But the Red Cross Knight, who is the creature, not the companion, of the narrator, must make his way through the mist as best he can, and his life, too, may go astray. His best is not very good; but Spenser is at pains to indicate that the obscurity in which he moves is only in part the consequence of willful blindness. It is also rooted in a congenital blindness that afflicts all of us and is echoed in the very structure of the world, "as the state of man now is." The poet, controlling a fictive version of this world, can strip away seemings and show us the naked principles themselves, as he does in the Cave of Night. He does it again in Canto iii, where the opposite principle is caused to reveal itself.

> One day nigh wearie of the yrkesome way,
>   From her unhastie beast she did alight,
>   And on the grasse her daintie limbs did lay
>   In secret shadow, farre from all mens sight:
>   From her faire head her fillet she undight,
>   And laid her stole aside. Her angels face
>   As the great eye of heaven shyned bright,
>   And made a sunshine in the shadie place;
> Did never mortall eye behold such heavenly grace.
>
> (I.iii.4)

In the context of its stanza the last line becomes more than a conventional formula for feminine beauty; *this* beauty is literally unearthly, and mortal eye cannot behold it because it never reveals itself except "farre from all mens sight." Far, that is, from all but the poet; for he can see, precisely, "things invisible to mortal sight." Milton's prayer, making a more explicit claim than Spenser ever does, reiterates the ancient equation of corporeal blindness with spiritual vision, both prophetic and poetic. Pico della Mirandola gives another version.

> Many ravish'd at the sight of Intellectual Beauty,
> become blinde to sensible; imply'd by Callimachus,
> Hymn 5 in the Fable of Tyresias, who viewing Pallas
> naked, lost his sight, yet by her was made a Prophet;
> closing the eyes of his Body, she open'd those of his
> Minde, by which he beheld both the Present and
> Future. The Ghost of Achilles, which inspired
> Homer with all Intellectual Contemplations in
> Poetry, deprived him of corporeal sight.[14]

The prophetic *character* of Book I of *The Faerie Queene* is Heavenly Contemplation.

> Great grace that old man to him given had;
>   For God he often saw from heavens hight,
>   All were his earthly eyen both blunt and bad,
>   And through great age had lost their kindly sight,
>   Yet wondrous quick and persant was his spright,
>   As Eagles eye, that can behold the Sunne. (I.x.47)

But this eagle eye is also possessed by the poem's maker, who has beheld the face of Una, bright as "the great eye of heaven," in Canto iii.

> The poet's eye, in a fine frenzy rolling,
>   Doth glance from heaven to earth, from earth to heaven.

The import of Shakespeare's lines is perhaps more precise than it is sometimes taken to be. The poet's sight-lines are not merely horizontal; they look up to Heaven and down to Hell. Spenser can go with Duessa to the underworld; he can go, unaccompanied by mere mortals, into the "shady place" where bright Truth is unveiled; and we as his readers can go with him, can see past and future and look on Pallas naked.

[14] *A Platonick Discourse upon Love*, tr. Thomas Stanley (1651), ed. E. G. Gardner (Boston, 1914), p. 46.

2. Learning to Read: The Tree and the Fountain

Yet the gods do not walk unveiled on Middle Earth, and this is what complicates the hero's life even beyond that confusion caused by the duplicities of evil. Both good *and* evil are "hardly to be discerned" in this world. Milton in *Areopagitica* warns that Truth, though "strong next to the Almighty," can be devious.

> Do not bind her when she sleeps, for then she speaks not true, as the old Proteus did, who spake oracles only when he was caught and bound, but then rather she turns herself into all shapes, except her own, and perhaps tunes her voice according to the time, . . . until she be adjured into her own likeness. Yet is it not impossible that she may have more shapes than one.
>
> (*SM*, p. 751)

Among other things, this passage is a fine gloss on Cantos i and ii of Spenser's poem. Sleeping truth ("drownd in deadly sleepe," i.36) can be bound and metamorphosed by demonic power, as she is by Archimago and by the Knight's own cooperating desires in Canto i. One of her false shapes is Duessa masquerading as Fidessa. In turning to her, the Red Cross Knight is rejecting what he thinks to be Una's own falsity; but this misdeeming is the consequence of his failure to understand the import of what Milton is talking about, the obscurity of Truth to fallen man. Una's name witnesses to the fact that ultimately she does *not* have "more shapes than one"; but because her true shape is hidden from us, desire and imagining often rule our sense of what the veil conceals. The Knight confuses a veil with a disguise. He sees the false Una "Under blake stole hyding her bayted hooke" (i.49). This is a description of Duessa, who in the shape of unacted desires enters the Knight's consciousness before she enters the poem. The veil of the real Una hides no baited hook; rather it hides a brightness that the Knight's unregenerate mortal sight *cannot*, in more than one sense, see. He cannot be allowed to look on Truth unveiled, lest he suffer the fate of Duessa's dragon when the veil is rent from Arthur's shield.

> And eke the fruitfull-headed beast, amaz'd
> At flashing beames of that sunshiny shield,
> Became starke blind, and all his senses daz'd.
> (I.viii.20)

Mortal sight also *cannot* see Truth because it is too feeble, too lacking in power—the power that Heavenly Contemplation has acquired by experience ("through great age") and by "great grace."

In the epistemological allegory of Book I, Spenser compels both his reader and his hero to confront the duplicity of seemings. The darkness of truth lies at the opposite pole from the darkness of "things that are not" in the kingdom of old Night. But like most opposites, these can be mistaken for each other. The Red Cross Knight cannot see Una as she "really is"; he will not see Duessa for what she is. "The false resemblance of Deceipt" is explored in two related episodes of the first book whose interaction allows us to see how the self-commentary of Spenserian allegory is informative in the larger context of its readers' lives. As we watch the Knight assenting to remain a mere allegorical character, inattentive to the poet's clues, we learn that the reading of allegory is a model for the honest reading of our own motives and self-deceptions.

This hero is making his way among veiled "shapes," but the veils are not impenetrable. *Frontis nulla fides*, says one of Whitney's emblems.

> But man is made, of suche a seemlie shape,
> That frende, or foe, is not discern'd by face:
> Then harde it is the wickeds wiles to scape,
> Since that the bad, doe maske with honest grace.[1]

The masks of wickedness confront the Red Cross Knight often enough in his early wanderings. But if "the bad, do maske with honest grace" in the "seemlie shape" of fair humanity, friends can appear in forbidding or even terrifying guise. This is illustrated in the encounter between the Knight and Fradubio in Canto ii, which deserves scrutiny both because it is proleptic with respect to later episodes, and because in it Spenser is saying something about the complex relation between deceptive appearance and veiled truth. Fraudubio's history is a parable of mistaken choice, a choice between ladies "unlike faire" in which deceptive seemings lead to error. Not only does Duessa masquerade "Like a faire Lady" as "a like faire Lady" (35)—the play on words directing our attention to the duplicity of likenesses, the poet's stock in trade; she also causes the true fairness of Fraelissa to be obscured.

> The wicked witch now seeing all this while
> The doubtfull ballaunce equally to sway,
> What not by right she cast to win by guile,
> And by her hellish science raisd streight way
> A foggy mist, that overcast the day,
> And a dull blast, that breathing on her face,
> Dimmed her former beauties shining ray,
> And with foule ugly forme did her disgrace.
>   (I.ii.38)

The darkness that rises up like a miasma from Hell (and later covers the ground before the Deadly Sins) restates, in another mode, the Red Cross Knight's misdeeming of the

---

[1] Geffrey Whitney, *A Choice of Emblemes*, ed. Henry Green (London, 1866; repr. New York, 1967), p. 100.

veiled Una. "Beauties shining ray" is dimmed in both cases; that is, the obscurity that overcame our powers of knowing at the Fall makes us unable to look upon the sun. "To a half-blind man, even when the sun is shining its brightest the sky looks cloudy." Beauty is in the eye of the beholder; and if the beholder's eye is half blind, fair and foul may well change places. The questioning of "appearances" that can lead us to truth can recoil ironically and produce the appearances that mislead us into error. The power of Duessa to confer a "foule ugly forme" on the beloved is "really" or is also a power of persuasion; she speaks of Fraelissa as a "deformed wight," and Fradubio at once assents: "Eftsoons I thought her such, as she me told" (39). The corresponding moment for the Red Cross Knight has come as he and Duessa rest in the deceptive shade of these two trees: "And in his falsed fancy he her takes / To be the fairest wight, that lived yit" (30). *His falsed fancy* has a beautifully precise ambivalence. The passive verbal adjective suggests that some power has wrought upon fancy, "falsing" it, so that now it *acts* falsely, taking the false for the true, or able to "see" only the false. "What we see is what we think." There is a bewilderment in these stanzas that reflects the bewilderment of half-blind men stumbling through a wandering wood, "That makes them doubt their wits be not their owne" (i.10). It is useless to talk about "inner" and "outer" worlds in such a context; the forces without and the forces within the psyche complement each other and owe their being to the same source. We are required to recall "how much we are the woods we wander in."[2] Wordsworth, celebrating the beautiful congruence between the eye and its object, wrote that "the external world is fitted to the mind";

[2] See Richard Wilbur's tiny poetic treatise on self and the world in "Ceremony" (*Ceremony and Other Poems* [New York, 1950], p. 55):

> But ceremony never did conceal,
> Save to the silly eye, which all allows,
> How much we are the woods we wander in.

but this fittingness can also be a distortion or deformation in the organ of sight and what it contemplates.

The result is not to absolve the Red Cross Knight or Fradubio of responsibility, but to suggest that responsibility and guilt are intrinsic to the human situation before they are actualized in any specific human event. Which is to say that no merely human power can right things: so Fradubio's "evill plight" cannot be corrected except by the power of the "living well" of grace (43). But it is also to say that virtuous action is impossible for any man who is not willing to understand his situation in other than merely private or personal terms, who refuses to learn to read the signs offered him by the sagacious elders, to see analogies and to make connections—to acquire, that is, the wisdom of an expert reader of allegory, whether composed by God or by the poet Spenser. Fradubio offers the Red Cross Knight a cautionary tale; his story is a little allegory within the larger allegory of *The Faerie Queene*, and the hero stands outside it, as capable of reading its message as Spenser's audience is capable of reading about *him* in the larger context of Book I. True, he is being asked to read, not merely a *book* by Virgil or Ariosto, but a living emblem. Anyone might find that "up his heare did hove" when confronted by an animated page out of *Orlando Furioso* (31). The Knight does recognize, however, that this voice speaks to him from another world, though from what world he is not sure. But at the end of it all he fastidiously retreats, the bleeding bough thrust back into the ground, "That from the bloud he might be innocent" (44). He is a dull or unwilling or easily distracted reader of allegory, turning aside from its mirror before he can see his own face there. Guyon "reads" in Tantalus an emblem that can teach men, including himself, "how to use their present state"; the Knight, though the outlines of the story repeat his own recent experience, refuses to make the inference that would connect Fradubio's

157

present state of arboreal paralysis with the result of a choice to which he himself is unwittingly being conducted.

Seeing, in the sense of understanding or reading sign-posts, dominates the Knight's adventures in the first part of Book I. He can defeat obvious adversaries like Error and Sansfoy, though even these conquests are in some sense illusory. But when Una cries, "Add faith unto your force, and be not faint," (i.19) in the first dragon-battle, she is defining the real problem he must solve. The names of the two "enclosed in wooden wals" in Canto ii, Fradubio and Fraelissa, echo and invert this line: doubt or faithlessness, and faintness or frailty. Their metamorphosis signifies not only a descent in the chain of being, but what that change means: isolation from the perceived world and atrophy of understanding. "All my senses were bereaved quight," says Fradubio; the sensitive soul has degenerated to the merely vegetal. We are reminded that when the Red Cross Knight meets the "wretched tree," he is himself cut off from Truth; and that truth and troth, faith, are intimately related.[3] Trust or faith is a source of strength; abusing it, he becomes merely a "fraile, feeble, fleshly wight" (ix.53). The frailty that results from faithlessness, the breaking of troth and loss of truth, is depicted in the book's second half, where Spenser moves on from epistemological dilemmas to their ruinous moral consequences.

At the opening of Canto vii, Spenser places a stanza that repeats the point of Whitney's emblem, *Frontis nulla fides.*

> What man so wise, what earthly wit so ware,
>   As to descry the crafty cunning traine,
>   By which deceipt doth maske in visour faire,

[3] "The meaning of the word truth which connects it with troth to an allegiance, and makes it include both veritas and fides, is a very important meaning in incident after incident of Book I. Both sides of Una's trueness are continually played upon. . . . Red Crosse learns nothing from seeing the exact parallel to his own situation [in Fradubio], because he has lost truth through failing to keep troth" (Tuve, *Allegorical Imagery*, p. 121).

And cast her coulours dyed deepe in graine,
To seeme like Truth, whose shape she well can faine,
And fitting gestures to her purpose frame,
The guiltlesse man with guile to entertaine?

(I.vii.1)

Like many of the contemplative stanzas that introduce
cantos, this encourages us to step back from the foreground
of the action to meditate on the relation of what we have
seen, and are about to see, to men in general. The lines usually do not refer specifically to the heroes, though they include them. The metaphors in this stanza—of masking,
painting, "entertaining"—have been and are being enacted
in the person of Duessa, "daughter of Deceipt." The Red
Cross Knight is certainly an "earthly wit," but in assimilating him to "what man," Spenser relieves him, to some degree, of the burden of private wickedness at the same time
that he implicates his reader in the general and inescapable
wickedness that he shares with the Knight and every "guiltlesse man" who attempts to make his way through the cunning byways of the world. It is difficult to explicate the precise weight of *guiltless* in this stanza. There is interaction
with *guile* in the same line, suggesting that no matter how
guiltless, a man is susceptible to guile; we are about to see,
in Canto vii, how the "entertainment" offered by Duessa can
draw the Knight into genuine guilt. But *guiltless*, falling
here at the mid-point of Book I,[4] more or less divides the
first half of the Red Cross Knight's career from the second,
marking the point at which his dallying with Falsehood and
her "baits and seeming pleasures" turns into something
more serious, a threat to his salvation. Hitherto he has made
plenty of mistakes, but he has more or less kept his distance
from mortal sin, though from no lofty motive where Lucifera and her band are concerned. Because he is led by

[4] The "arithmetical centre of Book I" comes at I.vii.12-13. See Michael
Baybak, Paul Delany, and A. Kent Hieatt, "Placement 'in the middest'
in *The Faerie Queene*," *Silent Poetry*, ed. Alastair Fowler (London,
1970), pp. 145-46.

159

Falsehood and has abandoned Truth, his actions cannot come to good; but hitherto he has conducted himself in knightly fashion, as Spenser suggests in introducing Canto v, where the Red Cross Knight will be victorious over Sans-joy, at least temporarily.[5]

> The noble hart, that harbours vertuous thought,
>   And is with child of glorious great intent,
>   Can never rest, untill it forth have brought
>   Th' eternall brood of glorie excellent:
>   Such restlesse passion did all night torment
>   The flaming corage of that Faery knight. . . .
>   (I.v.1)

Thought and intent are still "vertuous" and are directed to the pursuit of glory; but the stanza encourages us to regard our own thoughts and intents in the light of the Red Cross Knight's predicament, which *we* now know to be precariously susceptible to disaster. Virtuous thought and great intent are inadequate guides. "Vertue gives her selfe light through darknesse for to wade," the Knight has said; the kind of light that virtue gives *herself* is self-reflecting and self-pleasing; it is the light that emanates from the mirror of Lucifera as she contemplates her own "bright blazing beautie."

> And in her hand she held a mirrhour bright,
>   Wherein her face she often vewed fayne,
>   And in her selfe-lov'd semblance took delight;
> For she was wondrous faire, as any living wight.
>   (I.iv.10)

Here, as so often in *The Faerie Queene,* Spenser's allegory works by actualizing the vehicle of a metaphor. "Vertue gives her selfe light"; the fairest of living wights gazes into

---

[5] As Alpers points out, even his initial response to Duessa is prompted in part by "knightly obligation" (*Poetry of "The Faerie Queene,"* p. 148).

a mirror and sees her own light-bearing image, a semblance of the true sun. Virtue is not the only source of light.

Thus the Knight's situation at the beginning of Canto vii, having denied himself the benefit of Fradubio's lesson and barely escaped Lucifera's dungeon, is the situation of one who courts disaster, and this courtship is about to begin in the main action. But so far he is *guiltless*: that is, his failures and gropings have been those of any man born into the confusions of a wilderness-world he never made, though it was made for him by his ancestor Adam. I think Spenser is not pressing any precise theological point here or making distinctions that would bear technical scrutiny by the casuists; but only that up to now the Knight's enemies have been those that lie in wait to entrap any innocent "earthly wit," preparatory to entangling his soul, and that the tone of the poet's comments on his hero has hitherto been relatively indulgent. "Then harde it is the wickeds wiles to scape," as the emblem says, and Spenser is sympathetic to the Knight's vain efforts to contend with wicked wiles, up to a point.

The point comes when the Knight abandons his integrity as a knight, the identity he assumed when he put on the armor of God. This identity involved him in a particular relationship of submissiveness to God and acceptance of a model of virtuous life laid down by him: a life "whose only form is the form Christ gave it." It is symbolized by the armor, which Spenser thought important enough to explicate in the Letter to Ralegh, where the lady insists that unless the Knight can wield these arms "he could not succeed in that enterprise." Having been divested of armor, he ceases to have a man's "shape"; deliquescent, he lies "Pourd out in looseness on the grassy grownd" (7). (Una later speaks of him as *dissolute* [vii.51].) This line is a good example of the witty, self-commenting mode of Spenser's allegory. It literalizes an earlier line ("And chearefull bloud in faintnesse chill did melt," 6), describes the sexual act, and also comments on the Ovidian myth invented by Spenser to illuminate the Knight's willingness "to rest in middest of the

race." In "Pourd out in loosenesse," Spenser reinflects or re-
translates into metaphor the fable of the nymph turned into
a fountain, suggesting *why* myths of liquefaction are appropriate to such frailties as the Nymph's. Nymph and Knight
are analogous instances of failure to maintain a suitably rig-
orous life-style; the myth of the fountain and a phrase at
once metaphorical and literal like "Pourd out in loosenesse"
are complementary, equally appropriate ways of describing
such failure.

The myth is, however, read only by us, not by the Red
Cross Knight, who as a character in an allegory is enjoying,
in these stanzas, some "natural" pleasures, unaware of the
fountain's ominous history and unable to hear Spenser's
warnings. The relation between reader and action in
stanzas 1-7 of Canto vii is a complicated one, effectively illustrating the variety of ways in which Spenser's allegory
can work to instruct us. Alpers has explicated part of the effect, remarking that we are asked to respond positively to
the details in stanza 3, to feel "that the grove is genuinely
attractive and that the knight's desire to drink from the
fountain is natural."[6] So it is; but as the deluge of commentary on "Art and Nature" in Spenser has made plain, attitudes in *The Faerie Queene* toward what "is perfectly natural" are problematic indeed. Nature is innocent, to be
sure; the shade, the green boughs, the birdsong and "breath-
ing wynd" are not themselves threatening, but they are
vulnerable to abuse, as Milton's Lady in *Comus* says:

> Impostor do not charge most innocent nature,
> As if she would her children should be riotous
> With her abundance, she good cateress
> Means her provision only to the good
> That live according to her sober laws.
>
> (761-65)

The Knight has abandoned these sober laws, and abandonment to "nature" is dangerous for him. "For Nature giveth

[6] Ibid., p. 144.

not vertue; it is an art to be made good."[7] Spenser's lines project innocence and naturalness; they do make us aware that we share with the hero a susceptibility to these harmless seductions. But Spenser's intent in effecting this degree of identification between reader and hero is not simple. At the same time that the verse entices us into sympathy with the Knight's "natural" impulses, the narrator's commentary, the invented myth, and the allusiveness of the entire passage both within *The Faerie Queene* and beyond it instill a distrust of these very impulses. In the process of inducing this simultaneous attraction and recoil, Spenser is illustrating the way in which the benefits to be derived from the long perspectives of an allegorical poem, which makes available the history of imagining, can rescue us from the predicament of the Red Cross Knight. The Knight has been given some clues, and "ought" to know better; but we have been given more, and we do know better.

There is no doubt that Spenser in stanza 3 is deliberately recreating a *locus amoenus,* and this complex of images, at once paradisal and pastoral, would have been generically if not specifically recognizable to a reasonably instructed audience. The grove is one of Spenser's false paradises, of which the most famous instance is the Bower of Bliss. This one is false, not in the sense that its *décor* is "unnatural" or conceals a trap, but because the Red Cross Knight enters it at the wrong time.[8] The clearest analogy is Phaedria's island in Book II, to which Cymochles succumbs in Canto vi.

> Trees, braunches, birds, and songs, were framed fit,
> For to allure fraile mind to carelesse ease.
> Carelesse the man soone woxe, and his weake wit·

[7] This significant sentence, and the passage in Seneca where it appears, has been helpfully disinterred by Edward Tayler, *Nature and Art in Renaissance Literature* (New York, 1964), p. 50.

[8] For a discussion of the Bower as "a false, premature, or regressive Eden," see Williams, *World of Glass,* pp. 73-74.

> Was overcome of thing, that did him please;
> So pleased, did his wrathfull purpose faire appease.
>   (II.vi.13)

Cymochles succumbs; Guyon does not. A paradise prematurely regained is no paradise but a Garden of Proserpina. The Red Cross Knight is not yet ready for paradise; this is why Spenser insists that he is only "in middest of the race," and underlines the importance of due process in his colloquy with Heavenly Contemplation (I.x.63). Only in the fullness of time will man's nature be redeemed so that he can revel in the harmless pleasures of the natural world.

Phaedria's island belongs to a later canto and book; the Garden of Adonis, which is the ultimate prototype of all these "good" earthly paradises, will not be disclosed for two more books, and then will be visited not by any human character, but only by the bard who can make the way safe for the reader. Their illuminating power cannot therefore be brought to bear on Canto vii except for re-readers. But if we confine ourselves to what has already happened in Book I, we can observe Spenser repeatedly offering contexts within which a reader can make sense of successively unfolding episodes. One of the early readers of the poem remarked that "Although the beginning of his Allegory or mysticall sense, may be obscure, yet in the processe of it, he doth himselfe declare his own conceptions in such sort as they are obvious to any ordinary capacities."[9] There is a cumulative force within the books, sustained by a process of reflexive allusion. The allusion in vii.3 to a generic *locus amoenus* invokes other instances of this literary paradigm (both the details themselves and their arrangement, as in lines 3-5, are as "literary" as they are "natural"), and encourages us to speculate on the implications of a "paradise" at this point in the hero's adventures. The specific allusion refers within the poem's formal universe to the Fradubio

[9] Sir Kenelm Digby, *Var.* II, 472.

episode in Canto ii. The same combination of attractive detail and forbidding comment is visible there.

> But this good knight soone as he them can spie,
>   For the coole shade him thither hastly got:
>   For golden *Phoebus* now ymounted hie,
>   From fiery wheeles of his faire chariot
>   Hurled his beame so scorching cruell hot,
>   That living creature mote it not abide;
>   And his new Lady it endured not.
>   There they alight, in hope themselves to hide
> From the fierce heat, and rest their weary limbs a tide.
>
> Faire seemely pleasaunce each to other makes,
>   With goodly purposes, there as they sit: . . .
>
> (I.ii.29-30)

The rhetoric is heavily loaded with positive adjectives: "coole," "faire," "seemely," "goodly," and, as in Canto vii, Spenser insists on the "naturalness" of the impulse to rest and take shelter by assimilating the characters to all "living creatures." At the same time he fends off too-ready assent on the reader's part, following the description, in stanza 30, with references to the Knight's "falsed fancy," and preceding it with a stanza that reveals to us, though not to the hero, the dangers of the place.

> they came at last,
>   Where grew two goodly trees, that faire did spred
>   Their armes abroad, with gray mosse overcast,
>   And their greene leaves trembling with every blast,
>   Made a calm shadow far in compasse round:
>   The fearefull Shepheard often there aghast
>   Under them never sat, ne wont there sound
> His mery oaten pipe, but shund th' unlucky ground.
>
> (I.ii.28)

It is we who are "aghast" when the poet shifts gears in midstanza. The place has an air of sacredness; it is an encircled

165

center, and at the center is an emblem of metamorphosis, though we do not yet know that. "The fearefull Shepheard," whether he recognizes it or not, intuits the *numen* and shuns the unlucky ground. The Red Cross Knight lacks this intuition, just as he has somehow bypassed, or cut himself off from, the naive though idolatrous (or *therefore* idolatrous) faith in Una shown by "the woodborne people" in Canto vi, and the instinctive reverence of the lion in Canto iii. All these ways of responding to truth are put into the poem by Spenser for our instruction, though not necessarily for our imitation. He neither recommends nor dismisses the fearful shepherd's wariness; he merely records it, and having done so passes on to let us see the motive for it.

With this episode in Canto ii behind us we are equipped to respond with a complication of assent and dissent to the image and legend of the fountain in Canto vii. We assent insofar as the place is "really" attractive and satisfying to "natural" needs. Fradubio's grove and the nymph's are both attractive in this way. But the emblems at their centers give warning that these paradises are false *for us* (and for the Knight); these centers mark the point of departure for descents rather than ascents. Here the trees

> with greene boughes decking a gloomy glade,
> About the fountaine like a girlond made.
>
> (4)

This figure will be elaborately echoed in the Garden of Adonis ("A gloomy grove . . . like a girlond compassed the height," III.vi.43) and in the multiplied circles of Book VI (where, however, the "centers" are mountain-tops), as well as in the concentric circles of the Garden of Proserpina, "compast with a mound" and embraced by the black river Cocytus "which flow'd about it round" (II.vii.56). The last, which is actually underground and has a mound or earth-wall surrounding it, suggests by its three-dimensionality the "vertical" orientation of centers, from which the heavenly or demonic axes of Spenser's world proceed.

All of these contexts are ultimately relevant to the small circle around the Fountain of Sloth in I.vii. But when we first encounter it, only Fradubio's grove is relevant (with some echo as well, perhaps, of the danger of taking shelter, from the opening stanzas of the book). This relevance the poet conveys to us by a congruence of action (Knight and lady sheltering from the sun[10] and taking pleasure together), of setting (the magic circle), and of myth (the metamorphoses into trees and fountain). I have already commented upon the importance of the names Fradubio and Fraelissa. In Canto vii, the Knight enacts their meanings. Spenser reminds us in stanza 1 that the "false Dame" has a false name: "The false *Duessa*, cloked with *Fidessaes* name"; in consorting with her, the Knight reincarnates Fradubio, the falsing of faith. And shortly afterward, he "becomes" Fraelissa, unmanned and frail.

> Eftsoones his manly forces gan to faile,
> And mightie strong was turnd to feeble fraile.
>
> (6)

The two episodes are connected by the more obvious links noted above, and not much is lost if we fail to notice these subtler verbal innuendos.[11] I mention them as an instance of the way in which Spenser continually, almost instinctively, inflects his allegorical terms. Sage and serious though it may be, *The Faerie Queene* shows the poet at play. It also shows him alive to the ontological implications of figures

---

10 "Judgment comes when the knight turns aside from the heat of the summer sun in its power—from the righteousness and truth, that is, of the *Sol iustitiae*" (Fowler, *Numbers of Time*, p. 72). This description of the events of Canto vii also fits those of Canto ii.

11 This one seems to be insisted upon; the key word is repeated (not as a rhyme) in Stanza 11: "Through that fraile fountain which him feeble made."

of speech. The Knight is "like" Fraelissa not only in being frail, but in the sense that he has succumbed to the lower impulses in himself, traditionally signified by feminine personifications. He is a "womanish weake knight"—a phrase applied to Cymochles in Book II (v.36), who displays the Red Cross Knight's temporary proclivities at a pitch of higher ontological intensity.

The Fradubio episode and the Fountain of Sloth, with their echoing details, illuminate each other and introduce us to one of the ways in which symbolic places function in *The Faerie Queene.* Such places are often gateways through which other-wordly power can irrupt into life in the middest; they are equivalent, on the vertical axis, to a dangerous crossroads on the horizontal. Pausing here, human beings are standing, though they usually do not know it, on the brink of a definitive ascent or descent, toward a more final stage of moral being. Hence these places, like the circles around Fradubio and the fountain, are often scenes of metamorphoses where the immanent power, divine or demonic, has claimed a soul.

3. Spenserian Ontology: Pride and Despair

In the encounter with Orgoglio, prepared for by the opening details of Canto vii, we can observe the imagination at another of its fiction-making tasks and note how its procedure, as it answers the narrative's present needs, differs from earlier devisings of images for "the same" concepts. The question concerning Orgoglio that every reader of Book I has asked—why *another* representation of Pride? —identifies the issue. But this second incarnation stands in a different relation to the hero from that of the first one, Lucifera. There have been attempts to distinguish these characters on the basis of theological definitions of kinds of pride, but this seems to me mistaken. Pride is always a "spiritual" sin; the fact that pride's object may vary—that one may be proud of strength, beauty, or one's own virtue —does not alter the basic ingredient, which is a presumptuous declaration of independence from God. All positive gifts are from him, and pride trespasses upon his bounty. In Book I, rather than distinguishing the objects of pride, we ought to notice that its two versions inhabit two *kinds* of allegorical characters, and that therefore a logical and ontological distinction is involved. Lucifera embodies

> the thing which is half-concept, half-image, the
> universal which is itself thought of as a concrete
> object, *as an instance of itself*. . . . Philosophical
> jargon will give us a short-hand description of this
> phenomenon: the instantially viewed universal.[1]

Thus Womanliness is "something womanly," Venus "something which is both Love itself and enormously loving." This author calls such figures "logically very curious," but

[1] A. D. Nuttall, *Two Concepts of Allegory* (London, 1967), p. 36.

they are not curious to the imagination, and Spenser habitually gives us a virtue or a vice as an instance of itself, a
being that can be taken as representative because of the
intensity and exclusiveness of its possession by the vice or
virtue. Lucifera is surrounded by iconographical clues, and
we know that she is not just another human character. On
the other hand, she is *descended* from Lucifer, so she is not
the archetype either, but an emanation of it. She is a human
character raised to a higher power, and she stands at the
end of a road that we might all travel. Her recognizably human form places her on a low rung of the ontological ladder. A concept is educed from many instances; when an
instance is singled out as typical, it acquires conceptual
force as the incarnation of an Idea. An adjective hovers on
the frontiers of its noun, a proud person moves toward a
new role as a representative of Pride. As that frontier is
crossed, the image acquires its own attributes at the moment when it stops *being* an attribute. Spenser dramatizes
this process more explicitly in Book III when Malbecco
turns from a jealous human being to Jealousy, adjective to
noun:

> he through privy griefe, and horrour vaine,
> Is woxen so deform'd, that he has quight
> Forgot he was a man, and *Gealosie* is hight.
> (III.x.60)

Such exemplary figures exist in the *aevum*, their lives perpetually renewed by men who share their essences
attributively.

But in Orgoglio, the allegorical imagination produces a
different sort of being. Like Lucifera, the giant behaves
pridefully; but more than that, he "is" Pride anatomized, a
figure that only imagination can see, as it turns its gaze toward the world within. Joseph Spence, collecting instances
from *The Faerie Queene* to illustrate "what faults the great-

est allegorist may commit whilst the manner of allegorizing is left upon so unfixed and irregular a footing as it was in his time and is still among us," objects, for various but related reasons, to the Blatant Beast, Discord in Book IV, the Cave of Care, Munera in Book V, and finally, "such instances as I fear can scarce be called by any softer name than that of 'ridiculous imaginations.'" These last are all figures that are really animated metaphors, and like most metaphors they give us trouble if we attempt to visualize them as a whole; they include Ignaro, Daunger at the Temple of Venus, and Orgoglio. "The thought of a vast giant's shrinking into an empty form, like a bladder," struck Spence as a prime instance of ridiculous imagining, externally unlifelike.[2] Such images are the *causes* of behavior, visibly explicated. The realities they embody exist both as Ideas and as psychological facts. We may make the guess concerning Spenser's creation of them that A. D. Nuttall makes about Prudentius: "One cannot be confident that the poet has not asked himself, 'Now what must pride herself be like? . . .' and striven with some seriousness to depict her very soul."[3] What is it *like*—to feel pride, to act pridefully? The answer must be metaphorical; we are dealing with what Forster called "the inner life," the life that does not reveal itself in any overt gesture, an inarticulate level of being that must achieve articulation in images. At the same time, the intellect can intuit an essence, which it may name "Pride" but which is also entertained inarticulately. To both of these speechless modes of being, the psychic and the visionary, Spenser gives voice and body in Orgoglio.

The giant behaves like a prideful person, but that is only the beginning of our apprehension of him. When Spenser says that "His living like saw never living eye" (vii.8), he is being very precise about the *kind* of character he is depicting. To be proud is to feel oneself superior, "tall" in the

[2] *Var.* I, 365-66.
[3] *Two Concepts of Allegory*, pp. 34-35.

Elizabethan sense.[4] So Orgoglio, despising "all other powres and knighthood" (10), *seems* "to threat the skye" (8), and (like Lucifera) is proud of his "high descent" (10), a phrase that will look ironic when we see the mighty fallen in the next canto. In Canto vii Spenser stresses two features: his height and his earthiness, these being attributes immediately relevant to the Red Cross Knight's situation as a prideful "man of earth." The club with which he threatens the Knight is an alternative to the Christian man's proper armor, now laid aside; it too is earthy, "torne / Out of his mothers bowelles" (we remember the brood of dragonets in Canto i who "sucked up their dying mothers blood" [i.25]). This club betrays Orgoglio in his fight with Arthur; being of the earth, it returns to earth, and striving to free it the giant has his arm struck off. The sense of a grotesque presumptuousness, at once unstable and sluggish, a power unapt yet mortally dangerous, emerges in these episodes.

Under Orgoglio's stroke a man may be "pouldred all as thin as flowre" (12), the dominant image of flour-milling reinforced by the echo of mortal man's frailty, springing up like a flower to be cut down or, like the hero in the next canto, "shronk up like withered flowres" (viii.41). Images surrounding the giant's fall allude to the troubling of earth by thunderbolts (viii.9), earthquakes (8),[5] uprooted trees (22), and undermined castles (23). "Such was this Gyaunts fall, that seemd to shake / The stedfast globe of earth" (23).

---

[4] OED dates the first instance of the modern meaning, "high of stature," to 1530. The four primary definitions under Sense 1 all entail honorific adjectives: "quick, prompt, ready"; "meet, becoming, seemly"; "comely, goodly, fair, handsome"; "doughty, brave, bold, valiant." All of these senses remained current through the sixteenth century, and one is tempted to see in Orgoglio's gigantism—"The hight of three the tallest sonnes of mortall seed" (8)—another of Spenser's anatomized puns, this a quite complicated one playing on an archaic and a derived meaning, to suggest Orgoglio's (and the Red Cross Knight's) estimate of himself.

[5] For the apocalyptic connotations of the earthquake in Book I, see S. K. Heninger, "The Orgoglio Episode in *The Faerie Queene*," *ELH* XXVI (1959), 171-87.

Earth, throughout this episode, is metaphorically the flesh of the man of earth, Georgos; in Orgoglio's fall is figured the self-destructive ruin of the body by the prideful soul. Cantos vii and viii animate a principle later expressed by the disgruntled Body in Marvell's poem: "What but a Soul could have the wit / To build me up for Sin so fit?" Finally, in the giant's deflation (which disturbed Spence), the poet is pressing the metaphor through the stages of imagination's logic, as he does again when Duessa's "neather parts" are exposed, later in Canto viii (48).

The peculiar non-literalness of Orgoglio illustrates the energetic action of metaphor, working to make visible at least two normally invisible realities: the interior sense or psychological orientation—"what it feels like"—and the nature of the sin, Pride, as it looks *sub specie aeternitatis,* to God's eye. Weirdly surrealistic effects in art are frequently attempts to override the limits of our vision; so Maritain speculates that Picasso's "distorted human faces are perhaps our true likeness, when we are seen by the angels."[6] In contrast, Lucifera is an emblematic figure, Pride as it appears to a human observer who extrapolates from experience and arrives at what we call personification. Such a figure speaks to the senses through allusion and iconographical detail; it is only marginally metaphorical within the fiction. We respond to it contemplatively, not introspectively; it is a rationalized concept, not an expressive one.

In his characterization of Despair, Spenser unites the external and internal characteristics divided in the anatomy of Pride between Lucifera and Orgoglio. Despair gains entrance to the psyche by causing a division in it, forcing a man to see himself as he really is, a desperate sinner, and pressing this self-awareness to a logical and just, though ultimately false, conclusion. His chief weapons are "his charmed speaches" (30), weapons that seem to the Red

---

[6] Jacques Maritain, *Creative Intuition in Art and Poetry* (New York, 1953), p. 79.

Cross Knight, still insufficiently aware of the invisible world's strength, "idle" when he hears about them from Sir Trevisan.

> How may a man, (said he) with idle speach
>   Be wonne, to spoyle the Castle of his health?
>   (I.ix.31)

Living proof of the relation between self-division and self-destruction in Despair's victim is before his eyes; the relation is dramatized in Despair himself and the dialogue that follows, in which "idle speach" shows its terrible power. The masterly rhetoric of his argument has been often admired; its *effects* are carefully spelled out by the poet.

> The knight was much enmoved with his speach,
>   That as a swords poynt through his hart did perse,
>   And in his conscience made a secrete breach,
>   Well knowing true all, that he did reherse,
>   And to his fresh remembrance did reverse
>   The ugly vew of his deformed crimes,
>   That all his manly powres it did disperse,
>   As he were charmed with inchaunted rimes,
> That oftentimes he quakt, and fainted oftentimes.
>   (48)

This is the process that led to Sir Trevisan's plight: "of him selfe he seemd to be afrayd" (23). The secret breach of conscience divides the Knight's consciousness so that, for the first time, he sees *himself* in "the ugly vew" of sin; the sins are "*his* deformed crimes," as they were not when he visited the House of Pride, or even when he met himself in Orgoglio; that identification was made by the reader, not by the protagonist. Self-division and its consequences are depicted graphically in the next stanza; Despair

> shew'd him painted in a table plaine,
>   The damned ghosts, that doe in torments waile.
>   (49)

These damned souls have been "seen" by the Dwarf earlier, when he surveyed the "caytive wretched thralls, that wayled night and day" in Lucifera's dungeon (v.45). But only here does the sight become a self-confrontation for the hero, dramatized in the incident of Despair turning his gaze upon a *picture* of Hell's torments. The Red Cross Knight is now in the position of Britomart viewing Busirane's tapestries; each character sees the deplorable consequences of his or her pursuit of a particular line of action, but the confrontations affect them differently in response to their differing degrees of self-possession.

Despair is Orgoglio turned inside out, as commentators have long recognized; they are "two sins, one by excess, the other by defect, . . . opposed to the virtue of hope."[7] The differences between them are expressed in the details of their persons and behavior; the similarities, in the parallel effects they produce on the hero. And effects, in this narrative, are figures for motives, conscious or unconscious. The enervation and emasculation of the Knight when he meets Orgoglio—"faint in every joynt and vayne, / Through that fraile fountain which him feeble made" (vii.9)—is repeated when he hears Despair's argument. "His manly powres" are dispersed; we see him "waver, weake and fraile" (49) and faint repeatedly. In both cantos, the Red Cross Knight is confronting "the very source and fountainhead" of his sin,[8] though in the first instance he does not know it, and Spenser makes the point for the *reader* by having him drink from the "source"—the enervating fountain—before the giant actually appears. The secret connection between Pride and Despair is revealed in the hero's reiterated frailty and faintness. "When the soul gains self-knowledge, it moves from pride into conscious despair."[9] The Knight's limited self-

[7] Vern Torczon, "Spenser's Orgoglio and Despaire," *TSLL* III (1961), 126.

[8] Tuve, *Allegorical Imagery*, p. 107. This whole section of Miss Tuve's book deals in exemplary fashion with the subjects I am discussing.

[9] Susan Snyder, "The Left Hand of God: Despair in Medieval and Renaissance Tradition," *SR* XII (1965), 47.

knowledge must be emended through the disciplines of the House of Holiness and the vision unveiled on the Mount of Contemplation. In both Canto ix and Canto x, there is appeal to the *mind*'s eye, the power of "seeing" that is beyond ordinary sight; Despair shows the Knight a picture, Contemplation a vision of "the way, / That never yet was seene of Faeries sonne" (x.52).

Insofar as Despair's nature is expressed through his effects, we experience what it is like to *be in* despair, as in the figure of Orgoglio we "know" in a visceral sense what pride feels like. But Despair is *also* a "cursed man, low sitting on the ground" (ix.35), an instance as well as an instigator of his sin. His attitude displays the symptoms of Melancholy as they were conventionally diagnosed,[10] and when we last see him he is exemplary, like Malbecco. Both are doomed to endure till the upfolding of archetypes at the end of time. Despair demonstrates that he is an instance of himself when, having failed to persuade the Red Cross Knight, he succumbs to his own persuasions and attempts suicide. "Yet nathelesse it could not doe him die, / Till he should die his last, that is eternally" (I.ix.54).

Spenser augments his definition of Despair by causing him to live in one of the poem's magic places, a cave that opens into the nether regions, final destination of a despairing soul. The décor is thoroughly conventional:

> Caves, owls, graves, ruined trees, dead men, gibbets—
> these are the traditional symbols and the landscapes
> of death and despair. The poet is not describing a
> painting or emblem he has seen, he is composing a
> picture for us out of the common visual symbols of his
> time.[11]

[10] The note in the edition of Robert Kellogg and Oliver Steele (*The Faerie Queene, Books I and II* [New York, 1965], p. 183), cites a list of symptoms from the *Anatomy of Melancholy*.

[11] Kathrine Koller, "Art, Rhetoric, and Holy Dying in the *Faerie Queene* with Special Reference to the Despair Canto," *SP* LXI (1964), 135. See also Kenneth Clark, *Landscape into Art* (London, 1949), pp. 37-38, on the implications of an altarpiece by Grünewald (Pl. 34 & 35).

To despair is to see everywhere the emblems of death; this landscape anticipates the Knight's "amazement" later on: "nought but death before his eies he saw" (50). For Spenser's readers, this setting is reminiscent rather than proleptic. We are moving in the underworld which Spenser has allowed us to glimpse earlier in Book I; the environs of Lucifera's palace, where "many corses, like a great Laystall / Of murdred men . . . therein strowed lay" (v.53) dreadfully resemble the rocky knees of this cliff,

> On which had many wretches hanged beene,
> Whose carcases were scattered on the greene,
> And throwne about the cliffs.
>
> (ix.34)

The ultimate context for both is the "yawning gulfe of deepe *Avernus* hole" visited by Duessa in Canto v:

> an entrance darke and bace
> With smoake and sulphure hiding all the place.
>
> (v.31)

Despair is "a man of hell" (28), and by Canto ix we know what Hell is.

4. Inner and Outer Worlds

The characters in *The Faerie Queene* through whom the poet makes visible some ordinarily invisible truths about our psychic life do not always refer simply, or in the same way, to the human characters; that is a fact about Spenserian allegory which has, I hope, emerged from the analysis in the preceding section. It is essential to recognize the complications of reference in the poem if we are to read it properly, and such a recognition both arises from and leads to an awareness that Spenser is anatomizing the processes of mind in its relation to what we call "the outside world."

> From this the poem springs: that we live in a place
> That is not our own and, much more, not ourselves.[1]

If this is so, then it follows that there exist an "inside" and an "outside," a subjective and an objective realm, *within* the fiction. The relevant difference, here, between fiction and non-fiction is that within the poem both realms are *visible*, whereas in our ordinary lives we observe the consequences of our motives, but not their hidden springs. But allegory makes visible various sorts of invisibility, and not all of it is psychic. None of us has (yet) seen Hell or Heaven, but they are realized, even though briefly and fragmentarily, in Book I. Nor has anyone seen with his bodily eye the Idea of a perfect city. "Ideas" must certainly be said to have a psychic existence, insofar as they are entertained, but it is likely that Spenser and many of his contemporaries, though not Platonists or metaphysical realists in any systematic fashion, also attached to concepts some degree of indepen-

[1] "Notes toward a Supreme Fiction," *The Collected Poems of Wallace Stevens* (New York, 1954), p. 383.

178

dent reality.[2] These "exist" as permanent possibilities; Cleopolis, the Fairy Queen's city, refers to such an idea, or ideal, and beyond the poem to London as it might be. Even if we deny that Spenser was, philosophically, a realist, we must acknowledge that Cleopolis is not related to the Red Cross Knight in the same way that Despair's cave is.

An awareness of the various kinds of reality which Spenser understood to be the referents of his images must prevent us from saying that all the events of *The Faerie Queene* take place exclusively "in the mind" of one or another character. Spenser's dark conceit is not always metaphorical; as I have tried to show, Orgoglio is a metaphor for a state of the soul, but Lucifera is an instance of a concept as well as a participant in a large and complex metaphor, the House of Pride. The Red Cross Knight's disturbed sleep in Canto i is a metaphorical statement of the fact that he is, at that point in the narrative, a "sleepy mind." But Morpheus, from whom the enchanter borrows a dream, is not *in* that sleepy mind; he has an independent existence as an essence in which the hero participates when he submits to Archimago's charms.

An exclusively moral or psychological reading of *The Faerie Queene* seems to me mistaken, if only because it entails our seeing many episodes as redundant, decorative, or pointlessly "traditional." Duessa in the underworld must be read simply as a gesture of respect to a *topos* of epic, if we do not admit that Spenser had a larger purpose in mind in Canto v: that is, to follow "*Duessaes* race" back to its roots in a Hell that stands for something as real as Dante's Inferno. Its status within the fiction, despite its very different tonality, is as "objective" as that of Dickens' London in *Our Mutual Friend*. This is not to say that ingenuity cannot con-

---

[2] A sixteenth-century definition of *Idea* reads: "The figure conceived in Imagination, as it were a substance perpetuall, beying as paterne of all other sorte or kinde, as of one seale procedeth many printes, so of one Idea of man procede many thousandes of men." Thomas Cooper, *Thesaurus Linguae Romanae et Britannicae* (London, 1565), sig. Mmm 4r.

trive a psychological meaning for such digressions. An example can be found in a recent suggestive article by Judith Anderson, who argues that "In a figurative and spiritual sense we can say that Redcrosse is dreaming progressively from the time that he abandons Una and begins to accept the reality (truth) of falsehood." She interprets the Descent into Hell as a "second dream" of the Red Cross Knight.[3] We always "can say," if we like, that a character in *The Faerie Queene* is experiencing the poem's events somewhere in his unconscious when the fable shows him to be either asleep or absent. But the matter is more complicated in this case than this argument allows, because Spenser distinguishes between an actual fictive dream in Canto i and subsequent waking events about which the hero is obtuse, short-sighted, self-absorbed, or indifferent, and therefore mistaken. To show his initial mistakes as occurring in "a fit false dreame" concocted by a black magician is to say something, *by analogy*, about his subsequent mistakes. To be the victim of self-generated illusions as the Red Cross Knight is in his encounters with Duessa, Fradubio, and the Deadly Sins, is *like* being the victim of a demonically inspired dream; such illusions have their source in a demonic world to which the Knight is related by virtue of his vulnerability and self-destructive impulses as a fallen human being, and Spenser shows us this source in the events at Archimago's hermitage. But to say that his waking illusions *are* a dream, even "in a figurative and spiritual sense," is to collapse a metaphor and miss one of Spenser's characteristic distinctions, the distinction between a prototype and its ectypes, which in this case is also a distinction between a cause or source and its consequences.

To insist that all the poem's actions must occur in some character's psyche is to muddle the considerable complica-

---

[3] "Redcrosse and the Descent into Hell," *ELH* XXXVI (1969), 482. She also argues (p. 473) "that Morpheus is an aspect of Redcrosse's nature," a view I find ontologically unacceptable; rather, the Red Cross Knight participates in Morpheus' "nature."

tions of Spenser's ontology in *The Faerie Queene*. It will not do to rationalize the poem too far, or to say that the poet is invariably consistent in suggesting the kind of reality possessed by the various inhabitants of Fairy Land. If we insist, however, that the conjunction of Sansloy and Satyrane in Canto vi indicates that "Within the hero two opposed but equally self-directed impulses, lawless lust . . . and greedy hardiment . . . are deadlocked,"[4] we confuse two types of allegorical figuration that Spenser is usually careful to distinguish. Satyrane is a fairy knight, a possible version of humanity; Spenser defines his status by recounting his *enfances*, a birth and upbringing which anticipate at a more primitive stage the childhood of Artegal in Book V. Satyrane also has a career in the poem, turning up in Book III to rescue Florimell's girdle and the Squire of Dames (vii), and in Book IV to "make a Turneyment" (iv). He has, in short, a history, whereas principles like Sansloy generally exist in the vertical plane only, having a genealogy but no history, since their incarnate existence depends on the presence of human beings. To deploy both of these characters in an anatomy of "the hero's feelings," as Harry Berger does when he says that the events of the Una plot in Cantos iii and vi occur in "unconscious" regions of the Red Cross Knight's psyche, is again to miss a distinction that has point in the over-all scheme of *The Faerie Queene*. Spenser does not ordinarily embody in other human knights aspects of his heroes' psychic life; such minor characters are related to the hero rather as alternative versions of his virtue, or instances of it in other contexts. The most elaborately worked-out example of this relationship is that between Calidore, the hero of Book VI, and Sir Calepine, who takes over the narrative for several cantos.

The events that occur in the cantos of Book I where Una's separate adventures are traced are certainly not unrelated to the Red Cross Knight. The critic's problem lies in finding

[4] Harry Berger, "At Home and Abroad with Spenser," *MLQ* XXV (1964), 107.

the most accurate way of describing the relationship. "Una's separation from Redcross means that she has been banished from his consciousness."[5] Yes; but "means that" is a problematic phrase. Una has been banished from the hero's presence *as a means* to that end; the Knight hopes that out of sight will "mean" out of mind. This is a familiar enough stratagem of self-deceiving souls in "real life." But if "means" in Berger's sentence suggests that the action is exclusively a figure for some sort of psychological fact, then I think we must dissent. The separation of hero and heroine must be read literally: the Red Cross Knight deserts Una, he does not merely suppress her in his unconscious mind. What is going on in his psyche is straightforwardly described by Spenser:

> Still flying from his thoughts and gealous feare;
> Will was his guide, and griefe led him astray.
> (ii.12)

The narrative that ensues explores meaning in an expansive, not a reductive way; it elucidates the meaning of the poet's phrases, showing *what it means* to say that the hero has submitted to will's guidance. What Berger properly calls "the forked narrative" is the expression of choices made blindly and willfully: to reject the virtuous Una (love, faith, troth, in a *loved person*), and then to accept the unvirtuous Duessa. Neither of these characters "is" an aspect of the hero's psyche, nor are they aspects of a single principle. In turning from one to the other, the Knight is choosing to love someone (or something) else, not loving "the same" person in the wrong way. Each lady is exemplary of persons, principles, entities that may become the objects of decorous or perverse devotion for man.

With Una, the Red Cross Knight also rejects a certain role for himself, a role later assumed by Satyrane. The epithets Spenser chooses for the latter—"plaine, faithfull,

5 Ibid., 106.

true" (vi.20)—echo apocalyptic adjectives[6] earlier referring to the Red Cross Knight ("right faithfull true"), and
allude to the aspects of Una to which Satyrane responds
when he sits at her feet and becomes her protector.

> He wondred at her wisedome heavenly rare,
>   Whose like in womens wit he never knew;
>   And, when her curteous deeds he did compare,
>   Gan her admire, and her sad sorrowes rew,
>   Blaming of Fortune, which such troubles threw,
>   And joyd to make proofe of her cruelty
>   On gentle Dame, so hurtlesse, and so trew:
>   Thenceforth he kept her goodly company.
> And learnd her discipline of faith and veritie.
>
> (vi.31)

Satyrane is a product of mere Nature, as his parentage indicates. Yet he has assumed the discipline of chivalry, and can
go on (as the still-wild satyrs cannot) to understand the
revelation of Una. The stanza above is a precise account in
small compass of the natural man's positive response to revealed truth; it is the equivalent of the Utopians' glad acceptance of Christianity: "you would not believe how readily disposed they . . . were to join it."[7] Wonder, admiration,
and finally submission to "her discipline": these are the
stages through which Satyrane passes, and in passing he
indicates to us who read about him that the role which the
Red Cross Knight has temporarily rejected is a *possible* one
for a human being. He exemplifies what the Knight might
have become if he had not chosen the wrong fork in the

---

[6] The allusion in "right faithfull true" (i.2) to the warrior "faithful
and true" of *Revelation* 19:11 has been noted by Kermode, *Shakespeare,
Spenser, Donne*, p. 14. Spenser's description in vi.31 of Una's teaching
as the "discipline of faith and veritie" suggests that any knight who
dedicates himself to her can become a version of the apocalyptic model,
which is how I am identifying Satyrane.

[7] *Utopia*, ed. Edward Surtz and J. H. Hexter; *The Complete Works of
St. Thomas More*, IV (New Haven, 1965), 219.

path. And he is a negative example, as well; he is last seen inconclusively battling Sansloy, unable definitively to beat down "lawless lust" because no Arthur comes to his aid. This battle marks the limit of his power, virtuous though he is; he is in the position of Guyon in Book II, whose enemies are never finally defeated. The Red Cross Knight, on the other hand, has already succumbed to "lawless lust" in the form of his unlawful love for Duessa, immediately afterward made visible in the scene at the fountain that opens Canto vii.

To relegate the events of these cantos to "places of the soul not fully available to consciousness"[8] is, I think, reductive rather than anachronistic. Spenser knew as well as Shakespeare did that there is a significant psychic life flowing beneath ordinary consciousness; its presence, and its relation to an "objective" spiritual realm, is revealed during the Knight's sojourn with Archimago. To say that all of the poem's places are also "places of the soul," however, simplifies Spenser's allegory unduly because it blurs some of the statements he wants to make about the relations between psychic and non-psychic (but invisible) reality, a relationship that is primarily analogical, not figurative. These critics' manner of speaking tends to collapse all Spenser's meaning into a figurative meaning, when his purpose is often to explain how figurative meanings come to be, to anatomize the process of figuration which is in turn based upon some fundamental assumptions about the nature of reality.

Some of the events of *The Faerie Queene* are "analogous actions."[9] Satyrane is an analogue, a rejected model, for the Red Cross Knight; he cannot also *be* "greedy hardiment," an aspect of the hero's psyche, because these two ontologi-

---

[8] Berger, "At Home and Abroad," 107.

[9] I borrow this term from Francis Fergusson, who is describing the relationship between the hero and the mirroring characters who surround him in *Hamlet* (*The Idea of a Theater* [Princeton, 1949], pp. 140-41 and Ch. IV, *passim*). Young Fortinbras and Laertes, in different ways, embody possibilities for Hamlet; so does Satyrane for the Red Cross Knight.

cal roles exclude each other. A figure for psychic reality (e.g., the lustful and lawless Sansloy) cannot also function as a fully human analogue-character, or cannot without obfuscating the allegorical discourse in its analytic aspect. Spenser sometimes introduces images that have ambiguous, or multiple, ontological reference; these are the ganglia of meaning that attract the multiplied interpretations of critics. The phenomenon of multiple reference is explored, in Book I, in the final battle and its aftermath. But in most of the preceding episodes the narrative is analytic, which means that most of the personages have been simplified rather than complicated by the poet, so that each one individually refers simply, though their juxtapositions, confrontations, attractions and repellings, taken together, make up a complex set of meanings. Some of the characters exist "in" the hero's psyche; some of them exist "in" places that in the fiction's terms must be seen as objective. And they cannot be shifted about without disturbing the finely articulated system of meanings that compose *The Faerie Queene*. All the action takes place *in* the poem, where a reader is asked to make decisions as to whether the discourse is proceeding in "the material mode" or in "the formal mode," to use a philosopher's terms.[10] For each mode a different type of image or event is appropriate, and is appropriately indicated by the poet.

Spenser's road in *The Faerie Queene* winds not only "through places of the soul," but through fictive places that point toward or stand for actual locations in the macrocosm, to wit, Heaven, Hell, and the wilderness of this world. Macrocosm and microcosm are concentric, and in conse-

[10] "We do recognize a shift from talk of objects to talk of words. . . . It is the shift from talk of miles to talk of 'mile.' It is . . . what leads from the material (*inhaltlich*) mode into the formal mode. . . . It is the shift from talking in certain terms to talking about them" (W. V. Quine, *Word and Object* [Cambridge, Mass., 1960], p. 271). Quine calls this process "semantic ascent"; it is discussed in detail in §56 of his book. The distinction between "talking in" and "talking about" terms applies precisely to what Spenser is getting at when he devises such distinct allegorical entities as Satyrane and Sansloy.

quence at certain points they are related to each other by correspondence, or analogy, which provides the ontological basis for figures. Pico, in a famous passage of the *Heptaplus*, observed that "every principle of allegorical interpretation" is derived from the *fact* that, "tied by the chains of concord, all these worlds exchange both their natures and names." The wise ancients, "knowing all things and moved by that Spirit which not only knows but creates the Universe, . . . most aptly represented the nature of one world by what they knew corresponded to it in others." The human psyche is a "fourth world," analogically related to the other three—the elemental, the celestial, and the angelic. In this universe of correspondences, "whatever is in any of the worlds is contained in each."[11] But it is not necessarily "contained" in the same manner. Entities from the various worlds "exchange . . . natures and names" under the pressure of a poet's (or interpreter's) imaginings, but they do not thereby become each other. The brightness of truth, the sun in the sky, the eye in the body, the element of fire, a lion: these correspondent terms exist in a relationship of cross-reference which allows them to be figuratively, though not actually, interchanged. An emotion as we think about it, as we experience it in our flesh, as it looks to the angels' intuitive glance, or to the eye of God, as it is materially expressed in one of the four elements or the four humours: these are other realms of being whose correspondences encourage imaginative identification.

The Faerie Queene deals with the processes of thinking and imagining as they are carried on within this universe of correspondences which was designed by its Creator to be intelligible to the sovereign intellect of its highest creatures. That is one reason why the poet places first in his sequence of six books the one which deals thematically as well as formally with the subject of understanding. Book I lets

11 Tr. Douglas Carmichael; *On the Dignity of Man, On Being and the One, Heptaplus*, ed. P.J.W. Miller (Indianapolis, 1965), p. 80. The passage is cited and explicated by Roche, *The Kindly Flame*, pp. 7-8.

us see how epistemological and moral principles are inter-related, thereby suggesting how a poem that anatomizes the relation between the eye (I) and the object, the imagina-tion and its materials, the psyche and its environment, can also inform us about the moral life and contribute to the de-velopment of "vertuous and gentle discipline."

5. Typology: The Dragon-Battle

Spenser's allegory continually returns *ad fontes*. It moves backward, downward, inward, upward—and even forward, since the poem's future is our past—in search of sources and goals (both sources and goals partaking of the same reality). In this process, the poet establishes the ultimate contexts in which phenomenal or accidental events can be understood. These contexts are related to each other vertically along an ontological scale in the moral and metaphysical allegory, and horizontally in the historical allegory.

From Despair's cave Spenser moves, in the last third of Book I, toward the opposite pole of his poetic universe. In this segment of *The Faerie Queene*, the artist's design is atypically visible. Cantos x-xii are built to concentric patterns; at their centers are three cities, cognate in different but related realms of being: "The Citie of the great king," New Jerusalem (x.55); Cleopolis where the Fairy Queen reigns, "the fairest Citie . . . that might be seene" (58); and the besieged and barricaded city of Una's parents, threatened by the old serpent but now to be redeemed. These places are related not only to each other, but to "real" cities, notably the London of the 1590's, as More's Utopia is related to the real England of *Utopia*, Book I. Spenser's fiction points beyond itself, as More's does also, but its perspective is longer in both time and space. The full significance of Fairy Land as an image of the world in imagination's embrace is not altogether apparent until the *Mutabilitie Cantos*, where the entire range of the Spenserian world-picture is revealed; but it is intermittently visible in the poet's contextualizing of his images throughout the poem.

In these final cantos of Book I, of course, the Red Cross Knight is the focus: we are observing the last stages of his spiritual development. But we are also witnessing events in the *aevum*, actions once performed by Christ now re-enacted by a Christian man whose life has assumed "the form Christ gave it"; and actions that prefigure future acts to be performed in the last days. The allegory moves into a final *analytic* phase in the House of Holiness, preparatory to the "infolding" of the last two cantos. Its transparency in Canto x is appropriate to the stage that both reader and Knight have reached, "dull eyes" opened, "that light mote in them shine" (x.18). There is an innocent simplicity about the method of these stanzas. Fidelia holds a book "Wherein darke things were writ, hard to be understood" (13); yet under her tutelage the hard things become perfectly lucid.

> And that her sacred Booke, with bloud ywrit,
>> That none could read, except she did them teach,
>> She unto him disclosed every whit.
>>> (I.x.19)

"Wonder was to heare her goodly speach"; Faith makes scriptural mysteries plain, and the poet's goodly speech cooperates with hers to reveal the nature of his own discourse. Fidelia's method of "disclosing" enigmas for the benefit of "the weaker wit of man" is copied by Spenser with reference to the hero, now at the lowest ebb of his powers of understanding. Alluding to *Matthew* 7:14 in stanza 5, he surrounds the text with explication:

> He was an aged syre, all hory gray,
> With lookes full lowly cast, and gate full slow,
> Wont on a staffe his feeble steps to stay,
> Hight *Humilitá*. They passe in stouping low;
> For streight and narrow was the way, which he did show.

> Each goodly thing is hardest to begin. . . .
>> (I.x.5-6)

The perfect visibility of meaning here keeps decorum with the place where Holiness dwells, a place where dark things are made bright, eyes are opened, and language regains its innocence. In this condition of primal lucidity, no ambiguity or misunderstanding is possible. Whereas earlier in the poem personages appeared to the Knight, and often to the reader, as opaque, here image, name, and character are in perfect accord. Introducing Zeal, Spenser explicates a pun; this franklin is "faire and free."

> them does meet a francklin faire and free,
> And entertaines with comely courteous glee,
> His name was *Zele*, that him right well became,
> For in his speeches and behaviour hee
> Did labour lively to expresse the same,
> And gladly did them guide, till to the Hall they came.
>
> (I.x.6)

The many false guides are succeeded by a true one, the multiplied deceptions by the matching of name to nature.

It is appropriate that the climax of this canto should be the naming of the Knight: "thou Saint *George* shalt called bee" (x.61). An analogous moment of self-recognition crowns the *Purgatorio*.

> "Dante, perche Virgilio se ne vada,
> non pianger anco, non pianger ancora:
>
> . . . mi volsi al suon del nome mio.
> (xxx.55-6,62)

The pilgrim's Lady is about to reveal herself, but self-recognition precedes this consummation. In *The Faerie Queene*, the hero approaches the hermitage of Contemplation by way of the "holy Hospitall" where the seven bedesmen "Did spend their daies in doing godly thing" (36). The Corporal Works of Mercy honor the earthly nature of man; through them the Defaced Image, obscured by the Cardinal Sins, is restored. It is against the background of the "images of God in earthly clay" (39) that the hermit shortly afterward calls the Red Cross Knight "thou man of earth" (52). He cannot be named until he has been identified with those others who share God's image.

At the beginning of the penultimate canto, the man of earth has become "this man of God" (xi.7), a locution the poet is able to employ by virtue of the working out of its meaning in the allegory up to this point. The demonstration will be proved in the three-day battle, which not only concludes the hero's career and winds up the book's thematic threads, but also recapitulates Spenser's exploration of the allegorical mode. The battle contains all of the possible types (as some would say, "levels") of allegory, superimposed to produce a dense web of correspondences. As many scholarly articles have demonstrated, Spenser is here making use of all the various kinds of source material he drew on for his allegory: mystic historiography, commentary (especially on the Apocalypse), typology, and of course the many versions of the St. George legend, popular and esoteric, visual and literary.[1] Behind all these stands the life of Christ, which is itself an in-gathering of Old Testament history, a prefiguration of Revelation, a model for Christian knights, and a recapitulation of the life of Everyman from homeless birth to shameful death, and (by virtue of this reenactment) ultimate triumph. Christ's paradigmatic life made sense of the chaos of history; Alpha and Omega, the beginning and the end of time, are enfolded and reknit in him.[2] The ultimate adventure in the career of the Red Cross

---

[1] For these contexts see, *seriatim*: Kermode, "Spenser and the Allegorists"; John E. Hankins, *Source and Meaning in Spenser's Allegory* (Oxford, 1971), pp. 108-119; William Haller, *The Elect Nation* (New York, 1963); Carol V. Kaske, "The Dragon's Spark and Sting and the Structure of Red Cross's Dragon-fight: *The Faerie Queene*, I.xi-xii," *SP* LXVI (1969), 609-38; Kellogg and Steele, *Books I and II*, pp. 10-15; F. M. Padelford and Matthew O'Connor, "Spenser's Use of the St. George Legend," excerpted in *Var.* I, 386-87; Rosemond Tuve, "The Red Crosse Knight and Mediaeval Demon Stories," *PMLA* XLIV (1929), 706-14.

[2] The cross-referencing of images in *Genesis* and *Revelation* was regularly regarded as proof that the beginning and the end are one.

Knight makes sense out of the book in which it appears and provides the context for all future adventures the poem will unfold.

Spenser's images in Canto xi are recapitulative not only in terms of "the tradition," but in the terms of his own allegory. Not only is this dragon the archetype and summation of its three analogues—Errour; the "dreadfull Dragon with an hideous trayne" under Lucifera's feet (iv.10); and Duessa's "monstrous beast" (vii.16-18)—but the lengthy description of him assimilates many other key images of Book I. The ominous shadow is here ("made wide shadow under his huge wast," 8), and the "hollow glade" in which the Dragon's eyes are set (14) is the original of the "hollow cave" of Errour (i.11) and the dwelling of Despair (ix.33). In his stanza on the eyes, Spenser plays variations on the many-stranded eye/light imagery of this book.

> His blazing eyes, like two bright shining shields,
>   Did burne with wrath, and sparkled living fyre:
>   As two broad Beacons, set in open fields,
>   Send forth their flames farre off to every shyre,
>   And warning give, that enimies conspyre,
>   With fire and sword the region to invade;
>   So flam'd his eyne with rage and rancorous yre:
>   But farre within, as in a hollow glade,
> Those glaring lampes were set, that made a dreadfull
>   shade.
>
> (I.xi.14)

The initial simile makes the Dragon an instance of the false-heroic, alluding to Arthur's shield with its "blazing brightnesse" and "flashing beames." The actual shield partakes of the true sun's power, the Dragon's eyes of the power of false suns; we remember the Lucifera/Phaethon alignment.

The second simile is much more complicated, both in it-

So Spenser's Well of Life in I.xi.29 draws on both *Genesis* 2:10 and *Revelation* 22:1. Sacramental time or *aevum* is the referent and mode of existence of such images.

self and in relation to the stanza's final lines. It is not unique
in appearing to work against the grain of the stanza's, and
the episode's, main intent. During two earlier battles in
Book I, Spenser interpolates similes incongruent with the
major narrative movement. In his encounter with Errour,
the Red Cross Knight pauses to brush aside the dragon's
spawn, a swarm "of serpents small" that impede his movements; Spenser devotes a stanza to this pause, beginning,
"As gentle Shepheard in sweete even-tide, / When ruddy
Phebus gins to welke in west" (I.i.23).[3] The lines allude to
the concluding cadences of many pastoral poems, which
close with the drawing-in of evening; no literary context
could be more alien to the heroic posture of the tenor at this
point in *The Faerie Queene*. Again, when Arthur fights
Orgoglio in Canto viii, the giant directs a mis-aimed blow
at him and buries his own club in the ground. For this
stroke, Spenser devises another stanza-long simile, comparing it to Jove's thunderbolt, hurled "in wrathfull mood,
To wreake the guilt of mortall sins" (I.viii.9). But Orgoglio
is a mortal sin; how, then, can his hurtling club be "like"
the bolt directed against sinful humanity? There are several
answers, among them the probability that Spenser wants us
to see the self-destructive character of sin, the way in which
it can be "used" by God against itself, as Satan in *Paradise
Lost* turns into his own worst enemy.

Just now, however, I am not concerned with the interpretation of these similes, but with the kind of reading they
enforce—the position of the reader in relation to the text,
and what that implies about the position of the poet. All
three of the stanzas in question contain similes in which an
initial visual or kinaesthetic likeness is contradicted by tonal
and functional unlikeness. In this land of unlikeness live
friendly or beneficent or "good" powers, surviving in a context of "evil" powers: the "gentle Shepheard" in his peaceful
evening landscape, the wrath of Jove cutting down sinners,

[3] This stanza, and a sequence of congruent images generated by it,
has been well analyzed by Hamilton, *Structure of Allegory*, pp. 218-19.

and beacon-fires warning that an enemy is at hand.[4] We can, if we like, see them all pointing to an implied "super-plot," a design created by that providential care that presides over all events and insures that all, even the most overtly threatening, shall in the very long run work together for good. Some such effect is, I think, intended, though even to verbalize it gives too heavy-handed an impression of what is actually going on. The point is that to think this way at all about the stanzas, we have to step back for a moment from the events of the foreground, which in each case are energetic and precarious, and work out the problematic relation of those events to a "wider" context, a context to which the poet draws our attention by setting up an incongruity, tonal and thematic, between tenor and vehicle.[5]

The form of the comparison, the simile, encourages this distancing and contributes to it, because similes insist upon an analytic attitude toward a comparison.[6] The simile also tends to call attention to the controlling activity of the speaker who uses it—in this case, the narrator. Spenser's fondness for counter-logical similes insures, among other things, the *visibility* of his own function as poet, at least intermittently, in *The Faerie Queene*. Though Spenser's presence in the poem, compared to that of Dante or Ariosto, may be modest, it is there, all the same, as it must be insofar as Spenser is writing an allegory. A poet, in calling attention to his manipulation of narrative or rhetoric in an allegory, is making us see that the action takes place against

[4] Alpers has noted the complications arising from the fact that "the dragon's eyes are compared to friendly fires" (*Poetry of "The Faerie Queene,"* p. 363).

[5] The technique has often been described in discussions of epic simile. Cedric Whitman's sentence on simile in the *Iliad* suggests something of Spenser's effect: "Like a fountain, it rises from its point of comparison, . . . but falls back into the larger basin of meaning" (*Homer and the Heroic Tradition* [Cambridge, Mass., 1958], p. 117).

[6] "In simile . . . every word has its normal meaning and no semantic transference is incurred. . . . Metaphor is primarily a treatment of *language*, simile is primarily a treatment of thought" (W. B. Stanford, *Greek Metaphor* [Oxford, 1936], p. 30).

a background; the alienating or anti-dramatic effect of a counter-logical simile allows the background to become visible. That background is in the first instance contextual, a portion of the narrative pattern wider than that with which we have been engaged in the heat of battle: "the larger basin of meaning." It is, further, ideological, the *significatio* or tenor intimated by the whole vast metaphor that is *The Faerie Queene*: Heaven, Earth, and Hell, the space and time of the providentially ruled universe. This is grandiose talk; in relation to the dragon-eyes stanza, it means that the battle is taking place in a world where threatening enemies are everywhere, warnings are perpetually necessary, unwavering alertness against invasion is required of the resolved soul. The counter-logical element may disconcert us momentarily; warning-fires are not set by the enemy, but to rouse the forces against him. But the idea that "enimies conspyre" all the time makes its point through the complication of the unlikeness; a larger congruence succeeds an apparent, and temporary, incongruence, and we sense that the poet, like God in *his* Creation, is ultimately in control.

The context we are encouraged to recall is also the context of Book I, with its intertwining images of fire and light. Spenser tells us not what the Dragon sees, but what his eyes look like to an opponent. The Red Cross Knight has seen similar sights before—in particular, as he approached his first dragon in "a hollow cave, / Amid the thickest woods" (I.i.11). In Canto xi, the stanza's final couplet is peculiar in two respects, and its peculiarity is, again, a mode of emphasis that encourages recall of the earlier incident in Canto i. Spenser winds up the "beacon" simile predictably: "So flam'd his eyne with rage and rancourous yre"; he then adds, unpredictably, a self-correcting pair of lines:

> But farre within, as in a hollow glade,
> Those glaring lampes were set, that made
> a dreadfull shade.

The beacons, vehicle of the major comparison, were "set in open fields"; *but*, the poet adds, in reality they were set "far within," not in the open at all. So perhaps they were not so very much "like" beacon-fires after all; the Dragon is much more dangerous than that simile might suggest. The beacon-simile, having done its work, is allowed to retire behind a new image that to a certain degree disavows it. Again, the poet's manipulating hand is felt. We are forced to pay attention to what he is doing; the new simile has both corrective and retrospective force. The rhymes—*glade, made, shade*—assist the retrospection.

> But forth unto the darksome hole he went,
> And looked in: his glistring armor made
> A litle glooming light, much like a shade.
>
> (I.i.14)

The second peculiarity of the dragon-eye stanza, the assertion that these "glaring" objects produce not light, but "a dreadfull shade," is anticipated in the rhyming lines on the Knight's armor, whose "light," at that stage of his pilgrimage, was "like a shade." He was still very vulnerable to the false "light" whose source and effect is obfuscation; he was capable of becoming the victim of characters like Errour or Lucifera, false light-bearers. Now, in Canto xi, perfected in virtue, he "sees" this false light as his enemy, the Old Dragon whose attributes sum up those of all the previous enemies to which he has been exposed.

Stanza 14, therefore, with its triple-stranded comparison, functions in a manner typical of Spenser's method in the concluding cantos of Book I. The images and allusions of these cantos draw some of their power from earlier appearances in this book; at the same time, as the definitive versions of those images, they remind us of the center of meaning toward which earlier examples move. Milton, having several times described the archetypal Fall of Satan into

Hell, takes us "out" into history and the shadows of the myth that darkly reflect it in the human imagination:

> and in Ausonian land
> Men called him Mulciber; and how he fell
> From heaven, they fabled, thrown by angry Jove . . .
> (I.739-41)

Something like the reverse of this process occurs in the First Book of *The Faerie Queene* (though only once do we glimpse the archetype itself, in the brief vision of the Heavenly City). Beginning in the middest, in the dark wood, we move toward clarity and definition and the eventual infolding of images. True and false Suns have been visible, for instance, at several points: in the solitary epiphany of Una (iii), Arthur's "sunshiny shield" (viii.20), Lucifera the stepcousin of Phaethon (iv), Sansjoy who appears to Duessa as a "faire Sunne" (iv.48), to choose only the most obvious.[7] Now the Red Cross Knight assumes the power of the Sun itself, wielding its double power, natural and supernatural. George Herbert was later to celebrate the holy pun that our witty language permits:

> How neatly doe we give one onely name
> To parents issue and the sunnes bright starre![8]

Christ is the true Sun, the Son of God and "Sunne of Man," as Herbert insists. "As many as are led by the Spirit of God, they are the sons of God." The hero, having threaded the labyrinth with the help of the Spirit, rises up from the Well of Life after his first day's battle, in the likeness of the true light he imitates, in sunship and sonship. First, the paradigm, the Sun itself:

---

[7] According to Fowler's count, there are 40 "verbal mentions of the sun" in Book I, the closest rival being Book III with 32 (*Numbers of Time*, p. 71, n. 1).

[8] "The Sonne," *The Works of George Herbert*, ed. F. E. Hutchinson (Oxford, 1959), p. 168.

> The morrow next gan earely to appeare,
> That *Titan* rose to runne his daily race.
>
> (I.xi.33)

With Titan rises the sunlike Una, and finally the Knight, like the sun's bird, re-created by the night's immersion.

> At last she saw, where he upstarted brave
> Out of the well, wherein he drenched lay:
> As Eagle fresh out of the ocean wave,
> Where he hath lefte his plumes all hoary gray,
> And deckt himselfe with feathers youthly gay,
> Like Eyas hauke up mounts unto the skies,
> His newly budded pineons to assay,
> And marveiles at himselfe, stil as he flies:
> So new this new-borne knight to battell new did rise.
>
> (34)

The association (it is not an identification) of the Red Cross Knight with the Sun is apt in many ways, several of which have been demonstrated by Fowler in his analysis of "The Book of the Sun." I want mainly to stress the point that *this* appearance of the Sun, at the climax of Book I, assimilates earlier instances in the poem, and "places" the hero in relation to them. It also "places" him in relation to his ultimate model, the Son of God, for Spenser does not directly identify the Knight with the Sun itself. Rather, he is like the bird of the sun, the Eagle that was an emblem of resurrection and the birth of the New Man, the bird that can gaze upon the Sun without being blinded.[9] The relation of hero and Phoebus in this simile is oblique; in the immediately preceding stanzas, it is expressed as a parallelism, "stated" paratactically in terms of simultaneous occurrences. As "the golden Phoebus" sinks into the Ocean, the Dragon claps his wings to celebrate an imaginary victory, "having kest / His wearie foe into that living well" (31), whence he will rise

9 See T. H. White, tr., *The Book of Beasts* (London, 1954), pp. 105-107, on the Eagle.

again, like the Sun. Milton draws a similar parallel at the climax of *Lycidas*.

> For Lycidas your sorrow is not dead,
> Sunk though he be beneath the watery floor,
> So sinks the day-star in the ocean bed,
> And yet anon repairs his drooping head. . . .
>   (166-69)

The dead shepherd is "sunk low, but mounted high" through the power of the Son, who can tame the waves and bless the waters. In both poems there is visible a widening spiral of concentric circles, microcosmic, macrocosmic, and transcendent: the "dead" and reborn man, the setting and rising sun, the dead and resurrected Son of God.[10]

Spenser is, I think, making a careful point in Stanza 34. The simile forces us to call in question oversimple equations, to examine the ambiguous force of "is" in allegorical formulas. The Red Cross Knight is *like* an Eagle; his course parallels that of the Sun, which in turn serves as a punning metaphor for Son. These relationships deny identification. The Knight "is" not Holiness—all qualities find their perfection only in their single source. He "is" a holy man, a hero, adjectivally related to that source by virtue of faith and the power of grace, signified by the armor that he wears. At an earlier stage of his development, Spenser introduces the image of the rising Sun with ironic force to suggest a desired identification which has yet to be achieved, and which will in the end be supplanted by a more modest analogous, reflected glory. The Knight at Lucifera's Palace lies awake all night planning his next day's tournament with Sansjoy.

> At last, the golden Orientall gate
>   Of greatest heaven gan to open faire,
>   And *Phoebus* fresh, as bridegrome to his mate,

---

[10] See Alpers, *Poetry of "The Faerie Queene,"* p. 366.

> Came dauncing forth, shaking his deawie hayre:
> And hurld his glistring beames through gloomy aire.
> Which when the wakeful Elfe perceiv'd, streight way,
> He started up, and did him selfe prepaire,
> In sun-bright armes, and battailous array:
> For with that Pagan proud he combat will that day.
>
> (I.v.2)

Viewed from the standpoint of the moment in Canto v, this "up-starting" seems a properly heroic act; viewed with the hindsight of this battle's outcome, it looks like presumption, the zeal of an upstart—he is, after all, at the House of Pride. The hero cannot prepare *himself* for conclusive victory; his "sun-bright armes," though reflecting the light of their true source, will not serve him because they are worn without a sense of their import. Later, on the first day of the dragon-battle, this very armor burns him: "fyrie steele now burnt, that earst him arm'd" (xi.27), because he has still to feel the tempering balm of the living well. The parallel with Phoebus in Canto v is desired but not accomplished; the Knight hastens toward an identification to be presumptuously effected by donning "sun-bright armes," whereas all that he can properly aspire to is an *imitation* of the true Sun, a relationship established passively, and as it were stage-managed in Canto xi by the poet, who himself traces a pattern drawn by Providence. At that point, too, the Red Cross Knight will finally be fit to be a bridegroom; the third line of v.2 enforces its own irony with reference to one who has abandoned his destined bride. Nor is he the *Sol justitiae* shadowed in the allusion to Psalm 19.

Spenser establishes in Book I a structure of great steadfast images and points of reference which allude to a "real" system of values and truths in the divinely-constructed universe. I have said that the poet's hand obeys the design of Providence, and the point is seriously intended. Near the end of Canto xi, and the final battle, Spenser refers once more, as he so often has before (and will again) to chance, sometimes called Fortune, as the agent of an event. But this reference is different. As the Knight retreats before the Dragon's fiery breath,

> It chaunst (eternall God that chaunce did guide)
> As he recoyled backward, in the mire
> His nigh foreweried feeble feet did slide,
> And downe he fell, with dread of shame sore terrifide.
>
> (45)

"Chance," so often invoked to justify the twists and turns of the action, here merges with Providence, the guiding hand of God. The Knight falls at the foot of the Tree of Life, to be resuscitated by its balm. The poet's art, devising this episode in an allegory, is one with God's art, an art that can map the labyrinth and lead us to its center.

In fact Spenser is writing, in Canto xi, a rather different sort of allegory from that he composes elsewhere in the poem. It is a mode definitively expressed in the last movements of the *Purgatorio*. Writing of Dante's visions in the Earthly Paradise, Eliot compares the events to those in *Revelation*; his analogue for the poetic mode is "pageantry," a mode in which the symbolic and the literal are very close together, the events actualizing an ideal rather than merely shadowing it. The action described in Canto xi of *The Faerie Queene* would probably, in fact, have been witnessed *as* a pageant by many readers of the poem. But its nature can be apprehended by a careful reader without benefit of such a background. In the preceding canto, the hitherto nameless and changeling Knight receives a name and a genealogy; moving from Fairy Land to England, he emerges from fiction into history.

> O holy Sire (quoth he) how shall I quight
> The many favours I with thee have found,
> That hast my name and nation redd aright,
> And taught the way that does to heaven bound?
>
> (x.67)

His name, St. George, and his nation, England, possess both historical and fictive actuality; fiction and fact merge, as well, in the old man's other revelation: the way to Heaven. We arrive at Heaven by imitating Christ, and the new St. George is about to demonstrate this "way," by re-enacting the three-day battle against the Old Dragon.

That battle, the central event of Christian history, had often been graphically and fictively represented; so had St. George's victory. In European painting, the risen Christ emerging from the tomb carries the banner of the Red Cross which invariably figures in the St. George iconography. Depictions of the saint in the moment of victory almost as consistently show him piercing the dragon's mouth with his spear, and Spenser's stanza verbally reiterates the image.

> The weapon bright
> Taking advantage of his open jaw,
> Ran through his mouth with so importune might,
> That deepe emperst his darksome hollow maw,
> And back retyrd, his life bloud forth with all did draw.
>
> (xi.53)

The moment depicted in this stanza and in the St. George paintings alludes to representations of the Harrowing of Hell like that of the Credo Tapestry in the Metropolitan Museum, where a huge Hell-mouth (in other examples pierced with a tongue-depressor-like spear) gapes to let out Adam and Eve, assisted by Christ. Spenser has earlier told us that his Dragon's "deepe devouring jawes / Wide gaped, like the griesly mouth of hell" (xi.12). The *visibilia* in all these instances are literalized metaphors; the mouth of Hell is laid open before our eyes. All the metaphors point, with varying degrees of immediacy, to one historical source: events in the life of Christ. And those events contain and control the lives of actual men dedicated to "an ethical existence . . . whose only form is the form Christ gave it." In this retrospective typology, events in the centuries after the Incarnation are modeled upon that crucial occurrence, looking back to—rather than, like the history of the Old Testament, prefiguring—the events of A.D. 1-33. Those events, enacted in history, now belong to the *aevum*. They are sacramentally re-enacted in every Mass, and actually imitated in the lives of holy men. In a ritual re-enactment, *recurrent* aspects of the paradigm are stressed, but the saint's life "repeats" the life of Christ uniquely as well as paradigmatically. Each saint in the Christian calendar has his or her own attributes, is recognizably himself or herself.

The attributes of St. George the dragon-slayer, as I have said, are readily adaptable to certain events in the Gospels; the result is metaphorical interchange between the dragon-battle as enacted historically by the saint and "figuratively" by Christ.

> The Word Incarnate is our King, who came into the
> world to fight the devil; all the saints who were
> before his coming are as soldiers going before the
> royal presence; those who came after, and those
> to come, until the end of the world, are as soldiers
> following the King. And the King is in the midst
> of his army.[11]

Saints are "as soldiers"; some saints, including St. George, really are soldiers. The life of a soldier-saint itself actualizes a metaphor; the metaphor receives a fictive literalness when Christ is presented as an armed knight.

Some of the relationships involved here are suggested in the fine poem on the Resurrection by Dunbar that begins, "Done is a battell on the dragon blak," and uses the chivalric imagery in the first two stanzas, followed by a climactic ascension in the third, where the hero

---

11 Quoted from Hugh of St. Victor in Beryl Smalley, *The Study of the Bible in the Middle Ages* (Notre Dame, 1964), p. 89.

> Is lik a lyone rissin up agane,
> And as gyane raxit him on hicht:
> Sprungin is Aurora radius and bricht,
> On loft is gone the glorius Appollo,
> The blisfull day depairtit fro the nycht:
> *Surrexit Dominus de sepulchro.*

All these images appear in Book I, most of them with reference to the hero (the lion, the sun, the coming of "faire
Aurora" [*FQ* I.xi.51] to divide dark from light); the giant
appears in the parody-version of Orgoglio. I do not suggest
that Dunbar's poem was a "source" or even that Spenser
had read it; rather, it points to a normal conjunction of allusions in the context of this subject, based upon Biblical
texts from *Malachi* and Psalm 103. In the fourth stanza,
Dunbar recites the consequences of the fact that "The grit
victour agane is rissin on hicht":

> The knell of mercy fra the hevin is soundit,
> The Cristin ar deliverit of thair wo,
> The Jowis and thair errour ar confoundit:
> *Surrexit Dominus de sepulchro.*[12]

The present tense refers to the imagined scene, but also to
the moment of writing and imagining, the continuous presentness of Christ's sacrifice. The refrain, which is from the
Proper for Matins on Easter Sunday, makes clear this double reference to *now* and *then*, linked by sacramental re-
enactment and commemoration, united in the triumphant
Surrexit. The knell of mercy "is soundit"; it rings on the
Easter morning the poem celebrates, and the one on which
it is composed, or recited. The merging of fiction and reality, the dream and the dream's significance, is even more
clearly visible in the twenty-first Passus of *Piers Plowman*
where, after the great passage on the Harrowing of Hell,
the Daughters of God fulfill the prophecy of Psalm 85, and
the dreamer wakes.

[12] William Dunbar, *Poems*, ed. James Kinsley (Oxford, 1958), pp. 7-8.

Tyl the day dawede these damseles daunsede,
That men rang to the resurreccioun and with that ich
awakede,
And kallyd Kytte my wyf and Kalote my doughter,
"A-rys, and go reverence godes resurreccioun,
And creop on kneos to the croys and cusse hit for a
Juwel,
And ryghtfullokest a relyk non riccher on erthe."[13]

The day that dawns here is Resurrection Day, both unique and annually recurrent in history.

The events of Book I, Canto xi of *The Faerie Queene*, like all the rest of the poem, are part of a continued metaphor. But the vehicle of this metaphor is also continuously allusive, carrying us into history as well as into the history of imagining. It is therefore not *invented* in the sense, say, of Lucifera's palace, or the Virgilian and Ariostan bleeding tree, or the Ovidian fountain of Canto vii, with their sidelong glances at pagan fictions. All allusions take us outside the fictional frame; those in Canto xi, more than any other place in the poem, take us into Scripture, and therefore into history and the long tradition of typological commentary, where allegory and history are one.

The battle between St. George and the Dragon appropriately concludes Book I of *The Faerie Queene*, because it is the most comprehensive and resonant episode, allegorically, in the poem, being "polysemous" in the way that Dante describes in his letter to Can Grande. If we are looking for a literary instance of the traditional (but not very common) "fourfold significance," we can find it here. The Knight's battle figures, beyond the literal action, "our redemption wrought by Christ"; and, in the moral and anagogic senses, the soul's entry into a state of grace in this life, and a proleptic vision of its "departure . . . to the liberty of eternal glory."[14] The appropriateness of Canto xi is also a

---

[13] C-Text XXI.471-79; *The Vision of William Concerning Piers the Plowman*, ed. W. W. Skeat (2 vols., Oxford, 1924), I, 549-51.
[14] *Latin Works*, pp. 347-48.

function of Book I's historicity, the fact that Spenser makes his dark conceit shadow the life-history of the English Church. I have been speaking of the poet's task in this allegory as the providing of contexts for the reading of his images. The dragon-battle is the most important instance of this process, and the context it offers roots *The Faerie Queene* in history, both far away and here and now, thereby opening a commerce between fiction and actuality.

Spenser is not writing "allegory of the theologians." "The fiction of the *Divine Comedy* is that it is not fiction,"[15] but the poet of *The Faerie Queene* makes no such claim. He does, however, defend his poem as "a famous antique history" rather than "painted forgery" (II.Pro.1), and the history of imagining confers on many of his images the venerable weight of truthfulness if not of fact. The legend of St. George as "history" leaves something to be desired; Spenser and his contemporaries were aware of the shortcomings of Geoffrey of Monmouth and the *Legenda Aurea*. John Selden, one of the earliest practitioners in England of a scientific mythography, pondered and deplored, in his notes to Drayton's *Poly-Olbion*, the vicissitudes suffered by the story of St. George at the hands of gothic redactors.

> For S. *George*, that he is patron to the *English* . . .
> scarce any is, that knows not. Who he was, & when
> the *English* tooke him, is not so manifest. . . . His
> passion is supposed in *Diocletian*'s persecution. His
> country *Cappadoce*. His acts are divers and strange.
> . . . As for his Knightly forme, and the Dragon under
> him, as he is pictured in *Beryth*, a Citie of *Cyprus*,
> with a yong maide kneeling to him, an unwarrant-
> able report goes that it was for his martiall delivery
> of the Kings daughter from the *Dragon*, as *Hesione*
> and *Andromeda* were from the Whales by *Hercules*
> and *Perseus*. Your more neat judgements, finding no
> such matter in true antiquity, rather make it symboli-
> call then truely proper. So that some account him an

---

[15] Singleton, *Commedia: Elements of Structure*, p. 62.

allegory of our Saviour Christ; and our admired
Spencer hath made him an embleme of Religion.[16]

Selden goes on to dismiss as *"English* fictions" the legend
that St. George was "a *Coventry* man borne . . . or that he
descended from the *Saxon* race." This effort to sift the evidence offers an interesting instance of the Renaissance
scholar's readiness to conflate similarly patterned myths.
Selden describes the hero's "Knightly forme" as "symboli-
call," a metaphor, and such it clearly is, making reference
not only to St. George, but to his master in the metaphors
of Dunbar's poem and the young lord whom Langland
shows on his way to joust in Jerusalem. The terms and trappings of chivalry can refer metaphorically to the Cruci-
fixion; those who bear these trappings within the literalness
of a fiction, like Spenser's Knight of the Red Cross, reani-
mate the metaphor and remind us of its source in "historical" actuality when those who served Christ took up the
shield of faith in his behalf and made the words of St. Paul
truth.

[16] *Works of Drayton*, V, 84-85. An earlier note on Arthur indicates
that Selden was prepared to credit some of the legend, while lamenting
its accretions: "And it is wished that the poeticall Monkes in celebration
of him, *Arthur*, and such other Worthies had containd themselves
within bounds of likelyhood . . . but so farre have the indigested re-
ports of barren and Monkish invention expatiated out of the lists of
Truth, that from their intermixed and absurd fauxities hath proceeded
doubt; and, in some, even deniall of what was truth" (pp. 46-47).

6. Two Heroes and their Quests

The nature of Spenser's allegory in the final cantos of Book I, and the sense in which he can be said to provide a context for subsequent unfoldings, may be illuminated by looking at the corresponding episodes at the climax of Book II. This comparison has become a hackneyed examination question; since Woodhouse's classic article,[1] it has been rehearsed, in one version or another, by almost every critic of the poem.[2] Whether grace and nature, faith and reason, *mens* and *ratio*, or some other set of terms provides the conceptual matrix, descriptions of these twin events tend to sound much like each other. But those who want to emphasize a distinction between the episodes usually make things more difficult for themselves by failing to note the chief difference: that the dragon-battle and the Bower of Bliss are unlike as metaphors. Kellogg and Steele are on the right track when they observe that Guyon's adventures are "set forth in poetic images made philosophically significant by generations of medieval and Renaissance mythographers, but essentially independent of a mystical Christian significance."[3]

It is not really possible, of course, to argue that any images in *The Faerie Queene* are "independent of" Christian significance. They are all subsumed by a theory that saw pagan myths as versions of the one truth; and circumscribed, in the poem, by a system of cosmic references that

[1] A.S.P. Woodhouse, "Nature and Grace in *The Faerie Queene*," *ELH* XVI (1949), 194-228.

[2] For instance, by Nelson, *Poetry of Spenser*, pp. 178-79. Fowler, who questions Woodhouse's formula, nevertheless refers to "a division between the tasks appropriate to *mens* and *ratio* together, on the one hand, and those appropriate to *ratio* in its dealings with the lower parts of the mind, on the other" (*Numbers of Time*, p. 86), a division that also places Guyon in a more limited context than the hero of Book I.

[3] *Books I and II*, p. 72.

ultimately converge in a single source. Within the poem, however, Spenser makes a distinction between Guyon and the Red Cross Knight as a Faery knight and an English one, respectively; and this is reinforced in the canto of the chronicles where the same distinction is drawn between Guyon and Arthur. The hero of Book I appears briefly at the beginning of Book II; he is, Spenser says, "departed out of *Eden* lands, / To serve againe his soveraine Elfin Queene" (II.i.1). The Red Cross Knight moves freely across the boundaries between the globe of Earth and Gloriana's kingdom. It is possible for a "real" personage to appear in a fiction, but this one-way street is closed at the other end; it is not possible for an invented personage—a Faery knight —to enter into, or in Guyon's case, to comprehend, the spatio-temporal universe where human history unfolds and St. George's final battle takes place. Neither of Spenser's two chief Faery knights—Guyon and Calidore—has a history; we hear of the births of Arthur, St. George, Britomart, and Artegal, the "human" knights, but not of theirs. "The interaction of the two modes of heroic existence, faery and Briton, is an interaction of two aspects of time, its recurrent forms and its linear, evolutionary forms."[4] These two "forms" are not mutually exclusive—indeed, they are interdependent, and Spenser's poem, like God's creation, accommodates them both. The two aspects of time are both relevant to the dragon-battle, but the stress is on the divine or visionary point of view that sees the event as one open to re-enactment by others but closed and final as far as this particular hero is concerned.

Both these modes of time, the linear and the recurrent, are, of course, components of every human life. Spenserian allegory, as we particularly see when we compare Books I and II, analyzes the two modes and links each with a different type of human experience. In each of our lives, some

[4] Angus Fletcher, *The Prophetic Moment: An Essay on Spenser* (Chicago, 1971), p. 88. This distinction, too, is an old one; see Rathborne, *Meaning of Spenser's Fairyland*, pp. 203-204.

actions recur, must be constantly repeated and renewed; and some actions occur only once. Birth, marriage, death fall into the second category; to this group Christian theologians add rebirth or conversion, and the achievement of salvation. These experiences are definitive, irreversible, and unique; they are (sometimes, to be sure, conditionally) final. The idea that a soul can be "chosen" for salvation has been obscured by a thicket of theological hair-splitting, but behind it is always the sense that there is a *kind* of religious experience that is irreversible, however it may be denied, ignored, or obscured after it has occurred. The experiences of the Red Cross Knight in the last few cantos of Book I are of this nature. In the final episode he is betrothed to his one true love; earlier, he has slain in himself the principle of rebellion and disorder, with the aid of grace; he has received a "name and nation," and seen a vision of his last end. At the end of the encounter with Despair, Una speaks to him:

> Why shouldst thou then despeire, that chosen art?
>
> (I.ix.53)

The import of all the final adventures is that this knight is *chosen*, he is a unique being "singled out," as our idiom significantly puts it, for a conclusive fate. Every one of us participates in uniqueness in this way; every soul is unique in God's eye, and its life moves along a line from a beginning to an end.[5]

Spenser's hero in Book I develops, in the course of his adventures, in two ways, depending on our viewpoint. For most of the book, we, as readers, "see" him undergoing rec-

[5] Food for thought on temporality in fiction is provided by Frank Kermode in *The Sense of an Ending* (New York, 1967), especially Ch. 2, where he discusses some extrapolations of the terms *kairos* and *chronos*, linear and cyclical time. Kermode is also responsible for reviving the concept of *aevum* for literary criticism. I owe an obvious debt to his thoughtful book.

ognizable experiences, finally becoming perfected in moral virtue after his lessons in Canto x. From our point of view, therefore, he becomes more an "allegorical character," more completely transparent to a concept, less an adjective and more a noun, no longer a potentially holy man, but very nearly the embodiment of Holiness. Yet, viewed from God's point of vantage, which in the poem is located in the blind hermit Contemplation, his development is a growth into his destined selfhood, and the knight becomes not just *a* gentle knight, but *this* knight, St. George, a character in the divine fiction, which is perfectly "realistic" and unrepetitive, and in which every character is a major character (though, as Dante reveals in the *Paradiso*, some are more major than others). The Red Cross Knight/St. George is thus a mediating figure; he "imitates" Christ not only in slaying the Dragon, but in uniting possibility and actuality, destiny and a particular destiny. He is exemplary for the reader, a fulfillment and a prophecy of what he and we may some day become. In consequence the foreground of the allegory must have a definiteness, a historicity, that is not just psychic. Spenser spends three stanzas in Canto xi locating the action in a place which is the navel of the world, the site of "Christ's Cross and Adam's Tree." The Tree of Life which heals the hero is unique: "In all the world like was not to be found, / Save in that soile, where all good things did grow" (xi.47). This is *"Eden* lands."

Guyon's final adventure unfolds in a different sort of place:

> Within a wandring Island, that doth ronne
> And stray in perilous gulfe, her dwelling is.
> (II.i.51)

The sea is persistently an image of life's mutable, elemental on-goingness; and a wandering island cannot be a final stop in life's journey. Rather, it appears and disappears when the

211

imagination has need of it. Spenser's mythological description of the Bower helps us to identify its ontological nature.

> More sweet and holesome, then the pleasaunt hill
> Of *Rhodope*, on which the Nimphe, that bore
> A giaunt babe, her selfe for griefe did kill;
> Or the Thessalian *Tempe*, where of yore
> Faire *Daphne Phoebus* hart with love did gore;
> Or *Ida*, where the Gods lov'd to repaire,
> When ever they their heavenly bowres forlore;
> Or sweet *Parnasse*, the haunt of Muses faire;
> Or *Eden* selfe, if ought with *Eden* mote compaire.
>   (II.xii.52)

These lines may remind us of the stanzas in Book I where
the Mount of Contemplation is compared to Sinai, the
Mount of Olives, and Parnassus; the comparative form of
the reference ("*More* sweet . . .") suggests that this is not
just any analogue of Paradise, but *the* analogue, the definitively imagined version of the true Garden. It is not that
Garden itself, however. In the last line, Spenser takes back
part of what he has given and reminds us of what we know:
that nothing we now experience *can* compare with Eden.
The images that we experience with Guyon belong to Fairy
Land, not to "*Eden* lands," to the mode of invention, not
vision, though they insinuate themselves into our sensibili-
ties so winningly that we must actively resist succumbing
to the illusion that the poet's images have reference to a
geographical actuality rather than a "place" created by
imagination for its own self-pleasing ends.

The Palmer's adjuration as the boat approaches Acrasia's
island locates it accurately: "Lo where does appeare / The
sacred soile, where all our perils grow" (37). *Sacred* has its
old general force; the soil is imbued with *mana*, a doom-
laden potentiality for those who cannot rule it. It is the soil
of the incarnate, created world—our physical and psychological being that responds to the being of Nature. The
island and the Bower condense and focus, metaphorically,

the confrontation of the "inner" and "outer" worlds within Nature. Spenser's Banquet of Sense[6] in the Bower is designed to evoke our own sensory responses, including the admiration that is a valid reaction to the beauty of Creation —hence the reminders, in the vehicles of many similes, of Nature's genuine glories. Acrasia herself embodies untempered Sensuality; she makes visible the "feminine" principle which, from Eve downward, had been allegorically at war with Reason. The dominance of this principle in the life of the soul "causes" the corruption of Nature, including human nature; Spenser's metaphor for this process, in the Bower of Bliss, is the contamination of the natural (which left to itself is innocent) by human art. Marvell was to renew the metaphor a few decades later, in his miniature allegory, "The Mower against Gardens."

Spenser is composing here an "allegory of the poets" whose *primary* force is moral and psychological. The experiences which it contains belong to the realm of Nature, and compose the dissolving, constantly renewed scenario of our psychic lives. The rhetorical and metaphorical devices that Spenser employs are designed to take us into the dark world of somatic experience at the roots of our nature, as of Nature itself; the personages who inhabit this phase of the allegory are at once evanescent and permanent, the embodiments of physical and mental dispositions. The nature of the allegory in Canto xii is suggested in the two interesting stanzas on the good and bad Genii at the gate of the Bower. Good Genius is the self-preserving impulse in the psyche, a kind of life-force in which every living being participates.[7]

[6] For the background of this Renaissance sub-genre, see Ch. 4 in Kermode, *Shakespeare, Spenser, Donne.*

[7] C. S. Lewis, in his note on "Genius and Genius" (*Studies in . . . Literature*), distinguishes the generalized vital principle ("Genius A") from the individual's *daemon* ("Genius B"). The second can, however, be taken as a specialized (or psychically internalized) version of the first. For comment on the sources of Spenser's Genii, see Helen A. Kahin, "Spenser and the School of Alanus," *ELH* VIII (1941), 257-72.

> That is our Selfe, whom though we do not see,
> Yet each doth in him selfe it well perceive to bee.
>
> Therefore a God him sage Antiquity
> Did wisely make, and good *Agdistes* call.
>
> (II.xii.47-48)

Pagan gods are made, not born. The sages of antiquity gave the name of gods to invisible principles which we can "perceive" but not "see." The process is analogous to the allegorist's bodying-forth, as fictive personages, of other "celestiall powres." Bad Genius, "The foe of life. . . . That secretly doth us procure to fall," is the contrary, self-destructive principle in the soul; it in turn composes bad allegory, deceptive rather than revelatory, misleading us "Through guilefull semblaunts, which he makes us see" (48). As Berger has remarked, "The comparison suggests that both daemons exist in all men."[8] They are aspects of the soul's imaginative life, either warning us of "secret ill" (47), or creating it.

Spenser makes them visible in an allegory of the poets, analogous to the pagan mythology contrived by "sage Antiquity"; so Bad Genius is "devized to bee" the Porter (48). The stanzas are self-referring in a complicated way. Spenser is inventing characters that represent the power to invent, in both its celestial and its demonic aspects; and he is using them to introduce an allegory that is an example of what they do. Pleasure's Porter panders to the desires of the mind, persuading us of their innocence and of the "naturalness" of the self-deceiving artificial world that desire creates. Good Agdistes is a celestial power that can put us in

---

[8] *Allegorical Temper*, p. 214. Berger's discussion of these stanzas (pp. 212-15) is full of useful insights, and his reading, up to a point, is consistent with mine. It is weakened, in my view, by too much insistence on Guyon as a dramatic character rather than an "ensample" (or adjectival principle). I want to argue, in contrast, that Guyon is very much a hero of the indefinite article, unlike the historically oriented hero of Book I, whom Spenser calls quite early "the true *Saint George*" (I.ii.12).

touch with the true sources of our being and tell us "wondrous things concerning our welfare" (47); when Guyon listens to this voice in himself (perhaps objectified in the Palmer), he fares well and bids farewell to the Bower of Bliss.

Once we have entered the garden, we are participants in an allegory that requires a quite different sort of response from that demanded by the traditional typological allegory that concludes Book I. A second glance at the dragon-battle will help to define the difference. The fact that in the Red Cross Knight's encounter Spenser invokes a kind of history, whose claim to authenticity was more serious than that awarded to the adventures of Odysseus or Guyon, does not mean that the fiction's mode will be circumstantial. On this ritual occasion, when the invisible referents of the allegory, anagogical and tropological, are close to the surface, Spenser shifts the physical point of view repeatedly and rapidly. The visible action is foreshortened, stylized, dislocated, diminished, and enlarged; we are obliged to move quickly back and forth between long and short perspectives which telescope the enormous range of the allegorical references in this episode. The result is cinematic, and our familiarity with the technology of the movie camera means that we are less likely than some of Spenser's earlier readers to be troubled by inconsistencies of scale and other violations of a static realism. When "the dreadfull Beast drew nigh to hand," Spenser gives us a looming image of his body making a "wide shadow," and soon he is actually upon us:

> Approching nigh, he reared high afore
> His body monstrous, horrible, and vast.
>
> (I.xi.8)

Observed with this close-in foreshortening, it is no wonder that his wings appear "like two sayles" which, beating the air, cause the clouds to flee "for terrour great" (10). In Stanzas 12-13 we look right down his gullet; the effect is of peering over the rim of a volcano: "A cloud of smoothering smoke and sulphure seare / Out of his stinking gorge forth steemed still" (13). In Stanza 15, the camera moves away:

> So dreadfully he towards him did pas,
> Forelifting up aloft his speckled brest,
> And often bounding on the brused gras.

This Disney-like Dragon is "the same" as the monster three furlongs in length who from middle-distance resembled a ship under sail; but the sudden spatial alteration produces an alteration of scale that makes him look like a toy.

McLuhan's principle that the cinema is a "cool" medium is consistent with our experience of the dragon-battle, which is at once violent and detached, as it is with respect to many other divinely devised dream visions. A reader's involvement in the Bower of Bliss is, in contrast, more narrowly focused, intense, intimately affecting, even "realistic." It is, above all, sensuously immediate. There are plenty of pauses, where the Palmer or an allusion, or the rhetoric, warns us that we ought to question the nature and implications of the experience; but the action unfolds at an even pace in the same plane, and we feel ourselves to be inside it. The literalness of the "literal level," in this canto, is in the miming of sensory experience. The images that project or engender this experience are expendable, devised by the poetic imagination—with the aid of many forerunners who provided Spenser with precedents—to compose a fictive place whose features point beyond themselves to a *significatio*, at the same time that they elicit visual and visceral responses. They have psychological but not historical authenticity. The "story" this sequence of actions is telling is the story that Milton tells (also in an "allegory of the poets") in *Comus*. The dark conceit conceals the life-history of the resolved soul, making its way through the traps laid for it by its own responses to "natural" pleasure. In writing of the Bower, Spenser is reminding us of what it is like to experience the delicious lapse of the will into indolence and sensual delight. The lovely lay of *carpe diem* is one of those Lydian airs whose effect Milton describes at the end of *L'Allegro*; in the perfect innocence of that fictive world, from which the imagination has exorcised all the Stygian powers, they can be safely reveled in, but as Plato knew, such indulgence is dangerous in ordinary life, in the middest, where Guyon's quest takes place.[9] The poetic texture in the stanzas on the Bower is enriched not only by music, but by every kind of sensuous touching; the prevailing sensation is a kind of visceral languor combined with excitement and erotic suggestiveness. When Spenser says that the girl in the fountain showed Guyon "many sights, that courage cold could reare" (68), he is speaking about sexual arousal, and the suggestiveness is enhanced by other details, such as the naked cupids who

> fly about, playing their wanton toyes,
> Whilest others did them selves embay in liquid joyes.
> (II.xii.60)

The total effect of the canto is not pornographic, because the simple purpose of pornography is complicated and contradicted by other intents; but one part of the effect is to awaken those impulses to erotic wish-fulfillment in the human psyche that respond to pornography. They are both primitive and primitivistic; but they lie too deep to be given a simple moral label.

The reference to pornography is not without pertinence. Art's claim to be autotelic is a self-protective maneuver against abuse by kinetic emotions. As Stephen Dedalus remarked, art does not excite desire or loathing; when Spen-

---

[9] The music of he Bower has been analyzed by John Hollander as an illegitimate effort to imitate Arcadian harmonies through "a jumbling of musical conditions" ("Spenser and the Mingled Measure," *ELR* I [1971], 235). He adds that in the Garden of Adonis, birdsong is *not* music: "Their sound is a type of candid eloquence," reflecting "the openness, the nudity of the Garden (as opposed to the exposure, the nakedness, of the Bower)" (p. 236).

ser temporarily invokes desire in Canto xii, it is to suggest
how readily art can become pornography, or something
worse. He encourages in his reader an uncritical response
to illusion that collapses the contemplative decontamination
zone between art's power and vulnerable "life." He permits
us to enter his fiction and walk at the hero's side; to feast
our "hungry eies" on Acrasia, for whose charms he devises
one of his most beautiful, and most "natural," images.

> And her faire eyes sweet smyling in delight,
> Moystened their fierie beames, with which she thrild
> Fraile harts, yet quenched not; like starry light
> Which sparckling on the silent waves, does seeme more
> > bright.
> > (II.xii.78)

From this mesmerizing dazzle the poet abruptly withdraws
us; the next two stanzas show Verdant asleep in the ruins
of his nobility. It is a moment of self-confrontation for both
hero and reader; with critical powers re-awakened, we become once more readers of an allegory, not actors in it. But
we do not need to be told how Verdant came to his sorry
plight. Guyon, emerging from temporary victimization to
his own passions and senses, sees in the "goodly swayne" the
image of overturned natural order that leads to death in the
organism. He has seen its twin before in Mortdant, the dead
knight of the first canto; and both of these characterless
young men are *alter egos* for Guyon himself. Verdant need
only experience the little death of sleep, the hero's rescue
of him setting the seal on his own choice of temperance, or
life, over the way of excess, or death.

Mortdant, an "image of mortalitie" (II.i.57) in several
senses, and Verdant, whose name alludes to the reburgeon-
ing of organic life, are set by Spenser at the two portals of
the Book of Temperance. Their presence gives to the whole
a circular pattern consistent with the temporal recurrence

that is the normal mode of beings within Nature. And re-currence is the keynote of Book II's final stanza:

> Let *Grill* be *Grill*, and have his hoggish minde;
> But let us hence depart whilest wether serves and
> winde.
> (II.xii.87)

Guyon has destroyed the Bower. The soul has once more triumphed over the impulses that would persuade it of its own innocence. But the hero must still contend with wind and weather, in the macrocosm and in his own soul. The Palmer controls the witch Acrasia first with "A subtile net, which onely for the same / The skilfull Palmer formally did frame" (81), then with "chaines of adamant" (82). But she cannot be killed; she remains continually alive, like Sin and Death in *Paradise Lost*, because she is the source of some-thing persistently and recurrently present in every human soul. And she is also continuously available as the fictive representative of Sensuality in allegories. Her counterpart in Book I is Duessa, who is also immortal; though unmasked and exiled in "the wastfull wildernesse" (I.viii.50), she re-vives sufficiently to write the Red Cross Knight a letter in Canto xii—and, of course (after brief appearances at the opening of Books II and IV) to re-enter the poem in Book V, "royally arayed" (V.ix.40) in the costume of Mary Stuart. Her "death" takes place offstage, with a reference to "her wretched corse" (x.4) which we, as instructed read-ers of allegory, know full well to be the corpse of the Queen of Scots, but not of Duessa. The intermittent immortality of these characters links them with time in "its recurrent forms."

Guyon's victory over Acrasia is not final, but it is a sig-nificant stage in Spenser's instruction of his readers. The conversation between the hero and the Palmer at the end of Canto xii makes audible the colloquy of the rational mind with itself, and assures us of its power to withdraw from the solicitations of its own desires and choose its own fate. The myth of Circe is allegorically explicated in the final stanzas; in the process, Spenser also explicates the significance of Acrasia's island and the contemplative, analytical character of allegory which elucidates significance. He shuffles his "seemings" to demonstrate that these events are vehicles of a metaphor, *visibilia* making concrete an inward condition. "Then *Guyon* askt, what meant those beastes which there did ly" (84).

> Said he, These seeming beasts are men indeed,
> Whom this Enchauntresse hath transformed thus,
> Whylome her lovers, which her lusts did feed,
> Now turned into figures hideous,
> According to their mindes like monstruous.
>
> (xii.85)

We must, I think, allow a certain deliberate depth in the word "figures." And "indeed" in the first line makes "seeming" also bear its full weight; these creatures, who "look like" beasts, are "in deed" men, only "seeming beasts." But it is one of the basic principles of Spenserian allegory that the "literal level" when accurately read registers the nature of things, "shading a true case," even when the truth may be that appearance is deceptive. The veil of a dark conceit is in fact no veil at all, but revelation, a kind of light which, like the God-given daylight invoked by Prince Arthur,

> discovers all dishonest wayes,
> And sheweth each thing, as it is indeed.
>
> (III.iv.59)

The metamorphosis that inevitably ensues when men become Acrasia's lovers is therefore a violation of truth only if we stop with visible reality; but if we consider their "mindes like monstruous," we "perceive" and fictively "see" that the facts presented to the eye in the fiction register the true case of an inner reality. In this fictive universe, seeming accords with essence, just as words accurately name things. When the Palmer effects a counter-metamorphosis, one grudging former beast "did him miscall / That had from hoggish forme him brought to naturall" (86).

> Said *Guyon,* See the mind of beastly man,
> That hath so soone forgot the excellence
> Of his creation, when he life began,
> That now he chooseth, with vile difference,
> To be a beast, and lacke intelligence.
>
> (87)

The Palmer can restore things to their "natural" forms, but these may be less "true" than allegorical "figures hideous," in a universe where Nature has forsaken the excellence of its first creation. The task of the allegorist is to restore all things to their pristine clarity, but the Palmer is no allegorist, only a reader of allegory. The role of maker is reserved for the poet. Guyon, having seen the "seeming beasts" that Spenser has put into the poem, can "See *the mind* of beastly man" through a surface that is now a false-semblance. The metaphor has been once more internalized, the noun turned back to an adjective. Grill is a "beastly man," no longer visibly a beast. But we, along with Guyon, have learned a lesson from him. "Let *Grill* be *Grill*"; his restored semblance can no longer conceal his "hoggish mind."

Like Milton's Eden turned into "an island salt and bare," Acrasia's garden turns from the fairest to "the fowlest place." Guyon's action is a token that he has learned to see things as they "really are"—to read allegorically—so he can cause seemings to coincide with reality. He is the instrument of the allegorical poet in this episode, an invented agent in an invented world. The making of the soul of the Red Cross Knight, on the other hand, is narrated rather than contrived by the poet. The Knight comes to the relief of a city that he neither makes nor destroys, but releases

221

from its bondage. It is restored to its "free" condition, and this *kind* of action is what I have been calling typological allegory. St. George's victory restores the Golden Age; Guyon's reveals the actualities of our Iron Age. He also releases Verdant; but Verdant is still "alive" in the fiction, as Mortdant was not. Verdant can be given a second chance to live in conformity to "the excellence of his creation"; Mortdant cannot be restored to life.

Guyon, and "the allegory of the poets," can strip away appearances and false-seemings. They cannot pierce the veil that conceals a more ultimate truth. That is left for "the allegory of the theologians," who make the events of actuality transparent to vision. The theologian of Book I, who introduces this phase of Spenser's allegory, is Heavenly Contemplation. After the point of *anagnoresis*, the action ceases to be solely metaphorical; or rather, the poet's discourse, once exclusively the vehicle of a metaphor, now says what it means. Seeming and being are one in the visionary mode where veils are stripped away; we see "the literal and the metaphorical rushing together."[10] The dragon is the Dragon, not an invented version of dragonish guile. He *is* the essence or source concealed behind the assumed or perverted seemings of the wicked characters; he is what Duessa "looks like" when she is unmasked by the poet, or the poet's agent.[11] The Dragon looks like what he is, and his metamorphosis occurred long before: "Because thou hast done this, thou art cursed above all cattle, and above every beast of the field; upon thy belly shalt thou go, and dust shalt thou eat all the days of thy life." The history of Satan's serpentine metamorphoses, self-imposed and divinely im-

[10] C. S. Lewis, *Miracles* (New York, 1947), p. 192.

[11] The retreat of character into source is illustrated again in the Souldan's wife, that "bold woman" Adicia in Book V. She is compared to Ino, Medea, and "*Bacchus* Priests," all possessed by infernal powers; at the end, "they doe say that she transformed was / Into a Tygre . . . to prove her surname true" (V.viii.49). The relationship between name, false appearance, true appearance, and essence, is particularly visible here.

posed, is traced by Milton in the mythic narrative of *Paradise Lost*. The last two and a half cantos of *The Faerie Queene*, Book I are also "mythical" in that the cast of characters is archetypal. Since this action is unfolded on Middle Earth, however, the myth is *also* the vehicle of metaphors—the four senses, noticed above. It is myth-as-history, which is the mode adopted by the Holy Spirit in composing the Bible: typological allegory.

Homer, Virgil, Ovid, read by theologians, yield up theological meanings. But Odysseus and Aeneas do not become Christ, or even "Christ-figures," imitators of that Life; they remain inspired inventions, troubled mirrors showing, in brief gleams, the outlines of certain events whose pattern controls history. All truths participate in Truth; all virtues owe their source to a single energy. Commentators in the Renaissance were not surprised to find, in the myths of Hercules, Perseus, and other pagan heroes, "crooked images of some one true history." It was what they expected, what their theory of a unified truth required. The seventh canto of Book II lets us see that behind all truly heroic actions lies the pattern laid down by history's truest hero. But Guyon does not imitate Christ; the poet does that, by devising his narrative so that it reveals, somewhere in the middle distance, a certain structure. The action itself, like the action of *Comus*, unfolds "in" the wood of the world and the mind of man.

The model for Guyon's voyage in the first part of the final canto is the *Odyssey*, a text in "the scripture of the pagans." This pattern too, in its broadest outlines, has been assimilated to the master-model erected in Book I. In Canto xii of the first book a Christian knight, his life assuming the form Christ gave it, recites his adventures to the ancestors of mankind, as his hearers weep:

> Great pleasure mixt with pittifull regard,
> That godly King and Queene did passionate,
> Whiles they his pittifull adventures heard,

223

> That oft they did lament his lucklesse state,
> And often blame the too importune fate,
> That heapd on him so many wrathfull wreakes.
>
> (I.xii.16)

Behind this incident stand Odysseus and Aeneas, earlier voyagers recounting parallel "wrathfull wreakes"; they are related to this Christian hero by a sort of pagan typology. The Red Cross Knight's voyage on a "sea of deadly daungers" (17) has been figurative; Guyon's twelve cantos later will be fictively literal. But the King and Queen who preside over the dénouement of Book I are the "true" ancestors whose genuineness gives life to the many fictions derived from them, and the Knight, moving in a foreground of fictive history, is the source of metaphors and object of allusions by other instances of heroic endeavor.

The various significances of the betrothal in Canto xii require little glossing, being already quite explicit. The unveiling of Una, "Who, in her self-resemblance well beseene, / Did seeme, such as she was, a goodly maiden Queene," is followed by the exposure of Duessa and Archimago. The correct naming, by the hero, of the enchantress, is a token of his salvation, figured in his capacity to see things as they are "in deed." He "sees" both Una and Duessa accurately, becoming at last an accomplished reader of allegory; in this respect, his situation resembles Guyon's when Acrasia is captured.

> There did I find, or rather I was found
> Of this false woman, that *Fidessa* hight,
> *Fidessa* hight the falsest Dame on ground,
> Most false *Duessa*, royall richly dight,
> That easy was t' invegle weaker sight.
>
> (I.xii.32)

He has finally reached the stage which the poet, endowed with his special grace of tutored insight, has enjoyed all along. The poet was present when Una unveiled herself in Canto iii, witnessing what "mortall eye" rarely sees. Confronted by the mysteries of Canto xii, however, Spenser finds that words fail him even if sight does not. He makes use of the conventional rhetorical devices for expressing the inexpressible.[12] "What needs me tell their feast and goodly guize" (14)—though in fact he does tell us quite a bit about it. At the very end, however, he turns the poem inward and appeals to each reader's secret experience to help him "say" what cannot be said. Even Milton can give us only hints of the heavenly music made by those "Who sing, and singing in their glory move." Spenser says his characters heard something *like* this song.

> During the which there was an heavenly noise
>   Heard sound through all the Pallace pleasantly,
>   Like as it had bene many an Angels voice
>   Singing before th' eternall majesty,
>   In their trinall triplicities on hye;
>   Yet wist no creature, whence that hevenly sweet
>   Proceeded, yet eachone felt secretly
>   Himselfe thereby refte of his sences meet,
> And ravished with rare impression in his sprite.
>
> (I.xii.39)

When the senses are "refte," allegory ceases; poetry itself falls silent. The Feast of the Lamb can be only remotely approached, and Spenser with charming humility resigns from eloquence:

> their exceeding merth may not be told:
> Suffice it heare by signes to understand
> The usuall joyes at knitting of loves band.
>
> (40)

<hr>

[12] E. R. Curtius discusses "Inexpressibility Topoi" in *European Literature and the Latin Middle Ages*, tr. W. R. Trask (New York, 1953), pp. 159-62.

"The usuall joyes," indeed. It is a beautiful moment of simplicity, letting us down gently from the exigencies of vision.

Transcendent ineloquence may be the poet's only recourse at such moments. It is, at any rate, the most common mode for "the high dream," the moment of vision when we glimpse the promised end. Among the things that happen in Canto xii, time is redeemed. The old man who greets Una and her Knight "is" Adam, the Old Man. But we know who is the father of Truth; she is the daughter of Time.

> Then forth he called that his daughter faire,
> The fairest *Un'* his onely daughter deare,
> His onely daughter, and his onely heyre;
> Who forth proceeding with sad sober cheare,
> As bright as doth the morning starre appeare.
> (I.xii.21)

(Old spelling makes the pun on Una's name in *onely* unmistakable.) There are many pictorial representations of this scene in Renaissance iconography, the bright female figure being called forth out of darkness by the old man, Time.[13] The emergence of Truth and the redeeming of Time are twin manifestations of God's entry into history, fictively represented in *anagnoresis*, the visionary moment, the high dream. Eliot's own approximation of such a moment occurs at the crisis of *Ash Wednesday*. His version looks to Dante at the climax of the *Purgatorio* for its model, but the details are audible in Spenser's stanzas as well. Opaque "signs" replace words; silence falls; descending and ascending truth meet; time is redeemed.

> The new years walk, restoring
> Through a bright cloud of tears, the years, restoring
> With a new verse the ancient rhyme. Redeem
> The time. Redeem . . .

---

[13] See Erwin Panofsky, *Studies in Iconology* (New York, 1939), pp. 83ff.; and Fritz Saxl, "Veritas Filia Temporis," in *Philosophy and History: Essays Presented to Ernst Cassirer* (Oxford, 1936), pp. 197-222.

But the fountain sprang up and the bird sang down
Redeem the time, redeem the dream
The token of the word unheard, unspoken

Till the wind shake a thousand whispers from the yew

And after this our exile[14]

14 Eliot, *Ash Wednesday* IV; *Collected Poems*, pp. 90-91.

PART III

"Lovers Deare Debates": The Middle Books

1. Art and Love

"After this, our exile." Spenser exiles himself, along with the Red Cross Knight, from the Heavenly City, at the end of Book I. The rest of the poem unfolds in the field of this world, the appropriate arena for heroic effort, moral, intellectual, imaginative. Book I participates in Spenser's anatomy of imagination insofar as its theme is epistemological, and its poles of truth are the coordinates within which imagination discovers its proper tasks. In Books III and IV of *The Faerie Queene*, imagination is carried into new realms of human experience, and they will be the concern of this chapter. A second glance at Book II, whose hero lacks imagination, will reveal some negative instances that can lead into the middle books.

I have been exploring the causes and consequences of the notion, often advanced by Spenser's critics, that the hero of Book II embodies the rational soul of man beset by the toils and threats of created Nature. To say that this book moves within the realm of Nature is to suggest that Spenser wishes to comment upon the "naturalness" of reason in man; it is not to exclude the possibility of Christian references, patterns, allusions, and implications in the allegory of Book II. Many of these are in fact present, though they all, I think, are mediated by the poet's voice or by his presence as a manipulator of image and narrative, rather than in the "consciousness" of Guyon, whatever that may mean. Book II, like all the succeeding books of *The Faerie Queene*, is contained by the contexts of Book I, and the images of self-induced mortality, of fountain and bloody-handed babe at the opening of Book II are resonant with Christian meaning.[1] It is significant, however, that the elucidation of these

---

[1] Alastair Fowler, "The Image of Mortality: *The Faerie Queene*, II.i-ii," *HLQ* XXIV (1960-61), 91-110; "Emblems of Temperance in *The Faerie Queene*, Book II," *RES* (N.S.) XI (1960), 143-49.

spectacles by the hero and his Palmer includes no sentiment
that could not have been uttered by a virtuous pagan, aside
from a vague reference to "eternall doom."

> But after death the tryall is to come,
> When best shall be to them, that lived best.
>
> (II.i.59)

Guyon appears to have no imaginative grasp on this notion
as a living Christian reality; he turns aside from the sight
of the dead Amavia, "Accusing fortune, and too cruell fate"
(56). The canto ends with the burial of the dead in a setting of Roman piety, following a couplet on the shame of lying unburied that would have done credit to Sophocles. The
scene at the grave is subdued in tonality and classical in
range of reference.

> The great earthes wombe they open to the sky,
> And with sad Cypresse seemely it embrave,
> Then covering with a clod their closed eye,
> They lay therein those corses tenderly,
> And bid them sleepe in everlasting peace.
>
> (II.i.60)

This vacant landscape expresses the desolation of mortality
without articulate alternatives, and the sky above it is
empty. The final stanza records Guyon's vow of vengeance,
solemnized with pagan gestures: "he cut a locke of all their
heare, / Which medling with their bloud and earth, he
threw / Into the grave" (61).[2]

Guyon's recognition of the Red Cross Knight by virtue
of "the sacred badge of my Redeemers death" (II.i.27) alerts

[2] The Palmer solves Guyon's "great marvell" in the next canto by
accounting for Ruddymayne's affliction in terms of "a sacred Symbole"
that is to inspire "revengement" (ii.10); he prefaces this with an Ovidian
myth explaining the "secret vertue" of the fountain that will not allow
it to cleanse the babe's bloody hands. He does not suggest, as Spenser
does in the Fradubio episode, that a *different* water is required for
such cleansing.

us to a relationship between the books, but it has curiously little consequence where Guyon is concerned; he cannot understand the import of the bloody-handed babe, nor recognize Pilate in Hell. His shield bears the image of Gloriana, that Fairy Queen who presides over "the world," to whose realm the Red Cross Knight reluctantly returns after his sojourn with Heavenly Love. Everything in *The Faerie Queene* suggests that Spenser set great store by the heroism represented in Book II, and it is wholly alien to both his imaginative temperament and his expressed beliefs to suggest that Guyon's virtue is not compatible with, indeed congenial to, the virtues manifested by the explicitly Christian hero of Book I.[3] Hence, in fact, the plighting of friendship between them in Canto i, the mutual compliments. "So bene they both attone" (II.i.29); it is a profoundly Spenserian comment.

At the same time the poet is, I believe, carefully distinguishing the range of Guyon's aspirations from those of the Red Cross Knight when, in Canto vii, he composes the hero's reply to Mammon's offer of "the worldes blis" (32). The offer is that made by Satan to Christ in the wilderness, and the answer is couched, initially, in language compatible with scriptural reference.

Certes (sayd he) I n'ill thine offred grace,
    Ne to be made so happy do intend:
    Another blis before mine eyes I place,
    Another happinesse, another end.
    To them that list, these base regardes I lend:
    But I in armes, and in atchievements brave,
    Do rather choose my flitting houres to spend,
    And to be Lord of those, that riches have,
Then them to have my selfe, and be their servile sclave.
                         (II.vii.33)

[3] Kermode argues convincingly for Guyon as an exemplar of Heroic Virtue, a concept that in the Renaissance had both classical and Christian roots (*Shakespeare, Spenser, Donne*, Ch. 3). The recognition of this

The first five lines could have been spoken by the Red Cross Knight, or his model; the last four are the words of a Renaissance hero for whom secular glory is the limit of hope.[4] The Knight of Holiness has had "another blis" placed before his eyes, and has yearned after it even at the expense of his earthly quest, sponsored by Gloriana; Guyon's other bliss, however, though it is a "higher" and nobler one than any proposed by Mammon, is still something less than ultimate happiness. Classical wisdom could with equal sternness reject slavery to Mammon. The stanza as a whole follows the pattern, and the theme, of the famous speech by Marlowe's Tamburlaine:

> Nature, that framed us of four elements,
> Doth teach us all to have aspiring minds. . . .

The aspiration that Nature teaches is set out in Book II of *The Faerie Queene*; its conclusion, as Guyon's speech proclaims, is what Marlowe calls "The sweet fruition of an earthly crown"—"to be Lord of those that riches have." Guyon need not mean this literally, but its moral and psychological import are plain. In this episode Spenser is causing a confrontation between two interpretations of the *vita activa*, an ideal whose ambivalence has been set out in Harry Levin's discussion of *Tamburlaine.*

> The humanism of the Renaissance led directly from contemplation to action; intellectual curiosity was a means to a higher end; and the highest end of all the sciences was what Sir Philip Sidney terms *Architektonike* —an illuminating term in this context. . . . But, whereas a heavenly crown was the pious hope of every

---

paradigm by poet and reader seems to me compatible with my argument that there are limits placed upon the *character's* awareness within the fiction.

[4] This shift of point of view, indicating that Guyon is "firmly rooted in the here and now," is noted by Lewis H. Miller, "A Secular Reading of *The Faerie Queene*, Book II," *ELH* XXXIII (1966), 154.

Christian, an earthly crown is the notorious emblem of
worldliness, heterodoxy, and pride of life. In short, it
it not bathos, but blasphemy.[5]

There is a thin line between the "worldliness, heterodoxy,
and pride of life" embodied in Mammon, and the virtuous
architectonics of the resolved soul. Guyon is asked to tread
it in Canto vii, and he does so, avoiding both blasphemy
and bathos in rejecting Mammon's offer of "the end, / To
which all men doe ayme, rich to be made" (32).[6]

The demands of a virtuous life in the world are strenuous
and exigent, as Spenser suggests in the notorious episode
of the hero's swoon that follows the testing three days in
Mammon's world. And this exigency enforces a contraction
of Guyon's horizons, particularly with respect to his emotions. To this hero, love cannot present itself as anything
but a destructive force. It is a threat to that temperance that
is the enabling virtue of Guyon's rational heroism, and a
distraction from his true goal. It is, in short, a fatal Cleopatra. The "servile sclave" of Mammon, and the "seeming
beasts" of Acrasia's garden, the slaves of passion, are all
worldlings who have made the wrong choice. The Bower
of Bliss, with its abandoned arms—"the ydle instruments /
Of sleeping praise"—presents a version of love as seen by
a seeker for "fame"; another instance is the temptress Phaedria, whose distractions are designed to insure that "noyse
of armes, or vew of martiall guize / Might not revive desire
of knightly exercize" (II.vi.25). Thus Bacon sees love in the
tenth of his *Essays*.

The stage is more beholding to Love, than the life
of man. For as to the stage, love is ever matter of

---

[5] *The Overreacher* (Cambridge, Mass., 1952), p. 39.

[6] If blasphemy can be defined as the choice of a false god over the
true one—a version of idolatry—then Guyon's choice here is negatively
reflected in the two *exempla* that conclude the canto. Tantalus as an
instance of overreaching, "a type of blasphemous or intemperate
knowledge," has been discussed by Kermode (p. 73); Pilate chose "a
murdrer felonous" over "the Lord of life" (62).

comedies, and now and then of tragedies; but in life it doth much mischief; sometimes like a syren, sometimes like a fury. You may observe, that amongst all the great and worthy persons (whereof the memory remaineth, either ancient or recent,) there is not one that hath been transported to the mad degree of love: which shews that great spirits and great business do keep out this weak passion.[7]

"Whosoever esteemeth too much of amorous affection," he goes on, "quitteth both riches and wisdom." The love of Acrasia can override even the temptations of Mammon. But love as a siren or a fury will not do for Spenser in *The Faerie Queene*, though he allows the position to be expressed by Guyon's Palmer, moralizing the sad fate of Phedon who is among those "That to affections the bridle lend":

> Wrath is a fire, and gealosie a weede,
> Greife is a flood, and love a monster fell.
>
> (II.iv.35)

Love as siren, fury, monster: it is an attitude consistent with Guyon's statement that he will spend his life "in armes, and in atchievements brave," and consistent also with the narrator's comment upon a three-cornered battle in Canto ii. "So love does raine / In stoutest minds, and maketh monstrous warre" (ii.26). Guyon is one of the three knights, but he fights only to disengage the other two, lovers of Medina's excessive sisters. Medina herself does not love Guyon, but merely "entertaines" him (ii.16); the warrior and the politician must keep out this weak passion. For the poet himself, however, love, the ultimate blessing of Christian ethics, the motive power behind the universe, cannot continue to be ignored or dismissed by those who pursue the highest human virtues within the framework of heroic endeavor

---

[7] "Of Love," *Selected Writings*, p. 28.

236

Books III and IV alter the whole direction of *The Faerie Queene*. Consequently, when the siren love is confronted, one final time, by a Guyon-like hero in Book V, Artegal can repudiate the roles of Samson, Hercules, and Antony without being driven back upon the simple alternatives of the Palmer. Though he is enthralled by Radigund, whose beauty causes "his senses straunge astonishment" (V.v.12), he is released by Britomart, her *alter ego*, who has herself rejected the models offered by Cleopatra and Delila, and refused to become the new Helen for whose sake empires were ruined.[8] Together the lovers find new models in the chaste Penelope and her Ulysses (V.vii.39).

The middle cantos of Book V are one of Spenser's answers to the cold shoulder given to love by Baconian heroes like Guyon. "In reducing the confusions of the senses to reason, the intellect clarifies but it also contracts: for it clarifies by setting limits; and to transcend these limits we require a new and more lasting confusion, which is supplied by the blindness of love."[9] Love and heroic virtue are compatible, as Renaissance interpreters of the Mars/Venus myth, and the literary theorists who defended the importation of love as an epic theme, insisted. Love and war must be reconciled, and Spenser makes the case for their intimate union, explicitly, in the Proem to Book IV. But that is the least of it in *The Faerie Queene*. Between Book II and Book V, Spenser explores, with unmatched subtlety and inventiveness, the whole great subject of love. "Nuptial love maketh mankind; friendly love perfecteth it; but wanton love corrupteth and embaseth it." So Bacon in the final sentence of his essay. Spenser, having demonstrated the cor-

---

[8] Bacon, inevitably, cites among his bad examples in "Of Love," "he that preferred Helena, [and] quitted the gifts of Juno and Pallas." For Spenser, the alternative to the Judgment of Paris is not to repudiate Venus, but to choose a *Venus armata*, warded against unchastity; Britomart might be said also to unite the virtues of Juno, consort of the Jovian Artegal, and the armed maiden Pallas.

[9] Wind, *Pagan Mysteries*, pp. 55-56.

rupting force of wanton love in Book II, proceeds to examine nuptial and friendly love in the middle books.

Guyon's conquest lays the groundwork for the triumphs of Book III, but he does not himself participate in those triumphs. The angel who descends in Canto viii to protect the unconscious hero is "Like as *Cupido* on *Idaean* hill" (II.viii.6), a Cupid who has "laid his cruell bow away." But Guyon does not see him. The many faces of Cupid are manifested in Books III and IV, among them the angelic unarmed youth who, "laying his sad darts / Aside, with faire *Adonis* playes his wanton parts" (III.vi.49). The cantos of the poem over which this mighty god presides are not entered by the soul that clings to its rationality as the exclusive path to virtue. The colloquy between Glauce and love-wounded Britomart makes this plain.

> But mine is not (quoth she) like others wound;
>   For which no reason can finde remedy.
>   Was never such, but mote the like be found,
>   (Said she) and though no reason may apply
>   Salve to your sore, yet love can higher stye,
>   Then reasons reach, and oft hath wonders donne.
>   But neither God of love, nor God of sky
>   Can doe (said she) that, which cannot be donne.
> Things ofte impossible (quoth she) seeme, ere begonne.
>
> (III.ii.36)

This discussion explains, among other things, why Guyon has been laid low by Britomart in the opening encounter of Book III, as Artegal will be at the tournament of Book IV. The poet commiserates with the embarrassed knight.

> Ah gentlest knight, that ever armour bore,
>   Let not thee grieve dismounted to have beene,
>   And brought to ground, that never wast before;
>   For not thy fault, but secret powre unseene,
>   That speare enchaunted was, which layd thee on the
>   greene.
>
> (III.i.7)

The enchanted spear is a symbol for the "wonders done" by love, a "secret powre unseene" which Guyon, in fact, never does see.

The poet, of course, does see it, since things invisible, such as unveiled truth, are visible to him. The narrator of *The Faerie Queene*, possessed by the high-flying and deep-witted visionary power, can visit regions that reason never knows; so he alone sees the secret places of Book III. In the *Phaedrus*, Socrates identifies four types of "divine madness," among them the one dedicated to the Muses.

> In the divine kind we distinguished four types,
> ascribing them to four gods: the inspiration of the
> prophet to Apollo, that of the mystic to Dionysus,
> that of the poet to the Muses, and a fourth type
> which we declared to be the highest, the madness of
> the lover, to Aphrodite and Eros.[10]

This passage also provides the basis for the analogy between love and poetry that was to bear so many sweet and bitter fruits during the next two millennia. Both are visible in the middle books of *The Faerie Queene* (as well as the Apollonian or prophetic madness of Merlin), and the link was forged by Spenser in his earliest work. In the *October* eclogue, Piers, in language to be echoed by Glauce (III.ii.36), joins love and poetry in a mutually aspiring ardor.

> love does teach him climbe so hie,
> And lyftes him up out of the loathsome myre:
> Such immortall mirrhor, as he doth admire,
> Would rayse ones mynd above the starry skie.
> (91-94)

Poetry and love can both work wonders, fueled by a "secret powre unseene." The point is underlined in E. K.'s gloss for

[10] *Phaedrus* 265b, tr. R. Hackforth; *The Complete Dialogues of Plato*, ed. Edith Hamilton and Huntington Cairns (New York, 1961), p. 511.

the *October* emblem: "Poetry is a divine instinct and unnatural rage passing the reache of comen reason."

One of the metaphors for this secret power is magic: Britomart's enchanted spear, Merlin's enchanted glass that can reveal the future. But the mention of enchanters calls to mind the diabolic inventions of Archimago as well as the beneficent ones of Merlin, whose own begetting by "false illusion of a guilefull Spright" (III.iii.13) gives even his magic a slightly sinister tone. In Book III we read of the creation of the snowy Florimell by a witch who commands "hellish arts" and practices them in a hidden cottage (III.vii.6). This episode twines love, art, and magic, as we have earlier seen them wound together in the Merlin/Britomart encounter. The false Florimell is an emblem of love's power to alter appearances and "create" the desired being in defiance of Nature. The fact that she is composed out of the traditional materials of petrarchan convention implicates the poet in the making of illusions and animates the old suspicion that poetry and love are nothing but wish-fulfillment (a principle that has received a positive emphasis two cantos earlier when Timias awakens to see Belphoebe). The witch's power satisfies her son by embodying the desires of his mind in the shows of things, and the animation of the false Florimell's "carcas dead" by "A wicked Spright" is taken seriously enough by the poet to call forth the most deadly explanation. The animating spirit,

> with the Prince of Darknesse fell somewhile,
> From heavens blisse and everlasting rest;
> Him needed not instruct, which way were best
> Himselfe to fashion likest *Florimell*,
> Ne how to speake, ne how to use his gest,
> For he in counterfeisance did excell,
> And all the wyles of wemens wits knew passing well.
> (III.viii.8)

"Counterfeisance" of all kinds is malpractice, an abuse of reality for sinister purposes.

Yet, as Puttenham reminds us, the poet too is a "counterfaitor." We need not be surprised that Spenser gives an equivocal picture of imagination when he comes to describe the saturnine figure Phantastes at the Castle of Alma. A conservative attitude is confirmed repeatedly in the wariness with which, in *The Faerie Queene*, we are caused to approach the counterfeiting power—of which the poem itself is, of course, the supreme product. Spenser's description of Phantastes' chamber coincides with the opinion of Shakespeare's Theseus that "The lunatic, the lover, and the poet / Are of imagination all compact." This room is painted with "Infinite shapes of things"—

> Some such as in the world were never yit,
> Ne can devized be of mortall wit;
> Some daily seene and knowen by their names,
> Such as in idle fantasies doe flit:
> Infernall Hags, *Centaurs*, feendes, *Hippodames*,
> Apes, Lyons, Aegles, Owles, fooles, lovers, children,
> Dames.
>
> (II.ix.50)

Things which cannot "devized be of mortall wit" can nevertheless "exist" in fantasy—and presumably, when linked with the "secret powre" of the maker, can be caused to appear like the snowy Florimell. Most of the fantasies specified in the last two lines turn up somewhere in *The Faerie Queene* itself, which, looked on with a disapproving eye (like that of the "mighty Pere" who frowns at the end of Book VI), can itself resemble a vast Phantastes-chamber, full of

> Devices, dreames, opinions unsound,
> Shewes, visions, sooth-sayes, and prophesies;
> And all that fained is, as leasings, tales, and lies.
>
> (II.ix.51)

The stanzas devoted to Phantastes constitute one of Spenser's most visible efforts to defuse the potentially diabolic

energy of poetry by advertising imagination's inherent duplicity. A more subtle exploration of the topic runs like an
undergound river through the middle books, where Spenser suggests the serious potency of art by linking it with the
greatest of all powers, capable of raising a man to heaven
or casting him into hell. The counter-rational power of love
and the counter-factual power of imagination are close kin.
"Love can higher stye / Then reasons reach, and oft hath
wonders done"; Glauce's words are equally true applied to
imagination, and the connection was, in fact, made by theorists in the Renaissance. Ficino, in a chapter entitled "In
what Way Men are Captured by Love," focuses upon the
power of imagination to transform the images of sense into
"images like them, but much purer."

> Conception of this kind we call imagination and fancy;
> the images conceived here are kept in the memory.
> Through these, the eyes of the soul are wakened to be-
> hold the Universal Ideas of things which the soul holds
> within itself.[11]

Love and imagination are alike distinguished by their
aspiration towards "the Universal Ideas of things" ("things
ofte impossible"). For the discarnate impossible, however,
they would substitute the incarnate possible, and often they
succeed. Britomart complains that "neither God of love nor
God of skye / Can doe . . . that which cannot be done," but
she is wrong, and is proved wrong in the poem.

The Faerie Queene is not really a Phantastes-chamber;
it more nearly resembles the second room of Alma's turret,

> whose wals
> Were painted faire with memorable gestes,
> Of famous Wisards, and with picturals
> Of Magistrates, of courts, of tribunals,
> Of commen wealthes, of states, of pollicy,

---

[11] *Commentary of Marsilio Ficino on the "Symposium" of Plato*, tr.
Sears R. Jayne (Columbia, Mo., 1944), p. 189.

> Of lawes, of judgements, and of decretals;
> All artes, all science, all Philosophy,
> And all that in the world was aye thought wittily.
>
> (II.ix.53)

The "grave personage" who dwells here "is," of course, Reason, but the stanza shows how comprehensively Spenser understood that term. It is the source of all the productive, civilized human arts, all heroic "gestes," including, somewhat surprisingly, those "of famous Wisards"—like Merlin, who made the magic glass and caused Britomart to fall in love. The point, of course, is that imagination's mighty power for good or ill must incorporate with the ripe perfection of the fully-human rational soul if it is not to become the thrall of demonic impulses. "The longed-for lands" where the soul imagines itself dwelling can include *either* Heaven or Hell.

> But granted that imagination is necessary; nevertheless, it is irrational and devoid of correct judgment, unless aided by the guidance of a superior power. Hearkening to this, imagination beatifies man; disobedient to it, imagination dooms him. . . . If, yielding to the senses, phantasy shall decline to apply itself to the business of virtue, so great is its power that it afflicts the body and beclouds the mind, and finally brings it about that man divests himself of humanity, and takes on bestiality.[12]

The final sentence takes us into Acrasia's Bower, and a hell which must have seemed, to Mortdant and Verdant in the early stages, like a longed-for land. Following C. S. Lewis, critics have regularly read the Bower of Bliss canto in the context of Renaissance discussion of the problematic relations between Nature and Art. It is that, of course; and in the process it is also a commentary on the relations between Art and Love, exposing for us, before launching into

---

[12] Pico, *On the Imagination*, p. 43.

the celebration of *Venus urania* in III and IV, the death-wish concealed in both of these great powers. So the legitimate love of beauty and pleasure, which causes the knights irresistibly to pursue Florimell, can easily lead to self-deception. Spenser makes false Florimell "perfectly practiz'd in womans craft" (IV.ii.10), and this craft involves the short-circuiting of legitimate goals. The knight who succumbs to her is cast into "a foolish trance": "He seemed brought to bed in Paradise" (9). We are better able to discern this thread of the poem's fabric because Spenser has shown us the source from which false Florimells emanate—Acrasia, model for the witch who makes the snowy lady.

The definition of perverse or incomplete love at the end of Book II entails also a perversity of imagining. At the porch of the Bower there lounges "a comely dame" called Excess; her presence makes explicit the relation of this place to the major theme of the Book of Temperance. The Porter who admits pilgrims to the outermost wall of the Garden is also "a comely personage"; his allegorical import is more subtle and less entirely visible. As the master of "guilefull semblants which he makes us see," he is also "the foe of life." Commitment to illusion delivers us to death; a maker of illusions is necessarily implicated in pandering to the death-wish, if he fails to use his power responsibly. The Bad Genius of Acrasia's garden is, among other things, the embodiment of imagination's impulse to play us false. This impulse is made manifest in its works throughout the Garden, and initially in the ivory panels decorating the portals of the false paradise. The subject-matter is one of those Triumphs of Cupid of which we are to see several other instances in Book III: the ruination of heroic endeavor by the power of passion.

> And therein all the famous history
> Of *Jason* and *Medaea* was ywrit;
> Her mighty charmes, her furious loving fit,
> His goodly conquest of the golden fleece,

His falsed fayth, and love too lightly flit,
The wondred *Argo*, which in venturous peece
First through the *Euxine* seas bore all the flowr of
Greece.
(II.xii.44)

Other panels show the terrible fates of Apsyrtus and Creüsa.

This "piteous spectacle" makes plain the relation between the heroic quest and a love-passion that can subvert it; Jason, like Antony and Hercules, was one of the standard instances of this doom.[13] But the nature of the artifact through which the story is made visible is as significant as its subject-matter. The "work of admirable witt" is described, in a second stanza, in terms of its artfulness, the skill with which the maker has manipulated his materials. The effect is to place a fatal distance between the spectator and the sanguinary violence of the scenes; we are caused to dwell upon the artfully contrived surfaces and to ignore their import.

Ye might have seene the frothy billowes fry
Under the ship, as thorough them she went,
That seemd the waves were into yvory,
Or yvory into the waves were sent;
And other where the snowy substaunce sprent
With vermell, like the boyes bloud therein shed.
(II.xii.45)

The artist's hand can turn horror into beauty, but the consequence is to distance the ugliness and make it an object of contemplation. Spenser's paneled gateway offers a lesson in the dangers of aestheticism. Modern theorists write approvingly of "aesthetic distance" as a prerequisite for the disinterested contemplation of a work of art. But non-

---

[13] Lotspeich cites Natalis Comes on Jason's *voluptatem desiderium* (*Var.* II.373). Upton (Ibid., 372) observes that in the equivalent passage in Tasso, Hercules and Antony are included among *exempla* of destructive passion.

involvement of the emotions is intended to prepare us for the free action of reason and imagination in assessing the work's import, including its moral "meanings." Britomart standing before Busirane's tapestries demonstrates "aesthetic distance" properly understood. Yet the tapestries also solicit, from less controlled observers, a morally inappropriate submissiveness to superficial beauty which inhibits awareness of *significatio*. This amoral surrender to mere sensuous appeal, the appearance without the meaning, is repeatedly encouraged in the Bower of Bliss. A girl, viewed with the artful eyes of lust, becomes an object; the maiden in the fountain appears to Guyon as a chryselephantine work of art. Her locks unbound and veiling her body, she offers to the viewer "th' yvorie in golden mantle gownd" (67).

Harry Berger has devoted a chapter to the thesis that "Acrasia is a demonic allegorist. . . . She creates a world of false images which pretend to be real, yet which are completely dictated by a single intention."[14] But it is the poet who is the "creator" in this canto; Acrasia's power is metamorphic rather than creative. She can alter the appearance of things; so the sea-beasts are "into these fearefull shapes disguiz'd . . . to worke us dreed" (26). Her presence is a figure for the pleasure-principle in fallen man, causing every paradise to become a trap, its "natural" features to become the instruments of the soul's destruction. The Bower is a place

> In which what ever in this worldly state
> Is sweet, and pleasing unto living sense,
> Or that may dayntiest fantasie aggrate,
> Was poured forth with plentifull dispence.
>
> (42)

Sense and fantasy, that false secondary power, are here encouraged to do their destructive work. The means of per-

---

[14] *Allegorical Temper*, pp. 224 ff.

suasion, the "images," do not "pretend to be real"; they *are* real, but they are gilded by the human power of self-deception, and their sinister energy appears to the bemused spectator as a glamorous epiphany, like the girl's body "gownd" in her golden hair.

The ivory gate warns us both of the force of passion and of the parallel power of art to make us accept, even welcome, the morally unacceptable. Not art *simpliciter* is called in question, but bad art, art put to the service of untruth. The veils in this Garden—besides the body veiled in the maiden's hair, there are "snowy limbes" that "as through a vele, / So through the Christall waves appeared plaine" (64), and the "vele of silke and silver thin" (77) that does not hide Acrasia's "alablaster skin"—like the veil that shadows the truth of allegory, are contrived to let us "see" through them, up to a point. But a reader who has seen the point of the Jason/Medea panels will look further, will see through Acrasia's veils, not the lineaments of gratified desire, but the tormenting objects of a passion which cannot be satisfied.

The panels of the gate present us, therefore, with a cautionary tale in a double sense: through what they represent, and through what they are. Art is the handmaiden of this Garden's *Liebestod*. It disguises the wasting of our mortal being, as the intensity of sexual passion seems to arrest the rush of time; both offer illusory escapes from the limits of fallen nature.[15] The time-defying nature of art is matched only by the eternal vitality of passion itself. Acrasia, the pleasure-principle, never dies; but she must have constantly renewed human victims to prey upon, for though passions

15 In his discussion of the Bower, A. B. Giamatti identifies the flouting of the law of change as "the most illusory aspect of sexual self-indulgence"; it "pretends to make forever young, forever beautiful, that which is by nature fluid and in flux. This is the most profound perversion of the Bower and the radical deformity of Acrasia's way of life: its denial of the fact of death as an element of life; its refusal to face the necessity for decay in the midst of growth" (*The Earthly Paradise and the Renaissance Epic* [Princeton, 1966], p. 286).

are immortal their mortal vessels are not. The human being, body and soul, is quickly wasted and spent when possessed by demonic love, as Shakespeare's great sonnet, "Th' expense of spirit," insists. So every Mortdant, dying, must be succeeded by a Verdant; Spenser's names point to the terrifying rather than the benign implications of the natural cycle, which devours its own creations. Acrasia embodies, among many other forces, "Nature" in its aspect of indifference to man.[16] Dedication to passion on the part of a human being can be a kind of heroism; this aspect of it is unforgettably celebrated in Shakespeare's elegiac tragedy, *Antony and Cleopatra*. But like all tragic patterns this one involves *hubris*, a willed overriding of limits that is doomed to failure. A paradise of love is as false as any other paradise for those who must ride the stream of time. Possessed by an atemporal power, a fatal Cleopatra, man enters a world of immortal principles that quickly exhaust his glory and his might.[17]

Spenser isolates this single-minded dedication to passion first in the figure of Mortdant, killed by "raging passion with fierce tyrannie" (II.i.57), and later in Pyrochles.[18] This knight is the victim of a whole list of passions—

[16] Circe can be interpreted as "the generative principle in nature" (Lotspeich, *Var.* II.376). Hence the mytho-logic of her descent from Helios, which Spenser may be pursuing in making Belphoebe a daughter of the Sun. Her appearance in Canto iii of Acrasia's book would make additional sense if these two feminine principles could be seen, from the retrospect of the Book of Chastity, to polarize the problematic relation between human sexuality and the realm of essences.

[17] Shakespeare inflects the theme again in *Venus and Adonis*. And somewhere in the background of *The Merchant's Tale* lies an ironic version of Spenser's subject in II.xii. Chaucer makes the conjunction of Januarie and May a paradigm for the illegitimate attempt to turn the clock back, which is also an effort to gain premature entrance to Paradise. Januarie would have his youth again; declaring that "I shal have myn hevene in erthe heere" (E.1647), he weds "His freshe May, his paradys" (E.1822), but the garden in which he encloses her is no Garden of Adonis. Rather, he must play Mortdant to the verdant Damyan.

[18] This character illustrates how embodied principles in *The Faerie Queene* exist in a "vertical" dimension, literalizing the notion implied in genealogical "descent." Such personages irrupt into and disappear

> Outrageous anger, and woe-working jarre,
> Direful impatience, and hart-murdring love.
>
> (II.v.16)

His fate spells out the relation between passion and death, when he is metamorphosed into his own shield's emblem, *Burnt I doe burne* (II.iv.38).

> I burne, I burne, I burne then lowd he cryde,
> O how I burne with implacable fyre,
> Yet nought can quench mine inly flaming syde,
> Nor sea of licour cold, nor lake of myre,
> Nothing but death can doe me to respyre.
>
> (II.vi.44)

Passion regenerates itself—"dying dayly, dayly yet revives[s]" (45). Though it is temporarily abated by Archimago, death is indeed its only cure, and Pyrochles' failed suicide in this canto is consummated two cantos later in his battle with Arthur where, "all desperate as loathing light," he refuses the offered mercy: "I not overcome do dye, / But in despight of life, for death do call" (viii.47, 52). His quenchless fire has found its inevitable remedy. Immortality is torture for a mortal organism; but it is "natural" to Acrasia, whose eye-beams unite fire and water (the dominant elements of Book II) in sinister conjunction; her elemental powers "thrild / Fraile harts, yet quenched not" (xii.78).

The intemperance which leads men into this Garden is therefore an attempt to pass through the looking-glass and live in a world of art, to make literal that which for us is only safely encountered in imagination. "Our erected wit maketh us to know what perfection is, but our infected will keepeth us from attaining unto it." To become Acrasia's

---

from linear time; their permanence manifests a family resemblance on the abstraction ladder. Thus Spenser gives us Pyrochles' "immortall race": the son of Acrates, he can be traced through Phlegethon to "*Herebus* and *Night*; / But *Herebus* sonne of *Aeternitie* is hight" (II.iv.41). The brothers' claim to be more than mortal is firmly based.

thrall is to ignore the infection of the will. It is to aspire to the condition of the figures on Keats's Grecian Urn:

> More happy love! more happy, happy love!
>   For ever warm and still to be enjoy'd,
>   For ever panting, and for ever young;
> All breathing human passion far above,
>   That leaves a heart high-sorrowful and cloy'd,
>   A burning forehead, and a parching tongue.[19]

Passion parches us, as it does Pyrochles; those "far above" in the realms of art can enjoy it forever, but we cannot. Art can tame the destructive elements, as Stevens's jar "made the slovenly wilderness / Surround that hill." But set down in a genuine natural wilderness, Tennessee for example, all it ultimately brings is death.

The voice that chants the "lovely lay" at the center of the Bower of Bliss sings of *carpe diem*, and reminds the mortal lover that time is passing. The song, composed by a poet imitating another poet, is placed here by Spenser for the benefit primarily of his audience; its function is analogous to that of Time in the Garden of Adonis, whose puzzling presence has bemused so many readers. Both serve as salutary reminders to an alert reader; both speak over the characters' heads. But the song, of course, speaks also to Acrasia's prisoners, for as Marvell makes plain in the "Coy Mistress," the invitation to "Gather the Rose of love whilest yet is time," to narrow the pursuit to a single obsessive object, is an alternative that is the mirror-image of stretching time out into a "long love's day." Both alternatives beguile the time without redeeming it; both offer false models for the life of man. He may try to construct a heavenly bower of

---

[19] "Ode on a Grecian Urn," ll. 25-30; *Complete Poems and Selected Letters*, ed. C. D. Thorpe (New York, 1935), p. 353. The ambivalent relationship between the thirst for immortality through art or love, and the dyingness of organic life, submerged but visible in the "Grecian Urn," is elucidated by Keats in the "Bright Star" sonnet and explored at length in the "Ode to a Nightingale."

eternal bliss, a long love's day; or he may submit passively to the wheel of time that prevails in the merely natural world, carrying "the leafe, the bud, the flowre" down to darkness.

Two answers to the problem of life in time are thus offered in Acrasia's Garden, and both are unacceptable for man. They amount to the same thing in the end; both demand that the human being resign his proper humanity as the Great Amphibium, whose "goodly frame" Spenser has set out schematically in the famous "numerological stanza" of Canto ix. The "numbers" of the human constitution are both even and odd, circular and triangular:

> The one imperfect, mortall, foeminine;
> Th' other immortall, perfect, masculine.
> (II.ix.22)

The "quadrate" that mediates between the male and female principles is the well-tempered soul. This soul, in the armor of the Knight of Temperance, destroys in righteous wrath the "goodly workmanship" of bad Genius, which is bad because it offers a false mirror for man, misleading him as to his true nature, opening false options and concealing valid ones. To deny either the mortal or the immortal part of humanity is to betray it. In recognition of the "immortal, perfect" principle, the erected wit makes imaginary paradises; in recognition of the "imperfect, mortall" principle, the infected but instructed will keeps them imaginary, prophetic rather than nostalgic places of refuge. When the garden is entered by a fallen being it becomes a prison, and must be laid waste, as Milton lays it waste in *Paradise Lost,* lest we should try to re-enter it prematurely. And thus Guyon, inevitably, "of the fayrest late, now made the fowlest place" (83).

The violence of the hero's destructiveness does indeed, as many readers have suspected, draw its energy from a deep private source in the poet. But this source is not a puritanical fear of natural beauty in any simple sense; it is, rather, the rage of the artist who sees his gift of imagination abused by its dark twin, self-indulgent and self-destructive fantasy. The defacement or violation of Eden follows necessarily upon the abuse of edenic blessings, among them the blessing of imaginative innocence. Guyon's act is partly a self-protective gesture by the poet, what Wallace Stevens calls a cure of the ground. The golden world of *The Faerie Queene* encapsulates the gilded fiction of the Bower and dissolves it; a self-critical corrosiveness must be an element in valid human art. We remember that Spenser set the Bower in a context of allusions near the beginning of his description—allusions to Rhodope, Tempe "where of yore / Faire *Daphne Phoebus* hart with love did gore," Mount Ida —haunt of the gods but, more notoriously, site of the doom-burdened Judgment of Paris—Parnassus, and "*Eden* selfe" (52). All these places are either sites of memorable disaster —Ida, Eden—or, though neutral on the surface, are the scenes of particular events specified by the poet as melancholy. Daphne "gored" Apollo's heart and was herself metamorphosed; Rhodope, also a metamorphosed nymph, attracted the divine wrath and "her selfe for griefe did kill."[20] Rhodope was also the mountain where Orpheus retreated after the loss of Eurydice, and perhaps where he caused the trees to dance; this fact is interesting in light of the presence in this stanza of one famous place not obviously connected with disaster: "sweet *Parnasse*, the haunt of Muses faire." Thus surrounded by ominous portents, the reference at least raises the question of whether even the Muses' bower is immune to corruption and mortal grief. The ultimate fate of Orpheus suggests that it is not; the misgivings that Spenser arouses in this canto about the corruptibility of art confirm, and are confirmed by, this stanza.

[20] Jortin chided Spenser for this allusion: "Methinks he should not have singled out Rhodope, a mountain of Thrace, as an agreeable place. The Ancients are against him" (*Var.* II.378). Just so; but the poet is designedly "against" himself here.

In the final canto of Book II, therefore, Spenser exposes the varied duplicities of art. By forcing its artificiality upon us, it allows us to ignore the way things are "in deed," to admire the gold-and-ivory surface and forget "the boyes bloud therein shed." On the other hand, by concealing its artificiality and offering us the hope that a fictive world can be actualized, it tempts us to the abandonment of our own mortality and therefore of our humanity.

> Once out of nature I shall never take
> My bodily form from any natural thing,
> But such a form as Grecian goldsmiths make. . . .

But we are not out of nature yet. It is the great merit of Yeats's Byzantium poems that they recognize this, allowing the dying generations and "that dolphin-torn, that gong-tormented sea" to rage within the very poems that attempt to transcend them. Spenser, having practiced an ascetic self-effacement at the visionary climax of Book I, and an exorcism of the demons of art at the dénouement of Book II, prepares in the middle books to confront the flux and reflux of organic, temporal life and to see how (or whether) the mirror of art can accommodate it.

2. "Good Love": The Garden of Adonis and Belphoebe's Bower

The perpetual temptation of the artist is to become a magician. Prospero, at the conclusion of *The Tempest*, remains true to his vocation in breaking his staff and abjuring "this rough magic," acknowledging the fact that he and all the company must leave the island and return to Milan. Spenser lets us see what happens when magicians usurp the artist's powers in Book II, and he stresses, in Book III, the traditionally dubious paternity of Merlin, "wondrously begotten . . . / By false illusion of a guilefull Spright" (III.iii.13). Merlin uses his power responsibly in *The Faerie Queene*, but Spenser also records his legendary end, in thrall to the Lady of the Lake, and leaves us to meditate on this ambiguous fate. The irresponsibility of the artist turned magician panders to the restlessness endemic in the human condition, that "eternal restless change / Self-fed, and self-consumed" that Milton described as a condition of evil, though it is also the matrix for the energy that can eventually lead out of the labyrinth. "Thou hast made us for thyself, and our hearts are restless till they rest in thee." St. Augustine's poignant truth is terribly vulnerable to subversion. We are all traveling to "*Eden* laundes"; we all want to arrive there faster than we should, or by forbidden ways. This impulse is called by Milton "dis-obedience" when he sets out to trace it to its source in *Paradise Lost*; its other name is "im-patience." Its strength provides the fuel for our fatal habit of contriving false paradises, and the fatal power of the maker who can conjure them into being.

Hence we must admire the special tact of Spenser's art in Book III of *The Faerie Queene*. His cosmic poem, like all such fictions, reveals causes and sources, the reasons for "the way things are." In Book I, two of the vertical poles of

being were established: the Heaven of the "trinall triplici-
ties on high" and the New Jerusalem; the underworld
where Night has her kingdom. The latter is extended and
particularized in the description of Mammon's Cave, where
the universe's axle-tree has the form of

> a great gold chaine ylincked well,
> Whose upper end to highest heven was knit,
> And lower part did reach to lowest Hell.
>
> (II.vii.46)

Not only the virtues, but the vices, are thus linked, as Spenser demonstrates *in extenso* throughout the poem. The double resonance of the *gold* reference,[1] whose demonic aspect is explored in the Cave of Mammon, serves Spenser as
a symbol for the linkage between Heaven and Hell, which
involves an ontological continuity and a moral disjunction.
But between the two poles there lies the realm of Nature,
including human nature, where modes of being and moral
forces mingle. The peculiar difficulties of representing in
a fiction the dangerous potentialities of Nature have been
partly implied in the discussion of the Bower of Bliss. Non-
human Nature remains innocent, or at least amoral, and is
therefore not an appropriate model for the race of men who
have lost their innocence. The soul's longing to return to its
pristine state cannot, therefore, be satisfied within the natural world, however edenic it may appear. The beauties of
Nature can only adumbrate a more ultimate beauty. Those
who propose Nature as a model, like Acrasia and Comus,
are tempting human beings into a prematurely regained

---

[1] Spenser notes the duplicity of gold in *Mother Hubberds Tale*:

> That was the golden age of *Saturne* old,
> But this might better be the world of gold,
> For without golde now nothing wilbe got.
>
> (151-53)

Jonson's Lady Pecunia is another embodiment of this principle; he
plays on the Golden Age throughout *Volpone* and *The Alchemist*.

paradise, where the original harmony between man and the environment can exist only in a destructive parody-version. Having divided his soul into warring parts—Reason and Sensuality—at the Fall, the human being assents with only part of himself to this re-entry into bliss, since Right Reason (the Palmer in *The Faerie Queene*, Book II) is aware of the trap and its dangers. Everyman is weaker than the enduringly vital principles of Created Pleasure and will inevitably be overwhelmed and devoured by them unless his "higher" powers are awake. Some of these complications are dealt with by Marvell in that perfectly poised poem, "The Garden," where the presence of the poet's alert imagination holds Circean witchery at bay and dallies precariously with the devouring vegetation: "Stumbling on melons as I pass, / Ensnared with flowers, I fall on grass." The exclusion of Eve from Marvell's paradise is not mere misogyny; it implies the exclusion of the sensual principle which, as the state of man now is, prevents us from re-entering safely the secret world of "ordinary Nature."

Spenser's solution when he comes to deal with the nature of Nature in Book III anticipates Marvell in interesting ways. In "The Garden," the mind "withdraws into its happiness," and Spenser's vision of unspoiled Nature is also prepared by a withdrawal, "So hard it is for any living wight" to speak about her (VII.vii.9). In the *Mutabilitie Cantos* Nature (unlike Una) is never confronted unveiled. The poet as a man in the middest must approach her obliquely, and in Book III he does so by a manipulation of the narrative, distancing the Garden of Adonis from the foreground of the fictive present. It is the object of a quest undertaken by him, the deviser of the fiction, but not by any fictive personage in the main action. He arrives there through the byway of a sub-plot, led by the apparently casual narrative logic of the Ariostan mode. But this proves to be the instrument of his Muse's more farsighted logic, and what seemed a digression turns out to be the heart of the matter. One thing leads to another; the thread unwound half-wittingly by the poet takes us inward and downward in a movement that imitates the atavistic recoil of the psyche seeking its origins.

The august revelations of the *Cantos of Mutabilitie* do not really provide an alternative to the Bower of Bliss because they do not satisfy, as a genuine alternative must, the impulses that lead Mortdant and Verdant and all their siblings to the Bower in the first place. Spenser must somehow suggest that our physical being is a source of health as well as death. In the Bower of Bliss he shows the desperation and self-destructiveness of sensual indulgence, but he does not intend to evade the positive implications of this range of human experience in the poem as a whole. The Garden of Adonis is designed to answer some of the same needs of the human organism, but in a manner that will preserve the holiness of the heart's affections and keep intact an innocence that lies at the core of even human sexuality. It is a place which embodies the truth of the impulse in Sir Guyon to which the maidens in the fountain unsuccessfully appeal.

As that faire Starre, the messenger of morne,
  His deawy face out of the sea doth reare:
  Or as the *Cyprian* goddesse, newly borne
  Of th' Ocean's fruitfull froth, did first appeare:
  Such seemed they, and so their yellow heare
  Christalline humour dropped downe apace.
  Whom such when *Guyon* saw, he drew him neare,
  And somewhat gan relent his earnest pace,
His stubborne brest gan secret pleasaunce to embrace.
                                        (II.xii.65)

The splendor and solemnity of the allusions bear witness to the fact that we are in the presence of a mighty power, however unworthily manifested in this instance. The stanza records a genuine epiphany, and the poet honors it in the resonant stateliness of his verse. *Numen inest.* Acrasia's girls are not goddesses; a goddess is present in the Bower all the same.[2]

Spenser never underestimates this great deity and her son. Guyon seeing the maidens "gan secret pleasaunce to embrace"; misdirected in that instance, his impulse achieves its proper consummation in the secret places of the Garden of Adonis.

> There yet, some say, in secret he does ly,
> Lapped in flowres and pretious spycery,
> By her hid from the world, and from the skill
> Of *Stygian* Gods, which doe her love envy;
> But she her selfe, when ever that she will,
> Possesseth him, and of his sweetnesse takes her fill.
>
> (III.vi.46)

C. S. Lewis and many other writers have rightly applauded the frankness with which Spenser depicts these lovers, and contrasted the language of sexual communion in this stanza with the *voyeuse* Acrasia, feasting her eyes on her victim and "greedily depasturing delight" as she gazes at and kisses the sleeping Verdant. So much is true; and yet the stanzas describing Acrasia are without question more sensually exciting than anything in the Garden of Adonis canto, and the boy, "quite molten into lust and pleasure lewd," is certainly an emblem of the exhaustion of sexual passion. As I argued earlier, Spenser's rhetoric is deliberately designed, in the Bower of Bliss, to appeal to the "sensitive soul," to evoke the mindless somatic responses that so easily subvert rational temperance, and to suppress the objections that might be advanced by our severer contemplations. The Spenserian allusiveness is augmented by literal realization, so that, for example, we are not merely reminded of the

[2] The point is not affected, I think, by the fact that this stanza is derived, almost intact, from Tasso; rather, the presence of the allusion points to a similar seriousness in the Armida section of the *Gerusalemme*.

258

edenic harmonies of this paradise, but are given two actual examples of musical delight, which also suspend the narrative movement, and with it, our critical faculties. The "melodious lay" in which "Birdes, voyces, instruments, windes, waters, all agree" (II.xii.70) is reproduced in one of Spenser's virtuoso stanzas (71); shortly thereafter, we have the "lovely lay" filched from Tasso, two stanzas of irresistible persuasiveness. In contrast, though "the joyous birdes" are present in the Garden of Adonis, we do not hear them sing.

> The whiles the joyous birdes make their pastime
> Emongst the shadie leaves, their sweet abode,
> And their true loves without suspition tell abrode.
> (III.vi.42)

These lines conclude one of the few stanzas of undiluted direct description in the Garden of Adonis, and the rhetorical mode characteristically reflects the poet's approach to his subject in this canto. The *locus amoenus* is economically condensed into two heavily allusive stanzas (41-42), all of the details traditional and none engaging the poet's attention for more than a line or two, as he hastens toward the garden's center and its mysteries. Descriptive physical details alternate with the names of emotions, chiefly destructive emotions that are here excluded: "fell rancor, or fond gealosie," envy, suspicion. The effect is to surround the innocent physical details with a penumbra of knowingness on the part of the narrator—and, of course, the reader, who is acquainted with all the negative feelings associated with fallen love. Such counterpoint between innocence and experience is a feature, in one way or another, of most literary paradises; from it grows nostalgia, the enabling emotion of pastoral literature.[3] In stanzas 41-42, Spenser offers us a

---

[3] As Spenser launches into his description of Acrasia's garden, he offers a traditional stanza on the temperate weather; Nature permits

capsule version of this paradigm, an almost cursory instance of the way in which erected wit and infected will cooperate in the imaginative evocation of golden worlds.

The golden world *itself* is scarcely dwelt upon at all in its merely physical aspect. And that is because Spenser is dealing here with a kind of meaning that is both deeper and higher, or more general, than the direct mirroring of the mind's desires reflected in mimetic fantasies and exemplified in the Bower of Bliss. First of all, deeper: the experience imaged in Venus and Adonis lies below the level of consciously pleasurable "delight" associated with the isolated intemperate sexuality of Acrasia. Spenser is exploring what we mean by a source, a "sacred noursery" not merely of virtue, but of life itself. "Both Bower and Garden descend to a substratum, and show love not as a social form but as a natural appetite."[4] The substratum of the Bower lies, however, only just beneath the surface of "social form," and social forms themselves are often rationalized or ritualized developments of it. The substratum revealed in the Garden is the inarticulate life-force, the Freudian Eros at its eternal war with Thanatos; it involves a mode of experience that lies outside verbalization or, rather, renders words otiose, being, itself, simple, obvious, and profound. To capture it Spenser employs a style simple, sensuous, and passionate, but unlike the exposed and exhibitionist sensuality of the Bower, where, although the place is reached after the traverse of "many covert groves, and thickets close," there is nothing really private about the experience offered, "bare to readie spoyle / Of hungry eies." Compare this deeply moving journey to the interior:

> Right in the middest of that Paradise,
>   There stood a stately Mount, on whose round top

"Nor scorching heat, nor cold intemperate / T'afflict the creatures, which therein did dwell" (II.xii.51). But there is no parallel to the warding-off of dangerous emotions; rather, the stanza that follows contains the allusive catalogue of lovers' agonies (*supra*, p. 252).

[4] Lewis, *Images of Life*, p. 45.

A gloomy grove of mirtle trees did rise,
Whose shadie boughes sharpe steele did never lop,
Nor wicked beasts their tender buds did crop,
But like a girlond compassed the hight,
And from their fruitfull sides sweet gum did drop,
That all the ground with precious deaw bedight,
Threw forth most dainty odours, and most sweet delight.

(III.vi.43)

Of course this stanza "is" among other things a description
of the Mount of Venus; but the erotic anatomical suggestion
is undergirded by still deeper instincts and impulses, including the profound affinity of human beings with the
earth that breeds them, which makes possible metaphorical
linkages between the world's body and human anatomy.
The fact that we know this place sexually does not preclude
imaginative knowledge, but rather reinforces it. Here
"wicked beasts" do no harm, either because they cannot
enter this magic place, or because no beast *is* wicked here.
We are approaching a world of innocence where lions become golden and gentle—they no longer "rush dreadful."

> Saying: wrath by his meekness
> And by his health, sickness,
> Is driven away,
> From our immortal day.[5]

The meekness and health of Adonis turn aside the wrath of
fallen bestiality.

His bower is at the top of a mount, but Spenser contrives
to minimize the sensation of moving *up*; he leads us through
a labyrinth of foliage, among trees that tower over us, drop-
ping their "precious deaw." "In the thickest covert of that
shade" is the arbor itself where, again, the spectator has the
sense of an approach from below to within:

> With wanton yvie twyne entrayld athwart,
> And Eglantine, and Caprifole emong,

5 Blake, "Night," ll. 37-40; *Poetry and Prose*, p. 14.

> Fashiond above within their inmost part,
> That nether *Phoebus* beams could through them
> throng.
> Nor *Aeolus* sharp blast could worke them any wrong.
>
> (vi.44)

The sense of coming into a small, protected, intimately enclosed space probably satisfies an atavistic urge in all of us;
Milton learned from Spenser's stanzas when he came to
write of Adam and Eve's bower, where the effect of penetrating layer after layer as one approaches a center is vastly
elaborated. And, at this center, "in secret . . . hid from the
world," lies Adonis.

Like most other mountaintop paradises, this one appears
to be situated at the boundary of the celestial universe.[6]
Spenser's treatment of it, however, is consistent with his
quest for sources in Book III; in psychic terms, we tend to
think of sources as centers, a habit of imagining sustained,
perhaps inspired, by erotic fantasy. Donne's profane, punning, mock-heroic yet serious version of Love's Progress
in his eighteenth Elegy offers images coordinate with
Spenser's.

> Search every spheare
> And firmament, our *Cupid* is not there:
> He's an infernal god and under ground,
> With *Pluto* dwells, where gold and fire abound:
> Men to such Gods, their sacrificing Coles
> Did not in Altars lay, but pits and holes.
> Although we see Celestial bodies move
> Above the earth, the earth we Till and love.[7]

"We love the Centrique part." Spenser affirms the imaginative principles suggested here in *Mutabilitie*, when he ad-

---

[6] For commentary on this *topos*, see Frye, *Fables of Identity*, pp.
59-60.

[7] "Loves Progress" (Elegie XVIII), ll. 27-34; *The Elegies and the
Songs and Sonnets*, ed. Helen Gardner (Oxford, 1965), p. 17.

mits the chthonic deities to the parley on Arlo Hill: "*Pluto* and *Proserpina* were present there" (VII.vii.3). The cosmography of *The Faerie Queene* distinguishes between truly infernal powers—Night, Archimago, Mammon—and the "underground" energies that are part of Nature. The marriage of Pluto and Proserpina explains the revolution of the seasons within the fallen natural world; Adonis embraced by Venus is an image of that process.[8]

The secret center occupies Spenser for a single eloquent stanza in Canto vi; though "hid from the world," it is not hidden from imagination. But the poet preserves his humility: "There yet, *some say*, in secret he does ly." As, in *Mutabilitie*, he defers to his literary progenitors, so here Spenser invokes the anonymous *some* and *they* whose mythmaking has recurrently offered visions of the deepest truths known to man. Visceral or carnal knowledge, deeper than words, shapes itself in myths, profound images of what the body knows. But in the next stanza, Spenser returns to an alternative, though complementary, kind of knowledge. It too is remote from ordinary conscious experience, invisible, but accessible to imagination. In the "sooth" of the *conceptual* model is embodied the divine design that regulates the life-process imaged in the embrace of Venus and Adonis. To understand the meaning of sexual love, imagination must not only descend, but ascend.

"And sooth it seemes they say"; thus begins stanza 47, in which the poet reverts to the philosophical language that dominates his first survey of the Garden. Both parts of the description, the general and the concrete, are what "they say," versions of imagination's untiring effort to make visi-

[8] Adonis "is the entire biological cycle, conceived as subsisting in the *aevum*" (Kermode, *Sense of an Ending*, p. 78). Spenser is not altogether consistent in naming his underworld deities; context must be the determining factor. The "griesly *Pluto*" who is the sire of Lucifera (I.iv.11) is a stand-in for Satan; the Pluto and Proserpina of the *Mutabilitie Cantos* are Claudian's and Chaucer's: "Pluto, that is kyng of Fayerye" and "the queene Proserpyna, / Which that he ravysshed out of Ethna" (*Merch T* E.2227, 2229-30).

ble to the inner eye an ultimately imageless truth. One aspect of this truth in the Garden of Adonis is below the threshold of consciousness, and for it Spenser uses a mythic, obliquely articulated *image*. The other aspect is transcendent, beyond the limit of ordinary apprehension in an opposite direction, and for it he makes a *model*. "An image shows how something appears; a model shows how something works."[9] Although Spenser does not always employ his philosophical language lucidly or consistently, it is clear that he is partly concerned with process, with how the generative force "works," not merely with how one feels when participating in it. The juxtapositions and conjunctions in stanzas 30-40 are designed to suggest simultaneous relationships that may be experienced temporally or serially—that is, incompletely—by individuals involved in them. Cruel Cupid lays aside his "sad darts" in this place because when the life-process is viewed as a whole, instead of in the segments of unique lives where we ordinarily encounter it, it is endlessly triumphant and enduring. When we look at time from a sufficiently distant point, it appears as a spatial pattern, within which what we call birth and death can be seen as arrivals and departures.

> After that they againe returned beene,
>   They in that Gardin planted be againe;
>   And grow afresh, as they had never seene
>   Fleshly corruption, nor mortall paine.
>   Some thousand yeares so doen they there remaine;
>   And then of him are clad with other hew,
>   Or sent into the chaungefull world againe,
>   Till thither they returne, where first they grew:
> So like a wheele around they runne from old to new.
>   (III.vi.33)

The wheel of the final image is anticipated in the verbal wheels of the first eight lines; *returned* of line 1 comes around again in *returne* of line 8, and *againe* occurs thrice,

9 Langer, *Mind*, I, xix.

twice as a rhyme-word. The eye of the mind can "see" a thousand years as a turning wheel, and record its vision in a metaphor, or rather a sequence of metaphors. Each of Spenser's stanzas speaks of a different aspect of the phenomenon; to read them as a narrative progress or perambulation, like Marvell's tour of the estate in *Upon Appleton House*, is to translate his metaphors too literally. Analysis, in terms of human rationality, entails discursiveness; in fact, stanzas 30 through 40 need to be imaginatively superimposed, since they are simultaneous aspects of a single though complex idea: the point at which temporality and eternity, the material and the immaterial, unite to create the source of our mixed being.

Humphrey Tonkin has suggested that "It is characteristic of Spenser's narrative technique that when he wants to discuss principles or concepts he organizes them spatially,"[10] and he reminds us that spatial terms must be read as metaphors in the opening description of the Garden. Spenser gives us a diagram of the idea of generation, not a map; this "place" exists in the make of the mind, and like the mountaintop of Book VI it is a situation which "none can find, but who was taught them by the Muse" (VI.Pro.2). Spenser says, "I wote not well" where it is, refusing to commit himself to any of the visible haunts of Venus.

> But well I wote by triall, that this same
> All other pleasaunt places doth excell.
> (III.vi.29)

"I wote by triall" implies that the poet has experienced the pleasures of the Garden and also that he has visited them "deep within the mind," where alone sacred nurseries can be approached. He proceeds inductively, on a quest to discover what Herbert called "the callow principles within

[10] "Spenser's Garden of Adonis and Britomart's Quest," *PMLA* LXXXVIII (1973), 409.

their nest." Induction is a process of abstraction; but, as Bacon was soon to insist, its end-product is "not empty notions, but well defined, . . . and such as lie at the heart and marrow of things." In Bacon's topography of the mind, concrete language is employed for these "most general" notions. Bacon sees that general principles are, or ought to be, full of *content*, "not empty notions" but comprehensively significant ones. He uses terminology appropriate to essence and source, at once subjective and objective: "the depths of the mind," "the very bowels of nature." His purpose is to weight the heels of the investigator and direct his path inward and downward toward "the heart and marrow of things," where lie the first principles in all their fullness of implication.

> Now what the sciences stand in need of is a form of induction which shall analyse experience and take it to pieces. . . . And if that ordinary mode of judgment practised by the logicians was so laborious, and found exercise for such great wits, how much more labour must we be prepared to bestow upon this other, which is extracted not merely out of the depths of the mind, but out of the very bowels of nature.[11]

The logic of Spenser's progress follows the dictates of imagination, not of Baconian induction. But he too is led in and down on a journey toward the "huge eternall *Chaos*, which supplyes / The substances of natures fruitfull progenyes" (36). As in Bacon's diagram, this "most general" concept is reached near the end, and nothing could be a less "empty notion."

An inductive model (stanzas 30-41) and a traditional image (42-46) cooperate, therefore, to take the reader of *The Faerie Queene* away from the quotidian visible world to a place of ultimate deep hopes and fears lying at the center of both his own psyche and great creating Nature.

11 *The Great Instauration; Selected Writings*, pp. 442-43.

266

Microcosm and macrocosm are superimposed, and the power that shapes both in the same image is love. The poet makes this point in designing the narrative sequence at the beginning of Canto vi, which expresses the quest for sources and beginnings that is a major motive of the action of the middle books. The canto begins with the poet's promise to satisfy questions about the nature—that is, the source —of Belphoebe, by recounting her birth. The two newborn children, product of an innocent sexuality that is a paradigm of love within "mere Nature," are discovered by Venus and Diana in the process of their search for Cupid: that is, for Love, the source of all truly natural births. The goddesses' effort "To search the God of love" (vi.26) modulates into the poet's search for the Garden of Adonis, which "is" Love itself, as Cupid's harmless presence reveals in the end (vi.49).

The Garden of Adonis is a legitimate paradise because it is visited only by the poet, or the imagination. It satisfies our desire for immortality within Nature, where we are "by succession made perpetuall" (vi.47). There is another garden of the mind in Book III, where imagination anticipates a different sort of immortality: an ultimate bliss in the kingdom of archetypes. Belphoebe's bower is literal within the fictional foreground; a human character, Timias, is taken there, but he can remain only if he observes very stringent conditions.

The images of ascent that dominate the story of Belphoebe and Timias provide a clue to the nature of the experience, and contrast with the movements of descent and retreat in the Garden of Adonis. In the very long run, the way up and the way down may be the same, and Spenser makes the "ensamples" of his two kinds of love twin sisters; but in a human context one sort of love excludes the other. Heavenly love is defined in the canto preceding the vision of carnal love; together, they express the yearnings of the spirit and the flesh. To love Belphoebe is to mount the Platonic ladder in the manner prescribed by Bembo at the conclusion of the *Cortegiano*. Timias, who aspires to become such a lover, learns with difficulty to follow this program, which must be begun by laying aside "the blinde judgement of the sense."

> Whereupon the soule taketh a delite, and with a
> certaine wonder is agast, and yet enjoyeth she it, and
> (as it were) astonied together with the pleasure,
> feeleth the feare and reverence that men accustom-
> ably have towarde holy matters and thinketh her
> selfe to be in Paradise.[12]

We see this process, or at least its beginning, when Timias is rescued by Belphoebe after having suffered the wounds of lust; the "blinde judgement of the sense" is figured in the ambush of the three foresters who wait in "a covert glade" "with thicke woods overgrowne" (v.17). He awakens to "holy matters" in a garden of delight.

> Planted with mirtle trees and laurels greene,
> In which the birds song many a lovely lay
> Of gods high prayse, and of their loves sweet teene,
> As it an earthly Paradize had beene.
>
> (III.v.40)

Timias does not complete his education in the sage and seri-ous doctrine of virginity until he has suffered the "fall" and exile of Book IV; but already he knows instinctively that he must, as Bembo recommends, "recken her more deare to him than his owne life": "Dye rather, dye, then ever from her service swerve" (v.46). He dwells safely within Bel-phoebe's bower as long as he is faithful to the kind of love proper to her—a love, Castiglione assures us, that is "en-joyed" deep within the mind, in the imagination: "through

---

[12] Baldassare Castiglione, *The Book of the Courtier*, tr. Thomas Hoby, Everyman's Library (London, 1948), p. 316. Quotations later in this paragraph are from pp. 313 and 317.

the vertue of imagination, hee shall fashion with himselfe that beautie much more faire than it is in deede." The Platonic lover knows, or should know, that no literal embodiment of perfection can match the ideal which he is capable of imagining.

It is futile to deplore Belphoebe's "unjust" treatment of Timias when she finds him comforting Amoret in Book IV; she deserts him because he cannot have both her and her twin at once. They must be loved in different ways, and love of one excludes love of the other. The interpolated episode of Timias' exile and eventual reconciliation, with its sentimental machinery of dove and heart, probably owes its form to the circumstances of the Ralegh allusion;[13] even so, it sheds some light on the peculiar difficulties that may arise when life imitates art, when a human being—Queen though she may be—tries to demand the kind of allegiance proper to an ideal, or when men vest their ideals in an actual personage, however lofty. (Ontological disparity can also, however, be an appropriate figure for the social distance that separated Queen and courtier.)

Belphoebe's bower contrasts with Phaedria's island and other false or true paradises in *The Faerie Queene* not in its intrinsic nature—they are all versions of the *locus amoenus*—but in its imaginative status. Cymochles comes to the island willfully, to drown himself in ease and enjoy infantile unmanly pleasures, among them the pleasure of literalizing his desires. Timias comes to the "earthly Paradize" when he is unconscious; his awakening is like Adam's when he found his dream truth. In this waking dream the enraptured soul enjoys the "fruit of honour and all chast desire" (52): what Bembo calls "the fruites of most beautiful conditions," produced by the "sowing of vertue in the garden of that minde" that nourishes "vertue virginall."[14] As it

---

[13] The Ralegh/Spenser relationship is set out in Walter Oakeshott, *The Queen and the Poet* (London, 1960), pp. 81-99. See also H. M. English, Jr., "Spenser's Accommodation of Allegory to History in the Story of Timias and Belphoebe," *JEGP* LIX (1960), 417-29.

[14] *Courtier*, p. 314.

is created and contemplated by the mind, so it must be enjoyed only in the imagination's garden. Although Spenser is very far from recommending this kind of love as the only legitimate one, it must be included in *The Faerie Queene*, for it is a persistent resource of humanity, caught in the predicament eloquently described by Yeats: "the tragedy of sexual intercourse is the perpetual virginity of souls."[15] Longing for a different sort of communion, the soul finds it in one of imagination's golden worlds.

The Garden of Adonis and Belphoebe's bower are images of "good love," answers to the Bower of Bliss and Phaedria's island where "bad love" spreads its toils. Both are essential to Spenser's design in *The Faerie Queene*, where the secrets of all things must be revealed. Medieval exegetes knew that all the phenomena could be interpreted *in bono* and *in malo*; Spenser exposes the dubiety of allegorical reading and grounds it in the ambiguous powers of imagining, when he places Bower and Garden at the cores of Books II and III. The mind makes for itself healthy or unhealthy environments out of the "huge eternall *Chaos*" of hurtless and helpless Nature. To discover it at its invisible work, the poet can journey where he needs to go. He can "descend to a substratum, and show love . . . as a natural appetite"; he can also ascend, and show love as "an unnatural rage" in which the released soul finds a congenial resting-place as it prepares for a longer flight.

15 Yeats's remark was recorded by several of his friends but apparently appears nowhere in his writing. See A. Norman Jeffares, *A Commentary on the Complete Poems of W. B. Yeats* (London, 1968), p. 372.

3. Amoret and Belphoebe

Between the highly charged termini of the symbolic places in the middle books moves the field of folk subject to the rule of great Venus, those who must choose their fates.

> Wonder it is to see, in diverse minds
> How diversly love doth his pageants play,
> And shewes his powre in variable kinds:
> The baser wit, whose idle thoughts alway
> Are wont to cleave unto the lowly clay,
> It stirreth up to sensuall desire,
> And in lewd slouth to wast his carelesse day:
> But in brave spirite it kindles goodly fire,
> That to all high desert and honour doth aspire.
>
> (III.v.1)

Among the diverse minds are Cymochles, wasting his careless day in lewd sloth, in bondage to the lowly clay; and Timias, in whom the vision of Belphoebe kindles goodly fire.

Spenser's investigation of the many faces of Venus is supported within a structure of envisaged principles, in particular the twins, Amoret and Belphoebe. The Garden and Bower associated with them give important clues to their nature; I want now to turn directly to these important figures themselves and to describe more precisely their ontological status and the roles which that status defines for them. As Roche perceives, Belphoebe and Amoret are ontologically distinct from Britomart and the other human characters; they "are archetypes or universals."[1] The first of these terms is more appropriate than the second. A univer-

[1] *Kindly Flame*, p. 96. Lewis calls Belphoebe "an archetype," related to Artemis in *Hippolytus* and Diana in *Comus* (*Images of Life*, p. 47).

sal is a derived abstraction, an archetype a comprehensive model from which subsidiary instances are derived, which is precisely the relation between these twins and Britomart; as it is also the relation, moving further up the scale, between the twins and the divine sisters, Venus and Diana.

Spenser's myth of the twins' birth, engendered by the Sun upon a nymph "yborne of high degree" (vi.3), is also an effort to make visible to us a kind of reality not available experientially, in "real life." Chrysogonee conceives the twins "farre from all mens vew," a phrase habitually used by Spenser as a sign that he is moving into a realm of being that we must approach conceptually, and which can be "viewed" only by the imagination. Spenser interprets the myth in a stanza which explains that its events belong to the order of Nature:

> Miraculous may seeme to him, that reades
> So straunge ensample of conception;
> But reason teacheth that the fruitfull seades
> Of all things living, through impression
> Of the sunbeames in moyst complexion,
> Doe life conceive and quickned are by kynd.
> (III.vi.8)

The myth expresses a mystery, but not a miracle: "wondrously they were begot and bred" (6), but the wonder is an ordinary one, though not less wondrous for that. It is the life-process expressed at a level of generality which lies beyond even the reflection of it in the figure of Adonis. There, an immortal principle embraces a mortal being: an energy that outlasts its forms assumes a specific form, or many successive ones. This is the generative process as we know it. But the embrace of the nymph's body by the sunbeams unites two immortal principles: the life-force and matter, the "Great father . . . of generation" and "his faire sister." The incestuous brother/sister relationship suggests that the "two" principles are really aspects of a single auto-reproductive power. This process is something that does not "exist" for us except insofar as we can think about it and devise metaphors or myths for it.[2] "Reason teacheth" that every particular instance of engendering participates in this archetypal process; it is not known in unmediated experience. Spenser's observation that Belphoebe was created "Pure and unspotted from all loathly crime, / That is ingenerate in fleshly slime" (3) refers principally to the virginity of the character, but it can also be true of the process —"her whole creation"—because that process is the archetypal principle of generation as it was originally dictated by God. It can still be perceived by the erected wit, and can thus "exist" within the boundaries of Fairy Land, the land of imagination.[3]

The mode of existence of Belphoebe and Amoret in the ontological hierarchy of *The Faerie Queene* is established in the concluding stanzas of Cantos v and vi in Book III. Belphoebe is to be "a faire ensample" for human women (v.54); Amoret is brought forward "To be th' ensample of true love alone" (vi.52). *Exemplum* in the rhetoric books is synonymous with *paradigma*;[4] the logical category of paradigm, ensample, or archetype in *The Faerie Queene* is made up of characters like the twins or Arthur who are "ideal" models of perfection, mirrors of the potentiality

[2] Alpers' description of Chrysogonee is exact: "she is a model of human fertility and thus of the naturalness of human love, but she is not a model of human experience" (*Poetry of "The Faerie Queene,"* p. 391).

[3] Roche may be right to see the conception of the twins as "an analogue to the Incarnation" (*Kindly Flame*, p. 106); the language of Stanza 3 suggests it. But the relationship, if present at all, is peculiar; if Spenser means us to think of the Incarnation, he intends us to regard it as the sole instance *in history* of the perfected life-process which we know, ordinarily, only in imagination, in myths like that of Canto vi.

[4] *Exemplum* and *paradigma* are identified with each other in Isidore's *Etymologies*, I.xxxvii.31, 34; *Isidori Hispalensis Episcopi Etymologiarum sive Originum Libri XX*, ed. W. M. Lindsay (2 vols., Oxford, 1911). Henry Peacham says that "Paradigma is the same which the Latines called *Exemplum*, and we in English an example"; *exempla* may be drawn from history, or "made up," invented. This figure "is of great force to move, perswade, and enflame men with the love of vertue" (*Garden of Eloquence*, pp. 186-87).

which imagination continues to cherish even in its darkness. They belong to the "golden generation of mortal people" born into Hesiod's *Works and Days* and regularly reimagined since then.[5] In Spenser's poem they demonstrate the process described by Dame Nature in *Mutabilitie*: they "worke their owne perfection." Arthur is "perfected in the twelve private morall vertues," a living proof of the principle which undergirds *The Faerie Queene*, that the virtues are linked together by a "Goodly golden chaine" (I.ix.1). He is the appropriate lover of Gloriana, who manifests the ingathering of feminine virtue, "glory" being, like "magnificence," a blanket term or containing concept. Together they would compose a perfect hermaphroditic regal personage combining sun and moon, justice and mercy: the models for virtuous individuals in the realm of *human* history, i.e., Britomart and Artegal.

Amoret, Spenser says, "to perfect ripenesse grew" in the Garden; the plant growing into its perfection is a metaphor for the way in which time's creatures "their being doe dilate" toward complete realization of the ideal. This process rarely occurs within fallen nature, but paradigmatic characters are imagination's means of reminding us that it ought to occur.[6] Such characters are paradoxically related to temporality; they belong to that intermediate kind of time called *aevum*. Spenser is careful to note the births of

[5] *Hesiod*, tr. Richmond Lattimore (Ann Arbor, 1959), p. 31.

[6] Among the "antique books" that offer myths congruent with Spenser's is Bernard Silvestris' *Cosmographia*, where one finds the "metaphors of motherhood and birth that seemed to him to best express the elusive, creative aspects of substance."

> Matter, so to speak the nature and spirit of the world, although it does not seem to be born from the beginning, nonetheless has in itself the power and nature of being born and giving birth. . . .
> The material substance of the world, although it is not born, yet contains within itself the latent properties of all things since . . . it presents a highly fertile womb for conceiving.

The quotation is from the Hermetic *Asclepius*, one of the sources of Bernard's myth. (Brian Stock, *Myth and Science in the Twelfth Century* [Princeton, 1972], pp. 104-105.)

Arthur, Belphoebe, and Amoret, though these births are "heavenly" (II.iii.21); they do not occur *in* the Garden, the kingdom of mutable forms. Like aeviternity, of which they are denizens, they have a beginning but no end. Spenser refers to Belphoebe's "ensample dead" (III.v.54), but she is dead only in the sense that she was visible in Fairy Land, far away and long ago. She is perpetually resuscitated, like Arthur, whose legendary immortality—*rex quondam rexque futurus*—suggests his participation in this peculiar temporal mode.

An exact description of Belphoebe's ontological nature can be found in Samuel Daniel's account of the deities in his masque, *A Vision of the Twelve Goddesses*, who

> vouchsafe to recreate themselves upon this western
> mount of mighty Brittany, the land of civil music and
> rest, and are pleased to appear in the self-same figures
> wherein antiquity hath formerly clothed them and as
> they have been cast in the imagination of piety, who
> hath given mortal shapes to the gifts and effects of an
> eternal power for those beautiful characters of sense
> were easier to be read than their mystical *Ideas* dispersed
> in that wide and incomprehensible volume of nature.
> And well have mortal men apparelled all the graces,
> all the blessings, all virtues, with that shape wherein
> themselves are much delighted and which work the best
> motions and best represent the beauty of heavenly
> powers.[7]

Such beings are recurrently "recreated" by the pious imagination seeking to realize its intuitions. An example close to our own time is provided by Yeats:

> How shall I name you, immortal, mild, proud shadows?
> I only know that all we know comes from you,
> And that you come from Eden on flying feet.
> Is Eden far away, or do you hide

[7] *A Book of Masques, In Honour of Allardyce Nicoll* (Cambridge, 1967), p. 32.

275

From human thought, as hares and mice and coneys
That run before the reaping-hook and lie
In the last ridge of the barley? Do our woods
And winds and ponds cover more quiet woods,
More shining winds, more star-glimmering ponds?
Is Eden out of time and out of space?[8]

Belphoebe's glade, mountains, and "mighty woods" (v.39) belong to the same visionary geography.

When Timias awakens from his swoon and sees Belphoebe, he thinks she is an angel.

> Mercy deare Lord (said he) what grace is this,
>   That thou hast shewed to me sinfull wight,
>   To send thine Angell from her bowre of blis,
>   To comfort me in my distressed plight?
>   Angell, or Goddesse doe I call thee right?
>   (III.v.35)

But Belphoebe is only the fosterling of a divinity, and her modest reply associates her with other "mortall wights" (36). Timias' mistake is an advertent one, however, for angels, in Aquinas' scheme, are the principal denizens of the *aevum*.

> Angels . . . have, as regards their nature, an
> unchangeable being with changeableness as regards
> choice; moreover with changeableness of acts of
> understanding, of affections, and of places, in their
> own degree. Therefore, these are measured by
> aeviternity, which is a mean between eternity and
> time.
>   (*BW* I.81)

And Belphoebe is an angel-like being in another important way. As *aevum* mediates between time and eternity, so aeviternal beings mediate between men in the middest and their ultimate destination. "Ensamples" are fetched by God

8 Prologue to *The Shadowy Waters; Collected Poems*, pp. 401-402.

out of their "native place"; reaching down into time, he offers us models to lead us out of time.

> Eternall God in his almighty powre,
>   To make ensample of his heavenly grace,
>   In Paradize whilome did plant this flowre,
>   Whence he it fetcht out of her native place,
>   And did in stocke of earthly flesh enrace,
>   That mortall men her glory should admire.
>   (III.v.52)

God descends to man through such "ensamples," and through them we reascend to him. Planting and growing "up" make an inevitable metaphor for this process. Another is the ladder on which angels move to and fro between heaven and earth as mediators of divine compassion. Belphoebe performs this role too.

> Providence heavenly passeth living thought,
>   And doth for wretched mens reliefe make way;
>   For loe great grace or fortune thither brought
>   Comfort to him, that comfortless now lay.
>   (III.v.27)

The grace of providential concern is invoked by Timias himself, and we are encouraged to think of an earlier instance:

> How oft do they, their silver bowers leave,
>   To come to succour us, that succour want?
>   (II.viii.2)

These lines refer to the true angels, and Belphoebe is not one of them, though she too lives in a bower and brings "succor [to] wretched wights." But she is an angel-like being, imagined by the same need to envisage a mediate perfection that caused the angels themselves to come into being, for they too are earth-born, ultimately creatures of the human imagination. The "succour" all these figures bring is an alleviation of man's creaturely bondage to the limits of his mere earthiness. *Agape*, the heavenly power that condescends ("Meekely she bowed downe," v.31), is also the power that kindles in us the desire to ascend. Angels belong to the official version of this imagined reality; Belphoebe, a member of a cadet branch, incarnates the same desires. They endow the soul with upward mobility or, more accurately, witness to and foster its own heaven-born longing to return to its native place. Timias' gratitude is offered to the one "That hast from darkenesse me returnd to light" (III.v.35), and the phrase must be read in at least two senses. Belphoebe represents the "high bountie, which with her voice calleth and draweth to her al thinges."[9]

We can, therefore, speak of the twins as ideals, if we recognize that the word is too pale for the complexly imagined beings in which the Renaissance imagination figured forth its utopian and anagogic desires. Timias' awakening establishes Belphoebe's "celestiall" origin; she is also "mortal" in the sense that she is entertained by, and perceived in, the imaginations of "mortal wights."

These paradigmatic figures who embody humanity's recurrent dreams of perfection must be distinguished from personifications, and such distinctions can conveniently be made with reference to modes of temporality. The personified characters produced by analytical allegory refine our understanding of concepts by allowing us to observe them in action, but within Spenser's fiction they have only a local life. Their *ad hoc* incarnations sink beneath the narrative surface and are re-absorbed as it moves along; they are left behind, killed, forgotten, or otherwise disposed of—the

[9] Castiglione, *Courtier*, p. 320. The Christian doctrine of *agape* and *eros* was reformulated in the Renaissance. "The bounty bestowed by the gods upon lower beings was conceived by the Neoplatonists as a kind of overflowing (*emanatio*), which produced a vivifying rapture or conversion (called by Ficino *conversio*, *raptio*, or *vivificatio*) whereby the lower beings were drawn back to heaven and rejoined the gods (*remeatio*)" (Wind, *Pagan Mysteries*, p. 37).

most visible and comic instance being the evaporation of Orgoglio. Certain other personages in *The Faerie Queene* disappear and reappear, and in them Spenser is pointing to philosophical absolutes which have a "real" non-subjective status; they "exist" whether or not any mind is attending to them. Such personages are eternal and therefore, in the fiction, immortal: Duessa, Archimago, Despair, Acrasia. Ensamples or paradigms, on the other hand, are implicated in time, particularly the history of imagining, and their temporal dimension is normally indicated by attaching them to history, pseudo-history, or legend; they participate in history though they do not belong to it. In the Letter to Ralegh, Spenser cites Homer's heroes along with Aeneas, Orlando, and Rinaldo/Godfredo as "ensamples" of various excellences. The most conspicuous example is Arthur, "the image of a brave knight," a character not "made up" by the poet, but discovered in the Matter of Britain.

Spenser did, of course, "make up" Belphoebe and Amoret, but they too, in different ways, are presented so as to suggest their peculiar ontological status as beings that participate more completely than ordinary "mortal wights" in a realized perfection of being. This fullness of being can be indicated by weightiness, elaboration, and resonance of detail, and so it is with Arthur and Belphoebe, who are the subjects of Spenser's most extended, spectacular descriptive *tours de force*. In these passages he is attempting to clear imaginative spaces large enough, and fill them richly enough, to strike responsive chords in every reader no matter what his private history and tastes. It is not an accident that these descriptions have been praised as being especially "poetical"; in them the poet is creating concrete universals, the very stuff of poetry.

The blazon of Belphoebe in II.iii is, as Berger and others have indicated, expansive, cumulative, additive. Attributes are joined to attributes, allusions to allusions, decoration to decoration, in an effort to compose an inclusive image that will allow us to read in this character a wealth of significance that enables her to function in the poem as both a source and a goal of human action.[10] In the process, Spenser alludes to many of the different contexts within which human beings have expressed the power exerted over them by the notion of a love that transcends earthly limits and confirms our sense of an unsatisfied power within us. Among these contexts—scriptural, Neo-Platonic, Petrarchan—Spenser inserts an unspecific stanza at once eloquent and taciturn.

> Upon her eyelids many Graces sate,
>> Under the shadow of her even browes,
>> Working belgards, and amorous retrate,
>> And every one her with a grace endowes:
>> And every one with meekenesse to her bowes.
>> So glorious mirrhour of celestiall grace,
>> And soveraine moniment of mortall vowes,
>> How shall fraile pen descrive her heavenly face,
> For feare through want of skill her beautie to disgrace?
>>>> (II.iii.25)

As usual, Spenser does not employ the "Topos of Inexpressibility" carelessly; it almost always appears in *The Faerie Queene* at a point where in a genuine sense the subject is too lofty, protean, or complex to be pinned down in lan-

---

[10] Harry Berger's elaborate discussion of Stanza 31 makes it clear that the two exemplars belong to different realms, and to Diana and Penthesilea we might attach the terms "goal" and "source," respectively. "The Diana image focuses on a distinctly nonhistorical quality . . . the Penthesilea image evokes a context of history" (*Allegorical Temper*, pp. 126-27). Berger identifies Belphoebe primarily with the first, however, and emphasizes the difference between her and Penthesilea. But Belphoebe is both like and different from both. She exists between the genuine immortals who live in Heaven (or such surrogates as Olympus)—the realm of essences—and the stream of history. These two realms are represented in the stanza by Diana, for whose eternal presentness the present tense is used ("Wandreth alone . . ."); and by Penthesilea, whose epiphany to Priam occurred at a particular moment ("That day that first . . ."). Belphoebe is "like" them both; she is a mediating figure, the human imagination's embodied apprehension of perfected life in time, a self-generated model.

guage. Each reader can fill in these outlines as he chooses, select whichever of the unspecified "many Graces" he likes. Belphoebe is the object of many "mortall vowes" throughout history, our own included. The stanza's effect is to emphasize the literary quality of the entire description, encouraging us to see Belphoebe as a figure beyond the reach of expression while at the same time acknowledging her as one of the reasons why we find expression necessary. It is a technique appropriate to the subject within the ontological scheme of the poem.

The paradigmatic characters of *The Faerie Queene*, though not personifications in the usual sense, belong to and affect the continued metaphor of the allegory. As Aquinas said of aeviternal beings, they are endowed with "changeableness of acts of understanding, of affections, and of places," and quite capable of participation in the allegorical action. Most often they function as catalysts, evoking in those who encounter them intense reactions that produce motives. At her first appearance, in Book II, Belphoebe puts down Braggadocchio, the knight of vain-glory, and instructs him in the "painfull toile" required for the achievement of true honor (II.iii.40). But he burns for her "in filthy lust" (iii.42); his desire for honor is contaminated by self-love and worldly ends, notably the desire for advancement at court, which he describes as the seat of "happie blis / And all delight" (39). His scorn for the arduous self-discipline of pursuit and his mistaken view that "The wood is fit for beasts, the court is fit for thee," is echoed more seriously in Book IV when Timias takes to the wood and becomes beastlike. The wood of the world is something to master, not succumb to, and that mastery, not the scramble for favor, is the true source of "honour."[11] The interaction of Belphoebe with her two human lovers, the false and the true, is informative within the allegory. And the epiphany of Book II

[11] On the Timais/Belphoebe story as "an allegory of honor," see Roche, *Kindly Flame*, pp. 143-48; he assigns a narrower meaning to *honor* than I would wish to do.

is not merely parodistic; even the base knight and his squire are capable of recognizing and of responding to, however mistakenly, an ideal of behavior. Trompart, like Timias later, acknowledges Belphoebe as something unique: "For who can tell . . . / But that she is some powre celestiall?" and the knight concurs:

> And I (said *Braggadocchio*) thought no lesse,
> When first I heard her horne sound with such
> ghastlinesse.
> (iii.44)

The alexandrine conveys the genuine tremor of the numinous.

To turn from Braggadocchio to Timias is to discover another phase of the human imagination's long romance with its own dreams, as I suggested in the last section. And all such episodes are essential, indeed inevitable, threads in the allegory of *The Faerie Queene*. We must acknowledge that a character like Belphoebe is different in kind from one like, say, Lucifera, but this should not therefore involve us in an attitude toward Spenser's allegory that makes it a patchwork of "allegorical" and "non-allegorical," symbolic or mythical fragments. Belphoebe and Arthur may be mythical, but the allegory in *The Faerie Queene* has as one of its subjects precisely the relationship of human action and human imagining to myths and symbols. The seamless fabric of the poem accommodates many different sorts of beings, ontologically considered; its large subject is the nature of reality, and because much of reality is invisible or unsensed, the poet turns to allegory, most potent resource of imagination, "vis animae qua percipit homo figuram rei absentis." The kinds of meaning that Spenser expresses in employing characters like Amoret and Belphoebe are very difficult to describe accurately, in part because the self-reflexiveness of *The Faerie Queene*, its anatomizing of its own procedures, is so much in evidence. The complex nature of his continued metaphor may be rendered somewhat more visible, though scarcely less complicated, by examining some other examples of the twins' participation in the lives of mortal characters, particularly Britomart.

As most readers have recognized, Britomart's character and adventures are illuminated by our understanding of what Belphoebe and Amoret embody. She does not actually encounter the former within the fable, and her relationship to Belphoebe therefore remains oblique, a part of the meaning available to reader and poet only. One aspect of Britomart's adventures concerns her relationship to her titular virtue: the relationship between a human being and an idea of perfection, between existential and essential reality, between a "real" person and a world conceived in the erected wit. We do not "see" Holiness in Book I; we do not "see" Temperance in Book II (though an aspect of it is briefly visible in Shamefastness) ; nor, for that matter, do we "see" Justice in Book V (though we hear about her in the form of Astraea's supervision of Artegal's nurture) ; nor Courtesy in Book VI (though we see a figure for it). But in III and IV the crucial allegorical principle of adjective/noun is acted out within the poem's fictive historicity. We "see" a human character aspiring to perfect chastity; and we "see" how Chastity itself fares, in both its aspects, when it is subjected to the pressures of the quotidian. The result of the interlocking plots in which these three characters participate is to show us how essences must be to some degree adulterated or modified when they submit to human vicissitude within time. Britomart cannot "be" *either* Belphoebe or Amoret.[12] Virginity is an otherworldly virtue; in a fully

[12] A relationship has, of course, been regularly recognized. Nelson speaks of Britomart as combining "in even balance the qualities of the womanly and the maidenly twins" (*Poetry of Spenser*, p. 231). Roche, identifying Belphoebe with the Heavenly Venus and Amoret with the Earthly Venus, says that "Britomart is the human embodiment of both types, passing from the virginity of youth to the chaste married love of maturity" (*Kindly Flame*, pp. 102-03). I would modify this somewhat; Belphoebe and Amoret are *mirrors* of two aspects of Venus (or

human world sexuality is rooted in time, as Spenser reveals through the Garden of Adonis. Amoret is brought up there, and she is Britomart's chief model, but even she cannot be incarnated in a pure state as a human being. Like the pure truth of Una, Amoret's pure womanliness is passive and vulnerable to rape and other criminal abuses. The Red Cross Knight must protect Una; Britomart-as-Belphoebe must protect her own womanly chastity.

> Hence had the huntress *Dian* her dread bow
> Fair silver-shafted queen for ever chaste,
> Wherewith she tamed the brinded lioness
> And spotted mountain pard, but set at nought
> The frivolous bolt of *Cupid*; gods and men
> Fear'd her stern frown, and she was queen o' th' Woods.
>
> (441-46)

Milton's examination of virginity in *Comus* makes clear that it belongs to a supernatural order; it is *"saintly* chastity" to be achieved only by grace, or in the state of innocence which is the human analogue to grace. Diana's "dread bow" is like Britomart's magic spear, a weapon of unearthly power, and the Lady of *Comus* does not wield it. Its equivalent is the wand of Sabrina, which unlocks the charm. Britomart imitates Belphoebe during the early part of her adventures; the severity of her virtue enables her to rescue Amoret and subdue Busirane, who also draws power from trans-human sources. But as Britomart approaches the chastity embodied in Amoret, the weaknesses inherent in the state of being a female sexual partner manifest themselves; in the end her Belphoebe-like attributes must be laid aside and her safety

---

of Diana/Venus). Britomart's career demonstrates that the choice of Chastity as a motivating virtue can eventuate in more than one kind of behavior; there are choices to be made *within* the virtue itself, and the most important of these are allegorized in the division of Chastity into the twin sisters. Participation in these absolutes, for a human being, must be temporally sequential; hence the justice of Roche's reference to youth and maturity.

delivered into the hands of Artegal, though not before
many additional complications of the male-female relationship have been explored. When she comes to Artegal in
prison, Spenser uses an allusion that interestingly reverses
the roles that the two characters have filled hitherto; Britomart becomes not the pursuer, but the goal.

> Not so great wonder and astonishment,
>> Did the most chast *Penelope* possesse,
>> To see her Lord, that was reported drent,
>> And dead long since in dolorous distresse,
>> Come home to her in piteous wretchednesse,
>> After long travell of full twenty yeares,
>> That she knew not his favours likelynesse,
>> For many scarres and many hoary heares,
> But stood long staring on him, mongst uncertaine feares.
>
> (V.vii.39)

The allusion refers initially to the disguise that has "deformed" Artegal, and to the mixed emotions of half-recogni-
tion felt by the wife. But Penelope was also a famous instance of chastity, another human version of Amoret, and
by invoking her Spenser hints that the heroine is about to
take her womanly place at the center of an island or garden
to which all paths lead.

Neither Belphoebe nor Amoret is a totally appropriate
model for an historical heroine of love; each *in turn* supplies some useful guidelines for Britomart to follow, and for
us to follow in understanding Britomart.[13] We also come to

[13] I surmise that Harry Berger reaches a similar conclusion when he
speaks of the twins as "boundary figures": "temporary externalizations,
or personifications, whose fixed exemplary purposes are directly responsible for the dramatic and psychological dilemmas they cause and suffer"
("The Discarding of Malbecco," *SP* LXVI [1969], 152). Accordingly,
Amoret must be "discarded" as the "psychic disposition" she represents is "internalized" in Britomart. It is possible to subscribe to such
a reading as long as we recognize that it is a post-romantic, still more
a post-Freudian account, whereby imagined entities are considered to
be projections of the psyche and are re-attached to it, or "internalized,"
by the therapist. But if we read *The Faerie Queene* as a cosmic poem

understand something about the uses of imagined ideals, or myths, in human life, their powers and their limits. This range of meaning in Books III-IV is allegorical: it is metaphorically stated in a sequence of related actions. But what is being allegorized is not so much the state of the heroine's psyche (there are smaller allegorical episodes that do deal with this, such as Britomart's sojourn with Malecasta), as the relation of a human life, in the process of defining itself, to norms of behavior imaginatively conceived by an individual or a society, drawing upon models made available by prevailing philosophical systems. These may take the form of expectations, and the norms themselves can alter. Spenser was setting the convention of courtly love aside in favor of a different conception of sexual love, and so he shows the paradigm of female sexual virtue, Amoret, tortured and abused by a pattern of behavior that misconceives the true role of sexuality in human life.

The misadventures of Amoret in Book IV shed further light on her ontological nature and her relationship to the "human" characters. Like Una in Book I, and like Pastorella and Serena in Book VI, she is condemned to loss and suffering at the hands of demonic powers, to wandering in the desert places of the world, unprotected by the armor that human beings like Britomart and the Red Cross Knight learn to put on as necessary protection against principalities and powers, including the powers of their own subversive emotions. Amoret's role is, however, less strictly metaphorical than that of Una, who must enact the many perils, as well as the powers, of Truth made subject to the way of the

---

mirroring an ontologically complex universe, as I am doing, it is essential to accord paradigms independent existence. In such a universe, *exempla* are not "temporary," but absolute, timeless, perpetually living inhabitants of an invisible realm, realized in the imagination. It is perhaps true that in some unidentifiable sense, Spenser saw such figures as models that humanity necessarily, as part of its psychic life, contrives for its own entertainment, edification, and aspiration. But he would still have seen such contriving as a response to a stimulus coming from "outside," from an absolute though inaccessible reality.

world. On the other hand, she is more clearly visible to the eye of the mind than is Pastorella in Book VI, who is a human child in an archetypal situation. Pastorella's predicaments—lost parentage, bondage, rescue, and revival—give a pre-allegorical resonance to the actions in which she plays a part, but in Book VI Spenser does not provide his readers with interpretive keys to unlock and bring to light an intellectually coherent metaphorical complex of ideas.

There are such keys in Amoret's story. Her abduction in Book IV, Canto vii, resembles in some ways the trials of Serena in Book VI, who in Canto iii is seized by the Blatant Beast as she rambles in the woods "Without suspect of ill or daungers hidden dred" (23); and in Canto viii is abducted by the Salvage Nation when she has lain down to sleep, "Fearelesse of ought, that mote her peace molest" (34). Here is what Spenser says about Amoret:

> The whiles faire *Amoret*, of nought affeard,
>   Walkt through the wood, for pleasure, or for need;
>   When suddenly behind her backe she heard
>   One rushing forth out of the thickest weed,
>   That ere she backe could turne to taken heed,
>   Had unawares her snatched up from ground.
>   Feebly she shriekt, but so feebly indeed,
>   That *Britomart* heard not the shrilling sound,
> There where through weary travel she lay sleeping
>   sound.
>   (IV.vii.4)

There are verbal anticipations of Serena's fearless wandering; and ill-advised surrender to sleep is also involved (though here on the part of Amoret's protector, not the lady herself). Amoret's abductor, however, is a creature who belongs to a different order of being from that of the savages who steal away Serena in Book VI.

> It was to weet a wilde and salvage man,
>   Yet was no man, but onely like in shape

287

> And eke in stature higher by a span,
> All overgrowne with haire, that could awhape
> An hardy hart, and his wide mouth did gape
> With huge great teeth, like to a tusked Bore:
> For he liv'd all on ravin and on rape
> Of men and beasts; and fed on fleshly gore,
> The signe whereof yet stain'd his bloudy lips afore.
>
> (IV.vii.5)

There are two more stanzas of description; together, the details compose a fearsome figure who in some respects resembles Orgoglio—his stature, his weapon, an oak club with "knottie snags"—and is also an animated version of the male genitalia. The poet professes to be unsure of his lineage; he may be born "Of beasts, or of the earth" (7), but in either case he is linked with the lower parts of human nature. The Argument has named him: "greedie lust."

What follows is a small fable of canto length. It is encapsulated in the narrative and not witnessed by Britomart, though the fable's subject, the Amoret-Lust-Belphoebe encounter, is clearly relevant to the heroine's situation and the development of her affair with Artegal, which has reached a climax in the preceding canto. Here, at the center of Book IV and at a major crisis in Britomart's life, Spenser inserts an account of the principles that stand behind and control the actions of mortals. This paradigmatic drama, enacted exclusively for the reader's benefit, brings together for the first and only time since their birth the archetypal twin sisters. The terrified Amoret flees from Lust; pursuer and pursued are depicted in attitudes of classical lucidity and immortal relevance. This is a flight that can never end until it is interrupted by an equally potent countervailing power; and so it is.

> Long so she fled, and so he follow'd long;
> Ne living aide for her on earth appeares,
> But if the heavens helpe to redresse her wrong,
> Moved with pity of her plenteous teares.

> It fortuned *Belphebe* with her peares
> The woody Nimphs, and with that lovely boy,
> Was hunting then the Libbards and the Beares,
> In these wild woods, as was her wonted joy,
> To banish sloth, that oft doth noble mindes annoy.
>
> (IV.vii.23)

Amoret's perfect womanhood—she is compared to Myrrha and Daphne, Ovidian exemplars of vulnerable pure femininity—cannot be definitively defended except by the twin principle of armed and vigilant Chastity, embodied in Belphoebe. Belphoebe slays Lust, who has been merely held at bay by the squire Timias, himself incapable of killing the force that fuels his own masculinity. The monster reads his doom in her and flees: "Well knowing her to be his deaths sole instrument" (29). They are equal antagonists, wielding the power of archetypal principles. In Amoret and Belphoebe, the paradoxically related motives of the virtuous feminine soul are made visible: submissive, vulnerable, passive, on the one hand; actively defensive and invulnerably chaste on the other. The elements recede and advance in Britomart, who in her newly established relation to Artegal must transfer her allegiance from one to the other. Her success is given emblematic form in the dream of Book V, where the crocodile is first beaten back, then received as a lover.

The presence in Canto vii of two merely mortal characters, belonging to our own ambiguously mixed race, points up the ontological distinction between Spenser's depiction of principles, pure forces, and his unraveling of the predicaments that confront human beings. Æmylia and Timias are embroiled in situations partly of their own making. Æmylia relates the incautious actions that led to her captivity; planning an elopement with a Squire of Dames, concealing "th' intent, which in my heart did lurke," she arranges a rendezvous.

> But ah unhappy houre me thither brought:
>   For in that place where I him thought to find,
>   There was I found, contrary to my thought,
>   Of this accursed Carle of hellish kind,
>   The shame of men, and plague of womankind,
>   Who trussing me, as Eagle doth his pray,
>   Me hether brought with him, as swift as wind,
>   Where yet untouched till this present day,
> I rest his wretched thrall, the sad *Æmylia*.
>
>   (IV.vii.18)

Human beings like Æmylia meet Lust only if they create situations that permit lust to become manifest in them or their associates. But Amoret, without her twin counter-virtue, cannot help encountering Lust as long as she is unmarried: the definition of her nature requires it. She is the principle in woman that attracts male desire and proceeds to consummation in chaste marriage or in lustful union, as Belphoebe embodies the equally significant principle which insures that chastity shall prevail, either as permanent virginity or, united with her twin, as marriage. Spenser does not, in fact, return to Belphoebe (in the existing fragment of the poem) after IV.x, when Amoret and Scudamour are (it appears) happily reunited after their vicissitudes; it would be interesting to know whether or not she would have remained permanently invisible following the marriages of Amoret and Britomart.

4. Britomart, History, and Prophecy

Amoret's and Belphoebe's presences in the poem enable us to trace the process whereby the human imagination, relating its desires and its intuitions concerning the human soul to a realm of imaginatively apprehended forms, contrives for itself emblems of potentiality. Its goal is self-definition and self-control, often invoked as the enabling purpose of the *fonction fabulatrice*. The twin sisters are social models, too pure and complete to be realized in actuality, but possessing definitive and prophetic force. They are instances of how imagination shows the soul the way to become more than it is. Personifications tend to indicate how it may become less, like Malbecco who has "quight / Forgot he was a man, and *Gealosie* is hight" (III.x.60); or Pyrochles, coming to resemble his noun, Furor, and described by Guyon as "lesser, then himselfe" (II.v.15).

Turning from imagined beings who exemplify the transcendence or the debasement of human potentiality, we can see in the career of Britomart and other human characters further ramifications of Spenser's self-referring allegorical techniques and further facets of his anatomy of imagination. Britomart's vision of Artegal in the mirror wrought by Merlin's "deep science" (III.ii.18) initiates a progress from untested illusion to fulfilled prophecy which imitates not only the heroine's developing knowledge of her own identity, but a plumbing of the depths of its own "science" by the poetic imagination. Early in the third book, Spenser observes Britomart observing her own emotions and objectifying them in one of the hoariest images of Elizabethan love poetry. Her complaint to the sea conjures up the shadows of Petrarch and his many redactors—among them Wyatt's translation, "My galley charged with forgetfulness," and Gascoigne's poem cited by Puttenham to illustrate the figure *allegoria*. Britomart laments:

> Love my lewd Pilot hath a restlesse mind
> And fortune Boteswaine no assurance knowes,
> But saile withouten starres gainst tide and wind:
> How can they other do, sith both are bold and blind?
> (III.iv.9)

Reminding herself of the blindness of Cupid and Fortuna shows a degree of self-knowledge in the heroine—indeed, rather *too* cynical a view of destiny, since Merlin has just explained that her quest for Artegal is sanctioned by Providence. As for Cupid, the "blinded guest" who guides the heroine (iv.6), even his misbehavior may be read *in bono*. What is interesting, and even amusing, about this episode is that the address to Britomart's "Huge sea of sorrow, and tempestuous griefe" (8) is recited on the seashore. Thus, within the fiction, Spenser anatomizes a metaphor, giving us both tenor and vehicle in visible form. It is similar to the wit that contrives the composition of the false Florimell out of sonnet clichés. Spenser no doubt enjoyed playing these games, but the games have also a serious thematic point. I have already touched on the parallel between love and imagination, a similarity noted by Spenser as early as *The Shepheardes Calender* and developed at the end of Book II of *The Faerie Queene*. In Book III it is explored at some length, partly through a complicated play on the image of the mirror, that versatile figure for the duplicity of art, which is either self-revealing or self-deceiving, or both at once.

Britomart complaining on the sea-coast of her sorrow's "cruell billowes" could remind us of Colin Clout addressing a "dolefull dittie" to the frozen landscape in the *Januarye* eclogue.

> Thou barrein ground, whome winters wrath hath wasted,
> Art made a myrrhour, to behold my plight. (19-20)

Icicles become tears, tears icicles; a sympathetic Nature offers ready emblems for the human psyche. It is the basic justification for pastoral, and as numerous Renaissance texts testify, the reciprocity of inner and outer worlds was based on something more solid than what Ruskin later termed the pathetic fallacy. The complications of the relationship are almost infinite, and Spenser unfurls some of them in the succeeding eclogues of the *Calender*. Britomart's love affair illustrates the complexities that we must grapple with in *The Faerie Queene*, where the nature of allegory, metaphor, and analogy is part of the allegorical subject. The sea is a mirror in which Britomart beholds her plight, and Spenser's development of the sea's implications in Books III and IV justifies this analogy between sea and sorrow (as Shakespeare's shipwreck in *The Tempest* also does in its way). The sea is the setting for the sub-plot of Marinell and Florimell, characters in whom are crystallized certain of those forces we call "natural."[1] Florimell encounters both terrors and joys beneath the waves; and Proteus, the sea's presiding genius who holds her captive, is a notoriously slippery character both biologically and iconographically. The birth of Venus, that cruel and loving goddess, from "the fomy sea" (IV.xii.2), gives visible form to the birth of love which "with gall and hony doth abound" (IV.ix.1). One could go on and on, but this much may suffice to suggest that the metamorphoses of the literal sea in the foreground fiction of *The Faerie Queene* amply justify Britomart's use of it as a metaphor for psychic suffering.

The "literal" setting of the complaint therefore calls attention to the validity of this ancient poetic equation. Later on, Spenser compliments ancient poets for having devised, or discovered, the myth of Venus' birth.

> Therefore the antique wisards well invented,
> That *Venus* of the fomy sea was bred;
> For that the seas by her are most augmented.
> (IV.xii.2)

---

[1] Roche's fine chapter on Florimell and Marinell (*Kindly Flame*, Ch. III) is definitive; his identification of the emblems of Cupid holding flower and fish (p. 191) is a scholarly *trouvaille*.

The story of Britomart, introduced by Merlin's magic mirror and a prophecy which identifies imagining with truth, proceeds from the complaint beside the sea to the great vision of "the seas abundant progeny" (IV.xii.1) and the revival of Marinell, in the two final cantos of Book IV. These last events are not, strictly speaking, part of her "story," since no merely human character witnesses them. They occur behind, above, or below, the happenings in the middest, and are composed of actions and images invented by the poet in order to expose for us once more the cosmic forces which we participate in but do not see. The Venus who presides over the river-marriage is the same one who embraces Adonis in III.vi, but in IV.xi that deeply private occasion is given public form in a ritual. The union of fecundity and order that characterizes the nuptials of Thames and Medway constitutes Spenser's ultimate meditation upon the relation between love and art: the energy that brings together sexual partners in creative union, biological and social, is analogous to the energy that incessantly begets and re-begets images upon "that dolphin-torn, that gong-tormented sea."[2]

Between our introduction to Florimell and Britomart at the opening of Book III, and the great double climax at the end of Book IV, there stretches, however, a labyrinth of love to which only the poet can offer the clue. The careers of these two feminine characters tell us something about imagination's power to generate both illusion and truth; as these are gradually sorted out, the love-affairs move toward successful consummations. Antique wizards' inventions mirror the truth, and Nature is a mirror for man. But Britomart cannot afford to rest in the metaphor of her complaint, any more than, in the fable, she remains on the strand; having

[2] Even if the river-marriage canto of Book IV can be identified as a version of the *Epithalamion Thamesis* mentioned in Spenser's first letter to Harvey, the poem, revised and relocated in a complex narrative context, acquires ultimate force for a reader of *The Faerie Queene*. And every major imagination, as Shakespeare and Milton also bear witness, generates early the images that will be recomposed and inflected throughout its career.

dashed Marinell upon the precious shore, she "forward rode, and kept her ready way / Along the strond, . . . but would not stay" (iv.18). Colin Clout discovers to his dismay that Nature is a fickle mirror for his plight; and for Britomart to take the analogy between tempestuous life and tempestuous sea too seriously would be for her to submit to Fortune rather than cooperate with Providence. So Glauce chides her "with sharpe repriefe" and reminds her of her "immortall" destiny (11). The sea is the matrix of life and a figure for it, but human beings who identify themselves exclusively and literally with the "natural" world doom themselves to eternal childishness.

Identification of the sea with primitive and regressive tendencies in man is not peculiar to Jungian exegetes. Harry Berger has remarked that "The literal or metaphoric proximity to ocean is the sign of return or regression to an archaic condition."[3] Spenser tells us more about this "regression" and about the power of illusion in the final episode of Book III, Canto iv. Arthur, pursuing Florimell, is benighted and loses her; disgruntled, he prepares to wear out the night.

> Tho when her wayes he could no more descry,
>   But to and fro at disaventure strayd;
>   Like as a ship, whose Lodestarre suddenly
>   Covered with cloudes her Pilot hath dismayd;
>   His wearisome pursuit perforce he stayd.
>   (III.iv.53)

Here the narrator picks up the metaphor from Britomart's complaint earlier in the canto; Arthur in pursuit of Florimell is "like" Britomart at the mercy of the "lewd Pilot" love. Sea and Night are parallel "places," and Spenser causes Arthur to utter a parallel complaint: "Night thou foule Mother of annoyance sad . . ." (55). His recitation of Night's genealogy and attributes eloquently confirms her

[3] "The Discarding of Malbecco," p. 143.

hellish powers, already demonstrated in the action of Book
I. She is the metaphysical as well as the physical and meta-
phorical "cause" of woe, the "nurse of bitter cares" (57).
She is also the nourisher of dream and illusion.

> Indeed in sleepe
> The slouthfull bodie, that doth love to steepe
> His lustlesse limbes, and drowne his baser mind,
> Doth praise thee oft, and oft from *Stygian* deepe
> Calles thee, his goddesse in his error blind,
> And great Dame Natures handmaide, chearing
> every kind.
> (III.iv.56)

There is a certain sense in which Night *is* Nature's hand-
maid. The underworld that is her habitat is a matrix of vital
energy: "the wide wombe of the world" where, Spenser
tells us two cantos later, "there lyes . . . An huge eternall
Chaos," source of the seeds of the universe (vi.36). Most
often, however (and even in the Garden), he regards Night
with a shudder. The stanza in Canto iv recalls the many
perils that attend the sleeping heroes or anti-heroes of
Books I and II; and in it Night is specifically connected with
the oceanic principle that drowns consciousness in its pri-
meval depths. Error dwells in this Stygian deep, and something of its menace has already been experienced by Prince
Arthur, the very paradigm of virtue. Sleepless, he entertains
the phantoms of the night:

> sad sorow, and disdaine
> Of his hard hap did vexe his noble brest,
> And thousand fancies bet his idle braine
> With their light wings, the sights of semblants vaine:
> Oft did he wish, that Lady faire mote bee
> His Faery Queene, for whom he did complaine:
> Or that his Faery Queene were such, as shee:
> And ever hastie Night he blamed bitterlie.
> (III.iv.54)

This is the closest Arthur comes to infidelity, and it is not very close. Still, he has been pursuing Florimell, not her attackers, and Florimell, that will-o'-the-wisp, is the very essence of the elusive beauty that conjures away men's hearts; she is a *belle dame sans merci.* The poet affirms that she is truly fair; but also that she is ominous.

> All as a blazing starre doth farre outcast
> His hearie beames, and flaming lockes dispred,
> At sight whereof the people stand aghast:
> But the sage wisard telles, as he has red,
> That it importunes death and dolefull drerihed.
>
> (III.i.16)

This is his image for Florimell at her first appearance, and it connects her with the Night of Arthur's complaint, the source of "dreadfull visions, in the which alive / The drearie image of sad death appeares" (iv.57). Florimell herself is innocent, but she is the cause of irrational behavior in those who "love" her. "Like the comet, she does not seem harmful in herself, or by intention, but she brings the portent of harm."[4] She is always fleeing, always being swallowed up by night or by the sea; she is finally "captured" only by Proteus, the emblem of mutability. Florimell flickers through the middle books leaving chaos in her wake. Arthur's willful, benighted confusion of her with his true love is one example; the multiplied bewilderments spawned by the false Florimell come later. Insofar as beauty is in the eye of the beholder, Florimell is illusory, or at least elusive, and the readiness of virtuous as well as wicked characters to substitute a false version for the true attests to this ambiguousness, as do Arthur's shuffling thoughts of "that Lady faire" and his own lady. Paul Alpers is surely right in detecting in these stanzas a divergence between the Prince's point of view and the reader's.[5]

4 Williams, *World of Glass,* p. 83.
5 *The Poetry of "The Faerie Queene,"* p. 397.

The "sights of semblants vaine" that trouble Arthur are the products of the nighted elements in his own "idle braine." Britomart, surprised by love, shrinks from it for many reasons, but among others is the fear that she too may be enthralled by a vain semblant.

> Nor man it is, nor other living wight;
>   For then some hope I might unto me draw,
>   But th' only shade and semblant of a knight,
>   Whose shape or person yet I never saw,
>   Hath me subjected to loves cruell law:
>   The same one day, as me misfortune led,
>   I in my fathers wondrous mirrhour saw,
>   And, pleased with that seeming goodly-hed,
> Unwares the hidden hooke with baite I swallowed.
>   (III.ii.38)

There follows the colloquy with Glauce, who urges upon the heroine the naturalness of this process—

> For who with reason can you aye reprove
> To love the semblant pleasing most your mind. (ii.40)

Britomart rejects her comfort with a telling allusion.

> But wicked fortune mine, though mind be good,
>   Can have no end, nor hope of my desire,
>   But feed on shadowes, whiles I die for food,
>   And like a shadow wexe, whiles with entire
>   Affection, I doe languish and expire.
>   I fonder, then *Cephisus* foolish child,
>   Who having vewed in a fountaine shere
>   His face, was with the love thereof beguild;
> I fonder love a shade, the bodie farre exild.
>   (ii.44)

Glauce protests that Narcissus, after all, "Was of himselfe the idle Paramoure" (45). Yet to love a self-pleasing semblant, the projection of self, is a kind of self-love, and the allusion to Narcissus is a relevant warning. Earlier in this canto, in conversation with the Red Cross Knight, Britomart tells of her love and hears Artegal praised; Spenser adds a wise saw.

> Hart that is inly hurt, is greatly eased
> With hope of thing, that may allegge his smart;
> For pleasing words are like to Magick art,
> That doth the charmed Snake in slomber lay.
>
> (III.ii.15)

Pleasing words, magic art, and snake-charming; there is surely some reflexive irony here.

The course of Britomart's love-quest tells us various things about the pains and perplexities of love, among them that love's consummation ensues upon the recognition of the beloved as he is, not as a projection of desire. When she falls in love with Artegal, he exists for her only in the "world of glas" that is Merlin's mirror. Loving this "shade," she lives in the world of imagination, and that, Spenser makes clear, is not life at all, but a kind of death. Glauce reproaches her for imprisoning herself in "an huge *Aetn'* of deepe engulfed griefe":

> Ne tastest Princes pleasures, ne doest spred
> Abroad thy fresh youthes fairest flowre, but lose
> Both leafe and fruit, both too untimely shed,
> As one in wilfull bale for ever buried.
>
> (III.ii.31)

Britomart's situation is echoed in Book IV by that of Marinell, who cannot come to his true love, Florimell; in consequence "his wonted chearefull hew / Gan fade, and lively spirits deaded quight" (IV.xii.20). In part, this sort of language is Spenser's way of literalizing the cliché, "I die for love." But for him dying for love is connected with being cut off, for one reason or another, from the *true* presence of the beloved. Marinell, confronted by the "angels

face" of Florimell, revives like a flower—a flower identical
with that of "fresh youth" which Britomart, buried in her
wilful bale, had been unable to "spred." Marinell, feeling
the warmth of his sun,

> Liftes up his head, that did before decline
> And gins to spread his leafe before the faire sunshine.
>
> (IV.xii.34)[6]

In order to achieve this happy result, Britomart must pull
herself away from the self-regarding world of glass and
enter the world of actual men and women.

This is accomplished through several encounters with
Artegal, whose "wyld disguize" (IV.iv.42) as the Salvage
Knight allegorically figures the distance between Britomart's fantasy of the perfect knight and the actual man. At
the beginning of her quest to "seeke an unknowne Paramoure" (iii.3), she rides along dreaming of "Her lovers
shape, and chevalrous array":

> A thousand thoughts she fashioned in her mind,
> And in her feigning fancie did pourtray
> Him such as fittest she for love could find,
> Wise, warlike, personable, curteous, and kind.
>
> (III.iv.5)

---

6 In this canto, Spenser also works out a relationship between Marinell's unfulfilled love, narcissistic self-love, and loss of self as "death."
Florimell's complaint calls for death if she and Marinell cannot live
"as lovers ought to do"; "let him live unlov'd, or love him selfe alone"
(9). Marinell must be drawn away from unloving self-love and "learne
to love by learning lovers paines to rew" (13). This involves a period
of frustration when he knows *about* Florimell but cannot come to the
real woman, corresponding to Britomart's encounter with the "shade"
of Artegal. During this period his former selfhood is dissolved; he
roams "As he had lost him selfe, he wist not where" (17), and "nothing
like himselfe he seem'd in sight" (20). Self-love submits to "death" and
is replaced by a new birth. There is a parallel, perhaps, with the birth
of the New Man following Christian baptism, but Spenser does not
invoke it directly. It is present, if at all, as part of a comprehensive
parallelism between sacred and secular love, the second imitating and
adumbrating the first.

These, the poet informs us briskly, are "selfe-pleasing thoughts." The real Artegal is warlike, but the other honorific epithets do not fit him at all. At the tournament he "Far'd like a lyon," "That every one gan shun his dreadfull sight, / No lesse then death it selfe, in daungerous affright" (IV.iv.41). Britomart, of course, does not recognize in this ferocious figure the Boy Scout image she has fashioned for herself. Instead, she rides off again, "making blind love her guide" (v.29). Spenser is here interestingly varying the ancient image of blind Cupid. Love is blind to the faults of the beloved, and this can be regarded sentimentally as a virtue. But the blindness of Britomart has the effect of preventing her from loving Artegal in fact instead of in fancy. The epiphany of Canto vi is constructed so as to make clear that Britomart must, in effect, fall in love anew in order finally to lose the self-pleasing image. In this second encounter with the disguised Artegal, a truce is called by Glauce; the warriors, putting up their beavers, "shew'd themselves to her, such as indeed they were" (25). Britomart at last sees "the lovely face of *Artegall*, / Tempred with sternesse and stout majestie" (26). She identifies this knight with the one seen "long since in that enchaunted glasse," but does not fully yield until she hears his name and is reminded by Glauce that he represents the "secret fate" revealed by Merlin.

A further variation upon these related themes in Book III, intricately uniting isolation, infantile egotism and regression, fantasy, infidelity, and symbolic death, comes in the "odious argument" of Cantos ix and x, where Spenser reluctantly unfolds the history of Malbecco, Hellenore, and Paridell as a "paragone / Of evill" (ix.2). Hellenore is immured by her "withered" husband, "Depriv'd of kindly joy and naturall delight" (ix.5). As a result, her "womans will, which is disposd to go astray" (6), contrives the beguilement of her jailer, enlisting the power to delude in the interests of constrained self-love—a distortion of the instinct for self-preservation through "kindly joy." Denied an outlet,

301

the expansive love that could enjoy a natural fidelity in voluntary self-surrender turns back into itself and enacts its fantasies.

> For who wotes not, that womans subtiltyes
> Can guilen *Argus*, when she list misdonne?
> It is not yron bandes, nor hundred eyes,
> Nor brasen walls, nor many wakefull spyes,
> That can withhold her wilfull wandring feet;
> But fast good will with gentle curtesyes,
> And timely service to her pleasures meet.
>
> (III.ix.7)

The human spirit, for which stone walls do not a prison make, eludes physical constraint in one way or another; if need be, it takes refuge in those "phantasies / In wavering wemens wit, that none can tell" (III.xii.26), but that Spenser will attempt to unfold at the climax of Book III in the Masque of Cupid. He has already shown us their archetype in Phantastes' chamber: the "idle fantasies" entertained by "fooles, lovers, children, Dames" (II.ix.50). Fantasy leads to *"Death* with infamie" (III.xii.25), and, indeed, Hellenore dies to her own humanity; she is last glimpsed keeping house for satyrs in the greenwood, and being sexually "handeled."

She has come to this pass through force of circumstance —her old husband's foolish jealousy—which has exposed her to the dangerous power of fantasy in herself and the seductiveness of Paridell's "lewd lore." This weak knight has a fatal gift, which Spenser interestingly calls "a kindly pryde / Of gracious speach" (ix.32): speech is, after all, the proper mark of man, a natural and just source of pride. But Paridell uses "all that art," along with "speaking lookes" (28), to enchant Hellenore and nourish her fatal fancies.

> But all the while, that he these speaches spent,
> Upon his lips hong faire Dame *Hellenore*,
> With vigilant regard, and dew attent,

> Fashioning worlds of fancies evermore
> In her fraile wit, that now her quite forlore:
> The whiles unwares away her wondring eye,
> And greedy eares her weake hart from her bore.
>
> (ix.52)

The entire story, set into the story of Britomart, is a warning against the wrong sort of "dying for love." Hellenore surrenders her "fraile wit" as a result of having been forced into narcissistic fantasy, and loses her proper selfhood through the abuse of a natural human faculty. Britomart, protected by her armored chastity and constancy, moves through a series of adventures toward Artegal, fantasy checked by Merlin's lawful magic. Britomart will eventually surrender her self-enclosed virtue to the self-abnegating role of a wife. "The beginning of the *vita amorosa* proceeds from death," as the Florentine neo-Platonists liked to say[7]— that death which entails willingness to suffer the pains of love's wound to self-sufficiency. At the beginning of Britomart's story Spenser has described her, with a certain humorous and affectionate exaggeration, in sorry plight in a psychic underworld:

> she still did waste, and still did wayle,
> That through long languour, and hart-burning brame
> She shortly like a pyned ghost became,
> Which long hath waited by the Stygian strond.
>
> (III.ii.52)

She must, of course, move on from this stage of her adventure and emerge into the sunlight of the genuine Artegal, where the dream becomes truth.

Spenser's grotesque little tale of Hellenore is a satyr-play to the great epic of passion's doom, the fall of Troy. Choosing to model herself on Helen, for whose sake "fruitlesse lives were under furrow sowne" (ix.35), Hellenore enacts a parable of the infection of the will which results when its

---

[7] Quoted from Lorenzo de' Medici in Wind, *Pagan Mysteries*, p. 157.

desires are so severely frustrated as to be forced into fantasy. She travels a road not taken by Britomart, whose chaste desires, congruent with the purposes of both Nature and Providence, can flower into truth. For Britomart the ideal image of Artegal in Merlin's mirror is a talisman, and fantasy is the subjective counterpart of her chastity-preserving armor.

To trace the pattern of these episodes is to see the points at which the story of the heroine touches the subject of fantasy's relation to reality—of love and art as makers of illusion—which is one of Spenser's many themes in the middle books. The thematic role of Merlin in this pattern is indicated by a structural device. Spenser divides his references to the enchanter between the description of his "glassy globe" in Canto ii of Book III, and the heroine's visit to his cave in Canto iii, juxtaposing promise and fulfillment, dream and truth. The description of the glass turns first to its virtues; it can bring the truth to light, and discover "Whatever thing was in the world contaynd." The stanza concludes

> For thy it round and hollow shaped was,
> Like to the world it selfe, and seem'd a world of glas.
>
> (III.ii.19)

This microcosmic invention imitates or reflects or reveals *the* world, though exactly what it reflects at any moment depends selectively on the beholder; it can show anything, provided "that it to the looker appertaynd." It is *glass* in two senses. Like Momus' window it makes transparent what is opaque in reality, so that we see it for what it is, in this respect resembling Stevens' poet—

> He is the transparence of the place in which
> He is, and in his poems we find peace.[8]

8 "Asides on the Oboe," *Collected Poems*, p. 251.

In Spenser's terms, this virtue links the glass with heavenly light, the day that "discovers all dishonest wayes, / And sheweth each thing as it is indeed" (III.iv.59). Merlin's magic world is also, however, "a looking glasse, right wondrously aguiz'd" (18), and the mirror can be turned either inward or outward.[9] Spenser's example of a parallel wonder is not reassuring. He tells us of Phao, beloved of Ptolemy, who like the Lady of Shalott lived hidden from the world, viewing it from a distance in her glass tower. This story ended unhappily, with the lady's betrayal and the ruin of the world of glass. "Such was the glassie globe that *Merlin* made" (ii.21)—a valuable, potent, and, after such an introduction, surely dangerous gift.

Introducing us to Merlin himself in Canto iii, Spenser enumerates his awesome powers.

> For he by words could call out of the sky
>> Both Sunne and Moone, and make them him obay:
> The Land to sea, and sea to maineland dry,
> And darkesome night he eke could turne to day:
> Huge hostes of men he could alone dismay.
>> (III.iii.12)

Arthur in the next canto will pray for night to turn to day, and pray in vain until the hours have run their natural course; but Merlin can overgo Nature's power. In this respect he is like many other legendary enchanters, for example, Medea, who in Golding's Ovid boasts:

> By charms I make the calm seas rough, and make
>> the rough seas plain,
> And cover all the sky with clouds and chase them
>> thence again.
> By charms I raise and lay the winds, and burst the
>> viper's jaw,

[9] Kathleen Williams discusses the "false" and "true" valences of the mirror image in *World of Glass*, p. 94.

And from the bowels of the earth both stones and
trees do draw.

.   .   .   .

I call up dead men from their graves, and thee,
O lightsome moon,
I darken oft, though beaten brass abate thy peril
soon.
Our sorcery dims the morning fair and darks the
sun at noon.[10]

This speech was a source for Shakespeare when he made
Prospero describe his powers just before renouncing them.
It is perhaps significant that, though the sorceress boasts of
darkening the sun and moon, Spenser chooses rather to
stress Merlin's transformation of night into day. This would
be consistent with Merlin's mainly beneficent role in the
poem, and I do not suggest that we are meant to read him
as malignant. But his power, as its double source indicates
(his father an incubus, his mother a nun), can be either
rightly used, or abused, like so many other powers in *The
Faerie Queene*. In this episode, Spenser firmly corrects such
doubts as we might have about the ultimate efficacy of the
magic mirror. The world of glass is not something to live in,
however, but something to read. The visions it contains may
or may not correspond to "reality." If they do so correspond,
it is because Merlin is a white magician like Prospero,
whose enchantments are sanctioned by "the powers," otherwise called "destiny / That hath to instrument this lower
world" (III.3).[11] Merlin is likewise in league with destiny.

10 *Ovid's Metamorphoses: The Arthur Golding Translation*, ed. J. F.
Nims (New York, 1965), p. 168; in the original, VII.192-219.

11 Pico's discussion of magic, white and black, in the *Dignity of Man*,
identifies the source of the beneficent mage's power: "in calling forth
into the light as if from their hiding-places the powers scattered and
sown in the world by the loving-kindness of God, [he] does not so
much work wonders as diligently serve a wonder-working nature" (*The
Renaissance Philosophy of Man*, ed. Ernst Cassirer *et al.* [Chicago, 1948],
p. 248). On "natural magic," see French, *John Dee*, pp. 91-93.

306

It was not, *Britomart*, thy wandring eye,
  Glauncing unwares in charmed looking glas,
  But the streight course of hevenly destiny,
  Led with eternall providence, that has
  Guided thy glaunce, to bring his will to pas.
                                        (iii.24)

Art may, as Bacon feared, submit the shows of things to
the desires of the mind. But the desires of the mind are not
necessarily pernicious. Britomart's desires mislead her
somewhat in the course of her adventures, but fundamentally they are healthy, as Glauce insists when she distinguishes Britomart's affection from "uncouth" loves,
"contrary unto kinde" (ii.40). This concatenation of Nature,
Providence, and human desire is associated, in literary
terms, with comic forms, and Alpers is right in saying that
Britomart plays "a comic role" in Book III.[12] The plot of a
comedy—at least of the festive or pastoral kind that we as-
sociate with Shakespeare—imitates the union of desire and
reality that prevailed before the Fall. In the fallen world,
such a happy issue cannot come about except by "miracle,"
and Shakespeare regularly includes a *deus ex machina*
when he designs this sort of plot.[13] Spenser's reassurance—
to Britomart and to his readers—that Merlin's art mirrors
visionary truth, not mere wish-fulfilling illusion, indicates
that he too is composing in this mode. The agent of this reassurance is Merlin's prophecy, in which Britomart's life is
shown knit into the designs of Providence. It is a continuation of *Briton moniments*, the book that Arthur reads in
Alma's castle (II.x), which ends "Without full point, or
other Cesure right" (68). History does not come to a full
stop until Apocalypse, and only in Books I and VII does
Spenser give us glimpses of that. The other books of *The
Faerie Queene* are all bound into history in one way or an-

[12] *Poetry of "The Faerie Queene,"* p. 294.
[13] I am drawing on the model for Shakespearean comedy described
by Northrop Frye in *A Natural Perspective* (New York, 1965).

other. The womb of time lies at the center of Book III in the Garden of Adonis; from it emerge the anonymous organic beings produced by the life-force. But this force does not operate outside the purview of Providence, which is cosmic in scope. Providence is the name for God as he subdues himself to time; its central manifestation is the Incarnation, but Providence also rules the destinies of nations and of individual human beings. The Red Cross Knight learns his "name and nation" from Heavenly Contemplation (I.x.67); the episode of self-recognition is repeated, with a horizontal (or temporal) rather than a vertical (or anagogic) orientation, when Britomart learns her destiny from Merlin. She comes to him in disguise, but he is not taken in, and names her.

> Ne ye faire *Britomartis*, thus arayd,
> More hidden are, then Sunne in cloudy vele;
> Whom thy good fortune, having fate obayd,
> Hath hither brought, for succour to appele:
> The which the powres to thee are pleased to revele.
>
> (III.iii.19)

Britomart, "seeing her selfe descryde," blushes, and Spenser charmingly endows Merlin's figure with the narrator's authority, by actualizing it in his own similes of sunrise:

> As faire *Aurora* rising hastily,
> Doth by her blushing tell, that she did lye
> All night in old *Tithonus* frosen bed.
>
> (20)

The several epiphanies of Britomart within the action, appearing "like sunny beames" (III.ix.20) and "Like to the ruddie morne" (IV.vi.19), also affirm in the "real life" of the poem Merlin's insight.

Not only the name, but the nation, of the heroine is defined in this canto, where private history and public destiny are twined together. Merlin's prophecy of British history up to the Tudors recounts the fortunes of "the antique *Troian* blood" (42), sometimes obscured, sometimes breaking forth again like Britomart herself:

> Yet during this their most obscuritee,
> Their beames shall oft breake forth, that men them
>   faire may see.
>   (44)

Merlin uses a simile that is beautifully appropriate to the nature of Spenser's fiction in the central books, to describe the progress of Britomart's love and lineage.

> For so must all things excellent begin,
>   And eke enrooted deepe must be that Tree,
>   Whose big embodied braunches shall not lin,
>   Till they to heavens hight forth stretched bee.
>   For from thy wombe a famous Progenie
>   Shall spring, out of the auncient *Troian* blood,
>   Which shall revive the sleeping memorie
>   Of those same antique Peres, the heavens brood,
> Which *Greeke* and *Asian* rivers stained with their blood.
>   (22)

The stanza combines vertical and horizontal, spatial and temporal coordinates. The Tree of Commonwealth, "enrooted deepe" in the soil which Spenser will show us a few cantos later, touches Heaven at its other extremity. Yet it must grow toward that consummation in time, and the stanza moves forward and backward, as well as down and up, to indicate the historical dimensions of human experience. Another version of the tree image turns up later when Paridell recalls "aged Memnon's" continuation of the Troy story.

> Indeed he said (if I remember right,)
> That of the antique *Troian* stocke, there grew
> Another plant, that raught to wondrous hight,

And far abroad his mightie branches threw,
Into the utmost Angle of the world he knew.

(III.ix.47)

The "utmost Angle" is the future home of Angles, Saxons, and Britons.

Echoes in Paridell's story of Merlin's in Canto iii underline the parodistic relationship between the two tales. Paridell, as Roche has noted, is an irresponsible egotist who pursues his loves at the expense of "higher allegiance."[14] His pretense reminds us that, while destiny shapes the fates of nations, every individual can choose to cooperate or not with destiny. Paridell's dispassionate *ubi sunt* as he invokes the "idle name" of Troy indicates a limited conception of the role of human behavior in the providential scheme.

What boots it boast thy glorious descent,
And fetch from heaven thy great Genealogie,
Sith all thy worthy prayses being blent,
Their of-spring hath embaste, and later glory shent.

(ix.33)

His indifference contrasts with Britomart's tears for a kingdom "in one sad night consumd, and throwen downe" (39), and his uncommitted heart with her fidelity to destiny and Artegal. Paridell is submerged in meaningless linear time; having satisfied his lust for Hellenore he casts her off.

I take no keepe of her (said *Paridell*)
She wonneth in the forrest there before.
So forth he rode as his adventure fell.

(III.x.38)

The jostle of accident or "adventure" supplants the vision of history. Both Paridell and Hellenore have abdicated their roles in history, but Britomart's virtue insures a rela-

14 *Kindly Flame*, p. 64; I am indebted to Roche's account of the Britomart-Hellenore-Paridell relationship.

tionship to destiny that can protect her nation against the
fate of Troy. She will not play Hellenore to Artegal's Paridell, either as his lover or his queen. She is armed, and free
to pursue the "kindly joy and naturall delight" fatally denied to Hellenore, and she gives allegiance to a chaster
goddess than the one to whom Paris offered the apple.
Shortly before Paridell recites the tale of Troy, Spenser
pauses for one of Britomart's recurrent epiphanies.

> Like as *Minerva*, being late returnd
>   From slaughter of the Giaunts conquered;
>   Where proud *Encelade*, whose wide nosethrils burnd
>   With breathed flames, like to a furnace red,
>   Transfixed with the speare, downe tombled ded
>   From top of *Hemus*, by him heaped hye;
>   Hath loosd her helmet from her lofty hed,
>   And her *Gorgonian* shield gins to untye
> From her left arme, to rest in glorious victorye.
>
> (III.ix.22)

Had Paris chosen this goddess, Troy's stones might still be
standing, and Britomart's fidelity to the Minervan model
will insure a better fate for Troynovaunt.

Merlin's prophecy of Britomart's destiny is reconfirmed
and given divine sanction in the dream at the Temple of Isis
in Book V, where Spenser repeats, at a point near the end
of Britomart's quest, the pattern with which it began. Instead of the vision in the magic globe, we have a dream;
Britomart's self-beguilement with "shadowes," so that "no
powre / Nor guidance of her selfe in her did dwell"
(III.ii.49), is repeated in her bemusement after the dream,
"With thousand thoughts feeding her fantasie" (V.vii.17),
which leads her to seek the aid of the priests "in hope to
find / Your aide, to guide me out of errour blind" (19). The
priests of Isis retrospectively affirm and hallow the ambiguous magic of Merlin; the artist-sorcerer at his highest pitch
can serve a priestly function. The stanza of recognition
echoes that in which Merlin pierces Britomart's disguise.

Magnificke Virgin, that in queint disguise
  Of British armes doest maske thy royall blood,
  So to pursue a perillous emprize,
  How couldst thou weene, through that disguized hood,
  To hide thy state from being understood?
  Can from th' immortal Gods ought hidden bee?

(V.vii.21)

The visionary dream that expresses the gods' intention confirms the identity of the heroine, first revealed by the
magician who has made a world of glass. In that world, as
in *The Faerie Queene*, hidden things are made plain.

Britomart's story is, among other things, the story of the
vicissitudes of imagination. Two contrary impulses of the
imagining power are called in question: the impulse to seal
off the psyche in a self-created world of love, a dark glass;
and the impulse to serve a wonder-working natural providence. Spenser's awareness of the snares that fancy lays is
balanced by his sense that only the power to transcend "reasons reach," by love and imagination, can provide heroic
energy and ennoble the life of action. The two points of
view are balanced in the *apologia* that introduces Book IV,
halfway through the twenty-four cantos in which Spenser
explores "lovers deare debate." The grave statesman ad-
dressed in the first stanza is the spokesman for the dangers
of fiction; "looser rimes" lead to irresponsible folly in those

That better were in vertues discipled,
  Then with vaine poemes weeds to have their fancies fed.

(IV.Pro.1)

But this echo of Hellenore's story cannot be allowed to
stand. Poems are the sources not only of vain fancies, but
of "vertuous and gentle discipline." The poet speaks in his
own voice to defend the power of love to inspire virtue in
heroes and philosophers (3), and the poetry that celebrates
that power. Spenser appeals from "the rugged forehead" to
the true head of state, "The Queene of love, and Prince of

peace from heaven blest" (4). Compliment to Elizabeth can scarcely go further. The ruler of a peaceable kingdom, whether earthly or heavenly, is a decorous presiding power for the Book of Concord. Poetry can make that kingdom live, and therefore offer a model to human monarchs. Later in Book IV, Spenser describes the ideal innocence of his arcadian world—that visionary Fairy Land that is encapsulated within the wider world of the poem. And that land, "yet in the infancie / Of time" (IV.viii.30), to which only imagination has the key, *is* the peaceable kingdom.

> The Lyon there did with the Lambe consort,
>   And eke the Dove sate by the Faulcons side,
>   Ne each of other feared fraud or tort,
>   But did in safe securitie abide.
>
> (IV.viii.31)

5. The Order of Words and its Limits

In his stanzas on the state of innocence, Spenser connects moral probity and linguistic virtue. Ladies can converse with noble knights without being accused of "lightness" (IV.viii.29); innocence is a matter of "simple truth" and guilelessness. The poet, both truthful and guileful, necessarily plays an ambiguous role in such a world, and it is not without reason that makers of utopias exile fabulators from their commonwealths. Uttering the thing that is not for ulterior purposes, poets have no place in the philosopher's Republic. Critics have been noticing for some time that in the second part of *The Faerie Queene* Spenser is centrally concerned with what Northrop Frye calls the order of words. "Grace in religion implies revelation by the Word, and human grace depends much upon good human words. All through the second part of *The Faerie Queene*, slander is portrayed as the worst enemy of the human community."[1] Ate, who enters the poem at the beginning of Book IV, threatens the peaceable kingdom, and the poet treats her with eloquent loathing. She is related to the classical Rumor full of tongues, and Spenser, like Shakespeare in *Julius Caesar*, places her dwelling in Hell. It is decorated with the trophies of monumental disaster—"antique Babylon," "fatall Thebes," Rome, Salem, and "sad Ilion," all brought low by "evill wordes and factious deedes" (IV.i.22, 25), the former, by implication, inspiring the latter.

> Her lying tongue was in two parts divided,
> And both the parts did speake, and both contended.
>
> (i.27)

Ate is not a figure for the poet, but she is his constant bugbear and shadow, because he must practice the art of

[1] *Fables of Identity*, p. 86.

words in a world partly created by her. In *Paradise Lost* duplicity, in the form of shape-shifting and lying Satan, enters the created universe as the herald of Sin and Death. "Then faire grew foule, and foule grew faire in sight" (IV.viii.32). Along with the doubleness of being and seeming comes double-tongued Ate; her avatars, the abusers of language, jostle malignantly through the action of Books IV, V, and VI. There is Clarinda, Radegund's serving-woman, who deceives both her mistress and the imprisoned hero Artegal, employing "art, even womens witty trade, / The art of mightie words, that men can charme" (V.v.49); the two hags Envy and Detraction who meet and revile Artegal at the end of Book V; Malengin, or Guile himself, "smooth of tongue, and subtile in his tale" (V.ix.5), killed by the Iron Man who, incidentally, almost never speaks; Corflambo the blasphemer (IV.viii.45); and, of course, the Blatant Beast. Spenser's most melodramatic image for the abuse of words is the bad poet, Malfont, whom the heroes encounter at the palace of Queen Mercilla in Book V.

> There as they entred at the Scriene, they saw
> Some one, whose tongue was for his trespasse vyle
> Nayld to a post, adjudged so by law:
> For that therewith he falsely did revyle,
> And foule blaspheme that Queene for forged guyle,
> Both with bold speaches, which he blazed had,
> And with lewd poems, which he did compyle;
> For the bold title of a Poet bad
> He on himselfe had ta'en, and rayling rymes had sprad.
>   (V.ix.25)

The bad poet endures his spectacular punishment deservedly, for language is his special charge, and instead of cherishing and preserving it, he has made it hateful by hateful use. *Corruptio optimi pessima.* This maker of lewd poems is the poet Spenser is not, but is accused of being by the "rugged forhead" in the Proem (IV.Pro.1). In Malfont he acknowledges the accusation and dramatically dissociates himself, the character's creator, from it.

In Book IV, the Book of Concord, appears Spenser's famous tribute to "Dan *Chaucer*, well of English undefyled" (IV.ii.32). Malfont, "a welhed / Of evill words, and wicked sclaunders by him shed" (26), embodies a counter-force, poisoning the springs kept clear by Spenser's great predecessor. The poet of *The Faerie Queene* can claim, "I follow here the footing of thy feete" (32), but the path of linguistic probity is an intricate one for a writer who inhabits a radically deformed world and a universe of discourse as severely disabled. A poet cannot accept a counsel of despair, for then he must fall silent. Spenser puts several aphasic characters into *The Faerie Queene*, and though he accords them some sympathy, he does not shirk their limitations. The "good" Savage of Book VI has no language, only "a soft murmure, and confused sound / Of senselesse words" (VI.iv.11), and though he is invulnerable, he cannot master more articulate enemies. Timias, formerly a courtier, suffers self-imposed exile for love of Belphoebe; he takes to the woods and becomes a wild man, "mute, as if he had beene dum, / Ne signe of sence did shew, ne common wit" (IV.vii.44). In this state he is no use to anyone; he regains his knightly force when he returns to court and to articulate speech. The Savage Man and Timias are interesting subversions of pastoral primitivism, evidence that Spenser did not accept uncritically the equation between simplicity and eloquence, a primitive life-style and power of words.

In fact, the verbal artfulness that can survive among the confusions of fallen "civilized" life cannot be learned in Utopia. Swift's Houhynhmns, unable to understand "the thing that is not," produce verse characterized by "exactness," devoid of irony. The state of Nature knows nothing of guile or the abuse of words, and so it cannot cope with them. Virtuous art makes reference to the peaceable kingdom, the restored image of an "antique age," but it does not flourish there, because it must use the medium of a corrupt language. Utopian literature, if it exists at all, must be very unlike the radical allegory that is *The Faerie Queene*,[2] for Spenser's poem acknowledges, as it undertakes to correct, the corruption of art. It accepts, as any pre-utopian and post-arcadian poet must, the decadence of language and the guilefulness of those who use it. The allegorist speaks through an illusion while taking pains to clarify his own procedure, making the lie devour itself. He makes a mirror for man, and like the fool in the Tudor interludes, turns it upon the audience with a *tu quoque*.

Concord and Discord polarize the discourse in Book IV, and this polarity, like the wedded antagonism of Night and Day in Book I or Sea and Land in III, provides a basis for distinguishing between valid and invalid fictions. Double-tongued, hate-mongering Discord is the monster at the gate of Book IV, and we are not surprised to find her companioned by Duessa, that diabolic embodiment of the eternal feminine, now recovered from her late misfortunes. In the next canto, Spenser condenses his syntax into a succinct statement of the relation between Duessa, Ate, and their human victims, here the deceived knights Blandamour and Paridell.

> Both they unwise, and warelesse of the evill,
> That by themselves unto themselves is wrought,
> Through that false witch, and that foule aged drevill,
> The one a feend, the other an incarnate devill.
>
> (IV.ii.3)

The same two are later said to be "with hope of shadowes vaine inspyred" by Duessa (V.ix.41). The self-generated curse of discordant passion is manifest in the devilish woman who feeds men on the famishing shadows of their own desires; and in the "feend," related to the one that tormented Saul—and was exorcised by David, "that celestiall Psalmist" (2). The power of self-deception terminates in

---

[2] The problematical status of literature in Utopia is discussed by Robert C. Elliott, *The Shape of Utopia* (Chicago, 1970), pp. 121-28.

317

social falseness, and its instrument is language; the power to reveal truth and restore concord also employs words. "How shall we find the concord of this discord?" asks Shakespeare's Theseus; "Such Musicke is wise words, with time concented" is the answer supplied by Spenser in Book IV. Discord can be allayed only by those who can transpose the note:

> whose small sparkes once blowen
> None but a God or godlike man can slake;
> Such as was *Orpheus*, that when strife was growen
> Amongst those famous ympes of Greece, did take
> His silver Harpe in hand, and shortly friends them
> make.
> (IV.ii.1)

This is the art of words in its beneficent aspect. It becomes malignant in the mouth of Ate, who is the sibling of Jealousy—the former "borne of hellish brood, / And by infernall furies nourished" (IV.i.26), the latter also bred by a fury in "balefull house of *Proserpine* / Where in her bosome she thee long had nurst" (III.xi.1). Spenser's anatomy of Jealousy begins in Book III with the grotesque metamorphosis of Malbecco, where fact becomes fiction before our eyes as a human character becomes lost in his own passion. His retreat into "a cave with entrance small" (III.x.57) is expressive enough without calling it infantile regression; there he leads the implacably immortal life of an archetype, dreadfully embalmed in the imagination's idea of him. Jealousy then receives a stanza of exclamatory rhetoric from the poet: "Of all the passions in the mind thou vilest art" (III.xi.1); this is matched by the similar introductory stanza to IV.ii in which Discord is invoked as a "Firebrand of hell" (1). Jealousy and Discord are routed, only to reappear at the conclusion of Book V under the names Envy and Detraction, to harry Sir Artegal. Detraction, like Ate, "faynes to weave false tales and leasings bad" (V.xii.36).

Ate and Jealousy, both firebrands of hell, unite in several
of the imbroglios of Book IV. Scudamour spends a night in
the House of Care, "dismayd with gealous dread" (v.45),
jealousy being "The crime, which cursed *Ate* kindled earst"
(v.31). "His ydle braine" in sleep makes him dream of dis-
loyalty in Britomart and Amoret (v.43); Spenser in the next
canto says that Scudamour's misery is the result of "miscon-
ceipt" (vi.2). The very image of misconceit, false Florimell,
has been making trouble among both good and bad knights,
and in describing her blandishments the poet explicates the
relation between abused language, misbegotten fantasy,
self-deceiving passion, and the desire of the mind to win its
paradise too easily. Florimell, "So great a mistresse of her
art . . . And perfectly practiz'd in womans craft" (IV.ii.10),
sets out to charm Blandamour (whose name links him with
Discord's other victim, Scudamour).

> She in regard thereof him recompenst
> With golden words, and goodly countenance,
> And such fond favours sparingly dispenst:
> Sometimes him blessing with a light eye-glance,
> And coy lookes tempring with loose dalliance;
> Sometimes estranging him in sterner wise,
> That having cast him in a foolish trance,
> He seemed brought to bed in Paradise,
> And prov'd himselfe most foole in what he seem'd
> most wise.
>   (IV.ii.9)

This behavior is a terrible parody of a deity's varying aspect in the eyes of a worshipper, tempering sternness with
blessings; we have seen a proper version in Belphoebe's
condescension to Timias. And, of course, false Florimell *is*
the goddess of a literary religion of love. Her contrived
beauty parodies the true beauty which, Spenser says, "was
made to represent / The great Creatours owne resemblance
bright" (IV.viii.2). She is "the baite of bestiall delight"; she
leads men to a false paradise which resembles both Ate's

house and the spoiled Bower of Bliss, strewn with the tokens of ruined lovers, "Their girlonds rent, their bowres despoyled all" (IV.i.24); and "all without, / The baren ground was full of wicked weedes" (25).

The true garden of Book IV is that dedicated to Venus from which Scudamour wins Amoret. It is the second of the two places—two structural and thematic centers—associated with Amoret, and the difference between them is instructive. In both, we perceive "the characteristic motion of Spenser's allegory," described by Hamilton as "a moving ever inward, penetrating ever more deeply until we achieve some vision of perfection at the center."[3] At the center of the Garden of Adonis is a vision of the perfection of natural love, love within Nature. This is not, of course, peculiar to human beings; it is presided over by *Venus Pandemos*, the Venus of Lucretius and Boethius and Chaucer, who sponsors the generation of all things in the organic universe.[4] At the center of the Temple in Book IV there is a statue of *Venus Hermaphroditos*, and, as Roche has pointed out, it is important that the goddess "is here represented as an immutable artifact."[5] The two fostering-places of Amoret in *The Faerie Queene* express the nature of love first as instinct, then as conscious emotion. Venus' Castle and Temple in Book IV are artifacts because for human beings love is an art; we must find our way back to the concord of innocence by learning how to love. Scudamour at the beginning of his retrospective narrative speaks of the day "that first with deadly wound / My heart was launcht, and learned to have loved" (IV.x.1). His progress to the island's center records the early stages of his education, his loss and despair at the hands of Busirane a later one.

[3] *Structure of Allegory*, p. 164.

[4] That is, of course, the Venus of the Proem to Book III of *Troilus and Criseyde*. Chaucer's inflections of Venus illustrate the range of this figure's "meanings." The lightly veiled Venus of the *Parlement* figures the profane love that leads to a dead end and is, despite appearances, alienated from nature; this principle is embodied by Spenser in Acrasia.

[5] *Kindly Flame*, p. 132.

Scudamour associates love with grace which, working "gainst common sence," makes the pain of love seem sweet; he thus affirms Glauce's earlier claim that "love can higher stye / Then reasons reach." The Garden of Adonis reveals a sub-rational mystery, the Temple of Venus a supra-rational one. The "complementary relation between nature and nurture, between generation and civility, is imaged in the implicit correspondences" of these two places.[6] And civility is the product of a human design. The park of Venus' Temple, unlike the Garden, is framed by Nature and "Art playing second natures part" (x.21) to please the human lovers who enjoy it.

> And all without were walkes and alleyes dight
>   With divers trees, enrang'd in even rankes;
>   And here and there were pleasant arbors pight,
>   And shadie seates, and sundry flowring bankes,
>   To sit and rest the walkers wearie shankes,
>   And therein thousand payres of lovers walkt,
>   Praysing their god, and yeelding him great thankes,
>   Ne ever ought but of their true loves talkt,
> Ne ever for rebuke or blame of any balkt.
>   (IV.x.25)

These lovers are highly articulate (one of them later sings a Lucretian hymn to "Great *Venus*, Queene of beautie and of grace"), and the place where they learn to love is a carefully articulated image. It is full of echoes, in particular literary echoes. As in the Bower of Bliss, but with a different tonality, allusiveness makes plain its character as a product of human invention—its artfulness, using that term in a loose sense.

The Bower and the Temple, indeed, make a more revealing juxtaposition in some ways than do the Bower and the Garden, subject of C. S. Lewis's seminal discussion. Both Bower and Temple are made by the human imagination,

[6] Millar Maclure, "Nature and Art in *The Faerie Queene*," *ELH* XXVIII (1961), 18.

envisaging alternative possibilities for erotic life. The *potential* character of the human situation is the subject of Pico's great myth in the *Oration*; unlike other creatures, man makes himself, choosing his own model from those invented or perceived by the imagination. No particular way of life is "natural" to man; "each hath his fortune in his brest," in the words of Spenser's Melibee (VI.ix.29). The Elder Brother in *Comus* explains some of the choices open to every man; he can either "imbrute" himself or "converse with heavenly habitants" (458). Or (as Milton later came to recognize) he can choose to emulate his first parents, whose unfallen sexuality is mimed in the marriage service and St. Paul's assertion of the mystery: "They shall be one flesh." This union is imaged in the mystery of the hermaphrodite Venus;[7] it is elected by Scudamour, whereas Verdant and the other victims of Acrasia choose to follow the mindless course of mere sensuality. Neither choice is inherent in the human condition; each is the result of consciousness and self-consciousness; and each is expressed by Spenser in terms of artifice and artifact. The concealed art of the Bower exists to persuade man that he is acting spontaneously in entering the trap set by pleasure, but Guyon, like Marvell's Resolved Soul, knows better. The visible art of Venus' pleasance exists to initiate men, through a deliberate *ascesis*, into the paradisal idea: that love may be enjoyed without sin.

> In such luxurious plentie of all pleasure,
>   It seem'd a second paradise to ghesse,
>   So lavishly enricht with natures threasure,
>   That if the happie soules, which doe possesse
>   Th' Elysian fields and live in lasting blesse,

[7] Donald Cheney, "Spenser's Hermaphrodite and the 1590 *Faerie Queene*," *PMLA* LXXXVII (1972), 192-200, deals with the union of the lovers at the end of Book III in 1590; for the hermaphrodite Venus, see Roche, *Kindly Flame*, pp. 134-36; Fowler, *Numbers of Time*, pp. 162-65.

Should happen this with living eye to see,
They soone would loath their lesser happinesse,
And wish to life return'd againe to bee,
That in this joyous place they mote have joyance free.

(IV.x.23)

This "joyance free" belongs among the "unreproved pleasures free" of Milton's *L'Allegro*; the pleasure of this
Garden was born from the embrace of Cupid and Psyche,
whose story Spenser relates at the conclusion of the Garden
of Adonis canto (III.vi.50). Boccaccio, interpreting the
Apuleian myth, writes of the "Pleasure, which is eternal
bliss and joy," born of the Soul's union with Amor.[8] Spenser
has something more earthy in mind, but his pleasure too is
sanctified: "spotless pleasures and sweet loves concent"
(26).

Scudamour comes to it "by triall," through a discipline
that enacts the doubts, dangers, and delays that attend a
virtuous human love affair. The allegorical personages—
versions of whom appear in more sinister form at the House
of Busirane—express the emotions sometimes of the lover,
sometimes of the lady, sometimes of both. Doubt embodies
Scudamour's Janus-like reluctance to close one door and
open a new one (12); at the climax he is able to overcome
it, "shaking off all doubt and shamefast feare" (53).[9] Delay
is the lady's corresponding coyness, to which the knight responds much like Marvell's lover, accusing Amoret of

Feigning full many a fond excuse to prate,
And time to steale, the threasure of mans day,
Whose smallest minute lost, no riches render may.

(14)

[8] "Dum perituris dimissis rebus in eternam defertur gloriam, et ibi
ex amore parturit Voluptatem, id est delectationem et laetitiam sempi-
ternam" (V.xxii); *Genealogie deorum Gentilium libri*, ed. Vincenzo
Romano (2 vols., Bari, 1951), I, 261.

[9] Spenser connects Janus with the beginning of new love in *Amoretti*
iv; and see Fowler, *Numbers of Time*, p. 166.

This is the obverse of the *carpe diem* song in the Bower of Bliss which perverted a natural human impulse to demonic use. And so Scudamour proceeds through a series of encounters that reverberate with allusiveness; he is enacting the publicly condoned, familiar ritual of courtship, made available by the imagination in the *Roman de la Rose* and its analogues. The conventionality of the knight's adventures, in the context of literary allegory and romance, is recorded in the Variorum notes. Chaucerian allegory, in particular *The Parlement of Foules,* is very much present; it is not solely in completing the *Squire's Tale* that Spenser in Book IV experiences the "infusion sweet" of his great predecessor's spirit. The tree catalogue of Stanza 22 is only the beginning of his indebtedness. The effect of this Garden, as of Chaucer's, is to emphasize the artfulness of the natural order, "All which by nature made did nature selfe amaze" (24). What Nature achieves spontaneously with the aid of her sergeant Order, we achieve only through the laborious byways of art; her intricate inventions are thus inevitably "seen" by us, when we see them truly, in metaphors of art—they are the art which Nature makes.

Scudamour praises "the temple of great *Venus*" in a stanza that compares it to the Temple of Diana of the Ephesians and Solomon's Temple, and ends with a comprehensive reference to *all* such edifices:

> Nor all, that else through all the world is named
> To all the heathen Gods, might like to this be clamed.
>
> (30)

The form of the locution validates the claim of this Venus to be something more than a mere "heathen" deity, just as her Temple is more than a house made with hands. It is made, ultimately, by the human imagination to express its vision of the nature and power of Love, using Nature as a model. Its mode of existence is therefore "deep within the mind"; but in that depth is reflected "erthe and hevene, / And fer above the sterris sevene." As the product of man's "secret inwarde syght," the island of Venus, its Garden and Temple, is appropriately rendered as a conjunction of Nature and Art, since it is only by our art that we understand Nature.

> The "gardens" of Adonis could not be Spenser's last word. . . . It is rather to this pleasaunce in Book IV that Spenser would direct us; and in it, as in Chaucer and Alain, along with Venus there is Nature, and Nature is the goddess of orderly creation. . . . If there is a place for the Artist, the Maker, in this pleasaunce or in the world, it is because Nature herself is supreme artist.[10]

A similar conjunction appears for similar reasons, in the Acidalian vision of Book VI and the epiphany of Nature in the *Mutabilitie Cantos*. In all of them, the presence of artifacts or artfulness, and of fictive spectators, is a sign that we are dealing with a visible, socially available product of imagination, what we call a convention—cultural, literary, or both at once. The aspect of reality represented in the Garden of Adonis is experienced privately by the poet because it is apprehended only at the intuitive or visceral level by human beings, and also because our experience of the biological cycle insofar as it is merely organic does not demand a ritualized social context in order to be properly understood and entered into. Spenser and his allegory return to the daylight at the end of the canto with the myth of Cupid and Psyche, and that is the link between the Garden and the Temple of Book IV.

The Venus of Book IV is, then, Love as it emerges from the somatic darkness of physiological response and becomes a subject of discussion, representation, contemplation, and conscious experience both joyful and painful. She is "de-

[10] J.A.W. Bennett, *The Parlement of Foules, An Interpretation* (Oxford, 1957), p. 121.

scribed" twice: in terms of her effects in the Lucretian hymn of Stanzas 44-47, and in terms of her attributes in the veiled statue (39-41). Spenser repeats this goddess's claim to participate in a more nearly ultimate order of reality than that expressible by pagan mythology when he describes the statue as surpassing "All other Idoles, which the heathen adore" (40)—including Phidias' image of Paphian Venus, "with which that wretched Greeke . . . / Did fall in love." The allusion suggests that in this stanza the poet is claiming for his fiction a degree of validity that is superior to the art of Phidias, because it distinguishes more successfully between the fictive and the literal. The veil that covers the statue is a statement of the fiction's limits; we do not look directly upon ultimate mysteries unless we are granted the visionary power for which Milton prays in his epic, and Spenser is not invoking that here—he claims its privilege only in Book I to let us see Una unveiled, and the New Jerusalem. The androgynous nature of Venus—as of Nature in *Mutabilitie*—also expresses a mystery, that is, a realm of being more comprehensive and complex than any we know in the lower world. Paradox is one of the conventional means of suggesting the nature of this ultimate realm, as efforts to describe the deity, from earliest times to such Renaissance adepts as Nicholas of Cusa and Sir Thomas Browne, bear witness.[11] Though Scudamour in Book IV says of the statue that "The cause why she was covered with a vele, / Was hard to know" (41), the poet, speaking much later in his own voice about Nature, gives several reasons. One is that her essence is paradoxical, combining male and female, terrible ("like a Lion") and beautiful (VII.vii.6); it is thus "uncouth" to human understanding, in both senses of the word. Nature's countenance is, like Una's, so bright that it cannot "be seene, but like an image in a glass." And Spenser then solemnly invokes that most awesome of scriptural events, the Transfiguration, when the disciples "their

---

[11] See Rosalie L. Colie, *Paradoxia Epidemica: The Renaissance Tradition of Paradox* (Princeton, 1966), pp. 344-45 and Ch. 11 *passim*.

glorious Lord in strange disguise / Transfigur'd sawe" (7). The "disguise" in fact expressed the true ultimate nature of the Lord.

The ceremonies and images of IV.x are evidence of the human imagination's effort to make sense of its most intimate experiences in the light of what it understands of natural process. This is accomplished by the disciplines of love and art. The decorum of Scudamour's behavior is rewarded by Venus' smile and the proper degree of boldness required to win Amoret (56). He compares his feat to that of Orpheus winning "His Leman from the Stygian Princes boure" (58); the reference is designedly ironic in light of his later loss of the lady to another Stygian Prince, Busirane. But Orpheus in Book IV of *The Faerie Queene* is connected with another range of meanings, the power of Concord and her human instruments. In an earlier reference Spenser evokes Orpheus as the pacifier of the Argonauts' strife (ii.1); the music of his wise words makes concords out of discords. And Concord, "the nourse of pleasure and delight," sits in the porch of Venus' temple employing "powrefull speach" to tame Hatred (35-36). Book IV of *The Faerie Queene*, like Book III, suggests a number of analogies between love and art, which both flourish when imagination is healthy. If, as several critics have suggested, the concluding stanzas of Book III in the 1590 version of the poem were to be inserted at the end of Book IV, Canto ix in the revised version, we should have a conclusion within a conclusion, the reunion of the lovers followed by Scudamour's account of his initial triumph in Canto x. Even without rewriting Spenser's poem for him, or repairing his oversights, we can see a remnant of this pattern, for Scudamour prefaces his narrative by announcing his joy in finding that he has been wrong in believing Amoret unfaithful.

> So all that ever yet I have endured,
> I count as naught, and tread downe under feet,

> Since of my love at length I rest assured,
> That to disloyalty she will not be allured.
>
> (IV.x.2)

Doubt as Venus' porter looks back as well as forward, but the Scudamour/Orpheus who wins Amoret has not yet looked back, and the atemporality of Spenser's narrative, which places the Busirane crisis before the Temple of Venus, allows the triumph at the Temple to become part of the celebration of love and art in Book IV.

These triumphs include not only the union of Scudamour and Amoret, but the epiphany of Britomart to Artegal, the reconciliation of Belphoebe and Timias, the wedding of Thames and Medway, and the betrothal of Marinell and Florimell (not to mention the completion of *The Squire's Tale*).[12] As in Shakespearean comedy, multiple weddings express the concords emerging from preceding discords and anticipate a new reign of peace. Our gaze is directed forward to final things, as it is at the conclusion of Spenser's *Epithalamion*, where we hear of "a large posterity" and "heavenly tabernacles." This prayer is followed by the short stanza in which the poet offers his poem as "an endlesse moniment" to his lady. As at the end of Book IV, the poet's role is that of prophet, a role he assumes insofar as he commands an imagination that can conceive and embody the fulfillment of potentiality. Spenser incorporates two significant figures in the river-marriage of Canto xi which refer to the conjoint powers of prophecy and poetry. Ocean and Tethys, ancestors of bride and bridegroom, are heralded in the procession by Nereus, who is characterized as a true prophet, "Most voide of guile":

> Thereto he was expert in prophecies,
> And could the ledden of the Gods unfold;

---

12 Williams notes that Book IV "is built . . . around a series of meetings or assemblies," and that the resolution and knitting-up of situations replaces the "conflict, separation, complication" of Book III (*World of Glass*, p. 122).

Through which, when *Paris* brought his famous prise
The faire Tindarid lasse, he him fortold,
That her all *Greece* with many a champion bold
Should fetch againe, and finally destroy
Proud *Priams* towne. So wise is *Nereus* old,
And so well skild.

(IV.xi.19)

We need not conjecture that Spenser is alluding to his own
role as the prophet of a new Troy, in order to perceive the
relevance of this decorative stanza. Nereus' power as the interpreter of divine speech—"the ledden of the Gods"—and
the unfolder of mysteries, is analogous to that of the visionary poet; the suggestion is reinforced when, in the next
movement of the pageant, the bridegroom is preceded by
a figure "playing on the watery plaine": Arion the poet. As
Roche remarks, "he represents the power of order and harmony to curb the cruel and unlawful aspects of the sea";[13]
the description makes clear that this power is exerted
through powerful utterance.

Then was there heard a most celestiall sound,
Of dainty musicke, which did next ensew
Before the spouse: that was *Arion* crownd;
Who playing on his harpe, unto him drew
The eares and hearts of all that goodly crew,
That even yet the Dolphin, which him bore
Through the Ægaean seas from Pirates vew,
Stood still by him astonisht at his lore,
And all the raging seas for joy forgot to rore.

(IV.xi.23)

Spenser's Arion is a seagoing Orpheus. Milton was later to
portray the taming of the waters by the Omnific Word, and
the notion can be readily translated into a symbol for the
power of the mortal poet, a symbol which alludes to the
loftiest of analogues. Spenser himself is ordering chaos in

13 *Kindly Flame*, p. 181.

the Thames and Medway canto, a task which tires his
Muse (xi.53), and whose dimensions startle him into
exclamation—

O what an endlesse worke have I in hand,
To count the seas abundant progeny,
Whose fruitfull seede farre passeth those in land,
And also those which wonne in th' azure sky?
(IV.xii.1)

"Then blame me not, if I have err'd in count," he continues (2).

This apology is one note in an undertone of humility that
is associated with most of Spenser's allusions to his own
imagination in *The Faerie Queene*, whether direct or indi-
rect. The tone in which he introduces Nereus and Arion
into the procession is one of celebration and joy, but both
the prophetic and the poetic functions are qualified. The
poet's numbering of stars and floods does not claim accuracy; Nature escapes from the nets that imagination
weaves. One acknowledgment of the form-defeating fluidity
of experience within Nature and time is the presiding image
of *The Faerie Queene*, the poet in his ship wandering in the
perilous flood. He can tame the waters but not contain
them, and his stopping-places are concessions to the vessel's
weakness, rather than boundaries within the tireless unpas-
tured sea itself. For the imagination, every end is necessarily a new beginning, and the open-endedness of Spenser's poem is expressed in a pattern of reiterated inconclusiveness. Every book ends, Janus-like, with a backward and
a forward look; even the most conclusive, the first, anticipates in its final stanza a return by the mariner to "the long
voyage"; the "safe abode" of the haven is temporary
(I.xii.42). The ending of Book IV is particularly inconclusive. Having reached a climax, the revival of Marinell in the
light of his fulfilled love for Florimell, Spenser adds an an-
ticlimactic alexandrine to his last stanza: "Which to another

place I leave to be perfected" (IV.xii.35). The Marinell-Florimell story flows over—most appropriately—into Book V. There are many reasons why their union should be part of the Book of Justice; but its *non*-appearance in the preceding book brings home to us the arbitrariness of the formal patterns the poet is imposing on Nature. To say that the material is too abundant for the form, or that the form dictates a premature truncation of the story, is to offer two descriptions of the same phenomenon. A poetic structure is a procrustean bed on which life lies uneasily; the abrupt conclusion to Book IV is, among other things, a sign that the poet has allowed Proteus to triumph over Procrustes.[14]

And Proteus presides over the final canto of Book IV. As A. B. Giamatti has shown, the avatars of Proteus in Renaissance iconography are themselves protean, and the shepherd of the ocean is ambiguously beneficent and malevolent.[15] In *The Faerie Queene*, Proteus is viewed with suspicion, principally, I think, because of the primary associations of the figure with mutability, always a source of unease for Spenser. Bacon's allegorization of Proteus as matter was also traditional, however, and it is consistent with Spenser's reference throughout the poem to the sea as a matrix of life and figure for the "huge eternall Chaos" which supplies Nature with substance. Florimell is ultimately "freed from *Proteus* cruell band" by being married to Marinell (V.iii.2), but her protean captivity expresses the habitual subjection of natural forms to the limits of their material

14 Spenser could easily, in fact, have included the marriage of Marinell and Florimell within the elastic limits of his canto structure; IV.xii, at only 35 stanzas, is close to the minimal limit for *The Faerie Queene*, 30 stanzas (V.i), and far from the maximal (the 87 stanzas of II.xii). The abrupt lowering of the guillotine in Book IV is often attributed to weariness, but as with Shakespeare's "dotages," we may wish to give the poet the benefit of the doubt when reasonable explanations, based on designed control, suggest themselves.

15 "Proteus Unbound: Some Versions of the Sea God in the Renaissance," in *The Disciplines of Criticism*, ed. P. Demetz, T. Greene, and L. Nelson (New Haven, 1968). On the iconography of Proteus, see also Roche, *Kindly Flame*, pp. 159-60.

nature. Her union with Marinell indicates that cosmos contains chaos, that the changes which we witness and deplore in organic life are controlled by laws expressed through Nature's sergeant, Order (later made visible in *Mutabilitie*), and dictated by the God of Nature. The career of Florimell in Book IV thus "unfolds" some of the meanings superimposed in the Garden of Adonis canto.

More immediately relevant to the poet's role in Book IV is Proteus as the Old Man of the Sea who, when bound, utters prophecies. His freely given prophecy that Marinell's life will be endangered by "A virgin strange and stout" is recorded in Book III (iv.25), but its true significance is revealed only in the fullness of time by whatever providential design insures that truth shall ultimately emerge from darkness. Marinell, though in his fantasies he thinks "*Proteus* to constraine" (IV.xii.14), cannot bind him and release Florimell. Their love cannot flourish until his mother releases herself from her fear of Proteus' prophecy; she does so only when her son is near death.

> It was no time to scan the prophecie,
> Whether old *Proteus* true or false had sayd,
> That his decay should happen by a mayd.
>   (IV.xii.28)

Proteus has spoken truly; Marinell, overthrown on the Rich Strond by Britomart, experiences the second death of love for Florimell's sake. But this prophetic truth is confirmed in action, and by unforeseen ways; the designs of Cymoent cannot thwart it, for Proteus speaks for destiny; he is "the agent of a purpose beyond his own understanding."[16] And destiny, the poet warns,

> findeth dew effect or soone or late.
> So feeble is the powre of fleshly arme.
>   (III.iv.27)

[16] Williams, *World of Glass*, p. 139.

In the mirror of the universe that is *The Faerie Queene*, the poet, like Proteus, utters dark sayings; but they cannot be confirmed, or even properly understood, without the co-operation of natural powers. Unless imagination can overcome its urge to usurp Nature and to attempt the binding of Proteus, it cannot participate in the protean power, and the poet's prophecies will join the other images on the dump thoughtfully charted by Wallace Stevens—the sun and the moon, "the janitor's poems . . . the wrapper on the can of pears, / The cat in the paperbag."[17] Instead, imagination must commit itself to unpathed waters, at the mercy of waves and wind and Proteus' many changes that defy the imposition of a single form.

Spenser in *The Faerie Queene* drew upon whatever sources he had available to invent a form whose flux and reflux could accommodate the rhythms of the different clocks that measure our lives: biological, historical, providential. He controls the form, but in the calculated lapses of control that make part of the design he acknowledges that all structures must, like Proteus' prophecy, be responsive to uninvented reality. The story of Florimell and Marinell flows on like an underground river beneath many cantos, to surface at the end of Book IV and disappear again until its final emergence two cantos later. Ariostan narrative technique, and the medieval strategy of *entrelacement*, which provided Spenser with his most important structural models, can sometimes be used to suggest the maker's high-handed arbitrariness in the handling of his material, but in Spenser's poem these devices convey rather his fidelity to "eternal restless change" and the momentum of destiny. The interlaced narrative of Books III and IV mirrors its subject, the diversity of love's metamorphosing power in "divers minds." In Book IV, Spenser goes beyond this diversity to call in question the containing forms themselves: the grid of stanza and canto that together make up the poem's goodly frame.

17 Stevens, "The Man on the Dump," *Collected Poems*, p. 201.

In no other book are the canto-endings so defiant of narrative decorum, so rebellious toward their own conclusive
function. In all the other books, the customary ending for
a canto is the resolution of a knightly encounter or some
other "natural" stopping-place. Canto viii of Book II is typical: Arthur kills Pyrochles and Cymochles who are attacking the unconscious Guyon; Guyon awakens, the two
knights converse, and the canto ends:

> So goodly purpose they together fond,
> Of kindnesse and of curteous aggrace;
> The whiles false *Archimage* and *Atin* fled apace.
>
> (II.viii.56)

There is almost always a line left free for attachment to future events, but ordinarily Spenser allows the narrative to
catch its breath by making canto and event coincide. Not
so in Book IV. Of the twelve concluding stanzas, nine refer
to the poet himself and his conduct of the narrative; two
others stop but do not conclude an action (Scudamour raising his hand in wrath to kill Glauce in Canto i, and Arthur's promise to provide Æmylia with "remedie" in Canto
viii); only in Canto iii does Spenser offer anything like a
conclusive cadence, and that is at the end of a retrospective
narrative, the story of Cambel and Canacee which has already been completed when we meet these characters in
the foreground action. It is, in fact, an "antique story," the
"lost" conclusion to Chaucer's *Squire's Tale*, and so overflows the narrative limit in a retrospective direction.

> So all alike did love, and loved were,
> That since their dayes such lovers were not
> found elsewhere.
>
> (iii.52)

But this finality is unique in Book IV. The characteristic
note is rather that with which Spenser ends Canto ii:

> The which for length I will not here pursew,
> But rather will reserve it for a Canto new.
>
> (ii.54)

"It" is the impending battle of the three brothers with Cambell. Again, the narrative halts breathlessly in pursuit of the lost Amoret, a story which "Were long to tell; therefore I here will stay / Untill another tyde, that I it finish may" (vi.47); and droops with Timias in unconcluded anguish—"Which for it is too long here to abide, / I will deferre the end untill another tide" (vii.47). Canto ix almost comes to a decorous close with the reconciliation of Britomart and Scudamour, but the poet insists on marring its finality with Britomart's request to hear of Scudamour's adventures—

> Which sith they cannot in this Canto well
> Comprised be, I will them in another tell.
>
> (ix.41)

Twice he pleads weariness: in Canto xi after the exhausting labor of counting "th' Oceans seede," and in Canto v where he declines to follow Scudamour and Glauce in the next "prepared" peril.

> The end whereof and daungerous event
> Shall for another canticle be spared.
> But here my wearie teeme, nigh over spent,
> Shall breath it selfe awhile, after so long a went.
>
> (v.46)

"So long a went" is not so very long; forty-six stanzas are about average for a canto of *The Faerie Queene*, but the limit is often overpassed.

The consistency of this pattern, or lack of pattern, in the canto-endings of Book IV strikes me as a curious fact. As with most facts concerning the narrative of *The Faerie Queene*, we cannot be sure whether it can be attributed to deliberate design. But the indubitable persistence of the poet's self-conscious attention to his own story-telling may point to some underlying uneasiness, whether fully articulate or not. It is as if he abandoned his responsibility to order his protean material in a more than mechanical fashion. He is able to be conclusive only when he follows the footing of Chaucer, or when, in the only other truly *finished* canto, a character has concluded his tale. Scudamour winds up his account of his courtship in the penultimate line of Canto x; the poet speaks in the alexandrine: "So ended he his tale, where I this Canto end" (x.58). There is a note of relief here, as the fictive speaker is allowed to take control of the narrative.[18]

This enfeeblement of structural forms in Book IV is the more curious when it combines with the artfulness of the action and the many plot-resolutions which I spoke of earlier as characterizing this book. The combination reflects the basic tension in the Book of Concord between concordant and dissolving powers: Love and Art on the one hand, on the other "the stream of destiny" and the unruled forces of Chaos and old Night, whose activities are hidden from our understanding. Spenser makes explicit this tension in the confrontation of Agape and the Fates in Canto ii. These

---

[18] Book VI is the only other book in *The Faerie Queene* to approach IV in the inconclusiveness of its canto-structures. Six of the twelve cantos (ii, iii, v, vii, viii, ix) end with self-conscious wielding of the narrative shears, resembling those quoted above from Book IV, e.g., "The end whereof Ile keepe untill another cast" (VI.viii.51). One canto (iv) ends in the middle of an action, with Calepine "in anguish tost," lamenting the loss of Serena. Three cantos (i, vi, xi), on the other hand, are models of Spenserian conclusiveness, with the usual forward-cast thread to the next adventure, e.g., "The morrow next the Prince did early rize, / And passed forth to follow his first enterprize" (VI.vi. 44). The end of the final canto is in a class by itself. In my opinion, Book VI's violation of canto-boundaries, like that of Book IV, reflects the presence of the untamed sea of mortal life, which must somehow be acknowledged, though not contained, by legitimate art.

characters belong to the middle level of the poem's ontological range; they are immortal principles but not divini-
ties. Agape is a Fay who commands the art of white magic:

> the skill
> Of secret things, and all the powres of nature,
> Which she by art could use unto her will,
> And to her service bind each living creature,
> Through secret understanding of their feature.
>
> (IV.ii.44)

The "secret" nature of this power is a sign that it is ordinarily inaccessible to human beings; it is the paradigm for
human art, which also seeks to subdue Nature through understanding and "bind" it into a concordant pattern satisfying to human needs as an emblem of possibility. Agape, the
conscious, shaping impulse in Love, is a name for the desire
to redeem Nature from the ravages of temporality; but it
is effectually employed only by Love itself, which entered
the world once. Spenser's character Agape is the humanized
form of this impulse, doomed, like all our desires, to incomplete realization. The Fay's proposal cannot be altogether
translated into actuality. Her visit to "the three fatall sisters
house" is "an attempt on Spenser's part to foster an awed
respect for those dark forces that constitute the material
source of our being."[19] It also expresses our need to defy
these powers. The fatal sisters live in one of the intercon-
nected chambers of Spenser's underworld:

> Farre under ground from tract of living went,
> Downe in the bottome of the deepe *Abysse*,
> Where *Demogorgon* in dull darknesse pent
> Farre from the view of Gods and heavens blis,
> The hideous *Chaos* keepes, their dreadfull dwelling is.
>
> (IV.ii.47)

Spenser has mentioned Demogorgon once before, in the

19 Roche, *Kindly Flame*, pp. 19-20.

description of Night[20] in Book I, where he is associated with "the secrets of the world unmade" (I.v.22). So here, Agape is challenged as "Bold Fay, that durst / Come see the secret of the life of man" (ii.49). The place is obviously adjacent to that "strong rocky Cave" in which the wild boar of death is imprisoned, beneath the Garden of Adonis (III.vi.48). The central "secret of the life of man" is death, the moment of whose coming is mercifully veiled from each of us.

The confrontation of Love and Fate ends in a Spenserian compromise, a solution that we have seen before. It is mythically expressed in Adonis, "by succession made perpetuall" through the embrace of Venus. In Agape and her sons, Spenser gives a rationalized version of the same principle. "Succession" acquires a fictive literalness in the linked lives of Priamond, Diamond, and Triamond. "Through traduction" (iii.13) the life-force of each brother is re-embodied in the next; Spenser uses a familiar metamorphic image to describe the "traduction" of Diamond's life to Triamond's.

> Some newborne wight ye would him surely weene:
> So fresh he seemed and so fierce in sight;
> Like as a Snake, whom wearie winters teene
> Hath worne to nought, now feeling sommers might,
> Casts off his ragged skin and freshly doth him dight.
> (IV.iii.23)

These lines re-express the notion of a vital energy "eterne in mutabilitie"; Triamond looks like a "newborne wight" because he really is one, and the image of the snake renewing its winter weeds links the phenomenon to seasonal process within the natural cycle. Agape cannot succeed in evading this process; she leaves the Fates "with full contented mynd" (ii.53), but the contentment is really what *we* are expected to feel, and it is the consequence of knowledge, not power, for we are powerless to alter the order

[20] Noted by Roche, Ibid., p. 19 n., who gives a good account of the conflicting values assigned to Demogorgon by the mythographers, pp. 18-21.

"ordained by eternall fate" (ii.50). As Lachesis says, they are "fond" who suppose

> of things divine
> As of humane, that they may altred bee,
> And chaunged at pleasure.
>
> (IV.ii.51)

Agape's sons must still endure "the miserie of their estate": that is, they must fare on through the perilous flood of time—

> And thousand perills which them still awate,
> Tossing them like a boate amid the mayne.
>
> (iii.1)

It is the same ocean on which the poet's frail craft is tossed. Spenser's account of the Fates in Demogorgon's house completes his vision of the cosmic context of life and death in which the many experiences we call "love" must unfold. Together with the Temple of Venus, it expresses our conscious response to this great mystery; these two episodes of Book IV relate the chthonic powers revealed in the Garden of Adonis to human life, human understanding, and human art. Thus, although Spenser's imagining of Agape and her sons may have begun as "no more than a didactic exercise," his exploration of what happens psychologically when heavenly love is "unfolded" into human forms becomes a moving statement of those limits which only imagination and grace transcend.[21]

The bargain struck between Love and Fate illustrates the precariousness of Concord, who must mediate between the "contrarie natures" of her two sons, Love and Hate (IV.x.32). And those contrary natures are reflected in the contrasting aspects of formal structure in Book IV. Love, Spenser tells us, is "stronger in his state"; and his strength

21 Wind, *Pagan Mysteries*, p. 210.

is manifested in the many concorded loves and completed plots. But the invisible subterranean power that mars concords and subverts forms remains present in the book, as Hate, the elder brother, remains in the porch of Venus. Arion's music tames the ocean, and the poet controls the waters by naming them. But the floods, "so numberlesse their nation" (IV.xii.1), escape from his net at last, as the events of his fiction escape from the grid of twelve cantos that he has ordained for them. As he prepares to recite his catalogue of *"Neptunes* seed" Spenser movingly acknowledges the impossibility of the task, and the ultimate triumph of uninvented reality from which art draws its sustenance—as Yeats concludes his vision of Byzantium with a celebration of the image-spawning sea.

> But what doe I their names seeke to reherse,
> Which all the world have with their issue fild?
> How can they all in this so narrow verse
> Contayned be, and in small compasse hild?
>
> (IV.iv.17)

PART IV

Book VI: The Paradise Within

1. Centers and Sources

Book VI of *The Faerie Queene* has received its due from critics only since the renaissance of Spenserian studies over the past quarter-century. This is not surprising, for in his last completed book Spenser achieved the most original and unexpected of his imaginings, and one that is congenial to our modern taste for self-contemplation. Consequently, we are probably better equipped to understand what the poet is doing in this book than any previous generation of readers has been. The readings of Book VI by recent critics have made clear that the final book is a parable of the power and limitations of the imagination.

> The complete self-sufficiency of the second nature, the total inward mastery of experience—this is no triumph at all, only delusion, if it takes itself seriously. . . . Thus poetry, having triumphed, must dissolve its triumph again and again to show that it is still engaged in the ongoing process of life where experience is not yet ordered. On Mount Acidale, when the play of mind realizes its vision, the poet dissolves it and moves on. . . . So the poem returns to the blatant beast and to its own dissolution.[1]

Harry Berger's account, which concludes with these sentences, has been reaffirmed by a number of other writers, whose insights have made my task in this chapter easier.[2]

[1] Harry Berger, "A Secret Discipline: *The Faerie Queene*, Book VI," *Form and Convention in the Poetry of Edmund Spenser*, ed. William Nelson (New York, 1961), p. 74.

[2] I am indebted to the discussions of Book VI by Kathleen Williams, *World of Glass*, Ch. 6; and Donald Cheney, *Spenser's Image of Nature: Wild Man and Shepherd in "The Faerie Queene"* (New Haven, 1966). Tonkin calls Book VI "a poem talking about itself" (*Courteous Pastoral*, p. 142); in it, "Spenser dramatizes the battle against the enemies of poetry" (p. 110).

The theme of imagination's role in human life is a dominant one in Book VI; and that means that another of Spenser's subjects is necessarily close to the surface. *The Faerie Queene*, like *Paradise Lost*, examines the powerful attraction which the idea of paradise exerts upon the human imagination and considers various responses to this attraction, both innocent and dangerous. Innocence and danger are keynotes of the tone in Book VI; they come together in Canto xi, to remind us that the effort to actualize paradise and live there is satanic.

> The woods did nought but ecchoes vaine rebound;
> The playnes all waste and emptie did appeare:
> Where wont the shepheards oft their pypes resound,
> And feede an hundred flocks, there now not one he
> > found.
> > (VI.xi.26)

These lines describe the fate of the pastoral retreat at the hands of the brigands, and the major action of the book is framed to make us understand the nature of the disaster. An unearned literal eden can only be baleful now for a human soul; paradise has been definitively lost, and must be replaced, as Michael explains to fallen Adam and Eve, by a paradise within,

> New making Paradise, where we began,
> Not in a garden, but the heart of man.[3]

What this means, Spenser suggests in several ways: the fact that none of his virtuous knights is allowed to linger in a garden of delight; that he himself approaches the guarded precincts with the utmost circumspection; that a paradise within "means," for us, a place wrought by imagination, a place that "none can find but who was taught them by the

---

[3] Greville, *An Inquisition upon Fame and Honour*, st. 80; *Poems and Dramas*, I, 212.

Muse" (VI.Pro.2), as demonstrated in the central vision of Book VI.

This suggests that the poem's super-plot, which records the long quest or voyage of the poet himself, reaches its consummation in Book VI, as the narrator's flight through *Paradise Lost* concludes in the self-defining prologue to Book IX. There have been those who argue that this book is indeed the designed conclusion of *The Faerie Queene*, that Spenser, realizing that he would write no more, wound up this truncated epic with an appropriate finality.[4] Whatever the cause, Book VI looks inevitable in the light of Spenser's management of the first five—inevitable, that is, in the manner of artistic masterpieces, whose miraculous strangeness is immediately domesticated by the fidelity of their response to needs we do not recognize until they have been filled. Especially does Book VI look inevitable as it emerges out of the adventures of Artegal in the Book of Justice. The link between the two books, in plot and theme, is the Blatant Beast; and a comparison of the two Proems (the two longest of the six in *The Faerie Queene*) will make clear the sense in which Courtesy is a response to Justice. The Proem to Book V describes the crookedness of "the state of present time": it is a vision of history, establishing the temporal context of the poem, the equivalent of the "wider" Fairy Land in space. The decline from *then* to *now* is reiterated in the main action of Book V, which moves from "*Artegall* in justice . . . upbrought / Even from the cradle of his infancie" (V.i.5), to Artegal interrupted in his irenic mission by the howls of the Blatant Beast. Book V, as most readers have understood, is the most worldly, the most completely implicated in history of any part of *The Faerie*

4 See Frye, *Fables of Identity*, p. 70, and Richard Neuse's development of Frye's suggestion in "Book VI as Conclusion to *The Faerie Queene*," *ELH* XXXV (1968), 329-53. Various cases are made for the unity of the existing poem in the essays collected by Kenneth J. Atchity in *Eterne in Mutabilitie: The Unity of "The Faerie Queene"* (Hamden, Conn., 1972).

Queene. The necessary struggle against principalities and powers is succeeded, in the final Proem, by the quest for an invisible kingdom, the only kind that is invulnerable to the devastations of worldly rage.

> Revele to me the sacred noursery
>   Of vertue, which with you doth there remaine,
>   Where it in silver bowre does hidden ly
>   From view of men, and wicked worlds disdaine.
>   Since it at first was by the Gods with paine
>   Planted in earth, being derived at furst
>   From heavenly seedes of bounty soveraine,
>   And by them long with carefull labour nurst,
> Till it to ripenesse grew, and forth to honour burst.
>
> (VI.Pro.3)

In this stanza, Spenser moves from the horizontal axis of his microcosm to the vertical, from temporality to the spatial figures that will characterize Book VI. "At first," here has logical and ontological force; we are being reminded of a chain of being, a sequence of emanations, of giving, receiving, and returning that flows perpetually, without reference to the eddying of the stream of time. The process is the same as that which produces "son[s] of light / In a dark age" in the final books of *Paradise Lost.* Here in Spenser's poem, it produces the flower on a lowly stalk, "the bloosme of comely courtesie" (4).

The flower image has retrospective force; it helps to define the imaginative contrast between the world of Book VI and that of Artegal's book. His world has declined from the Saturnian age when

> Peace universall rayn'd mongst men and beasts,
> And all things freely grew out of the ground.
>
> (V.Pro.9)

As a result, the knight must be "trayn'd in Justice lore" (Arg.i); he cannot be left to develop spontaneously in a state of nature. The situation calls for heroic action, the pressure of the will upon circumstance:

> then likewise the wicked seede of vice
> Began to spring which shortly grew full great,
> And with their boughes the gentle plants did beat.
> But evermore some of the vertuous race
> Rose up, inspired with heroicke heat,
> That cropt the branches of the sient base,
> And with strong hand their fruitfull ranckness did
> > deface.
> > (V.i.1)

Calidore's virtue flourishes on its lowly stalk, freely growing from the ground of an uncorrupted "nature"; Artegal's strong (and instructed) hand prunes the rankness of branches that grow from a corrupt root. In the clash between these two images, the essence of Spenser's distinction between Justice and Courtesy is expressed. The patron of Justice requires strong hands, for he must enforce "the Law of a Commonweal, the very soul of a politic body." This law, as Hooker explains and Spenser assumes, is a response to the "rankness" of human nature.

> Laws politic, ordained for external order and regiment amongst men, are never framed as they should be, unless presuming the will of men to be inwardly obstinate, rebellious, and averse from all obedience unto the sacred laws of his nature; in a word, unless presuming man to be in regard of his depraved mind little better than a wild beast, they do accordingly provide notwithstanding so to frame his outward actions, that they be no hinderance unto the common good for which societies are instituted.[5]

It is appropriate that Artegal's first triumph over an "uncivill fo," Sir Sanglier, concludes with the victim "Bound

[5] Richard Hooker, *Of the Laws of Ecclesiastical Polity*, Everyman's Library (2 vols., London, 1954), I, 188.

like a beast" (V.i.22). Restraint, not reform, is the aim of Artegal's exploits.

The Knight of Justice belongs, therefore, to history; like the Red Cross Knight, he is a British changeling in Fairy Land, "sprong of seed terrestriall" (III.iii.26). He is, in fact, a step-sibling of Arthur, "the sonne of *Gorlois*" (27). But Calidore springs from different seed, and we hear nothing of his breeding. History-less like the other Faeries, he simply turns up at court, a full-made knight in whom "manners mylde were planted naturall" (VI.i.2). He can "steale mens hearts away" without trying. We learn from Calidore's effortless charm and his Faerie heritage that the principle of courtesy defies circumstance and the pressures of environment. Spenser's figure for this mystery is the idea of innate, congenital virtue or "noble birth" which can reveal itself in a savage or a shepherd's daughter as well as in a courtly knight. The old romance motif of the lost child is given conceptual weight as a *tertium quid* in which the debate between nature and nurture is resolved.[6] The Proem stanza (VI.Pro.3) describes a nuture *within* Nature that reproduces the pre-lapsarian state of affairs before nature was overtaken by process and began to "runne quite out of square, / From the first point of his appointed sourse" (V.Pro.1). Spenser translates his pun, the point of the appointed source, into vision in Book VI: the source is the central point of an invisible circle from which "all goodly vertues well / Into the rest, which round about you ring" (Pro.7).

"You" is the Queen in her aspect of Astraea/Gloriana, ruler of an invisible kingdom celebrated by her poets. The "silver bowre" where virtue is nurtured cannot be seen by mortal eye, but is revealed by the Muses to whom the poet prays in Stanza 2. This fact may remind us of the Garden of Adonis, another secret bower and sacred nursery, and I would like for a moment to return to Book III, which closes the first part of *The Faerie Queene* as Book VI closes the

6 See Nelson, *Poetry of Spenser*, p. 277.

second. The Garden also reflects an "inner" world of psychic experience, though at a level which we should now call unconscious, and Aristotelian psychology, the realm of the vegetal and sensitive souls. It is the fostering-place of Amoret, where she is nurtured within Nature until "she to perfect ripenes grew, / Of grace and beautie noble Paragone" (III.vi.52). The image of the growth to perfect ripeness and flowering "forth to honour" is similar to that in the Proem to Book VI. And the later book also echoes the passage which describes the origin of the second twin, Belphoebe. Her chastity is the treasure "whose flowre / The girlond of her honour did adorne" (III.v.51); this flower, like that of Courtesy, was planted first in Paradise.

> Eternall God in his almighty powre,
>   To make ensample of his heavenly grace,
>   In Paradize whilome did plant this flowre,
>   Whence he it fetcht out of her native place,
>   And did in stocke of earthly flesh enrace,
>   That mortall men her glory should admire:
>   In gentle Ladies brest, and bounteous race
> Of woman kind it fairest flowre doth spire,
> And beareth fruit of honour and all chast desire.
>   (III.v.52)

We need not argue that the similarities between this stanza and the "sacred noursery" stanza of Book VI were deliberately planted by Spenser. It is rather a habit of imagining that is in question. The fact that a particular configuration of "meanings" persistently takes flesh in a particular verbal and imagistic matrix has been established for Shakespeare, beginning with the writings of Caroline Spurgeon and Wilson Knight. Similar iterations sound throughout the poetry and prose of Milton, and they may be taken as a sign that we have to do with a major imagination, powerfully inventive and self-nourishing. Spenser in both these stanzas is elucidating the meaning of *source* as a permanent "place" of origin which will account for—that is, satisfy the imag-

349

ination's need to explain—the kinship of virtue that persists despite the darkness of times. Defiance of temporality entails a conceptual or imagined mode of existence: the notion of an atemporal realm of recurrences, the *aevum*. Hence the concept of a garden of origins that has been transposed from the mode of time—the temporally distant point from which history flows—to the mode of inner space—a "first point" that focuses ontological priority. In the two quoted stanzas, this "place" is made actual within the fiction and gives rise to a miniature myth of divine nurture and transplantation "in stocke of earthly flesh."[7]

Spenser's other metaphor for this process is elaborated in the Proem to Book VI, where he wishes to create an imaginative linkage between divine virtue and "learnings threasures"—the products of human invention that make those virtues visible to the eye of the mind, providing "secret comfort and . . . heavenly pleasures" (2) to those burdened by "tedious travell" in the world. Spenser is here writing about an imagined place of refreshment like Marvell's Garden, where the mind, wearied by incessant labours, "Withdraws into its happiness." The "first point" or source of these pleasures is the top of Parnassus, whence the pleasures and treasures of learning "Into the mindes of mortall men doe well." The fountain that overflows from center to circumference provides an image again at the end of the Proem: "Right so from you all goodly vertues well." The home of the Muses, and the idealized court of Elizabeth, are drawn together as concentric circles, sources of virtue *on earth* which correspond to the hidden heavenly

[7] The effort of archaic religions to transcend and transfigure time by inventing the mode of recurrence has been lucidly set out by Mircea Eliade, *Cosmos and History: The Myth of the Eternal Return*, tr. Willard R. Trask, Torchbooks ed. (New York, 1959). Eliade remarks that for Christians, "the *illud tempus* is eternally of the present and accessible to anyone, at any moment. . . . Christianity translates the periodic regeneration of the world into a regeneration of the human individual" (p. 129): hence the "paradise within."

bower that is the ultimate source.[8] This conjunction dates from Spenser's earliest years as a poet. In the three eclogues of *The Shepheardes Calender* which offer some hope of escape from the wheel of time, these three "sources" of virtue are reflected. *Aprill* contains a vision of the peaceable kingdom, a pastoral arcadian world presided over by "fayre *Eliza*, Queene of shepheardes all" (34), Spenser's first version of Gloriana. In *October* the "divine instinct" of imagination is invoked as Piers describes the power of "musicks might the hellish hound [to] tame" (30)—Cerberus, whose descendant is the Blatant Beast. Finally, in *November* Spenser gives us a glimpse of the ultimate happy place —"The fieldes ay fresh, the grasse ay greene" (189)—in his elegy for Dido.

The quest of Book VI, then, is a quest for sources[9] and its design links it, again, with Book III, where the sources lie both deep and high, *altus*, ranged along a vertical pole. Alastair Fowler's suggestion that both books are dedicated to a version of Venus is interesting in this connection. The Venus who embraces Adonis in the Garden is "the same" as, but different from, the Venus who sports with the Graces on Mt. Acidale. As Wind notes, the avatars of Venus are concordant: she is one of the deities who, "inherently composite and contrarious contain multiplicity within their own natures and are hence not agonized when their power is spread out, or paired with that of other deities."[10] Both Venuses are sources, both concordant powers. Fowler in his discussion of the numerological import of Book VI observes that "there is no symbolic conception of the hexad

[8] On circles in Book VI, see Williams, *World of Glass*, p. 217; Berger, "Secret Discipline," pp. 49-50.

[9] Berger discusses the theme of return to "the ideal mythic place of origins" in "'Faerie Queene' Book III: A General Description," *Criticism* XI (1969), 253. His stress on "the backward and downward pull exerted by the matrix or chaos on figures struggling to emerge and break free" strikes me, however, as more reductive than the poem itself allows.

[10] *Pagan Mysteries*, p. 138.

351

known to me that can constitute a centre for all the themes of the sixth book."[11] The two suggestions he does make—of six as a "marriage number" related to the "concern with children" in Book VI, and as a symbol of harmony, based on the six tones of the octave—are very convincing guesses. To them might be added the association of six with perfection and completeness—though again it is right to remind ourselves that the notion that Book VI "completes" *The Faerie Queene* rests on a dubious basis. Augustine devotes a brief chapter to "The perfection of the number six, the first that is complete in all the parts," basing his discussion on the Six Days' Works and the arithmetical concordance whereby the factors of six add up to six. It is thus the first number "that is made of the conjunction of the parts; and in this did God make perfect all His works."[12] In addition, like all the other even numbers six is "empty in the center" and feminine—a biological and geometrical analogy which is certainly consistent with a book presided over by a female deity, and in which the major symbol is the hollow-centered circle of perfection.[13]

Interestingly, Spenser introduces Mt. Acidale into the poem as the fostering-place of Florimell, one of the protégées of Venus—

> her secret bowre,
> On *Acidalian* mount, where many an howre
> She with the pleasant *Graces* wont to play.
> There *Florimell* in her first ages flowre
> Was fostered by those *Graces*, (as they say)
> And brought with her from thence that goodly belt away.
>
> (IV.v.5)

It is appropriate that Florimell, who perfectly embodies the inexplicable power that can "steal mens hearts away,"

---

[11] *Numbers of Time,* p. 48.

[12] *The City of God,* XI.xxx; tr. John Healey, ed. R.V.G. Tasker, Everyman's Library (2 vols., London, 1945), I, 338-39.

[13] See Vincent F. Hopper, *Medieval Number Symbolism* (New York, 1938), p. 40.

should be reared by the Graces, dispensers of that causeless bounty that must ultimately be linked with a divine source. We have already seen how various personages in the middle books focus their fantasy-life on Florimell. She "is" beauty—that is, the principle which elicits love; but it is unsafe to love her "in herself," since such love leads to permanent entrapment in a fantasy world. Hence the baleful images that are associated with Florimell. But the principle she embodies can be fittingly loved when it is "planted" in an actual, mortal person and recreated in the eye of the beholder. It is therefore altogether decorous that Colin's vision of the Florimell-principle should be centered upon "that faire one, . . . to whom that shepheard pypt alone" (VI.x.15), as Calidore's initiation into love is centered upon Pastorella: "a faire damzell, which did weare a crowne / Of sundry flowres" (VI.ix.7). Spenser tells us that she participates in heavenly beauty

> As if some miracle of heavenly hew
> Were downe to them descended in that earthly vew.
> (VI.ix.8)

The heroines of Book VI are instances of mortal ladies to whom the "flowers" of heavenly grace have been handed down.

Colin's unknown maiden dances at the center of the innermost circle in the vision of Canto x.

> Who can aread, what creature mote she bee,
> Whether a creature, or a goddesse graced
> With heavenly gifts from heven first enraced?
> But what so sure she was, she worthy was,
> To be the fourth with those three other placed:
> Yet was she certes but a countrey lasse,
> Yet she all other countrey lasses farre did passe.
> (VI.x.25)

A lass unparalleled, she is one in whom all the graces are "gathered" (27). In her, many principles are symbolically "upfolded" in the manner of Renaissance iconography; indeed, in this most self-conscious passage of the poem, she is an ultimate model for this mode of imagining, earlier manifested in Belphoebe. Colin's refusal to name her points to the privacy and inwardness of the vision, but it also calls attention to the lady's paradigmatic function. The rhetoric of the stanza deliberately leaves open her ontological status, in the rhetorical question and the inconclusive "Yet, . . . Yet."[14] The poet does not say whether she is a goddess or a creature because she is both; she embodies the imagination's power to invent "goddesses" in, and out of, "creatures," universals out of particulars, concepts out of percepts. And such invention is, in turn, a discovery of the way back to the sources in which all human virtues participate, that heaven from which they are "enraced." That verb echoes the stanza on Belphoebe in III.v: "in stocke of earthly flesh enrace." Heaven plants virtues in earthly creatures, where they become *visibilia* that will lead us back to their source. This downpouring and uprising through the power of grace is figured in the forward-and-back circle of the Graces, consistent in iconography through many centuries.[15] "That fourth Mayd" is "graced . . . to be another Grace" (26), uniting the downward movement of *agape* with the upward surge of *eros*.

And *eros*, as Spenser has been suggesting all through the poem, is the twin of imagination.[16] Thus the vision is the

14 It is relevant to recall Timias' waking questions in Belphoebe's bower: "Mercy deare Lord (said he) what grace is this . . . ? / Angell, or Goddesse do I call thee right?" (III.v.35).

15 Wind, *Pagan Mysteries*, Ch. III, *passim*.

16 Berger discusses the "dialectic between the soul and its environment" produced by *eros*, and the manner in which the "given" phenomena "supply the vocabulary through which the soul defines its desire . . . [and] articulates its experience" ("Secret Discipline," p. 59). He overstresses, I think, "the poverty of the actual" and imagination's urge to transcend it. For Spenser the actual was abundant, not impoverished—though, of course, often infected and blighted. The problem

culmination of Spenser's quest for sources in Book VI, in a double sense. It expresses, first, the heavenly source of Calidore's virtue—by analogy, of all genuine virtues:

> These three on men all gracious gifts bestow,
> Which decke the body or adorne the mynde.
>
> (x.23)

The Graces are also, of course, sources of Colin Clout's virtuous imagination. But the song has, in addition, an earthly source, the "other Grace" that is the country lass: "She made me often pipe and now to pipe apace" (27). "Love does teach him climbe so hie," as Piers insists in *October* (91). In the stanzas at the visionary center of Book VI, invisible heavenly Grace becomes incarnate; and at the same time, the visible maiden is made transparent to the peculiar virtue she embodies, as the ambiguous rhetoric of Stanza 25 gives us access to the ideal behind or within the actual woman. In the intersection between visible actuality and invisible transcendence, where *agape* merges with *eros*, poetry has its life. Spenser's visionary stanzas allow us to see the dance of imagination, the concrete universal emerging from the figure the poem makes.

Love and imagination embrace particulars, and the embrace can provide the means whereby we transcend mortality. Every "poore handmayd" shadows "divine resemblaunce" (27) when looked upon with imagination's loving eye. Hence, though the poet asks pardon of Gloriana for linking her with a country lass, the apology actually shows why apology is unnecessary. Gloriana is "Sunne of the world, great glory of the sky," enlightening the earth; but so is the poet's fourth grace:

---

was, rather, to contain and order actuality as God contained Chaos, "in number, weight, and measure." This poet's images are in Stevens' phrase, "fully made, fully apparent, fully found," luminous with the power of actuality in a union with imaginative energy. Spenser is not Blake, though he is one of Blake's ancestors.

> So farre as doth the daughter of the day,
> All other lesser lights in light excell,
> So farre doth she in beautyfull array,
> Above all other lasses beare the bell.
> (26)

The Queen has inspired "many layes," and in this respect too she is like Colin's lass. From both of them virtues emanate, and in both are they gathered. Ultimately all centers are one center, and the lady's anonymity draws our gaze toward the deep truth that is nameless and imageless. All names are finally inadequate, and the name of what we love most will serve most appropriately, whether it is the name of Gloriana, or that of a country lass.

2. Finding What Will Suffice

The vision on Mount Acidale[1] lies at the center of the Book of Courtesy, evoked by the supreme adept in the art of words, the poet. It is an "answer" to the depredations of the Blatant Beast, and so also an essential feature in the experience of the knight who pursues the Beast. This creature enters the poem as the monstrous pet of the hags Envy and Detraction, at the end of Book V. Spenser allows these characters to attack the Knight of Justice, hurling at him a "cursed Serpent" which bites him in the back (another instance of literalized metaphor, V.xii.39). The Beast, like its mistresses, is the enemy of truth and fair speaking, a destroyer of reputations with its "vile tongue and venomous intent" (VI.i.8). Calidore pursues it from court to city, from cities to the towns, from towns into the country, and finally "into the open fields," where he finds "shepheards singing to their flockes" (ix.4), and inquires after the Beast.

> They answer'd him, that no such beast they saw,
> Nor any wicked feend, that mote offend
> Their happie flockes, nor daunger to them draw:
> But if that such there were (as none they kend)
> They prayd high God them farre from them to send.
> (VI.ix.6)

The Blatant Beast is Spenser's most formidable and explicit symbol for the misuse of language; in preserving the pastoral retreat from his ravages, the poet is honoring once more the tradition that makes shepherds' songs the purest instance of human eloquence, the product of spontaneous impulse and innocent intent. Virgil's shepherds, "Arcades

[1] Spenser notes that the hill where he places his paradise "rightly cleeped was mount *Acidale*" (x.8). This consonance of etymology and actuality signifies that it is a place where language is in control.

ambo / et cantare pares, et respondere parati," always ready with a song, are important models.[2] But Spenser's Knight of Courtesy cannot learn the art of perfect eloquence, though in a lower key he can be persuasive. His love, Pastorella, prefers the poet's songs to the knight's "queint usage"—

> But cared more for *Colins* carolings
> Then all that he could doe, or ever devize:
> His layes, his loves, his lookes she did them all despize.
>
> (VI.ix.35)

Having "lost himselfe" (26) in an unfamiliar context, Calidore sets out to remake himself, "And doffing his bright armes, himselfe addrest / In shepheards weed" (36); like the young heroes in Sidney's *Arcadia*, he must divest himself of superficial refinement and learn the lessons of love and art in pastoral innocence. Yet, as Sidney designs his great romance to expose the limitations as well as the felicities of Arcadia, so Spenser in Book VI shapes his narrative to reveal the fragility of pastoral harmonies and the naiveté of innocence. In the very canto of the Acidalian vision, brigands rape the rural retreat, a consummation foreshadowed by the beautiful allusive stanza describing the dance and the "bloudy fray" that interrupted another festival (VI.x.13).

Calidore, as the patron of Courtesy, is associated with the proper use of words: he "loathd leasing, and base flattery, / And loved simple truth and stedfast honesty" (i.3). But Calidore's virtue implies more, or less, than simplicity and naked truth. For him, even virtuous speech must use the weapons of its adversaries, and on occasion, literal truth gives way to a higher principle. Calidore lies to Priscilla's father, devising a "counter-cast of slight" (iii.16) in order to persuade the old man that the lady is "Most perfect pure,

2 Eclogue VII, 4-5; *Virgil*, tr. H. Rushton Fairclough, LCL (2 vols., London, 1953), I, 48.

and guiltlesse innocent" (18)—as, indeed, she is, in fact if not in appearance. This truth is hidden, and must be brought to light by indirection, like many truths in the fallen world, where false-seeming is the rule. Calidore acts courteously in the sense that his behavior is appropriate to the needs of the occasion. Though the words of Mercury are harsh after the songs of Apollo, there is a deep affinity between Courtesy and the poetic art: both are ruled by decorum—a delicate conformity of demand to answer; both depend for effectiveness on the best words in the best order. "Goodly manners" and "civill conversation," Spenser says, are both rooted in Courtesy (i.1); and Courtesy is first made visible in the poem as the principle of decorum:

> comely *Curtesie,*
> That unto every person knew her part.
> (IV.x.51)

Spenser makes the point explicitly in Book VI.

> What vertue is so fitting for a knight,
>   Or for a Ladie, whom a knight should love,
> As Curtesie, to beare themselves aright
>   To all of each degree, as doth behove?
> (VI.ii.1)

To this decorum, whose essential instrument is the art of words, is opposed the Blatant Beast,

> A wicked Monster, that his tongue doth whet
> Gainst all, both good and bad, both most and least.
> (vi.12)

This is Courtesy turned inside-out in hellish parody. For attentiveness to distinctions, a fitting relation between meed and need, is substituted indiscriminate malice toward "good and bad" alike, "low and hie"; for the persuasiveness of "civill conversation," the slander of a "vile tongue and venemous intent."[3] The leveling of distinctions is rebuked in Book V by Artegal in his colloquy with the Giant; in Book VI it is associated with the forces marshaled against Courtesy. It is a sign of lovelessness, for love cherishes the unique. Spenser makes the point again when, in the "huge havocke" of the Brigants' quarrel, the candles go out, leaving "no skill nor difference of wight" (xi.16). The darkness that blots out distinctions is the enemy of Courtesy.

The anatomy of Courtesy in the opening cantos demonstrates that this virtue is the peculiar essence of "milde humanity," of human-kindness itself.

> For seldome yet did living creature see,
> That curtesie and manhood ever disagree.
>
> (VI.iii.40)

Hence its greatest inhibitor is what Spenser calls "inhumanitie"—the special kind of pride that refuses to acknowledge our common predicament as human beings. Courtesy is one of the "virtues . . . forced upon us by our impudent crimes," those crimes that have made our condition unstable and vulnerable to ruin. "The reproch of pride and cruelnesse" is the special enemy of those who profess Courtesy, and Calidore proceeds to show why:

> All flesh is frayle, and full of ficklenesse,
> Subject to fortunes chance, still chaunging new;
> What haps to day to me, to morrow may to you.
>
> Who will not mercie unto others shew,
> How can he mercy ever hope to have?
> To pay each with his owne is right and dew.
> Yet since ye mercie now doe need to crave,
> I will it graunt.
>
> (VI.i.41-42)

---

[3] Spenser again falls into parody, conscious or unconscious, when he describes the Beast's fostering "in *Stygian* fen, / Till he to perfect ripenesse grew" (VI.i.8); it is the demonic equivalent of Calidore's virtue, "long with carefull labour nurst, / Till it to ripenesse grew" (Pro.3).

Crudor, to whom Calidore grants mercy, is one who scorns love "through high disdaine / And proud despight of his selfe pleasing mynd"; his lady, Briana, is herself "a prouder Lady" than any alive (i.14,15). In humbling their pride, Calidore makes them accessible to Courtesy, and potentially courteous themselves; self-contemplation no longer blocks out the view of their fellow men. The link between Courtesy and the Mercie of Book V here becomes obvious; each of them "Oft spilles the principall, to save the part," working through "powre and art" to preserve the spirit, even if it means denying the letter (V.x.2). Both acknowledge, but ultimately transcend, the principle of measure for measure—"to pay each with his owne." The notion of absolute justice is of limited efficacy in a world as perilously balanced as the one we all live in. Book VI is haunted by mutability in its most painful form—not merely the "natural" metamorphoses inherent in the life-process, but "fickleness," the unforeseeable *bouleversements* traditionally attributed to Fortune, whose emblem is a globe on an unstable sea.

> On rolling ball doth fickle fortune stande;
> on firme and setled square sitts Mercurie,
> The god of Arts, with wisdomes rodd in hande:
> which covertlie to us doth signifie,
> that fortunes power, unconstant and still frayle,
> against wisdome and art cannot prevaile.[4]

Art, this writer observes, is "the antidote against fortune." Courtesy too may artfully prevail over the unexpected, and one of its wisdoms is Mercy, a necessary virtue in a world ruled by Fortuna; its model is the God who takes on flesh in order to bring us the undeserved meed of salvation.

The problematic relation between meed and desert, and between meed and need, grows out of the definition of Courtesy as a decorum of action. It is one of Shakespeare's concerns in *King Lear*, where the hero's commitment to the

---

[4] Francis Thynne, *Emblemes and Epigrames*, ed. F. J. Furnivall, EETS (O.S.), LXIV (London, 1876), 8.

measure-for-measure principle eventually gives way, beneath the playwright's unremitting pressure, to the recognition that for love there is "No cause, no cause," and no merit either. The king's moral bargaining is terribly avenged when his daughters haggle with him over the number of his retainers, winding up with Regan's contemptuous question, "What need one?" Lear's answer is one of the play's basic moral statements:

> O! reason not the need; our basest beggars
> Are in the poorest thing superfluous:
> Allow not nature more than nature needs,
> Man's life is cheap as beast's.
> (II.iv.266-69)

"But for true need—" he goes on, only to break off in the confusions of impatience and impending madness. Spenser in Book VI is also concerned with true and false needs and the responses appropriate to them.[5] Like Shakespeare, he construes *need* as that which legitimately evokes charitable compassion: not the reductive need of Regan, properly spurned by her father, but Lear's own unrecognized need for spontaneous, unsolicited love, a love whose existence he comes painfully to recognize in Cordelia and Kent. Courteous behavior in *The Faerie Queene* is decorous response to need; so Timias will not desert Serena "in great extremity"—

[5] There are a number of points of connection between *Lear* and the last book of *The Faerie Queene*, attributable, I think, to a congruity of imagining when certain thematic patterns are treated. Among these is the theme of valid and invalid relationships among human beings: the bonds of love and duty, the shackles of economic and emotional dependence. Thus Briana, "converted" from pride by Calidore, "With all due thanks, and dutifull respect, / Her selfe acknowledg'd bound for that accord" (VI.i.45). It is like the filial dutifulness of Cordelia, acknowledging her love "according to my bond" (I.i.93). There are several contrasting characters in Book VI who, like the villains of *Lear*, insist upon absolute disconnection of their wills from the common good. Chief among them is Mirabella, "borne free, not bound to any wight" (vii.30); an "unmeete array" follows her in her penance, including the Squire fast bound by Disdain with "an hempen cord . . . like a dog" (viii.5).

for that he courteous was indeed,
Would not her leave alone in her great need.
(VI.vi.16)

Discourteous pride, on the other hand, refuses to recognize
need, as when Turpine encounters a knight and a distressed
lady:

Whom *Calepine* saluting (as became)
Besought of courtesie in that his neede,
For safe conducting of his sickely Dame,
Through that same perillous foord with better heede,
To take him up behinde upon his steed.
To whom that other did this taunt returne.
Perdy thou peasant Knight, mightst rightly reed
Me then to be full base and evill borne,
If I would beare behinde a burden of such scorne.
(VI.iii.31)

It is a characteristic of Spenserian *gentilesse* that it is not
ashamed to dirty its hands and stoop to humble burdens.
"Entire affection hateth nicer hands" (I.viii.40); "So love
does loath disdainfull nicitee" (II.ii.3); "No service loth-
some to a gentle kind" (IV.viii.22): these parenthetical au-
thorial comments link Prince Arthur and Guyon in a community of self-forgetfulness, against the pride that thinks
it base to bend one's back. The point becomes part of the
main plot in the Book of Courtesy, as Calidore gently but
firmly corrects the fastidiousness of Priscilla.

Yet could she not devise by any wit,
How thence she might convay him to some place.
For him [Calidore] to trouble she it thought unfit,
That was a straunger to her wretched case;
And him [Aladine] to beare, she thought it
thing too base.
Which when as he perceiv'd, he thus bespake;
Faire Lady let it not you seeme disgrace,

> To beare this burden on your dainty backe;
> My selfe will beare a part, coportion of your packe.
>
> (VI.ii.47)

Squeamishness and love are incompatibles; immaculate art, similarly, can only indicate a self-regarding pride in the maker. The poet, Stevens says, is one modestly engaged in "the act of finding / What will suffice," and this is the task as well of Spenser's courteous knights, awarding to others "their rightfull meed" (i.47), claiming no recompense for themselves. For, although generosity rules Calidore's relations with others, parsimony is the foundation of his relationship with himself. The process of finding what "*true need*" means, involves reducing life to its lowest terms, peeling away the shows of things and retreating to the paradise within. This is, once more, a description of the plot of *Lear*. The king learns "the art of our necessities" and in consequence can speak, for the first time, to the "houseless poverty" of his subjects, the "poor naked wretches . . . / That bide the pelting of this pitiless storm" that is the storm of the world's great rage. Spenser's hero is more gently initiated into the realities of life close to the bone, in the soft pastoralism of Canto ix. His pursuit of the Beast through the diminishing succession of "civilized" societies—court, city, town, country, "private farms"—is simultaneously a sloughing-off of the abuses which the Beast embodies, and it leads him "into the open fields" to Pastorella, his heart's desire. He is surprised by "the blynd boy" and, struck with wonder, "Caught like the bird, which gazing still on others stands" (ix.11). Thus caught, he enters the harmless but easily harmed world of innocence, a world to which we have already been introduced in the hermitage of Canto vi where the wise old man lives "like carelesse bird in cage" (vi.4). Lear, too, imagines an inner sanctum where he and Cordelia can be safe: "We two alone will sing like birds i' the cage" (V.iii.9). These cages are like the woodland re-

364

treat in which the poet of Marvell's *Appleton House* takes refuge:

> How safe, methinks, and strong, behind
> These trees, have I encamped my mind.
> (601-602)[6]

They are all places where the soul can "fleet the time carelessly as they did in the golden world." And they all look, to the eyes of the worldly, like prisons, like poverty, like exile.

Spenser explores the venerable tradition of virtuous *otium* in the colloquy between Melibee and Calidore in Canto ix. The old man has reduced nature, not to beastliness, but to the limits of "true need."

> If happie, then it is in this intent,
> That having small, yet doe I not complaine
> Of want, ne wish for more it to augment,
> But doe my self, with that I have, content;
> So taught of nature, which doth little need
> Of forreine helpes to lifes due nourishment:
> The fields my food, my flocke my rayment breed;
> No better doe I weare, no better doe I feed.
> (VI.ix.20)

This self-sufficiency is not the pride of a "selfe pleasing mynd," but the humbleness of Courtesy, which understands the indecorous "inhumanitie" of exploitation. It is to be contrasted with the customs of the ignoble savages who abduct Serena—"on the labours of poore men to feed, / And serve their owne necessities with others need" (viii.35)—and the brigands who eventually kill Melibee,

---

[6] Marvell's retreat is designed to protect him from the arrows of "Beauty, aiming at the heart" (603)—the very power that induces Calidore to enter the retreat. These two contexts illustrate the dubious value of love in pastoral literature; it can be, alternatively, the consummation or the ruination of the paradisal place.

> That never usde to live by plough nor spade,
> But fed on spoile and booty, which they made
> Upon their neighbours.
>
> (VI.x.39)

Plough and spade are essential implements in Melibee's homestead, where even the poet's art cannot restore the *otium* of the Golden Age completely. The need to create for oneself what will suffice, rather than simply finding (or stealing) it, is a condition of our fallenness. And so is the pattern of life which Spenser's wise old men illustrate in *The Faerie Queene*, a pattern initiated in Virgil's first *Eclogue*. In that poem, Tityrus journeys to Rome and receives the surety of his farm from the young Augustus, returning to a perpetuity of country pleasures.

> O Meliboee, deus nobis haec otia fecit.
> namque erit ille mihi semper deus, illius aram
> saepe tener nostris ab ovilibus imbuet agnus.
> ille meas errare boves, ut cernis, et ipsum
> ludere quae vellem calamo permisit agresti.[7]

This formula of out-and-back is made harsher, and turned inward, by later pastoral poets. For Augustan Rome is substituted "this wicked world" (VI.i.8), the decadent city or court, which nevertheless teaches the man who sojourns there an essential lesson. So he returns to the country, not with economic security, but with a surer sense of what he possesses. Wisdom is added to innocence, through experience of a contrasting way of life. Having labored in the vineyard, "Old John with white hair / Doth laugh away care."

Spenser evidently attached important meanings to this pattern, for it occurs at least four times in his poetry. One poem, *Colin Clouts Come Home Againe*, derives its tripartite structure from this paradigm, and in *The Faerie*

---

[7] Eclogue I, 6-10; *Virgil*, I, 2.

Queene the interlocutors and instructors of the heroes in
the first and last books express it in different ways. The Red
Cross Knight learns from Heavenly Contemplation that he
cannot retreat to "Pilgrims poore estate" until he has accomplished his mission in the world.

> But when thou famous victorie hast wonne,
> And high emongst all knights hast hong thy shield,
> Thence forth the suit of earthly conquest shonne,
> And wash thy hands from guilt of bloudy field.
>
> (I.x.60)

Here the paradigm, keeping decorum with the lofty reach
of Book I, is given anagogic significance; as in Peele's song
for Sir Henry Lee, his helmet now shall make a hive for
bees, and he will turn from sonnets to psalms. In Book VI,
both the Hermit and Melibee have sojourned in "the
world." The Hermit, once "Renowmed much in armes and
derring doe," has renounced incessant labours—"worlds
contentious toyle,"

> And hanging up his armes and warlike spoyle,
> From all this worlds incombraunce did himselfe assoyle.
>
> (VI.v.37)

Melibee's autobiographical discourse to Calidore offers a
more proletarian and more severely moralized version of
the pattern:

> leaving home, to roiall court I sought;
> Where I did sell my selfe for yearely hire,
> And in the Princes gardin daily wrought:
> There I beheld such vainenesse, as I never thought.
>
> (VI.ix.24)

The lesson is well learned. "I from thenceforth have learn'd
to love more deare / This lowly quiet life, which I inherit
here" (25).

In the following stanzas, Spenser explicates the meaning of "This lowly quiet life" through the dialogue between his two characters. What is being recommended is not necessarily a change in outward vocation, but a finding of what will suffice in a paradise within.[8] Calidore longs to resign from his chivalric quest and "live in like condition" to the shepherds—

> Or that my fortunes might transposed bee
> From pitch of higher place, unto this low degree.
>
> (VI.ix.28)

Such transposition of Fortune is, however, outside the permitted limits for human beings; it offends against the decorum, or courtesy, of Providence. Melibee's conclusion —"Each unto himselfe his life may fortunize" (30)—is misunderstood by Calidore, who interprets it to mean that he can choose between vocations in the "real" world, remaking it in the image of his desires.

> Since then in each mans self (said *Calidore*)
>   It is to fashion his own lyfes estate,
>   Give leave awhyle, good father, in this shore
>   To rest my barcke, which hath bene beaten late
>   With stormes of fortune and tempestuous fate
>   In seas of troubles and of toylesome paine,
>   That whether quite from them for to retrate

---

[8] Here my reading differs from Berger's. Though avoiding the errors of commentators who have "atrociously glamorized" Melibee, one can yet demur at his judgment that the old man is offering an "excuse for laziness." Satisfaction with "lifes due nourishment" does not indicate simple-minded trust in the "sufficiency of the first nature," as an examination of the later part of the argument reveals. Melibee argues for an internalizing of fortune, a "second nature" that acknowledges our constraint within necessary limits. See "Secret Discipline," p. 61, and p. 173, n. 25.

Alpers' principle that Spenser's imagination resists simplistic judgments is more to the point. Rhetoric is used "not to make a decision, but to complicate an issue" (*Poetry of "Faerie Queene,"* p. 292). Alpers' discussion of the Melibee dialogue (pp. 292-96), turning on a contrast with Sidney, is alert to the claims of both "sides" in the debate.

I shall resolve, or backe to turne againe,
I may here with your selfe some small repose obtaine.
                                                    (VI.ix.31)

He does not seem to take Melibee's point, that a man should choose to embrace his fortune, to incorporate it into his being so that a right choice leads to the paradise within.

But fittest is, that all contented rest
With that they hold: each hath his fortune in his brest.
                                                    (29)

Calidore's reaction is natural enough for one trained in chivalry and the exercise of heroic force. But Melibee's discourse solicits a less literal reading. To make one's soul, or fortune, is not to discover (or create) a place that offers contentment, but rather to find one's true vocation and dwell, like Artegal, in the inward peace it offers. "It is the mynd, that maketh good or ill" (30), but the realities that sustain themselves in the make of the mind are invisible. Calidore's literal-mindedness leads him to a worldly and literal interpretation of meed and need, and a sin against decorum: the offer to pay Melibee for his room and board. It is a venial sin, no doubt, but it has a special visibility in a book that celebrates the power of the Graces, of unconstrained giving and undeserved receiving.

In the dire circumstances of ordinary life, "some small repose" in a temporarily realized idyllic "place" is the best one can hope for. Calidore complains, as the narrator himself has often done, of the hardships of his voyage. In the end, it is the narrator, as the instrument of a higher law, who must interrupt the idyll and set him on his course again, for the choice defined in Stanza 31 is made by default when Calidore lingers with Pastorella. Destiny demands that Calidore complete the circuit of withdrawal and return; he must, however reluctantly, come home again to court. For Melibee, who belongs to the country, homecoming means perpetuation of a "lowly quiet life" after an excursion into the worldly experience of the prince's garden. The pattern is reversed for Calidore, though like the Red Cross Knight he can look forward, ultimately, to the hermitage of an innocent and quiet mind. The Hermit demonstrates the ultimate meaning of coming "home again."

> For whylome he had bene a doughty Knight,
>   As any one, that lived in his daies,
>   And proved oft in many perillous fight,
>   Of which he grace and glory wonne alwaies,
>   And in all battels bore away the baies.
>   But being now attacht with timely age,
>   And weary of this worlds unquiet waies,
>   He tooke him selfe unto this Hermitage,
> In which he liv'd alone, like carelesse bird in cage.
>   (VI.vi.4)

3. Fortune and the Limits of Heroism

It should be evident from this brief description that the action of Book VI departs radically in its implications from the patterns and significances of the earlier books. As I suggested above, its structure resembles that of Book III; Venus dwells at the centers of both, and the respective epiphanies are conjured into view by the poet's wit rather than by the effortful deservingness of any questing knight. And in both books we are aware, as well, of the pressure of a power that circumscribes and limits the human will. In Book III it is love, which, like Britomart's spear, has the force of a "secret powre unseene" (III.i.7).

In Book VI, the name of the power is Fortune.[1] In Renaissance poetry, the goddess Fortuna presides over all the aspects of life that lie beyond our control, or our understanding.

> But indeede, this name of Fortune, Chaunce, Hap,
> or Hazard, was onely invented by such as knewe not
> the first cause, Gods providence: And therefore when
> any thing fell out contrary to theyr expectation, where-

---

[1] Fowler identifies Fortune as "one of the most persistent themes of Book VI" (*Numbers of Time*, p. 223); and see Dorothy Culp's article, cited below, note 3. Tonkin discusses misfortune and its remedies, *Courteous Pastoral*, pp. 268-70.

The impression that Fortune is often invoked in Book VI is confirmed by a word-count. Lexical details can never be an exact register of the poet's preoccupations in *The Faerie Queene*, where the tyranny of rhyme and reliance on formulas exert powerful pressures. But the occurrence of *fortune* and related words in Book VI so strikingly outdistances the count for other books as to suggest that formal exigency is not the whole story. There are 51 instances in VI, the closest rival (perhaps significantly) being Book III with 33. (For the remaining books: I, 18; II, 22; IV, 29; V, 24.) Add to this the fact that *chance* and *chanced* occur 30 times in Book VI, as against 21 in the runner-up, Book I.

of they neyther understoode the cause, nor could yeeld
any reason, they said it came by chaunce, fortune and
hazard.[2]

The hand of Providence is often visible behind the wayward events of Book VI, as the poet's hand can be seen to
control the apparently haphazard turnings of the interact-
ing plots. The design is not, however, produced by the wills
or intentions of the participants. More than in any other
book, we are made aware of how feebly the well-laid plans
of men control the actual events of their lives. In choosing
his plot-motifs, Spenser selects "those which seem to emphasize the role of chance and fortune."[3] Calidore, pursuing his
quest, is led astray, and into the greatest adventure of his
life, by "the blynd boy" Cupid, whose working offered Renaissance poets an easily available figure for the blind activity of Fortune.

> He was unwares surprisd in subtile bands
> Of the blynd boy, ne thence could be redeemed
> By any skill out of his cruell hands,
> Caught like the bird, which gazing still on others stands.
>
> (VI.ix.11)

The arbitrariness of love's wound, and its incurability as
well, connects it with a more malign power in Book VI, the
Blatant Beast itself. Spenser describes Calidore's love-sick-
ness in language that curiously echoes earlier stanzas describing the Beast's bite; it is an "envenimd sting," a "poysnous point deepe fixed in his hart" (x.31),

> Which to recure, no skill of Leaches art
> Mote him availe, but to return againe
> To his wounds worker.

---

[2] Abraham Fraunce, *The Lawiers Logike* . . . (London, 1588), p. 17 v.
[3] Dorothy W. Culp, "Courtesy and Fortune's Chance in Book 6 of
The Faerie Queene," *MP* LXVIII (1970-71), 255.

Fortune operates both benignly and malignantly in Book VI, though within the fiction most of the good characters ultimately find their adventures ending happily. As Dante knew, Providence writes comic plots.

> Fayre Pastorella by great hap
> Her parents understands,

in the final canto (Arg.xii); the long arm of coincidence, beloved of primitive storytellers, provides a mysterious birthmark and a fortuitous recognition scene. Pastorella has been "fortunes spoile," but in the end she is restored to her mother, who finds that "the heavens had her graste, / To save her chylde, which in misfortunes mouth was plaste" (xii.16).

The emphasis on Fortune in Book VI, and its formal equivalent, the rambling criss-cross of the plot-structure, reflects the movement that leads the poet from the world of Book V to the haunts of virtue, "deep within the mynd," in the last book. Artegal is a hero in the traditional mold, bringing to bear the powers of intellect and will, as well as his "mightie hands" (V.iv.1), upon the disorders of a fallen world. He is trying to reform the ragged commonweal, to educe Irena's ravaged island from a state of primitive savagery to the discipline of civilization that imitates the lost spontaneities of innocence. In this task he is only partly successful, and Spenser ascribes the interruption of his program to the work of "occasion," another of Fortune's many names. Even if the occasion was the recall of Lord Grey from Ireland, or perhaps *especially* if it refers to a depressing analogue in real life disrupting the decorums of the fiction, it marks one of the limits of the hero's power:

> of necessity
> His course of Justice he was forst to stay,
> And *Talus* to revoke from the right way,

373

> In which he was that Realme for to redresse.
> But envies cloud still dimmeth vertues ray.
> (V.xii.27)

The light of virtue, like the sun of Una's truth in Book I, is dimmed by the world's sinfulness and must appear, in action, behind a veil. But the light itself remains, "deep within the mynd," undimmed. Artegal preserves his virtue from the Beast's bite, safe behind the disfiguring veil of slander.

> But I that knew my selfe from perill free,
> Did nought regard his malice nor his powre.
> (VI.i.9)

The only place "from perill free," unbeaten by the storms of Fortune, lies deep within, and to it the poet retreats when he realizes that heroic virtue, however mighty its hands, will always to some degree fail in its undertakings. In the conversation between Artegal and Calidore, the Knight of Courtesy describes his quest; it is very unlike the forthright progress of Justice, thoroughly mapped ahead of time by the just dooms of Astraea.

> But where ye ended have, now I begin
>   To tread an endlesse trace, withouten guyde,
>   Or good direction, how to enter in,
>   Or how to issue forth in waies untryde,
>   In perils strange, in labours long and wide,
>   In which although good Fortune me befall,
>   Yet shall it not by none be testifyde.
>   (VI.i.6)

We are back to Book I and the labyrinthine wood of the world, but whereas Providence controls the actions of both I and VI, it remains veiled, "untestified," in the final book. Book VI is a world of "hap," of surprising conversions, moving accidents by flood and field, purposes mistook or diverted. In such a world there is little scope for the heroic control of fate; Calidore can rescue Pastorella, hiding his sword under his shepherd's cloak, but he cannot prevent her abduction. In Book VI, the stoically relaxed will is often the only strategy that will suffice. The resignation that causes Hamlet to yield himself into the hands of a special providence must be accepted, by Spenser's protagonists, with much less assurance of ultimate design. "Since no man, of aught he leaves, knows what is't to leave betimes, let be" (*Hamlet* V.ii.23-24). "The readiness is all": Spenser's name for readiness is Courtesy, the power to answer any occasion with the appropriate response, without seeking occasions. Calidore's progress through Book VI is marked, as Kathleen Williams has said, by "a sense of release from tension and difficulty," by "delight and liberty," which paradoxically follow upon accepting the burdens of fate.[4] Love itself, the happiest of these burdens, is a sweet yoke, though we may find lasting freedoms there.

The tether of permitted liberty is short, however, and delight and liberty are accompanied by brutal reminders that hap places all our joys in hazard. Witness Calepine's woodland walk after his rescue by the Salvage Man.

> Upon a day he cast abrode to wend,
> To take the ayre, and heare the thrushes song,
> Unarm'd, as fearing neither foe nor frend,
> And without sword his person to defend.
> There him befell, unlooked for before,
> An hard adventure with unhappie end.
>
> (VI.iv.17)

The movement of this stanza precisely reflects the characteristic action of Book VI, the realm of "hap," both good and bad. Events occur "unlooked for," and a wise man will never venture forth unarmed. But this simple moral is not allowed to stand in Book VI. The unaccustomed lightness felt by Calepine without his armor is what allows him to

---

[4] *World of Glass*, p. 190.

succeed in this hard adventure: "Him seem'd his feet did fly, and in their speed delight" (iv.19). He quickly overtakes "the wearie Beare" and rescues the baby. The events that follow in Canto iv provide an object-lesson in the curious ways of Providence and are moralized by the hero when he has thankfully handed over "his lovely litle spoile" to Matilde, the mother who needs a baby.

> Oftimes it haps, that sorrowes of the mynd
> Find remedie unsought, which seeking cannot fynd.
>
> (28)

Calepine's own seeking has brought him "nought the nearer to his journeys end" (25); Spenser's description of his perplexities catches perfectly the very nature of the mortal labyrinth we all wander in.

> But when he lookt about on every syde,
> To weet which way were best to entertaine,
> To bring him to the place, where he would faine,
> He could no path nor tract of foot descry,
> Ne by inquirie learne, nor ghesse by ayme.
> For nought but woods and forrests farre and nye,
> That all about did close the compasse of his eye.
>
> (VI.iv.24)

We reach the places we would fain not by any rational process, but by good hap, and by the grace of the poet, leading us into strange ways. Spenser traces in the alexandrine the curve of the limited horizon that bounds the vision of man in the middest; it is the tightest of the many circles in Book VI. "The compasse of his eye" alone cannot make sense of the apparently planless accidents that confront him; his only recourse is faith that the plan will become plain to a more distant view, which he may achieve with the aid of imagination. And so he falls back, again, on a kind of stoicism that is anti-heroic in the limits it sets on human action. Another of the wise old men in Book VI makes the point—Aldus, whom life has taught to "temper his griefe."

> Such is the weakenesse of all mortall hope;
>> So tickle is the state of earthly things,
>> That ere they come unto their aymed scope,
>> They fall too short of our fraile reckonings,
>> And bring us bale and bitter sorrowings,
>> In stead of comfort, which we should embrace:
>> This is the state of Keasars and of Kings.
>> Let none therefore, that is in meaner place,
> Too greatly grieve at any his unlucky case.
>
>> (VI.iii.5)

This stanza, occurring early in Book VI, is unfolded in the remaining action of the book. An appropriate emblem is provided on the shield of the uncourteous knight who attacked Priscilla and Aladine in the preceding canto: "A Ladie on rough waves, row'd in a sommer barge" (ii.44). All the ladies, and most of the gentlemen, in Book VI are committed to unpathed waters in very frail craft indeed. Only the poet's craft, guided by Providence, can bring them safely to land. The wild wood, or rough waves, of the world are unsafe, as Serena discovers in an episode to be echoed by her knight.

> Allur'd with myldnesse of the gentle wether,
> And pleasaunce of the place, the which was dight
> With divers flowres distinct with rare delight,
> Wandred about the fields, as liking led
> Her wavering lust after her wandring sight,
> To make a garland to adorne her hed,
> Without suspect of ill or daungers hidden dred.

> All sodainely out of the forrest nere
> The Blatant Beast forth rushing unaware,
> Caught her thus loosely wandring here and there.
>> (VI.iii.23-24)

We have seen something like this before, when Amoret in Book IV, "of nought affeard, / Walkt through the wood, for pleasure, or for need" (IV.vii.4) into mortal danger. Serena's pleasures are similarly innocent, but *wavering lust* and *loosely wandring* are warning signals; innocence is vulnerable precisely because it permits itself to wander "without suspect of ill." It can survive only when it has completed its circuit through experience and become what Blake called organized innocence. Then it protects itself against "daungers hidden dred" by an armor like Britomart's, or by a self-created refuge, the Hermit's "little cage" that signifies his immunity to the maladies of the world.

This immunity is the direct result of the old man's exposure of himself to the corruptions of life in the middest and his recognition that the springs of virtue are deep within the mind. "In your selfe your onely helpe doth lie" (vi.7), he tells his guests. He can heal Serena and Timias because he has access to fortune's remedy.

> For he right well in Leaches craft was seene,
> And through the long experience of his dayes,
> Which had in many fortunes tossed beene,
> And past through many perillous assayes,
> He knew the diverse went of mortall wayes,
> And in the mindes of men had great insight;
> Which with sage counsell, when they went astray,
> He could enforme, and them reduce aright,
> And al the passions heale which wound the weaker spright.
> (VI.vi.3)

To "enforme" through insight into the recesses of the mind and thread the labyrinth of the world: this is the role played by the poet as well in Book VI. And the Hermit's wisdom, too, is effective through "fit speaches": "he the art of words knew wondrous well" (6).

The art of words is linked with the wisdom of experience, and both of these are wanting in that other woods-

man, the Salvage Man, whose presence in the middle cantos
allows Spenser to define the limits of primitive virtue. The
Salvage Man's natural *gentilesse* distinguishes him from the
other Savages who in Canto viii attack Serena as she
"drowned in the depth of sleepe all fearelesse lay" (viii.36).
He is naked, unarmed, and vegetarian—

> neither plough'd nor sowed,
> Ne fcd on flesh, ne ever of wyld beast
> Did taste the bloud, obaying natures first beheast.
> (VI.iv.14)

The Salvage Nation, in contrast, though they also refuse "to
drive / The painefull plough," prey on other human beings:

> they usde one most accursed order,
> To eate the flesh of men, whom they mote fynde,
> And straungers to devoure, which on their border
> Were brought by errour, or by wreckfull wynde.
> A monstrous cruelty gainst course of kynde.
> (VI.viii.36)

Nature is invoked in both these stanzas as a measure of
moral instinct, and the different versions of Natural Man
exemplify respectively soft and hard pastoral. "Natural"
courtesy, or discourtesy, manifests itself in a spontaneous
reaction, either decorous or "unkind," to hap, the unforeseen chances of fortune. The knights and ladies of Book VI
who are regularly surprised in their dalliance are safe so
long as it is the Knight of Courtesy who interrupts them;
the Salvage Man, too, upon finding the wounded strangers,
responds humanely. The shepherds receive Calidore with
a "gentle offer" of sustenance and shelter (ix.7); Calepine
rescues Serena (and so, finally, deserves her) without recognizing her except as "a woman spoyld of all attire"
(viii.48), a poor naked wretch. The inhumanity of the Salvage Nation, in contrast, is demonstrated by their readiness

to prey upon the "straungers . . . brought by errour or by wreckfull wynde" to their shores. The treatment of strangers, not friends, is the test of courtesy, as Calidore indicates when he accepts the burden of the "straunger," Aladine (ii.47). Those who would practice this virtue must heed St. Paul's injunction: "Be not forgetful to entertain strangers, for thereby some have entertained angels unawares" (Hebrews 13:2).

The decorum of Courtesy, like many other responses once "natural" to man, must now—except for a fortunate few like Calidore—be re-learned by civilized men. Therefore the solution to the monstrous indecorums of the Salvage Nation lies, not in retreat to the primitive ways of the Salvage Man, but in that artfulness which carries us beyond an abused and deformed Nature.[5] The Salvage Man can heal only physical wounds; his artless pharmacopoea knows nothing of "the passions . . . which wound the weaker spright." The symbol of his limitations, which are those of "mere" Nature in a fallen world, is his speechlessness. The "senseless words, which nature did him teach" (iv.11) are insufficient when he is confronted by the powers of the Blatant Beast who can be subdued only by a matching, but virtuous, courtly sophistication. "The ideal figure of courtesy combines both nature and nurture, each complementing the other."[6] Spenser's most revealing analogue for this comple-

---

[5] The later career of the Salvage Man in Book VI is instructive. He follows Arthur and takes him for a model, "greatly growne in love of that brave pere" (v.41). The spontaneous aptness to learn through love is a mark of courtesy and is reiterated on another level in Calidore's love of Pastorella. The persistent ambiguities associated with nurture are also illustrated in our final glimpse of the Salvage Man, however, who begins his knightly education by learning to shed blood: "environed about / With slaughtred bodies, which his hand had slaine" (vi.38).

[6] William V. Nestrick, "The Virtuous and Gentle Discipline of Gentlemen and Poets," in *Spenser: A Collection of Critical Essays*, ed. Harry Berger (Englewood Cliffs, N.J., 1968), p. 139. Nestrick also discusses the continuity between nature and nurture in Spenser's images of the seed's growth.

mentarity, which unites freedom and discipline, is the poet's art itself. A poem is both made and found, the product of both inspiration and labor. Like Calidore's courtesy, it is a "grace" that requires cultivation: "a divine gift and heavenly instinct not to bee gotten by laboure and learning, but adorned with both" (*October*, Arg.).

It is, therefore, accurate up to a point to read Book VI as a confirmation of the power of words. The Hermit's "sage counsell" has guided men through "the diverse went of mortall wayes," "when they went astray" (vi.3)—a typical Spenserian pun in which the poet's artifice demonstrates the skill he speaks of. And Spenser's art contrives both the labyrinth of the plot and the clue that leads out of the maze. Nevertheless, no more than Colin Clout does he control the coming and going of poetic grace. The poet guides his reader, and his hero, but the Muse guides him. She alone can take us deep within the mind, and lead us out again in safety.

> Guyde ye my footing, and conduct me well
> In these strange waies, where never foote did use,
> Ne none can find, but who was taught them by the Muse.
> (VI.Pro.2)

Scorners of the Muse, and those who pay insufficient attention to wise words, get into trouble in Book VI. Calidore's most serious deviation from perfect courtesy comes at the end of his colloquy with Melibee, whose discourse entrances him but fails of its designed effect. The hero is distracted, dividing his attention between the old man and "the object of his vew," Pastorella.

> Whylest thus he talkt, the knight with greedy eare
> Hong still upon his melting mouth attent;
> Whose sensefull words empierst his hart so neare,
> That he was rapt with double ravishment,
> Both of his speach that wrought him great content,

And also of the object of his vew,
On which his hungry eye was alwayes bent;
That twixt his pleasing tongue, and her faire hew,
He lost himselfe, and like one half entraunced grew.
(VI.ix.26)

It is to Calidore's credit that he is willing to lose himself, but, as I suggested earlier, the stanzas that follow show that he is reading Melibee's lesson over-literally.

The precise sense of the old man's "sensefull words" contributes to Spenser's consideration, in Book VI, of the limits of chivalric action and, by implication, of the poetry that celebrates it. Berger is right to see in Melibee's quietism a disparagement of "aspiration and unfulfilled desire"; he is wrong, I think, in suggesting that Spenser repudiates this position.[7] It is confirmed at many other points in this book, and not least in the constraint with which the poet treats his own vocation as a maker of heroic lays. When Calidore describes the sort of quest on which he is about to embark, he concludes with a curious comment:

In which although good Fortune me befall,
Yet shall it not by none be testifyde.
(VI.i.6)

This victory will occur in a place where "feeble eies" cannot see it; for virtue "in silver bowre does hidden ly / From view of men, and wicked worlds disdaine" (Pro.3). No testimony will be returned to the wicked public world from this place. And the poet, though he prays to be granted access to "the sacred noursery / Of vertue," will not celebrate it in the heroic vein.

The Knight of Courtesy and his poet are thus set apart, at the opening of Book VI, from the familiar world of heroic virtue and heroic poetry. To have one's deeds "testifyde" by the poet's song is one of the chief reasons for performing

[7] "Secret Discipline," p. 61. Some useful comments on Chance and Providence are made by Williams, *World of Glass*, pp. 208-10.

them, according to epic tradition, and in the earlier books of *The Faerie Queene* this tradition is repeatedly affirmed. Of Satyrane, Spenser says, "through all Faery lond his famous worth was blown" (I.vi.29); Guyon and Arthur "hunt for glorie and renowmed praise" (III.i.3), and are not rebuked. Spenser's first exhortation to himself to attempt a higher flight is the *October* eclogue, and E. K.'s gloss explains that the poet's loftiest task is to celebrate "manhoode and chevalrie."

> He sheweth the cause, why Poetes were wont be
> had in such honor of noble men; that is, that by
> them their worthines and valor shold through theyr
> famous Posies be commended to al posterities.
> Wherfore it is sayd, that Achilles had never bene
> so famous, as he is, but for Homeres immortal
> verses.

E. K. continues with the catalogue: Alexander, Cicero, Scipio all testify to the significance of poetic testimony. Unless our fame lives registered by poets upon our brazen tombs, it is hardly worth achieving.

> For deeds doe die, how ever noblie donne,
> And thoughts of men do as themselves decay,
> But wise words taught in numbers for to runne,
> Recorded by the Muses, live for ay.
>   (*Ruines of Time*, 400-403)

Calidore is not Achilles, however, and the Muses of Book VI decline to stay for an answer when he approaches them. Calidore as captor of the Blatant Beast is portrayed with some acknowledgment of conventional heroic postures. He is compared to Hercules, and leads his prey through Fairy Land, where he is greeted by crowds that "much admyr'd the Beast, but more admyr'd the Knight" (xii.37). But Calidore as the courteous shepherd and witness to the Graces' dance is not "testifyed" to the great world.

Spenser *does*, of course, make visible to us his hero's peculiar virtue; but in order to do it, he turns his plough-share to a different furrow, abandoning, even though temporarily, his own pursuit of heroism through *The Faerie Queene*. The narrator's truancy parallels that of the hero; in the middle cantos he deserts Calidore altogether, to follow the fortunes of Calepine and Serena, Timias, Arthur, and the Salvage Man. He excuses himself at the opening of Canto ix and vows to return to the main furrow.

> Now turne againe my teme thou jolly swayne,
>> Backe to the furrow which I lately left;
>> I lately left a furrow, one or twayne
>> Unplough'd, the which my coulter hath not cleft:
>> Yet seem'd the soyle both fayre and frutefull eft,
>> As I it past, that were too great a shame,
>> That so rich frute should be from us bereft;
>> Besides the great dishonour and defame,
> Which should befall to *Calidores* immortall name.
>> (VI.ix.1)

The truancy is to be repaired, and Calidore's immortal name celebrated; but the rustic metaphor establishes the key of the adventures to follow, where Calidore will doff his bright arms and "chaunge the manner of his loftie looke" (ix.36) by abandoning his sword for a shepherd's crook.

At the opening of the crucial tenth canto, Spenser devotes four stanzas to an account of Calidore's dawdling entrapment and, unexpectedly, a qualified justification of it; the passage is the most explicit statement of Book VI's anti-heroic theme. "Who now does follow the foule *Blatant Beast*"; the poet begins accusingly with a rhetorical question, reminding us of the hero's "vow and high beheast" and his betrayal by love. It might be Aeneas led astray by Dido. But the next stanza swerves unpredictably.

> That from henceforth he meanes no more to sew
>> His former quest, so full of toile and paine;

> Another quest, another game in vew
> He hath, the guerdon of his love to gaine:
> With whom he myndes for ever to remaine,
> And set his rest amonst the rusticke sort,
> Rather then hunt still after shadows vaine
> Of courtly favour, fed with light report
> Of every blaste, and sayling alwaies in the port.
>
> (x.2)

In this unexpectedly harsh light, Calidore's quest looks less like the heroic pursuit of a dangerous beast, more like a self-aggrandizing search for the flimsy rewards of "report" —which, in a way, it is, since the capture of the Beast would seal the lips of hostile rumor and allow "courtly favour" to flourish. The stanza makes us think again about the significance of the Blatant Beast as an object of heroic endeavor; it is not Spenser's last word, and the Beast will later appear in far more sinister aspect, but the stanza reflects a danger inherent in all heroism: that even a legitimate quest can be accepted for the wrong reasons. Fame, that all hunt after in their lives, is a fleeting thing, a "light report" and vain shadow compared with more enduring rewards; it is the last infirmity of noble minds. In allowing Calidore to abandon it for a while, Spenser is protecting him against the glamor of false heroism. He has made the point once before, in Belphoebe's lecture to the cowardly knight of Book II.

> Who so in pompe of proud estate (quoth she)
> Does swim, and bathes himselfe in courtly blis,
> Does waste his dayes in darke obscuritee,
> And in oblivion ever buried is:
> Where ease abounds, yt's eath to doe amis.
>
> (II.iii.40)

Honor is to be pursued "Abroad in armes, at home in studious kind"—and the last phrase anticipates the quest of virtue in the inner world which Spenser elaborates in Book VI. The easy satisfactions of superficial "report" can be obtained by "sayling alwaies in the port," never venturing into the untried regions where the deep sources of human virtue wait to enlighten the hero and redeem him from the glitter of an earthly guerdon.

The modulations of Stanza 2 are designed to bring us to an inflection of our ideas about "reality." What appeared to be a quest "full of toile and paine" is really "sailing in the port": Calidore will not have moved beyond the vain shadows of courtly favor unless his quest is informed by a sense of the meaning for which all such pursuits are metaphors. The poet is leading Calidore toward the hiding-places of his power, the point of the appointed source, in order to stimulate that power and inoculate it against self-serving motives. This movement involves a passage from one sort of prison to a different kind; an earlier statement of it is the Hermit's retreat from "the worlds unquiet waies" to the "little cage" of his hermitage. Calidore, "entrapt of love" (x.1), can see through the false delights at court, "set . . . / T' entrap unwary fooles" (x.3). The trap of love is preferred to the trap of vanity, and Spenser is going to show us why, in the vision of the poet's love transfigured to an image of eternal bliss. Calidore has been permitted by aesthetic providence to venture into the trap and love Pastorella in order that the poet may lead him on further.

> For what hath all that goodly glorious gaze
> Like to one sight, which *Calidore* did vew?
> The glaunce whereof their dimmed eies would daze,
> That never more they should endure the shew
> Of that sunne-shine, that makes them look askew.
>
> (VI.x.4)

We are back in the world of true and false suns, Lucifera and Una blazing in the sky of Book I, real and invented Florimell in Book V.

Spenser's distinctions between real and unreal objects of

devotion produce a more exact definition of the titular virtue. Genuine courtesy has its roots in the generosity of love;
false courtesy, in the "pompe of proud estate" that scorns
love and seeks public adulation. Spenser begins to unfold
these equivalences in the episode of Mirabella who, in
origin at least, is the feminine equivalent of Calidore.

> In prime of youthly yeares, when first the flowre
> Of beauty gan to bud, and bloosme delight,
> And nature me endu'd with plenteous dowre,
> Of all her gifts, that pleasde each living sight,
> I was belov'd of many a gentle Knight.
>
> (viii.20)

Like Calidore, she can steal men's hearts away, but instead
of responding with an appropriate *agape*, she withdraws
into her pride rather than be lured into the trap of love: "ne
list me leave my loved libertie" (viii.21).[8] Those who love
liberty alone are narcissists—"To love my selfe I learned
had in schoole." But the god of love is not mocked, and a
snare avoided is merely another snare. Refusing to be "entrapt of love," Mirabella is now enthralled to Disdain, a
giant whose name speaks for itself and who is "sib to great
Orgoglio" (vii.41).

The mention of Orgoglio suggests that Spenser had Book
I in mind when he composed Book VI, which carries further a number of principles left undeveloped in the poem's
first movement. One of these concerns the Christian paradox that underlies the pursuit of heroic virtue in the New
Covenant, perplexing and complicating it. Heroism demands a self-willed confidence not only in the righteousness
of a cause, but in the power of one's arm in establishing that

---

[8] As Berger has pointed out, Mirabella's "popularity reflects on the
love entertained by her suitors" as well ("Secret Discipline," p. 52).
Their love is self-generated rather than inspired by "grace," and is
therefore a version of false art, presumptuous and untransfiguring.

cause. But the will is infected, and at the heart of Christian heroism there must lie a kind of humility, a willingness to resign that will into the hands of another power.

> His be the praise, that this atchiev'ment wrought,
> Who made my hand the organ of his might;
> More then goodwill to me attribute nought:
> For all I did, I did but as I ought.
>
> (II.i.33)

Will becomes good will when the knight surrenders the design of his quest to the superior artistry of a divine artificer. The theme of art in Book VI, therefore, offers a new perspective on some of the lessons of Book I. Providence is here called Fortune, and the poet's hand is the organ of its might, causing Calidore to be "unwares surprisd in subtile bands" of love. In effecting this, he is first of all drawing attention to the ordinary way of love's working, which is always to bring about surprising conversions. The arbitrary nature of "falling in love" has made it through many centuries a natural analogue for the grace of divine love, which comes and goes in obedience to a law too dark for us to fathom. The Fortune that brings Calidore to Pastorella is the poet's design, expressing an *agape* that offers unexpected bounty.[9] But the hero is not undeserving, because he has offered similar grace to unarmed enemies and strangers; his courtesy is a generosity untainted by the loveless self-regard of Book VI's many discourteous characters, from Crudor to Mirabella. Courtesy thus resembles the central Christian virtues of Charity and Mercy; it testifies that grace has touched the mortals who manifest it.[10] So the Graces dance on Mt. Acidale.

[9] It is interesting that Mammon's offer to Guyon of "the worldes blis" should be seen in similar terms; like love, it is unearned, but unlike love, has a demonic source. Both could be called "offred grace" (II.vii.33).

[10] Several writers have considered the analogies between Christian virtues and the values defined in Book VI. On Courtesy and Charity,

Calidore's falling in love with Pastorella is a necessary prelude to his vision of the Graces, and Spenser makes the point by using his favorite strategies: juxtaposition and a reiterated visual pattern.

> Upon a little hillocke she was placed
>   Higher then all the rest, and round about
>   Environ'd with a girland, goodly graced,
>   Of lovely lasses, and them all without
>   The lustie shepheard swaynes sate in a rout,
>   The which did pype and sing her prayses dew,
>   And oft rejoyce, and oft for wonder shout,
>   As if some miracle of heavenly hew
> Were downe to them descended in that earthly vew.
>
> (VI.ix.8)

In the next canto we, and Calidore, are to see "a troupe of Ladies dauncing," the three Graces in the midst "The whilest the rest them round about did hemme," and in the very center another damsel, "That with her goodly presence all the rest much graced" (x.11-12). The vision of Pastorella is a "lower" version of the vision on Acidale; the lady is more particularized (she has a name), and the miracle of her presence is qualified by *As if*. Spenser is here imaging the transfiguration of everyday reality that occurs when love graces an "ordinary" human being; the commonness of the event must not be allowed to blind us to the fact that a miracle has occurred. The congruence of the two visions, which becomes apparent in Canto x, works in two directions. It gives Colin Clout's vision roots in ordinary experience; his lady is "but a countrey lasse" (25), and the experience that brought her to the center of Mt. Acidale does

---

see P. C. Bayley, "Order, Grace and Courtesy in Spenser's World," *Patterns of Love and Courtesy: Essays in Memory of C. S. Lewis*, ed. John Lawlor (Evanston, 1966), pp. 198-99. On the Graces of Canto x and divine grace, see Tonkin, *Courteous Pastoral*, pp. 254-57, and Lila Geller, "The Acidalian Vision: Spenser's Graces in Book VI of *The Faerie Queene*," *RES* XXIII (1972), 267-77.

not differ in quality from that which caused Calidore to be "caught like the bird" gazing at Pastorella. At the same time, the knight's experience in the preceding canto is exalted; the *As if* that introduced the miracle can be expunged, for we now know how true a miracle she was. In addition, the concentric visions enable the poet to forge a link between love and poetic inspiration that is more visible than any he has hitherto suggested, though the love/art parallel, as I have argued, is pervasive also in Books III and IV. To refer again to Plato's anatomy of divine madness in the *Phaedrus*: Apollo presides over Book I in the prophetic mode; Dionysus is intermittently present, for example in the dream of Book V; the Muses and the erotic powers together shape the epiphanies of Part II of *The Faerie Queene*.

Love and art become, in turn, instances of divine or at least other-worldly *agape*. Spenser rhymes six times in Canto x on the word *grace*, using the rhyme thrice in the stanzas that cluster around the fourth "Grace." The penultimate instance is the most emphatic: the Graces themselves have "graced her so much to be another Grace" (26). Spenser has already told us that love derives its power from these Graces:

> Those three to men all gifts of grace do graunt,
> And all, that *Venus* in her selfe doth vaunt,
> Is borrowed of them.
>
> (x.15)

Similarly, they endow Colin Clout with the power to pipe; it can be wielded by none "But whom they of them selves list so to grace" (20). There is nothing especially elegant or euphonious about *grace* as a rhyme-word; Spenser must have been aware of the echoes he was stirring up in employing it so frequently in so few stanzas. The Acidalian vision unfolds the implications of the Red Cross Knight's humility and sanctification.

In heavenly mercies hast thou not a part?
Why shoudst thou then despeire, that chosen art?
Where justice growes, there grows eke greater grace.

(I.ix.53)

We have watched the development of Justice in Book V; in
Book VI the poet reveals the sacred nursery of grace, growing on the lowly stalk that paradoxically figures its divine
origin.

The Acidalian vision is an analogue of the true visionary
experience that climaxes Book I. Only saints "really" see the
New Jerusalem. Ordinary mortals, of whom Colin Clout is
certainly one, must "see" the ultimate truth mediately,
through the creations of art, though in making *grace* re-
sound through Canto x, Spenser is insisting that the two
visions have the same root. And, in different ways, they
both adumbrate a reality inaccessible to those still in the
middest. Heavenly Contemplation tells the Red Cross
Knight that he cannot approach the "blessed end" until he
has completed his earthly quest and become sanctified. He
must accept, for the time being, Cleopolis and its lady,
the bearers, on earth, of divine intimation.

Yet is *Cleopolis* for earthly frame,
The fairest peece, that eye beholden can:
And well beseemes all knights of noble name,
That covet in th'immortal booke of fame
To be eternized, that same to haunt,
And doen their service to that soveraigne Dame,
That glorie does to them for guerdon graunt:
For she is heavenly borne, and heaven may justly vaunt.

(I.x.59)

The heavenly birth of Gloriana unites her with Colin Clout's
nameless maiden who, Spenser says, manifests "divine resemblaunce" in a degree second only to the Queen's. Both
of them are "suns" of their worlds, both therefore also re-

391

lated to Una, whose truth "as the great eye of heaven shyned bright." Una cannot be beheld directly by mortal eye, but her substitutes are personages "that eye beholden can"—the eye, at any rate, of one who has been properly initiated.

They can be beheld but they cannot, any more than the ultimate vision, be grasped. Calidore's initiation, in Canto x, repeats the lesson more discursively offered by Melibee one canto earlier. As he was literal-minded then, so he is literal-minded now, and must be instructed by the poet in the nature of the beings he has just seen and caused to vanish.

> Much wondred *Calidore* at this straunge sight,
>   Whose like before his eye had never seene,
>   And standing long astonished in spright,
>   And rapt with pleasaunce, wist not what to weene;
>   Whether it were the traine of beauties Queene,
>   Or Nymphes, or Faeries, or enchaunted show,
>   With which his eyes mote have deluded beene.
>   Therefore resolving, what it was, to know,
> Out of the wood he rose, and toward them did go.
>
> (VI.x.17)

Rapt and *astonished* are clues to the nature of this experience, which anticipates or imitates the rapture of mystical experience at the top of the Platonic ladder. Spenser describes this in some eloquent stanzas at the end of the *Hymne of Heavenly Beautie*. Earth is left behind, along with "all that pompe, to which proud minds aspyre / By name of honor"; the happy souls rejoice "in th'aspect of that felicitie / Which they have written in their inward ey" (*HHB* 277-78, 284-85). Calidore, having cast off aspiration and the vain pursuit of honor, approaches the paradise within. He comes close to realizing the vision's nature, but not close enough, because he confuses the inward truth of symbolic vision with mimetic literalness. He breaks the fiction's frame, introducing into it the literalness of his own presence. For, while he can "see" the vision, the dancing maidens, absorbed in the pattern which gives them their being, cannot "see" beyond its limits. Therefore, "soone as he appeared to their vew," they necessarily vanish. Their disappearance may remind us of an earlier visitation and departure: Arthur's loss of his dream-maiden in Book I. "Whether dreames delude, or true it were" (I.ix.14), he has vowed to seek her all his days. She is the stuff that dreams are made on, and she cannot be "known" any more than can the vision Calidore is granted in Book VI. Both exemplify the great Yeatsian principle that "man can embody truth but he cannot know it." And the embodiment is a gift of imagination, unfolding its truth deep within the mind.

4. The Return of the Beast

The recovery of a lost paradise, or a lost maiden (they may be in the end the same thing), takes place either in an interior world or in a transcendent one. Between these two invisibilities lies life in the middest. The most audacious claim a poet can make has always been that the world his imagination creates and the world revealed in visionary experience are the same. Blake's version of the claim is most convincing because it is the most passionate and unqualified; Spenser's is rather a hint than a claim, for it was not really possible for anyone in his century to state the point openly and without equivocation, or even to think of it in terms recognizable by post-romantic asethetics. The hint comes in the patterning of the vision on Acidale. The *locus amoenus* evoked by the poet surrounds and contains, not only its transcendent center—the "Damzell, as a precious gemme" environed by her peers (x.12)—but also a small patch of darkness. When Spenser comes to the climax of the vision, he describes the center twice: first in the straightforward narrative mode that characterizes his other visionary moments; and then—also a characteristic of such passages—in a "digressive" simile.

> Looke how the Crowne, which *Ariadne* wore
> Upon her yvory forehead that same day
> That *Theseus* her unto his bridale bore,
> When the bold *Centaures* made that bloudy fray,
> With the fierce *Lapithes*, which did them dismay;
> Being now placed in the firmament,
> Through the bright heaven doth her beams display,
> And is unto the starres an ornament,
> Which round about her move in order excellent.
>
> (VI.x.13)

The poet announces this epiphany with the same sort of proud ostensive gesture that introduces earlier manifestations of "great triumphant joy"—

> Such as *Diana* by the sandie shore
> Of swift *Eurotas*. . . .
>
> (II.iii.31)
>
> Like as *Cupido* on *Idaean* hill. . . .
> (II.viii.6)

The allusion to Ariadne's stellification suggests, as Kathleen Williams has said, a transcendent order, "the divine art itself" that is imitated in human art and human love.[1] "The comparison unites the heavenly and imaginary dances, the physical and mental orders, the actual zodiac and the zodiac of the poet's wit."[2]

This union of "heavenly" and "imaginary" circles lends validity to the aesthetic order of truth: both orders participate in a timeless invisible mode of being. But we do not live, ordinarily, in heaven or in poems. We live in a world where "the bold *Centaures* made that bloudy fray"—or if not centaurs, then other representatives of our mixed race. Stellification—the immortalizing of pattern in stars or words—is a "solution" to bloody frays that may delight poets but that even they do not usually regard with ultimate seriousness. When Pope allows *The Rape of the Lock* to conclude with a stellification he is testifying to "both the fragility and strength, the triviality and dignity, of art."[3]

> A sudden Star, it shot thro' liquid Air,
> And drew behind a radiant *Trail of Hair*.
> Not *Berenice*'s Locks first rose so bright,
> The Heav'ns bespangling with dishevel'd Light.

[1] *World of Glass*, p. 217.
[2] Berger, "Secret Discipline," p. 67.
[3] Martin Price, *To the Palace of Wisdom* (New York, 1964), p. 154.

> The *Sylphs* behold it kindling as it flies,
> And pleas'd pursue its Progress through the Skies.[4]

"The elevated lock is, in a sense, the poem," but the poem has also contained the Cave of Spleen and the battle of the gaming table. There is no place for them among the constellations, so the analogy must remain incomplete, insofar as the poem—and every poem—has roots in the disorder of mere being and suffers the malady of the quotidian. The "order excellent" of the heavens succeeds the destructive passion of lapiths and centaurs but does not cancel it.

> We move above the moving tree
> In light upon the figured leaf
> And hear upon the sodden floor
> Below, the boarhound and the boar
> Pursue their pattern as before
> But reconciled among the stars.[5]

Reconciliation occurs in some ultimate kingdom, and in the vision of that kingdom which the poet can transiently provide. But the curiously conflated myths, the bloody fray interrupting the bridal festivities, remain in the middle of Spenser's stanza to perpetuate the unreconciled darkness of those in the middest.[6] The point is reiterated in the total structure of Book VI, which turns inside-out the containing, reconciling pattern of Colin's vision. Among the many circles, those which make up the vision constitute a bright border with a darkness at the center, in the allusion to lapiths and centaurs. The canto itself, however, has a dark frame: first, the poet's reminder of the "foule Blatant Beast" and the corruptions of court (x.1-3); and finally the abduction of Pastorella by the Brigants, "her wretched life, shut

---

[4] V. 145-50; *The Poems of Alexander Pope*, ed. John Butt, One-volume ed. (London, 1963), p. 242.

[5] Eliot, *Burnt Norton* II; *Collected Poems*, p. 177.

[6] Stanza 13 is intensively explicated, and the allusions unraveled, in Cheney, *Image of Nature*, pp. 231-35.

up in deadly shade" (x.44). At the center is the brightness of Acidale, the lost garden where we are forbidden to linger; and at the center of the book itself, the pastoral place that is destroyed in order to bring Calidore back to his mission in a world ravaged by the Beast's "outragious spoile" (xii.22). Calidore has left childhood and its vision behind forever; and for us, Spenser's audience, it is revisited only when we follow the Muses' directions.

Blake saw that absolute fidelity to imagination allows one to live perpetually in the paradise within. The fountain overflows, and the contained imagination rushes forth to embrace and encircle the world, like the river in Wordsworth's great image at climax of *The Prelude*:

> the soul . . .
> Strong in herself and in beatitude
> That hides her, like the mighty flood of Nile
> Poured from his fount of Abyssinian clouds
> To fertilise the whole Egyptian plain.
> (VI.609-16)

For such imaginations life is a perpetual fountain of transcendent sweets, and history a divine comedy. But it may be a heresy to suppose that any *human* imagination can enjoy "close felicity" for more than a short time. Colin cannot recall the Graces, nor, pursued by "fortune fraught with malice, blinde, and brute" (x.38), can Calidore prevent the rape of Pastorella. So in the final book of *The Faerie Queene* Spenser surrounds his comic patterns with the marred perfection of a tragic paradigm, a fictive strategy which shatters the mirror of fiction in order to remain faithful to the brutal truncations of reality among the withered stumps of time.

Spenser's imagination in *The Faerie Queene* is closer to the chastened power of Wordsworth than to Blake. Wordsworth habitually renders his visions in terms of glimpses, flashes, and gleams, lamenting the brevity of their visitation.

His causal metaphor for this phenomenon is the process of organic decay, but in the *Immortality Ode* he reconstitutes the myth of the soul's fall into the darkness of the world that lies behind this metaphor, and behind Book VI of Spenser's poem as well. Both poets exert pressure upon the pastoral vision. Spenser does this by allowing the enemies of language and imagination to break the charmed circles of Courtesy. The fierce Lapiths, the Brigants,[7] the mighty Peer whose displeasure makes *The Faerie Queene* end on a dying fall (VI.xii.41) are all agents of the Blatant Beast; all victimize those who engage in "civill conversation." Satan, the father of lies and ruler of a kingdom of death, is their ultimate ancestor. Spenser makes this plain on the two occasions when Hell rises up to engulf his innocent heroines, daughters of Eve and Proserpina. Both episodes are realized nightmares, the Savages coming upon Serena "in the depth of sleepe" (viii.36), the Brigants immuring Pastorella "in dreadfull darknesse layd" (xi.2) on their little island. Both unfold in a terrible chiaroscuro—"by th' uncertaine glims of starry night" (viii.48) and in "continuall candlelight, which delt / A doubtfull sense of things, not so well seene, as felt" (x.42). The Salvage Nation embody the corruption of Nature, the Brigants the corruption of Art.[8] The consequence of such corruption is the instability of earthly joy.

[7] The Brigants destroy themselves when approached by the merchants, because they cannot control language:

> Thus as they words amongst them multiply,
> They fall to strokes, the frute of too much talke.
>
> (xi.16)

[8] This formula is, of course, too neat for the realities of Spenser's poem, and a more exact sense of its import can be gained by comparing these bad characters with the contrasted sorts of badness manifested in *The Tempest* by Caliban on the one hand, and on the other by the corrupt citizens of "civilized" Italy—Antonio, Sebastian, Stephano, and Trinculo. Caliban's attempt to violate Miranda recalls the abduction of Serena; dreamless Antonio and Sebastian, superstitious Stephano and Trinculo fall victim to the subtler temptations of Prospero's and Ariel's art.

The joyes of love, if they should ever last
  Without affliction or disquietnesse,
  That worldly chaunces doe amongst them cast,
  Would be on earth too great a blessednesse,
  Liker to heaven, then mortall wretchednesse.
Therefore the winged God, to let men weet,
  That here on earth is no sure happinesse,
  A thousand sowres hath tempred with one sweet,
To make it seeme more deare and dainty, as is meet.

                (VI.xi.1)

The winged God is the lover of Psyche. But their union is
beset by tribulation on earth, where comic or concordant
endings occur only in fictions. Marvell's unfortunate lovers
cannot remain in the kingdom of "infant Love":

    Alas, how pleasant are their days
    With whom the infant Love yet plays!
    Sorted by pairs, they still are seen
    By fountains cool, and shadows green,
    But soon those flames do lose their light,
    Like meteors of a summer's night.[9]

The light of Pastorella becomes, inevitably, "Like the faire
Morning clad in misty fog" (xi.3)—or like the light of Una,
veiled "as one that inly mournd" (I.i.4). At the hands of
their tormenters the innocent maidens of Book VI suffer a
kind of death: the loss of innocence that overtakes every
human soul. It is not a question, here, of moral judgments,
but of the traditional pattern of the soul's life. Pastorella
and Serena are not "guilty" of anything, except being born
into a fallen world; they undergo descents into the dark
places as one of the penalties of incarnation. Shades of the
prison-house close upon them as upon all growing boys and
girls.

    The main plot of Book VI is allowed a consummation;
Pastorella revives after Hell is harrowed by her lover.

[9] "The unfortunate Lover," 1-6.

> Like him that being long in tempest tost,
> Looking each houre into deathes mouth to fall,
> At length espyes at hand the happie cost,
> On which he safety hopes, that earst feard to be lost.
> (VI.xi.44)

But this action is visibly what we call a fairy-tale. As Maurice Evans has said, Spenser "is not postulating a Golden Age returned but using the appropriate poetic 'kind' as an allegory to express the poet's ideal vision of life. It is the product of the erected wit which can escape in imagination but not in action from the corrupted will."[10] The action of "ideal visions" is no stronger than a flower, for instance, the flower of Courtesy. That peculiar strength has been defined for us by Shakespeare; it lies in persistence rather than weight. Having allowed it to triumph briefly, Spenser moves beyond the tale of Pastorella to conclude Book VI and, whether by hap or not, *The Faerie Queene*. The conclusion is not fortunate.

The poet who steers his course through the poem does not reach a haven, and not merely because he was prevented from finishing his work. Spenser's actual death occurred less than three years after he published the six completed books of *The Faerie Queene*, but a different sort of death overtook the poem before that happened. The final canto of Book VI terminates in the moment of writing, and life invades art as Calidore spoiled Colin's vision, as the Brigants ravaged the homestead of Melibee. The Blatant Beast is a monster whose presence blurs the boundaries of fiction. England of the 1590's becomes an extension of the allegorical landscape as the Beast "raungeth through the world againe" (xii.40); the indecorum of its behavior, rending "without regard of person or of time," causes the leaching away of the poet's strength. He can no longer maintain the power of his fiction to resist simplistic reading and the malice of the envious. For one who traffics in words, this

10 *Anatomy of Heroism*, p. 225.

failure of his words to defend their own integrity is a kind of death, and Spenser reinforces this notion in his final descriptions of the Beast. "As the poem ends we are left in no doubt whatsoever that Spenser regards the Blatant Beast as the particular enemy of poetry and of himself as a poet."[11] And the enemies of poetry work through the poet's medium, by attacking and finally silencing his words. That silence is death, and so the Beast is appropriately a sibling of the first and last enemy in *The Faerie Queene*. It "realizes completely the Dragon figure of earlier books," in particular the Dragon of Book I whose mouth opens into Hell.[12] So this Beast:

> With open mouth, that seemed to containe
> A full good pecke within the utmost brim,
> All set with yron teeth in raunges twaine,
> That terrifide his foes, and armed him,
> Appearing like the mouth of *Orcus* griesly grim.
> (VI.xii.26)

Tonally, these lines move from the homely diction of a child's fairy-tale ("How big was the dragon?" "His mouth could hold a peck.") to the terrible allusion of the last line. Like Serena in the woods, the poet awakens from his nightmare and finds it truth.

He can invent a knight who, imitating "that strong *Tirynthian* swaine," can tame "the dreadfull dog of hell" (xii.35),

---

[11] Fletcher, *The Prophetic Moment*, p. 291. Fletcher also notes in passing that the Beast is "unmeasurable, like death" (p. 293).

[12] Hamilton, *Structure of Allegory*, pp. 205-206. The many filiations between Book I and Book VI still need to be worked out in detail. Roche devotes a few sentences to the notion that there is "a mirror relationship between individual books," so that "that virtue, which in individuals is called holiness, manifests itself socially as courtesy" (*Kindly Flame*, p. 200). Alastair Fowler says that I and VI "match" structurally (*Triumphal Forms: Structural Patterns in Elizabethan Poetry* [Cambridge, 1970], p. 111); Evans, that "*The Faerie Queene* turns upon an axis of which faith and poetry are the two poles, the vision which God sends to man and the vision which man attains of God" (*Anatomy of Heroism*, pp. 18-19).

but Colin Clout is not Hercules nor was meant to be. His acknowledgment of his own weakness is a virtue of Spenser's self-critical imagination, like Shakespeare's in *The Tempest*. "The pastoral passage is Spenser's comment on his own creation, on the kind of strength and the kind of fragility poetry has,"[13] and the comment continues to the last bitter alexandrine of Book VI.

> Therefore do you my rimes keep bitter measure,
> And seeke to please, that now is counted wisemens
> threasure.
> (xii.41)

Dulce has devoured *utile*; this is one meaning of the Blatant Beast's triumph. And necessarily, for the poet who had set before himself the serious aim of fashioning a gentleman in virtue, the rest is silence.

[13] Williams, *World of Glass*, p. 215.

5. The Recession of Allegory

It is ironic that Book VI, the most relaxed and joyous part of *The Faerie Queene*, manifesting the happiest union between pleasure and profit, should end with this weary admission of defeat. Yet Spenser gives us intimations of this conclusion even in the Proem, reminding us that for many of the members of this courtly audience, virtue

> indeed is nought but forgerie,
> Fashion'd to please the eies of them, that pas,
> Which see not perfect things but in a glas:
> Yet is that glasse so gay, that it can blynd
> The wisest sight, to thinke gold that is bras.
> But vertues seat is deepe within the mynd,
> And not in outward shows, but inward thoughts
> defynd.
> (VI.Pro.5)

The logic of these lines is not easy to untangle. It is true that mortal sight can see "perfect things but in a glas"—but glass is itself a treacherous concept. "Now we see through a glass darkly"; as fallen creatures we can know the vision only in mediated form. And poetry is one of the "glasses" that can mediate for us. But it *may* be simply a flattering delusion in which we see ourselves as we would wish to be, not as we are: a "glasse so gay, that it can blynd / The wisest sight," as Duessa blinded the Red Cross Knight. A popinjay courtier may be a glass of fashion and a mold of form in an age that confuses brass with gold; poetry that merely "seeks to please" can be mistakenly treasured. "But vertues seat is deepe within the mynd," and an art that captures it must be more than the distorting surface of a mirror; it must be a *speculum* that will turn our gaze upon that invisible deep

403

virtue. Seeking for an alternative to "forgerie," the poet finds, in the next stanza, a fair "patterne" in the Queen,

> In whose pure minde, as in a mirrour sheene,
> It showes, and with her brightnesse doth inflame
> The eyes of all, which thereon fixed beene;
> But meriteth indeede an higher name.
>
> (VI.Pro.6)

In these two stanzas, Spenser explores the different ways in which poetry can mirror reality. It can reflect surfaces, or it can imitate the pattern of virtue that lies in a pure mind, visible to those who have eyes to see: those, in fact, who have been taught by the Muse. It is necessary to think again about the kind of mirror *The Faerie Queene* itself is; and, more particularly, the manner in which we are to understand the relationship between the mirror's surface and the mirrored objects in Book VI. That is, we must consider again the nature of Spenser's allegory, for Book VI marks the poet's final and most radical manipulation of his venerable mode.

Critics discussing this book often assume that the allegory has disappeared, and that it may therefore be ignored. Most analyses of Book VI are not allegorical interpretations —or at least, not in a way that demonstrates those habits of interpreting that Spenser has taught us in the first five books. In order to look more closely at the *allegorical* relevance of the final book, I want to recall Susanne Langer's distinction between model and image. I observed earlier that her discussion offers useful terms for describing the alternative angles from which we view Spenser's fiction; the phenomenal vividness of the image and the projective power of the model are in constant interplay in the action of *The Faerie Queene*. In Book VI, image dominates and model becomes submerged in the "immediate effect on our sensibility" produced by the stories of Calidore and Calepine, Priscilla, Serena, and Pastorella.[1] The warmth of

[1] For Langer's image/model distinction, see above, p. 264.

response usually accorded to Book VI is partly, as Lewis noted, a reaction to the harsh landscapes of Book V. That is its negative aspect. But it is also a response to a world which is presented to us as simply as an old tale. The introductory stanza to Canto i etymologizes Courtesy in a straightforward, even simple-minded way: "Of Court it seemes, men Courtesie doe call, . . . / Right so in Faery court it did redound." With that, we are introduced to Sir Calidore, "beloved over all," the pattern of Courtesy.

> Ne was there Knight, ne was there Lady found
> In Faery court, but him did deare embrace,
> In his faire usage and conditions sound,
> The which in all mens liking gayned place,
> And with the greatest purchast greatest grace.
> (VI.i.3)

It is the world of the *Morte d'Arthur*; one thinks of the arrival at court of Gareth, "Beaumains":

> Ryght so com into the halle two men well besayne
> and rychely, and uppon their sholdyrs there lened
> the goodlyest yonge man and the fayreste that ever
> they all sawe. And he was large and longe and brode
> in the shuldyrs, well-vysaged.

Calidore "did steale mens hearts away," says Spenser; Gareth "never dyspleased man nother chylde, but allwayes he was meke and mylde," says Malory.[2] The motif of the young man, nobly born, who rises from obscurity to become a famous knight, is recounted first by Spenser in the Letter with reference to the Red Cross Knight; in Book VI, he redevelops it in the story of Tristram—which he drew, in part, from the Arthurian material used by Malory.[3]

[2] *The Works of Sir Thomas Malory*, ed. Eugene Vinaver, Oxford Standard Authors (Oxford, 1954), pp. 212, 214.

[3] C. S. Lewis long ago identified "distinct traces of the influence of Malory" in Book VI, as well as "the high proportion of unallegorical, or faintly allegorical, scenes (*Allegory of Love*, p. 353).

To say this much is merely to repeat what all readers of Book VI have noticed: that Spenser is here relaxing his narrative into its romance origins more completely than he does elsewhere in *The Faerie Queene*. This formal fact must be assumed to have thematic relevance: what aspects of Spenser's subject in Book VI make it appropriate for the image to displace the model, for the analytic and projective powers of allegory to recede into the middle distance or go underground? The question can best be explored, I think, under two headings. The first is thematic and concerns the primitivism of Book VI, its retreat to simplicity and the wellsprings of virtue, its evocation of edenic conditions. The second concerns the peculiar ontology of Spenser's allegory in *The Faerie Queene*. These thematic and formal aspects of the problem are intertwined, and may in fact be two ways of verbalizing the same phenomena.

At several places in *The Faerie Queene*, Spenser pauses to describe the characteristics of the "antique age" he invokes as a standard of behavior. It is not, as I have already argued, to be identified uncritically with the poem's world; rather, it is an ideal whose remoteness in time puts it beyond the grasp even of most of the characters within the fiction. But it does materialize now and then, in the form of an interlude when "simple truth" prevails. The House of Holiness, an island of simplicity in a sea of duplicity, is one such interlude. There language reassumes its pristine purity. The squire Reverence greets the travelers with "speeches meet":

> no courting nicetie,
> But simple true, and eke unfained sweet.
>
> (I.x.7)[4]

---

[4] Spenser says that Reverence "knew his good to all of each degree"; the phrase is echoed when he describes Courtesy as one of the handmaidens of Womanhood in the Temple of Venus: "comely *Curtesie,* / That unto every person knew her part" (IV.x.51). I do not attach great weight to this parallel, since Spenser almost certainly had not projected the Book of Courtesy when he wrote either line; but it does speak for the instinctive consistency of his imagination.

In the antique age, "simple Truth did rayne, and was of all admyred" (V.Pro.3). As Spenser's phrase, "no courting nicetie," suggests (the point is made explicitly in *Colin Clouts Come Home Againe*), this simplicity is not often found at court; rather, we must journey into the country on the other side of the mirror, the pastoral place where the Muses are at home. The truancy that takes Calidore into Melibee's cottage is a confirmation of the knight's deepest nature, for, Spenser insists on first introducing him, he always "loathd leasing, and base flattery, / And loved simple truth and stedfast honesty" (i.3). He embodies the virtue that Spenser's friend Bryskett calls Verity:

> by which a man . . . sheweth himselfe sincere and
> ful of truth, making his words and his deeds always
> to agree. . . . This is that excellent vertue that is of
> all others the best fitting a Gentleman, . . . whose
> contrary likewise is of all other things the most un-
> fitting, the very destroier of humane conversation
> the mother of scandals, and the deadly enemy of
> friendship.[5]

Simple truth or verity is envisioned in the naked Graces who dance on Mt. Acidale: they

> naked are, that without guile
> Or false dissemblaunce all them plaine may see,
> Simple and true from covert malice free.
> (x.24)

As Bacon was shortly to affirm, "nakedness of mind is still, as nakedness of the body once was, the companion of innocence and simplicity."[6]

---

[5] Lodowick Bryskett, *A Discourse of Civill Life* (London, 1606), pp. 242-43.

[6] Plan of *The Great Instauration; Selected Writings*, p. 439. For the iconography of nakedness, see Ch. 8 and 9 of Wind, *Pagan Mysteries*.

The "warm nude ages of instinctive poise" are gone forever, and the world of Book VI is not innocent; it conceals
brigands and cannibals and discourteous knights like Turpine. But it also harbors the benevolent Salvage Man, the
wise hermit, the beautiful squire Tristram who is compared
to "*Latonaes* sonne, / After his chace on woodie *Cynthus*
donne" (ii.25), and the shepherd and his daughter, as well
as several loving couples who "shew all lovely courtesyes"
to each other (ii.16). These personages embody various
kinds of innocence, and though they are discomfited by hostile forces which severely limit their free action, their presence in Book VI and the relative joyousness the poet allows
them suggest an ambiance less contaminated than that of the
rest of *The Faerie Queene*. The innocent in this book are all
human characters, neither personifications nor "ensamples"
like Una or Florimell or Amoret; so are most of the wicked
(with exceptions shortly to be noted). Spenser is imagining
a world in which "primitive" or primal virtue has not yet
become so infected by the confusions that have fallen upon
Nature and human nature that it must retreat behind a veil
or manifest itself solely to the visionary eye of imagination
or revelation. This world is postlapsarian, but closer to the
time when "simple Truth did rayne"; in consequence, good
and bad are visible to the naked eye, unobscured by the
confusion of seemings that perplex the heroes of the other
books, set in a time after "the world woxe old." In his
lengthiest description of the "antique age," Spenser explains
that it "Ne then of guile had made experiment"; but later,
"faire grew foule, and foule grew faire in sight" (IV.viii.
30-32) and the "glorious flowre" of divine beauty languished.

> And now it is so utterly decayd,
>> That any bud thereof doth scarse remaine,
>> But if few plants preserv'd through heavenly ayd,
>> In Princes Court doe hap to sprout againe,
>> Dew'd with her drops of bountie Soveraine,
>> Which from that goodly glorious flowre proceed,

> Sprung of the auncient stocke of Princes straine,
> Now th'onely remnant of that royall breed,
> Whose noble kind at first was sure of heavenly seed.
>
> (IV.viii.33)

Calidore is born of this seed; so are Tristram, the Salvage Man, and Pastorella. And in Book VI, Spenser recreates, more completely than anywhere else in the poem, the early time when virtue's stock still flourished. Here, uniquely in *The Faerie Queene*, the entire action unfolds within the fictive literalness of Fairy Land itself, as distinct from the larger world of the total poetic fiction. In the first canto, Spenser for the first and only time initiates an action in "Faery court"—a place we have hitherto encountered only in retrospect or anticipation (and in the Letter to Ralegh) ; as when the Red Cross Knight refers to "that great *Cleopolis*, where I have beene, / In which that fairest *Faerie Queene* doth dwell" (I.x.58). We are only in Fairy court for three stanzas of Book VI, and they are mostly devoted to praise of Calidore. Nevertheless, the fact that his quest takes him from that court into and through *the place* called "Faerie Land" is an important clue to the nature of Spenser's fiction in Book VI. It is significant, too, that Calidore is the only patron of a book besides Guyon to have been born in Fairy Land.

In Book VI, then, Spenser is revealing to us the true meaning of "Faerie Land" as a place that lives within the mind, to be reached only by "these strange waies, where never foote did use, / Ne none can find, but who was taught them by the Muse" (VI.Pro.2). These famous lines must be taken seriously as exactly prophesying the nature of the discourse they introduce. Only "in Faery court" does Courtesy justify its etymology; only in Guyon's book, *Antiquitie of Faerie lond*, does history reveal the orderly sequences which we would have it do. "The romance is nearest of all literary forms to the wish-fulfilment dream."[7] This does not

---

[7] Frye, *Anatomy of Criticism*, p. 186.

mean that it ignores nightmares, for romances contain villains as well as heroes, but it does mean that villain and hero are easily recognizable. In Eden, Adam could name the beasts because he "understood their nature" (*PL* VIII.352-53); romance, more than any other literary form, reproduces that condition of intuitive apprehension and primal lucidity. The peculiar simplicities of Book VI, the fact that the epistemological muddles that snare characters and readers from Book I to Book V have fallen away, suggest that Spenser is here giving us "poetry" in its essence, an exemplary instance of the erected wit contriving its golden worlds. All the more, therefore, must we admire the poet's honesty, and lament our rude awakening, when this simplicity is first invaded, then contaminated and ruined, by a messenger from our own uncivil culture, the Blatant Beast.

If it is Spenser's intention to take us back into "our first world," then allegory as I have described it hitherto will be indecorous. A primitive society can neither generate nor comprehend ironic modes—most notably, the mode of allegory, "the figure of false semblant" in which "our wordes and our meanings meete not."[8] Calidore must capture the Blatant Beast in order that allegorical fictions may remain unnecessary in Fairy Land. The Beast itself, undeniably an allegorical creature, is able to flourish only in situations where being and seeming have parted company. Its strategy is to suggest "reproch, or secrete shame" in noble knights and ladies; where there are no secrets, its bite must be ineffectual. Hence the Hermit who cures Serena and Timias advises them to

> Shun secresie, and talke in open sight:
> So shall you soone repaire your present evill plight.
> (VI.vi.14)

[8] When Puttenham speaks of pastoral as inherently allegorical, a fiction devised to "insinuate and glaunce at greater matters" (*Arte of English Poesie*, I.xviii; p. 38), he describes a version of pastoral employed by Spenser in *The Shepheardes Calender*. Book VI, in contrast, shows us the innocent life before the birth of allegory.

Spenser alludes twice to the hellish birth of the Beast, casually producing two genealogies for it. The first briefly refers to its begetting by Cerberus upon "fell *Chimaera* in her darkesome den" (i.8); the second gives a lengthier and more revealing account. The Beast's dam is Echidna, an incarnation of the female snake so often depicted in paintings of the Fall, and recurrently visible in *The Faerie Queene* from Errour on.[9]

> Yet did her face and former parts professe
> A faire young Mayden, full of comely glee;
> But all her hinder parts did plaine expresse
> A monstrous Dragon, full of fearefull uglinesse.
> (VI.vi.10)

This creature dwells undergound, "In hideous horrour and obscurity, / Wasting the strength of her immortall age": her endurance, like that of other immortal beings in *The Faerie Queene*, betokens the endless vitality of the principle she embodies. Echidna is clearly related to Satan the father of lies; the lying truth of allegory is an effort to counterbalance their power and that of Echidna's child, the Blatant Beast. Where these beings are powerless, in a place centered upon a vision of the naked Graces, allegory can be abandoned.

It erupts into Book VI, therefore, only when Spenser makes us feel the pressure of corrupt "civilized" behavior upon the simplicities of the antique age. Canto vii contains the story of Mirabella, who began life under auspicious circumstances.

> Famous through all the land of Faerie,
> Though of meane parentage and kindred base,

---

[9] A history of this icon, and many interesting reproductions, can be found in J. B. Trapp's essay, "The Iconography of the Fall of Man," in *Approaches to "Paradise Lost,"* ed. C. A. Patrides (London, 1968). Jane Aptekar considers Spenser's serpent-women in *Icons of Justice: Iconography and Thematic Imagery in Book V of the Faerie Queene* (New York, 1969), pp. 141-44.

411

> Yet deckt with wondrous giftes of natures grace,
> That all men did her person much admire.
>
> (VI.vii.28)

Unlike Calidore, who also steals men's hearts, she becomes vainglorious as a result and turns into the archetypal cruel mistress. Her mean parentage is a key to her bad behavior; Calidore and Tristram, who also possess the "giftes of natures grace," belong to a stock rooted in the "noble kind . . . of heavenly seed" that is Spenser's metaphor for the mysterious strength of innate virtue. Without it, the outward gifts of nature are of no account. So Mirabella is a prime instance of the fair face concealing a psyche that is less than fair: *Frontes nulla fides.* In order to dissect her career, the poet resorts inevitably to allegory: the doom in Cupid's court, the Giant Disdain, and the fool Scorne. Timias, whose earlier encounters with allegorical beings have alerted us to the presence of a secret life in him, valiantly but unwisely assaults the Giant and is made prisoner. In the next canto Mirabella is left to work out her fate, moving through the allegorical mirror to become an analyzed "case" (viii.2) for other "gentle Ladies." A self-explanatory rhetorical mode returns to the narrative.

> Here in this bottle (sayd the sory Mayd)
> I put the teares of my contrition,
> Till to the brim I have it full defrayd:
> And in this bag which I behinde me don,
> I put repentaunce for things past and gon.
>
> (VI.viii.24)

The note struck here, and throughout the tale of Mirabella, is out of key with the dominant of Book VI. The passage's stylistic crudeness need not be admired, but it insures that the reader notices a distinction significant within the book as a whole. At any rate, Pastorella could not put her tears in a bottle labeled contrition, even though she sheds some.

But her story is enacted within a different literary convention.

To define this convention, we must reconsider the sense in which the action of Book VI unfolds "in the mind." Turning back for a moment to Book V, where one of Spenser's aims is to define the limits of effective human action, let us observe the Giant with whom Artegal converses in Canto ii. This Giant is not only an egalitarian; he is also, perforce, a simple-minded allegorist. He is first seen

> Upon a rocke, and holding forth on hie
> An huge great paire of ballance in his hand,
> With which he boasted in his surquedrie,
> That all the world he would weigh equallie.
>
> (V.ii.30)

Artegal's reply to the Giant's boast concerns, first of all, its political implications: the nature of hierarchy, the nature of limit. Eventually he comes to the theoretical basis of the argument:

> Of things unseene how canst thou deeme aright,
>   Then answered the righteous *Artegall*,
> Sith thou misdeem'st so much of things in sight?
>
> (V.ii.39)

He proceeds to instruct the Giant in the various senses of the word *weigh*.

> For take thy ballaunce, if thou be so wise,
>   And weigh the winde, that under heaven doth blow;
> Or weigh the light, that in the East doth rise;
> Or weigh the thought, that from mans mind doth flow.
>
> (V.ii.43)

And words cannot be "weighed" any more than thoughts— or cannot as long as we are taking the notion of a "ballaunce" as literally as the Giant. He does not know how to read, or compose, allegory, though his balance was given him by the allegorical poet. When he attempts to "weigh" right and wrong, he fails, because wrong or evil does not "weigh" anything compared with right. He is using the balance properly—the poet and his instructed reader can "see" the metaphorical point—but interpreting its message mistakenly. Enraged, he tries to break his instrument, but Artegal intervenes.

> Be not upon thy balance wroken:
> For they doe nought but right or wrong betoken;
> But in the mind the doome of right must bee;
> And so likewise of words, the which be spoken,
> The eare must be the ballance, to decree
> And judge, whether with truth or falshood they agree.
>
> (V.ii.47)

The balance metaphorically "betokens" the relation between right and wrong; but the doom or judgment concerning that relation and its meaning takes place "in the mind," just as the mind or "eare" receives the speaking pictures of words and translates them into a judgment. The psychological model of the senses as receptors and transmitters of images to an "inward sense" which fits them together and judges them, lies behind Spenser's stanza, and indeed the whole episode, which is not only an allegorical rendering of the Knight's just doom, but a directive as to how we should read it. The balance is a typical allegorical image: taciturn, visible, explicated; signifying the imponderability of the invisible world where its meaning lies, it is also a metaphor that insists upon its own metaphorical status.

"The doome of right" is "in the mind"; so is "vertues seat," in the Proem to Book VI. The mind itself is both a source and a goal, a sacred nursery of allegories and the place to which allegorical images must return to receive "doome"— the judgment and interpretation of meaning. The Book of Justice is centrally concerned with the act of judgment, with the mind as the arena in which visible tokens of mean-

ing are rightly weighed. Book V repeatedly shows us Artegal rendering judgment, after contemplation of initially
enigmatic circumstances; the book is like Book I in that the
process of allegorical reading is a model of its own subject-
matter, the life of the mind in its confrontation with the
world "outside." In the Book of Courtesy, Spenser takes us
into that part of the psyche that is a *source* of both allegories and judgments, a "primitive" place self-haunted by
mighty forms that move slowly through the mind in daydream and nightmare. In many parts of the book, he is
showing us what goes on "in the mind" before it has articulated its judgments into the rhetorical tropes of allegory
and metaphor for the instruction or self-instruction of the
soul. The Fairy Land of the final book is a pre-allegorical
realm, in which the psychological materials from which allegory is shaped flourish in their "natural" state.

Deep within the mind, as it is sometimes described by
modern psychiatry, the primordial elements of our fantasy-
life pursue their existence, shadowy but potent, imaging the
soul's life before it has been made external and rationalized.

> The romancer does not attempt to create "real
> people" so much as stylized figures which expand
> into psychological archetypes. It is in the romance
> that we find Jung's libido, anima, and shadow
> reflected in the hero, heroine, and villain respec-
> tively. That is why the romance so often radiates a glow
> of subjective intensity . . . and why a suggestion of
> allegory is constantly creeping in around its fringes.[10]

The notion that romance is a kind of ur-allegory offers an
important clue to the narrative mode of Book VI. The "glow
of subjective intensity" emanating from old tales and traced
to a psychic source by modern theorists turns the reader's
gaze to the invisible world deep within the mind, to which
the Muse holds the key. In nightmare and daydream these
forms manifest themselves to a passive observer; in mythic

---

[10] Frye, *Anatomy of Criticism*, p. 304.

poetry like *The Faerie Queene* VI, the active imagination draws them up from the well of the past and gives them stability in the magical fixities of language.

Although ancient fictional motifs are a staple of Spenser's narrative in every book of *The Faerie Queene*, the examples of old stories in Book VI are invested with a "glow of subjective intensity" that is generated by a power greater than that of the poet's visible thematic elaboration of the virtue of Courtesy. Two of the commonest "adolescent fantasies" described by Jung are the changeling motif—the child's notion that he is begotten by "a rich and elegant count and . . . merely brought up by foster-parents"—and the "dream of sexual assault: the robber who breaks in and does something dangerous."[11] Both of these primitive "stories" embodying fears and wishes are enacted by the heroines of Book VI: Serena is assaulted sexually by the Salvage Nation in a nightmare sequence with herself as the focal point; Pastorella discovers that she is the daughter of "the good Sir *Bellamour*," and was brought up by foster-parents. Pastorella's adventures in Canto xi also trace the outlines of an ancient story. Abducted by the primitive, pre-agricultural brigands, she is taken to a cave on a woody island and incarcerated in perpetual darkness, barely lit with candles which produce "A doubtfull sense of things, not so well seene, as felt" (xi.42). The maiden "thought her self in hell," as well she might, since the place is a kind of psychic ancestor of all our hells, including those which Spenser embodies in earlier books of *The Faerie Queene*. Fantasies of this kind are rich with potentiality for the interpreter, and their recurrent embodiment in literature, legend, and religious rite through the centuries has shown what some of the possibilities are. The interpretive contexts may be Freudian or Jungian, may concern the enactment of sexual fears and wishes, or the quest for identity, the "endlessly repeated

[11] C. G. Jung, *Symbols of Transformation*, tr. R.F.C. Hull, Torchbooks ed. (2 vols., New York, 1962), I, 26.

drama of coming-to-be and passing-away."[12] Neo-Platonic interpreters read into such images myths of the soul's descent into matter, "the body [in] its prison or tomb, the kosmos its cave or cavern."[13] Plotinus' description of the fallen soul might be a description of Pastorella among the brigands:

> It has fallen: it is at the chain: debarred from
> expressing itself now through its intellectual phase,
> it operates through sense ["a doubtfull sense of
> things"]; it is a captive; this is the burial, the
> encavernment, of the Soul.[14]

The point, of course, is not that Spenser was a Neo-Platonic adept, or that his Merlin-like prophetic eye pierced the mists of twentieth-century psychological theory. The plot of Book VI is a sequence of fairy tales from which almost any number of rationalizations or "doomes" can be derived. Deep within the mind they lie unanalyzed but potent, ready to be magically awakened by the interpreter's scrutiny.

It is the unanalyzed character of Spenser's allegory that has led readers of Book VI, with some reason, to say that he has forgotten allegory altogether in the final movement of *The Faerie Queene*. If, as I argued in the first chapter, the analytical examination of images is part of the definition of allegory, then many stretches of Book VI do not qualify. I also argued, however, that Spenser incorporates into the wide fabric of *The Faerie Queene* a consideration of the nature of allegorical poetry itself. In Book VI he returns *ad fontes* to write about sources and the search for sources. As

---

[12] C. G. Jung and C. Kerenyi, *Introduction to a Science of Mythology*, tr. R.F.C. Hull (London, 1951), p. 172. The phrase appears in a discussion by Kerenyi of the Demeter-Persephone myth. Tonkin calls the Proserpina story "one of the most important of the mythic structures which serve as correlatives for the action of the book" (*Courteous Pastoral*, p. 310).

[13] *Plotinus on the Nature of the Soul, Being the Fourth Ennead*, tr. Stephen MacKenna (London, 1924), p. 146.

[14] Ibid., p. 148.

the poet revealed in Book III, these sources lie both deep and high, "in the mind" and in the realm of "sky ruling Jove" that is the native place of the Graces and the sacred nursery of "heavenly seedes of bounty" (Pro.3).

> So from the Ocean all rivers spring,
> And tribute back repay as to their King.
>   (Pro.7)

To call the action of Book VI pre-allegorical is also to say that it is predominantly non-metaphorical. The personages —lost maiden, old shepherd, hermit, wild man, young squire, discourteous knight—are what they are. They are not figural shadowings of invisible truths, but shadowy types which live in our minds and enact the imagination's never-ending primitive romance with the world. The stories handed down through tradition acquire the permanence of repeated reincarnation; they link the workings of the primitive imagination to the literary products of more sophisticated ages. The dénouement of *The Winter's Tale* is "like an old tale" itself; and so is the story of the shepherd lass and her stepfather that Spenser unravels at the end of Book VI.

> He was to weet by common voice esteemed
>   The father of the fayrest *Pastorell*,
>   And of her selfe in very deede so deemed;
>   Yet was not so, but as old stories tell
>   Found her by fortune, which to him befell,
>   In th' open fields an Infant left alone,
>   And taking up brought home, and noursed well
>   As his owne chyld; for other he had none,
> That she in tract of time accompted was his owne.
>   (VI.ix.14)

But tract of time has further revelations in store, and like other old stories this one ends with a reunion of child and true parents. Pastorella, like Perdita, is destined to play out a tale told not twice but many times. Insofar as any lost child, like Blake's Little Girl Lost, shows us the soul wandering through the wood of the world,[15] the places where it sojourns can be read as aspects of its own psychic life. But the stories are not metaphors, not consciously designed tropes, but enactments of fears and desires, like dreams. They do not give metaphorical life to moral struggles in the invisible world of spirit; rather, they transport our dreams to an imaginary realm where they can be magically realized. When dream-life and moral life are traced to a common origin by the self-aware, self-contemplating imagination, then the allegory on the fringes of romance moves to the center and invests the dream images with metaphorical import. This happens in the first five books of *The Faerie Queene*; in Book VI, the roots of the great tree are exposed.

The peculiar permanence of old stories cannot be absolute. Muses and Graces vanish, visions fade, childhood recedes, and poems end. Spenser's great poem ends on a peculiarly unhappy note, manifesting itself in a certain slackness of style; some implications of that ending have already been discussed. It is an appropriately realistic conclusion as well to the poet's examination of imagining, in

[15] Neo-Platonic readings of Blake are provided by Kathleen Raine, *Blake and Tradition* (2 vols., Princeton, 1968); she concludes that "The soul's sufferings in this world, the cruel laws to which she is here subjected, and her inextinguishable longing for eternity are the theme of all the poems" in *Songs of Experience*, pre-eminently "The Little Girl Lost" (I, 149). The cruel, apparently meaningless "laws" that constrain human souls certainly weight also the lives of Spenser's maidens in Book VI, but those lives are rather instances of a common human fate which gave rise to such myths as Plotinus', than allegorical developments of the adventuring soul. C. S. Lewis speaks of Florimell enthralled by Proteus as "the *anima semplicetta* come from the sweet golden clime into the sea of matter . . . an allegory of the descent of the soul into material embodiment," and compares the story to that of Blake's Lyca (*Images of Life*, p. 126). But Florimell is a deeply allegorical figure whose many significances are unfolded in the course of her varied adventures. Spenser by contrast quickly establishes Pastorella as a typical fictional heroine, lost and found "as old stories tell" (VI.ix.14).

419

Book VI and the entire poem. "Homely verse" of the kind that he has composed in the twice-told tales of Book VI cannot survive the sophisticated corruptions of civilization, any more than Serena can wander unharmed in the gentle weather. The violent conclusion to Calidore's pastoral sojourn is the poet's way of returning him to the place where his duty lies; it is also a statement about the dangers of lingering too long in the golden worlds the poet makes. An interesting discrepancy in the text of Canto x reveals the hidden sense of this canto's narrative: that Calidore's dalliance with the poet and the Graces is the enabling cause of his loss of the pastoral paradise. In the narrative proper, the knight leaves Acidale and rejoins Pastorella:

> So taking leave of that same gentle swaine,
> He backe returned to his rusticke wonne.
>
> (VI.x.32)

Several stanzas are then devoted to his wooing, the defeat of his rival Coridon, and his ultimate success with the lady: "at the last unto his will he brought her" (38). Not only several stanzas, but several days have passed. And after the lovers' accord, they "joyed long in close felicity." Nevertheless, twin time-clocks are ticking here. Recorded time is telescoped in memory; and most readers of Book VI have the impression that Pastorella is abducted while Calidore is with Colin Clout on Acidale. This impression is confirmed and enshrined in the Argument to Canto x; and here, above all, we should like to know for certain who is responsible for these often misleadingly illuminating little quatrains.[16]

> Calidore sees the Graces daunce,
>   To Colins melody:
> The whiles his Pastorell is led,
>   Into captivity.

[16] Townsend Rich has a note on the problematic character of the Arguments (*Harington and Ariosto: A Study in Elizabethan Verse Translation* [New Haven, 1940], p. 60 n.). He points out that Ariosto

We cannot help reading into these lines a causal link: Calidore's love is ravished *because* he is absent gazing at the visionary maidens. Spenser uses juxtaposition throughout the paratactic narrative of *The Faerie Queene* to indicate causes: Orgoglio attacks the Red Cross Knight *because* he has doffed his armor and poured out his vital force in Duessa's arms. The brigands succeed in abducting Pastorella *because* she has been left vulnerable to the brutalities of the "lawless people" who live in the fallen world. Spenser treats his protagonists in Book VI more gently than those of Book I, and we are not to moralize this episode. Calidore's glimpse of the fountain of his Courtesy was necessary; but the ravishment of Colin Clout's song, and his explanation of it, can become a distracting *cul de sac*. The abduction itself is attributed to fortune's envy, and Spenser's stanzas resemble a later lament for a Nymph and her pet, slain by the wanton troopers who happen to be "riding by."

The point is that they always are riding by, and we have to be prepared to meet them. Therefore we grow up and acquire the means to defend ourselves against wicked tongues and the venomous despite of those who envy the innocent. The simple visible fictions of childhood cannot sustain the complex meanings with which adult life must grapple. Book VI is only a short segment of the immense poem, and it expires under the renewed assaults of the Blatant Beast.

> . . . the hiding-places of man's power
> Open; I would approach them, but they close.
> I see by glimpses now; when age comes on,
> May scarcely see at all.
>   (*Prelude* XII.279-82)

---

did not provide *Argomenti* for the cantos of the *Furioso*, the verses being supplied by the editors from "another hand." He suggests that "William Ponsonby would probably have provided verses for Spenser's poem, if the author himself had not furnished them."

Having visited the hiding-places of his own power, Spenser succumbs to the coming-on of night and the late age of the world. His retreat in Book VI to a world "deep within the mind" was perhaps a response to his disillusionment with the political expediency of iron men like Talus, who has no mind. To lose faith in external order was also to lose the foothold in "some underlying reality, something in the nature of things" that makes allegory possible. Book VI explores the subjective part of the allegorical equation; if for Spenser by this time there was nothing else, then this book is, from profound necessity, the end of *The Faerie Queene*. In the last stanzas, he turns to the only alternative for a poet in the middest, a final wordlessness.

Conclusion

The Promised End in Mutabilitie

Whatever the facts about the composition of the *Muta-bilitie Cantos* may be, they are now unavailable, and aesthetic judgment must assume the task of relating this great fragment to the rest of *The Faerie Queene*. The relationship is as eminently appropriate as it is problematic; as many critics have realized, the *Cantos* make a sufficient, if not a necessary, conclusion to the six books that Spenser completed. Among other themes here reconsidered and wound up is the anatomy of imagination. The vision of Book VII affirms that, for man, the good of life is bound up with change, so the exercise of imagination cannot be divorced from mutability without turning into its demonic form, idolatry. All the places from which time is excluded are dangerous in *The Faerie Queene*: the Bower of Bliss; Busirane's castle, with its claustrophobic revels, ceaselessly reiterated; the explicitly idolatrous temple reared by Geryoneo. All these places are *necessarily* ruined by the poem's heroes—Guyon, Britomart, Arthur—whose missions involve the purging of ragged commonweals so that human virtue, including imaginative virtue, can function in health.

Those missions, however, as we have seen, are invariably incomplete. And all restorations or recreations of golden worlds must be, until time ends. "Poetry concerns itself with the creation of Paradises,"[1] but the many versions of paradise, and the poet's treatment of them in *The Faerie Queene*, testify to Spenser's awareness that the imagination cannot safely fall in love with its own creations. They all vanish when we attempt to confer any sort of literalness on

[1] J. B. Yeats, *Letters to his Son W. B. Yeats and Others* (New York, 1946), p. 179.

them. The imagination mediates the truths of Eden for us now; Spenser, when he approaches the abiding gardens, offers us a decontaminated magic, going before us with his golden bough—

> sed non ante datur telluris operta subire,
> auricomos quam qui decerpserit arbore fetus.[2]

The major instance of safe felicity in the poem, the Garden of Adonis, is situated in a narrative loop and visited for us by the poet. Spenser insulates his mirrors of perfection from the rash gazer's eye *within* the fiction; the sorrows of Timias, as well as the brashness of Braggadocchio and the foolhardiness of Calidore, attest to some of the difficulties that ensue when denizens of imagination's paradise manifest themselves to the merely natural vision.

Calidore, temporarily discourteous and Trompart-like, fails to keep decorum with the vision on Mt. Acidale, and those maidens flee away even more quickly than Belphoebe. Later in the same canto, Melibee's farm is reduced to a waste land. It is the result of Fortune's malice, "blinde, and brute" (VI.x.38), but Fortune is the instrument of the principle that no pastoral retreat can be safe unless it remains deep within the mind. The pattern is reiterated in *Mutabilitie*, in the mythical farce of "foolish God *Faunus*." We might say that Faunus like Calidore fails to preserve an appropriately contemplative attitude when he observes "*Diana*, with her Nymphes about her"; aesthetic distance is violated by laughter. Faunus is an ancestor of Lynch in Joyce's *Portrait*, symbol of the unaesthetic *kinesis*: "one day I wrote my name in pencil on the backside of the Venus of Praxiteles in the Museum."[3]

[2] *Aeneid* VI.140-41; *Virgil*, I, 516. For comments on the golden bough in *The Faerie Queene*, see Nelson, *Poetry of Spenser*, p. 159; Hankins, *Source and Meaning*, pp. 65-68. The usual allegorization for the bough was *sapientia*.

[3] *A Portrait of the Artist as a Young Man*, Modern Library (New York, 1928), p. 240.

There *Faunus* saw that pleased much his eye,
   And made his hart to tickle in his brest,
   That for great joy of some-what he did spy,
   He could him not containe in silent rest;
   But breaking forth in laughter, loud profest
His foolish thought. A foolish *Faune* indeed,
   That couldst not hold thy selfe so hidden blest,
   But wouldest needs thine owne conceit areed.
Babblers unworthy been of so divine a meed.
                      (VII.vi.46)

The conceit that prefers itself to the hidden blessing of divine meed gets its just comic deserts; but, more seriously, it leads to the punishment of the river-nymph Molanna and, eventually, a new waste land, when Diana departs in anger.

Thence-forth she left; and parting from the place,
   There-on an heavy haplesse curse did lay,
   To weet, that Wolves, where she was wont to space,
   Should harbour'd be, and all those Woods deface,
And Thieves should rob and spoile that Coast around.
                      (VII.vi.55)

It is from this defaced island, a ragged war-wearied Ireland, that Spenser addresses the lords of the kingdom in offering them his poem. *The Faerie Queene* is itself an eden raised in the waste wilderness.

Receive most noble Lord a simple taste
   Of the wilde fruit, which salvage soyl hath bred,
   Which being through long wars left almost waste,
   With brutish barbarisme is overspredd:
And in so faire a land, as may be redd,
   Not one *Parnassus*, nor one *Helicone*
   Left for sweete Muses to be harboured.
           (To the Earl of Ormond and Ossory)

The great poem is a harbor for the Muses, but it is rudely shattered at the end of the sixth book, and it contains the destructiveness that periodically ruins paradises, as well as the energy that persistently restores them. Spenser performs his recreative task one final time in *Mutabilitie*, invoking Nature to repair the ruin wrought by the *contretemps* of Faunus' violation in Canto vi. As Apollo himself returned to sing on Mt. Haemus, so his poets come to Arlo: "old *Dan Geffrey*" and Alanus, who had earlier greeted Nature. Finally, the earth is rejuvenated to a richness surpassing that of "Princes bowres adorne[d] with painted imagery":

> And all the earth far underneath her feete
> Was dight with flowres, that voluntary grew
> Out of the ground, and sent forth odours sweet;
> Tenne thousand mores of sundry sent and hew,
> That might delight the smell, or please the vew.
>   (VII.vii.10)

From this vantage point, the Golden Age restored, Spenser's audience can view the majestic order of the cosmos and rejoice in the wisdom of Nature, the assurance that all things "worke their owne perfection" within time and thereby triumph over it.

The myth that Spenser recounts in *Mutabilitie* is mediated by faery historians; the poet has come upon it, "registred of old, / In *Faery* Land mongst records permanent" (vi.2). At least two voices intervene between us, the readers, and the actuality of the great events; this paradise cannot be visited except in memory.[4] Memory need not, of course, go far—the story is a version of the Titans' rebellion, often retold, imbedded in the mind of Europe. The

---

[4] Berger notes that "Faery Land" in Stanza 2 can refer both to Spenser's "own literary world or imagination," and to the "scryne" or casket of the Muses, "the fictions, myths, and legends recorded throughout history" ("The *Mutabilitie Cantos*: Archaism and Evolution in Retrospect," *Critical Essays*, p. 150).

426

Mutabilitie Cantos, like many other poems in the visionary mode, hark back to remote times in order to make a prophetic statement. The personages are allegorical in the sense that in them normally invisible principles are given voices and apprehensible (though not fully visible) shapes. The story itself is not an allegory, however, not continued metaphorical discourse, but Blake's "Eternal Vision or Imagination," "a Representation of what Eternally Exists, Really and Unchangeably." The poet's purpose in reanimating the myth is to bring us the comfort of knowing that there is a sense-making order hidden in the apparent chaos of mortality; this purpose is enunciated in the opening stanza, though the rhetoric betrays a deep unease beneath the speaker's confidence.

> What man that sees the ever-whirling wheele
>   Of *Change,* the which all mortall things doth sway,
>   But that therby doth find, and plainly feele,
>   How MUTABILITY in them doth play
>   Her cruell sports, to many mens decay?
>   Which that to all may better yet appeare,
>   I will rehearse that whylome I heard say.
>
> (VII.vi.1)

The transformation of this ever-whirling wheel to the circles of seasons and months, "the sundry motions" of the spheres that are the handwriting of Nature's God, is designed to temper the organism's instinctive sensory recoil from its cruel adversary. "What man"—whatever man, every man—who is limited to his ordinary sight and "plain" feeling, cannot help concluding that he is the plaything of a ruthless blind power. The antecedent of *Which* in line 6 is deliberately vague; it refers to the whole dismaying picture of Mutabilitie sketched in the first five lines. The task of the visionary poet is to make the outlines of orderly truth "appeare" behind the whirling wheel.

The myth designed to effect this change in point of view

427

—and with it, an alteration of our feelings about change it-self—focuses on the confrontation between Nature and Mutabilitie. They are the last of the great feminine figures that Spenser associates, in *The Faerie Queene,* with the ver-tical axis of his universe, embodying in them the eternal principles that are the objects of mankind's love or loathing. Sapience in the *Hymne of Heavenly Beautie* is a final in-stance; like Nature's, "The fairenesse of her face no tongue can tell" (204). Mutabilitie confronting Nature may remind us of the meeting between Agape and Atropos in Book IV. In fact, the distance between these two episodes is instruc-tive. The Fates embody changelessness, and Lachesis re-bukes Agape for supposing that divine law "may altred bee, / And chaung'd at pleasure" (IV.ii.51). The gods themselves, she says, must bow before the superior decrees of Fate. So, in *Mutabilitie,* the planetary deities obey the laws of Nature, whereby things "are not changed from their first estate" (VII.vii.58). Yet Nature's dictum is seen in the *Cantos* as beneficent, whereas the cruel Fates have dictated an irrevocable doom for the sons of Agape, and for all other beloved mortal sons. The difference, of course, is in point of view. In the *Mutabilitie Cantos,* the poet's visionary pow-er removes us from the immediate scene of suffering and loss so that, like Chaucer's Troilus, we can look down upon the universe with the eyes of God. Doing so, we find the rage for order satisfied; the lovely processions of temporal alteration unfold with perfect decorum, assuring us that re-newal within Nature has no end.[5] This vision is certainly preferable to the anguished close-up of the first stanza, where the fickle hand of Mutability reaches out to turn the capricious wheel of Fortune, "blinde and brute." Blindness is replaced by far-sightedness, and to such opening of the eyes of the mind some part of every human imagination must gratefully respond.

[5] An eloquent argument for a positive reading of the *Cantos* is of-fered by Sherman Hawkins, "Mutabilitie and the Cycle of the Months," *Form and Convention,* ed. Nelson, pp. 76-102.

The *Cantos* do not end, however, with Nature's doom.
The voice of the goddess is followed by her disappearance
(and that of Mutabilitie as well, since these two beings are,
in the end, versions of the same principle);[6] and then the
musing voice of the poet strikes in with two final stanzas of
an "unperfite" eighth canto. Hearing him speak, we hear
again the voice that describes Adonis in the Garden, persuading us to accede to mortality, rather than to disguise
it. Spenser in Book III shows us a mystery: though we shall
all sleep, we shall all be changed, and he is able to contemplate that change with a degree of equanimity. The Garden
is not Eden, for death is there; Adonis dies, he simply does
not "for ever die" (III.vi.47). But our woe is subdued by
the mystery of continuing generation, which Spenser celebrated again in a different mode but similar tonality, at the
end of his marriage song.

> And thou glad Genius, in whose gentle hand,
> The bridale bowre and geniall bed remaine,
> Without blemish or staine,
> And the sweet pleasures of theyr loves delight
> With secret ayde doest succour and supply,

6 In the same stanza, Mutabilitie is "put downe and whist," and
"*Natur*'s selfe did vanish, whither no man wist" (VII.vii.59). These are
their normal and proper situations: Mutabilitie visible in the everyday
flux of things, but silent; Nature, eloquent but invisible. The first is
the mirror of the second, as the *Cantos* have demonstrated; it is a
relationship revealed, at a higher level, when Spenser explains the relation between the Creator and his beautiful universe in the *Hymne of
Heavenly Beautie*.

> Those unto all he daily doth display,
> And shew himselfe in th' image of his grace,
> As in a looking glasse, through which he may
> Be seene, of all his creatures vile and base,
> That are unable else to see his face.

(113-17)

Nature is veiled in the *Cantos*, but Jove himself is dazzled by the beauty
of Mutabilitie—"her lovely face, / In which, faire beames of beauty did
appeare, / That could the greatest wrath soone turne to grace" (vi.31).
An essential action in the *Cantos* is the reader's coming to perceive that
the relation between the two central figures is that of identity, not
antagonism.

Till they bring forth the fruitfull progeny,
Send us the timely fruit of this same night.
(Epithalamion, 398-404)

The language and tone of this passage bear an obvious relation, whether deliberate or not we cannot know, to the climactic stanzas in the Garden of Adonis. Venus, like Acrasia, is an immortal being; her lover participates in immortality, but within time.

All be he subject to mortalitie,
Yet is eterne in mutabilitie,
And by succession made perpetuall,
Transformed oft, and chaunged diverslie.
(III.vi.47)

Adonis lives "by succession," and Venus, that great and ruthless goddess, enjoys him. This seems good to that part of us that can rejoice in the ministrations of glad Genius, to the loving poet who can write of his "gentle hand." But it is not quite good enough at the last end. The final cantos of *The Faerie Queene* are full of grief, for defaced monuments at the end of Book VI and for the fading, fickle beauty of mortal lives in *Mutabilitie*. Eventually, Spenser wearies of his role as visionary and returns to the emotion of an ordinary mortal, the emotion of the first stanza. Mutabilitie's sports are cruel; no man can evade the "love of things":

Which makes me loath this state of life so tickle,
And love of things so vaine to cast away;
Whose flowring pride, so fading and so fickle,
Short *Time* shall soon cut down with his consuming
sickle.
(VII.viii.1)

"Things" are loved vainly, not just because they are vanity, but because our love is helpless to preserve them. And, like Chaucer's in *Troilus and Criseyde*, the poet's visionary dispassion cannot cancel human suffering.

As he confesses his helplessness, Spenser also acknowledges the limits of his art. Having accomplished his highest flight, he descends again to the realm of Time, where the imagination can make sorrowful truth beautiful but cannot negate it. At the center of Book III, imagination exercises its legitimate magic, "lawful as eating," to convince us that we should rejoice in change, which is the source of life as well as of death. Spenser cannot resist interjecting there a reminder that poetry, too, is the source of a different, and possibly superior, kind of life. In an Ovidian stanza, he catalogues metamorphosed lovers, including

> Sad *Amaranthus*, in whose purple gore
> Me seemes I see *Amintas* wretched fate,
> To whom sweet Poets verse hath given endlesse date.
> (III.vi.45)

Wretched fates can be transfigured by imagination, which thus triumphs over time. But in *Mutabilitie*, Spenser has passed beyond the self-delighted praise of poetry. All golden worlds are substitutes, alluding to a loss that no merely human power can repair. And so the great poem ends with a repudiation of fictions and a confession of the human limits of imagining. The logic of the *Cantos*, and of the whole of *The Faerie Queene*, has insisted that permanence is unattainable for us, that the temptation to make eternal monuments is demonic, that the end is not yet. But poets' verses cannot really be endless; poems end, and, like every other thing we make, they die. Wallace Stevens, at the close of his life, was able to accept the mortality of his own work:

> His self and the sun were one
> And his poems, although makings of his self,
> Were no less makings of the sun.
>
> It was not important that they survive.[7]

---

[7] "The Planet on the Table," *Collected Poems*, p. 532.

Imagination, in the end, is part of Nature, and participates in its relentless alterations.

Nature says that "all things stedfastnes doe hate"; if they are healthy, they must change. She adds that "being rightly wayd / They are not changed from their first estate" (vii.58). The key word is *rightly*. The "right" meaning of the word *change* exists in the mind of God, and the poet attempts to read it. Finally, however, Spenser's God, like Milton's, is unreadable. The poet does not see Nature's face; still less does he see God's. All creaturely powers, even those of the angels, are inadequate; we are "unable else to see his face," except as mediated in Creation (*HHB* 117). So the final stanza of *Mutabilitie* takes us beyond vision. The poet ceases to be the active shaper of an allegorical poem. He utters a prayer, which ends in silence and passivity:

> O that great Sabbaoth God,
> graunt me that Sabaoths sight.
> (VII.viii.2)

Only God can write the ultimately satisfying poem, and it will not be an allegorical fiction. Now we see through a glass darkly; but dark conceits and Mutabilitie alike will vanish when all the veils are cast aside.

The prayer of the final line has, to be sure, its own audacity; it is as close as Spenser comes to the Milton of the great prologues, seeking the visionary power. If this poet will write no more, he may yet glimpse the grand poem of God. "That Sabaoths sight" is a notorious crux, but it certainly refers to an ultimate vision. The literary prototype is the *Paradiso* and the poet who reads "the scattered leaves of all the universe" gathered into one volume. But Spenser is inadequate to the task of describing this volume, though it may be an analogue, in some distant way, of his own, *The Faerie Queene*. His imagination measures the spaces of the universe in *Mutabilitie*, for an instant outdistancing Jove and Nature herself. "We say God and the imagination are one,"[8] but Spenser does not say it. He merely links his poem with the source of all gracious gifts, including imagination, by leaving it open to space and silence, breaking the fiction along the vertical axis of timeless reality. At the end of Book VI, it was broken along the horizontal axis, to admit the filthy modern tide of history. Both of these breakings-off, rendering *The Faerie Queene* "unperfite" in several necessary senses, mark the honest imagination's final self-recognition. The poet confesses; he prays; he reads the book he has not written. It might open to the last chapter of Paul's Epistle to the Hebrews: "Remember them that are in bonds, as bound with them. . . . For here have we no continuing city, but we seek one to come."

[8] Stevens, "Final Soliloquy of the Internal Paramour," *Collected Poems*, p. 524.

Index to *The Faerie Queene*

A. Passages Discussed

B. Characters and Places

General Index

Abrams, M. H., 5n
aenigma, 126-27
aevum, 93, 170, 203, 210n, 274-76, 350
Alain de Lille, 116n, 426
allegory, accuracy of, 220-21;
adjective/noun relation in, 83-84, 170, 211, 283, 291;
"darkness" of, 40, 60-63; duplicity of, 56-57, 317; and history, 211, 215; inexplicitness of, 51; and irony, 57, 410-11; and journey plot, 39; and knowledge, 37, 39; and "levels," 27, 30, 191; and logical priority, 29-30; and "mental space," 6-8, 413-17; ontological diversity of, 282; polysemous, 205; psychological, 178-84, 213, 216-18; and reality, 23-24, 26, 28-29, 61, 178-79; relation to reader, 45, 50, 57-58, 79-80, 97, 154; self-referring, 37, 47, 59, 81-82, 84, 86-87; unanalyzed, 417; "veil" of, 137-38, 247
allusion, 51, 103, 205
Alpers, Paul, 44n, 47, 51, 147n, 160n, 162, 194n, 273n, 297, 307, 368n, 426n
analogy, 27, 180, 184-86
Anderson, Judith, 180
Anglo, Sydney, 49n
Aptekar, Jane, 411n
Aquinas, 26, 92-93, 276
Ariosto, Lodovico, 50, 157, 420n
Aristotle, 14, 15, 29, 46, 349
art, as alternative world, 20-22; and death, 249-50; deceptiveness of, 107-109, 244-47, 252, 292; divine, 200-201, 388; and dreams, 3; as imitation, 22,

106, 124; limits of, 115, 431; and love, 240-43, 320-22, 327-28; and pornography, 217-18; self-commenting, 104, 251-52
Atchity, Kenneth, 345n
Auerbach, Erich, 48
Augustine, 4, 17, 56, 62n, 73, 254, 352

Bachelard, Gaston, 149
Bacon, Francis, 34, 35-37, 235-37, 266, 307, 331, 407
Barfield, Owen, 5n, 30
Barthes, Roland, 104n
Bayley, P. C., 389n
Bender, John B., 104n
Bennett, J. A. W., 325
Berger, Harry, 87n, 90, 91n, 181-82, 184, 214, 246, 279, 280n, 285n, 295, 343, 351n, 354n, 368n, 382, 387n, 395
Bergson, Henri, 31-32n
Bernard Silvestris, 274n
Bible, 47, 66, 145, 189, 223; *Hebrews*, 380, 433; *Malachi*, 204; *Psalms*, 200, 204; *Revelation*, 23, 35, 183n, 191, 201
Blackmur, Richard, 23-24
Blake, William, 23, 100, 141, 261, 355n, 366, 394, 397, 419, 427
Blitch, Alice, 53n
Bloom, Harold, 133
Bloomfield, M. W., 14n, 28n, 61n, 88n
Boccaccio, 56, 62n, 136-37, 147, 323
Boethius, 17, 35, 125n, 320
Botticelli, 117-18, 122
Bryskett, Lodowick, 407
Bundy, M. W., 14, 15n, 17

440

LIBRARY OF CONGRESS CATALOGING IN PUBLICATION DATA

MacCaffrey, Isabel Gamble.
  Spenser's allegory.

  Includes index.
  1. Spenser, Edmund, 1552?-1599. Faerie queene.
  2. Spenser, Edmund, 1552?-1599—Allegory and symbolism. I. Title.
PR2358.M3   821'.3   75-30197
ISBN 0-691-06306-0
ISBN 0-691-10043-8 pbk.